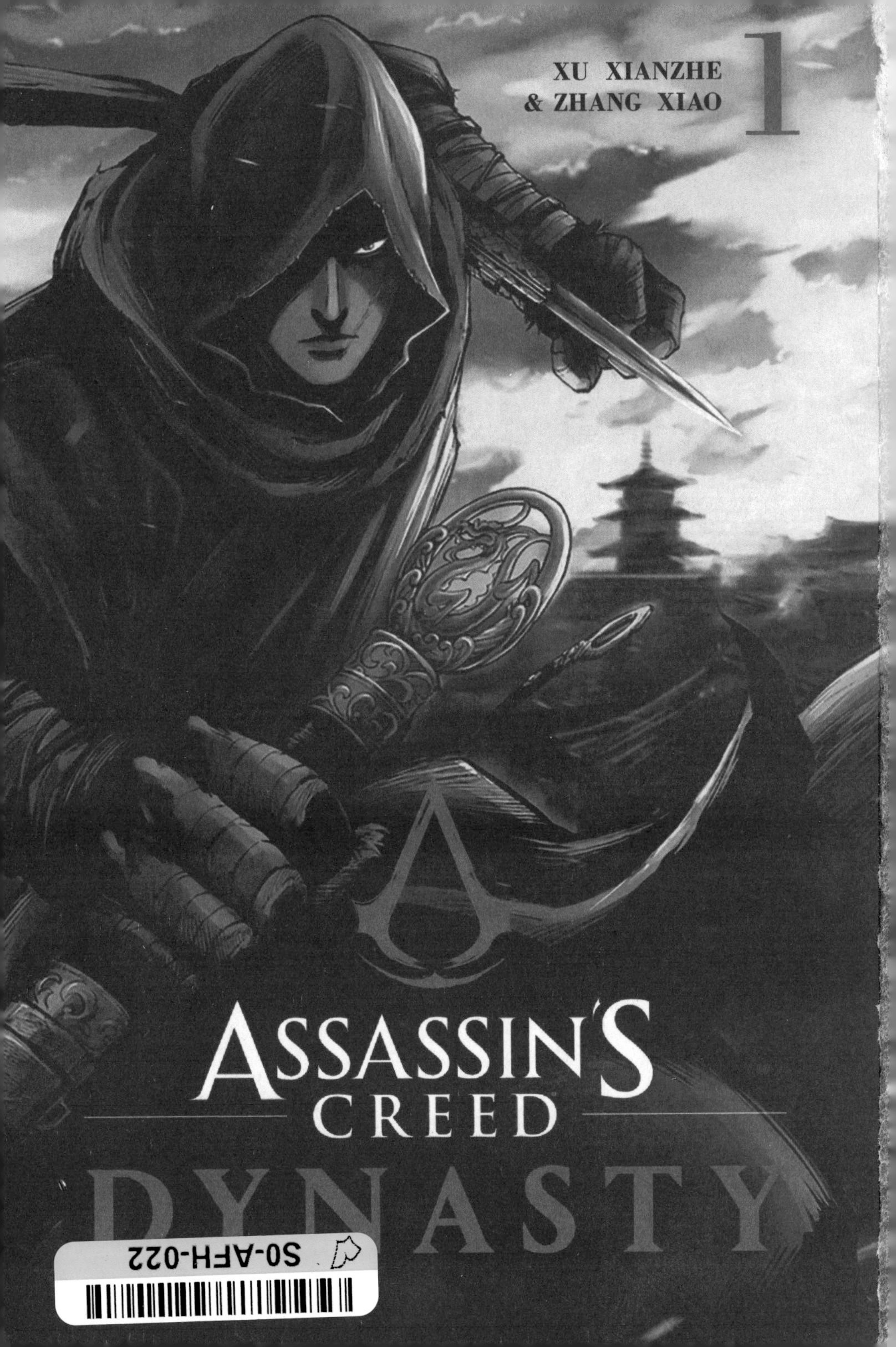
XU XIANZHE
& ZHANG XIAO
1
ASSASSIN'S
CREED
DYNASTY

BOOK ONE:

THE FLOWER BANQUET

TABLE OF CONTENTS

THE EARLIEST RECORDS OF ASSASSINS
IN CHINA CAN BE FOUND IN SIMA QIAN'S
"RECORDS OF THE GRAND HISTORIAN."

OF THESE, THE MOST INFAMOUS
FIVE WERE CAO MO, ZHUAN ZHU,
NIE ZHENG, YU RANG, AND JING KE.

THEY WERE LATER REFERRED TO
AS "THE FIVE GREAT ASSASSINS."

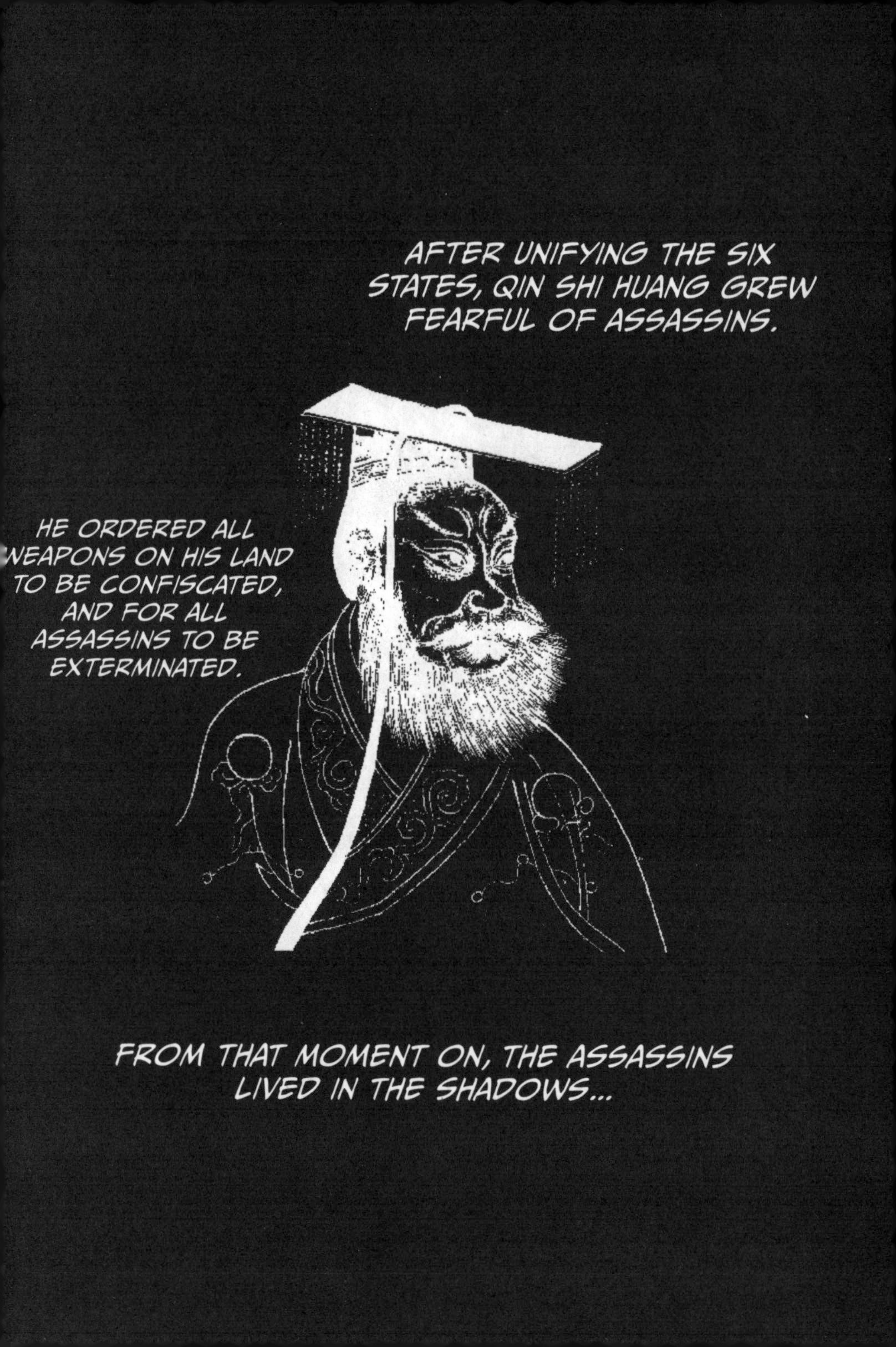
AFTER UNIFYING THE SIX STATES, QIN SHI HUANG GREW FEARFUL OF ASSASSINS.
HE ORDERED ALL WEAPONS ON HIS LAND TO BE CONFISCATED, AND FOR ALL ASSASSINS TO BE EXTERMINATED.
FROM THAT MOMENT ON, THE ASSASSINS LIVED IN THE SHADOWS...

IT IS THE THIRTEENTH YEAR OF
TIANBAO IN THE TANG DYNASTY.
AN ASSASSIN HAS APPEARED IN CHANG'AN...

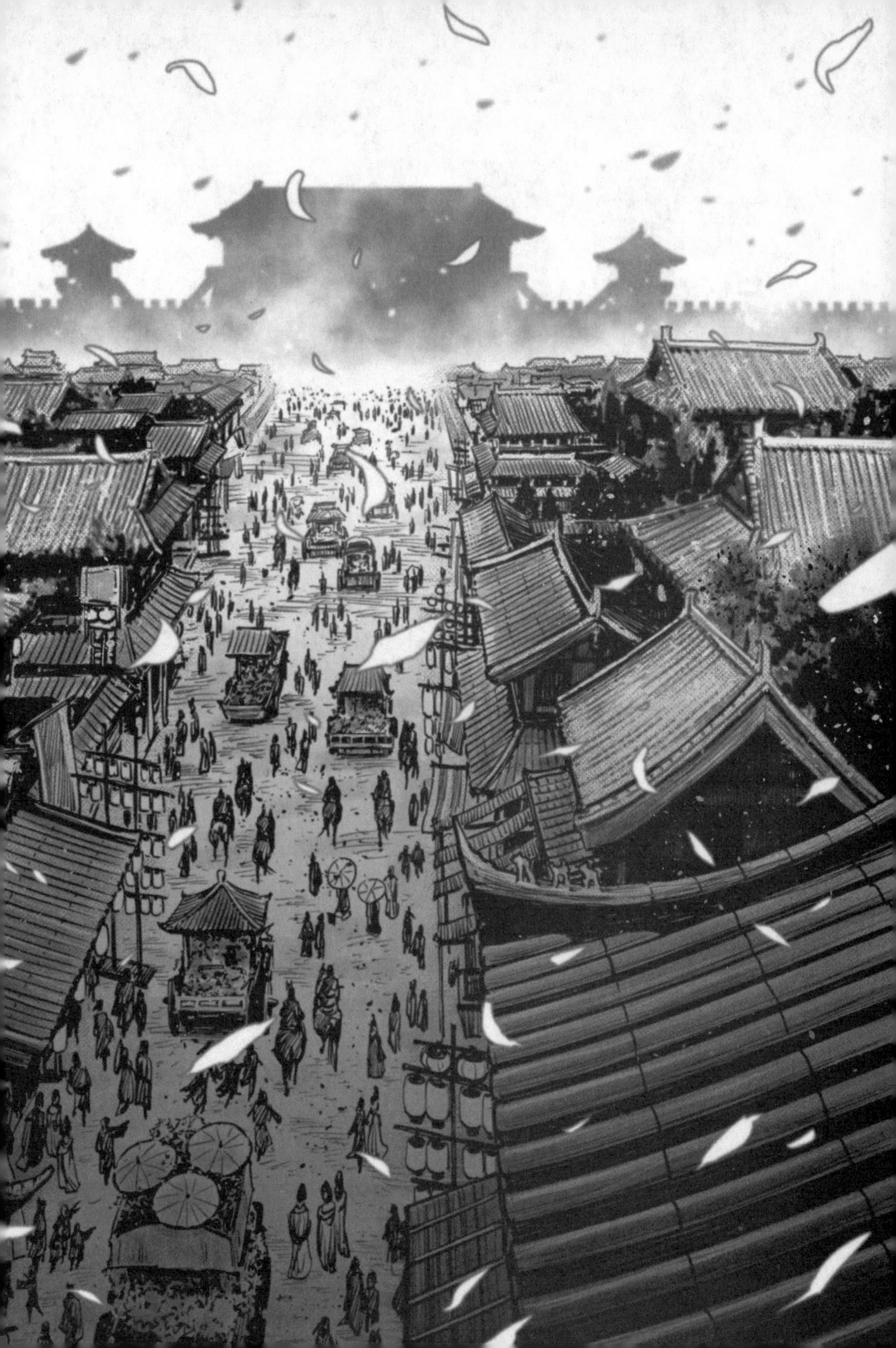

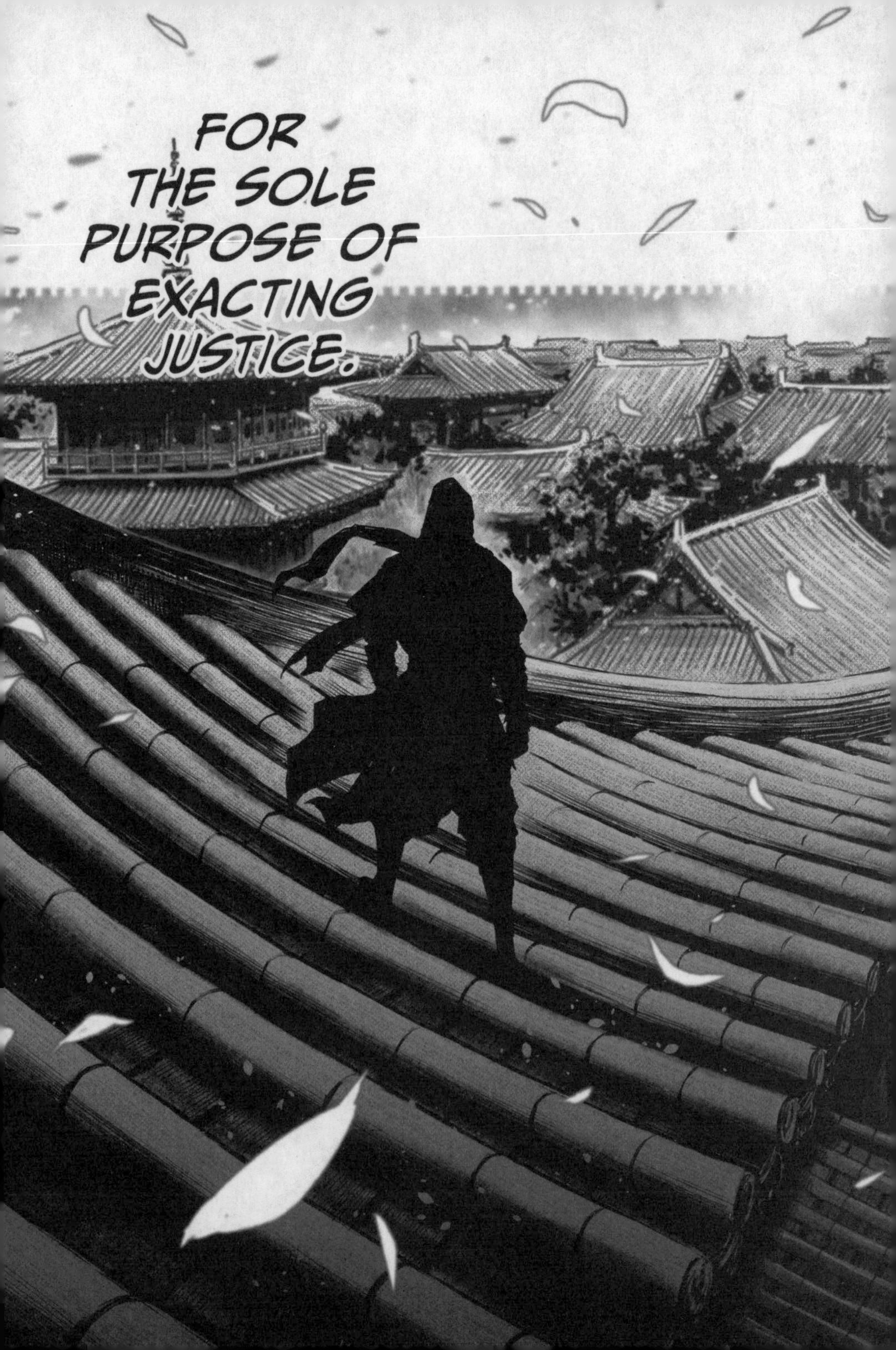
FOR THE SOLE PURPOSE OF EXACTING JUSTICE.

NOTHING IS TRUE;
EVERYTHING IS
PERMITTED.

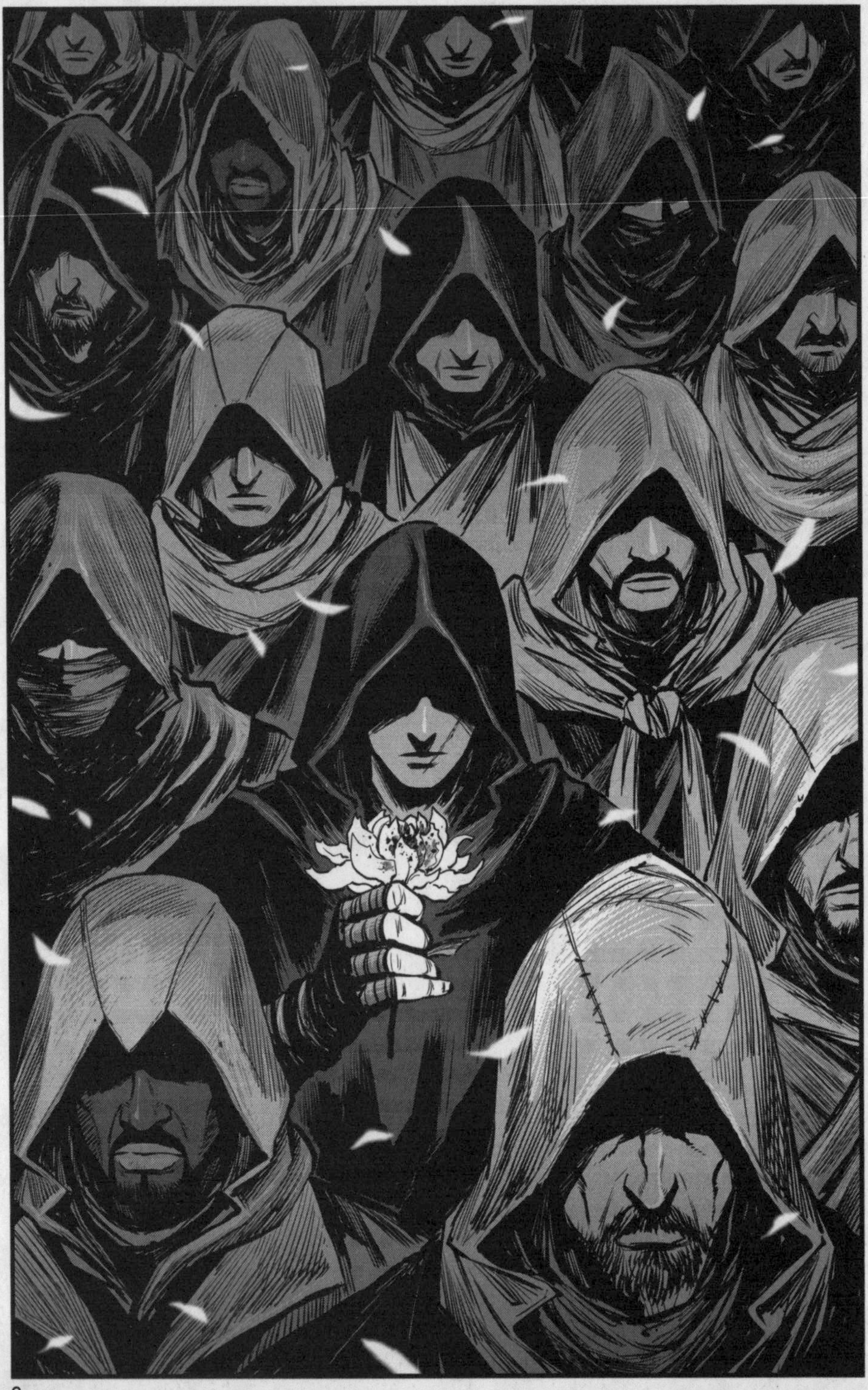

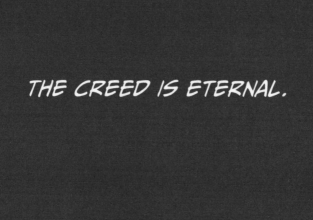

THE CREED IS ETERNAL.

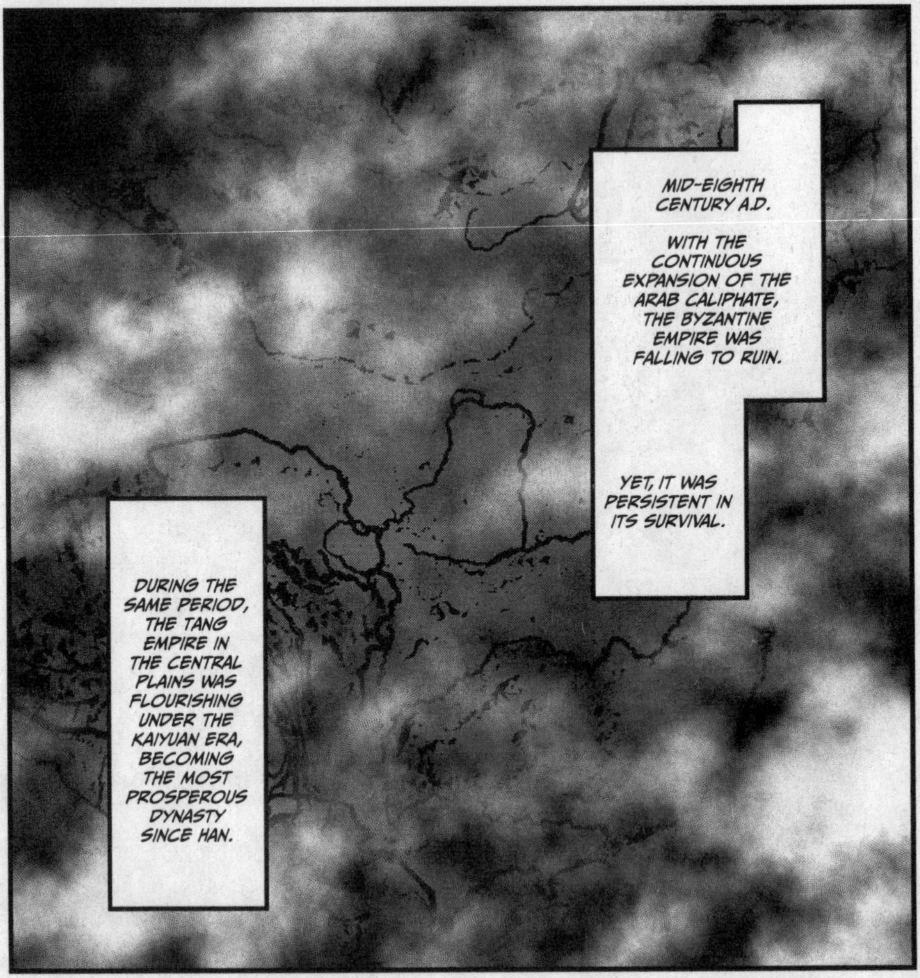
MID-EIGHTH CENTURY A.D.
WITH THE CONTINUOUS EXPANSION OF THE ARAB CALIPHATE, THE BYZANTINE EMPIRE WAS FALLING TO RUIN.
YET, IT WAS PERSISTENT IN ITS SURVIVAL.
DURING THE SAME PERIOD, THE TANG EMPIRE IN THE CENTRAL PLAINS WAS FLOURISHING UNDER THE KAIYUAN ERA, BECOMING THE MOST PROSPEROUS DYNASTY SINCE HAN.
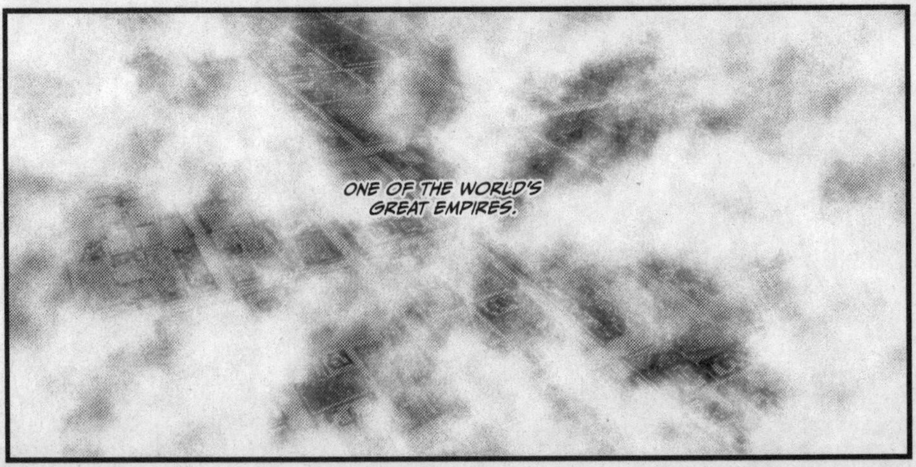
ONE OF THE WORLD'S GREAT EMPIRES.

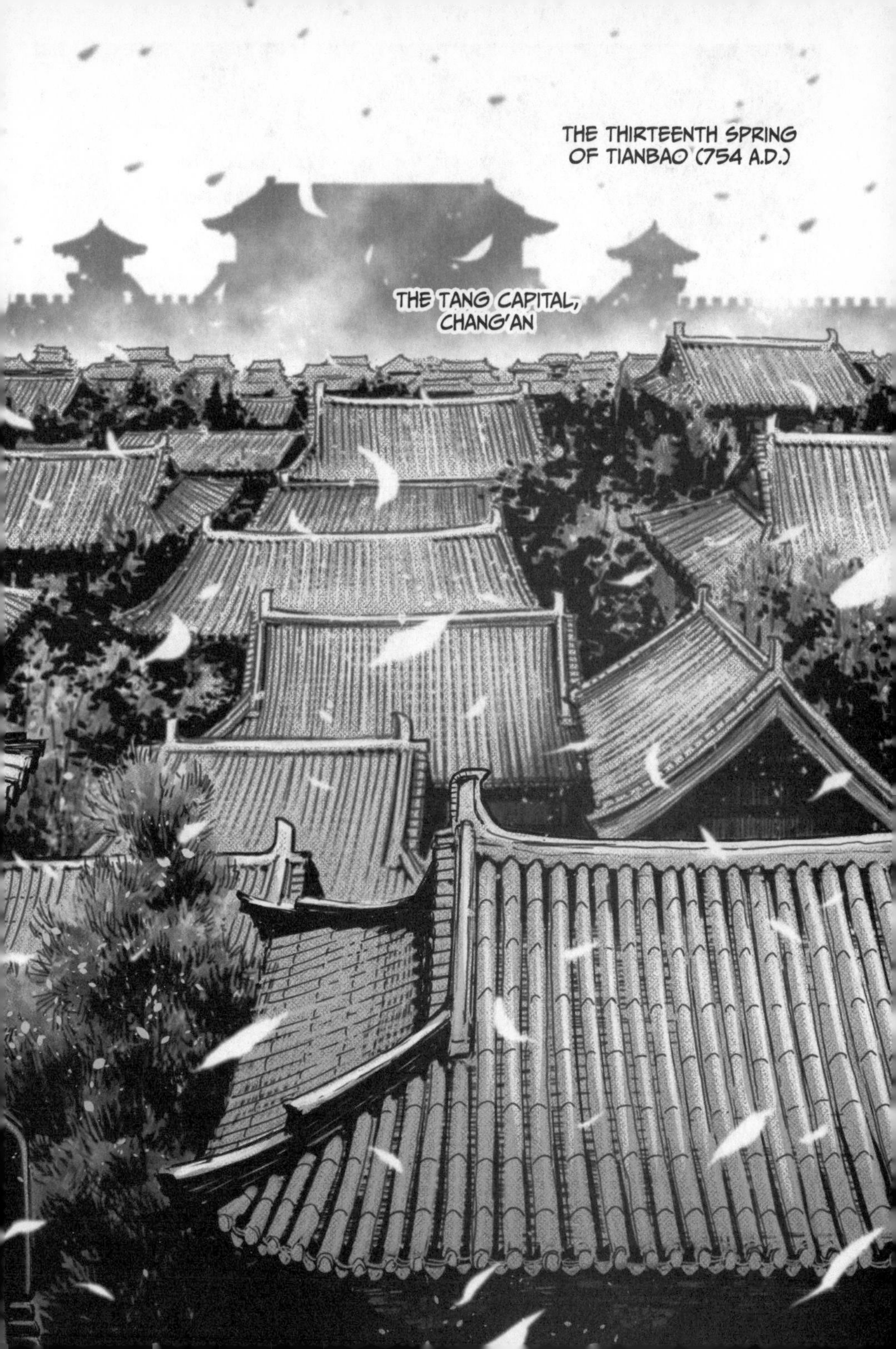
THE THIRTEENTH SPRING OF TIANBAO (754 A.D.)
THE TANG CAPITAL, CHANG'AN

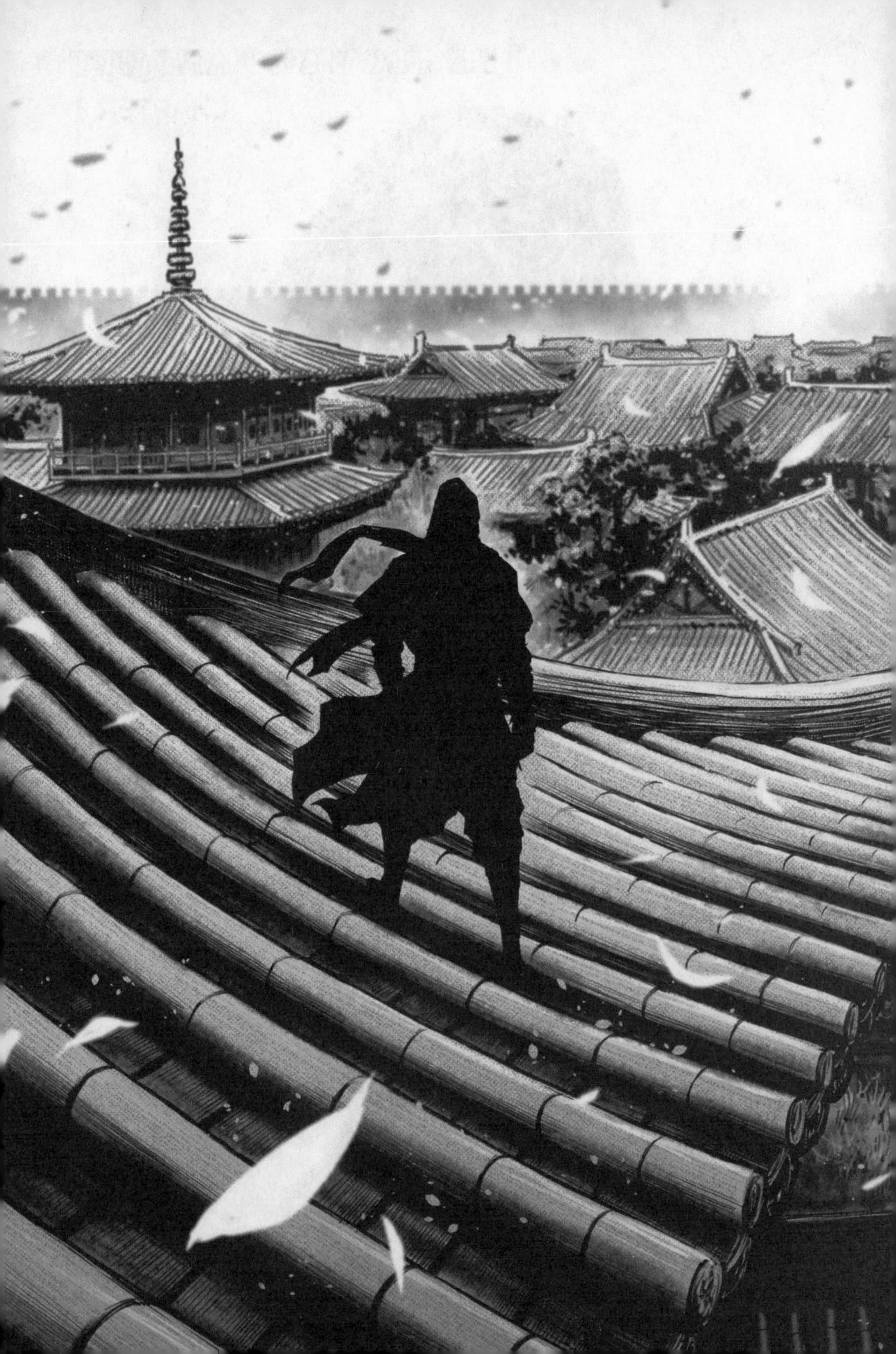

The Flower Banquet

Chapter I

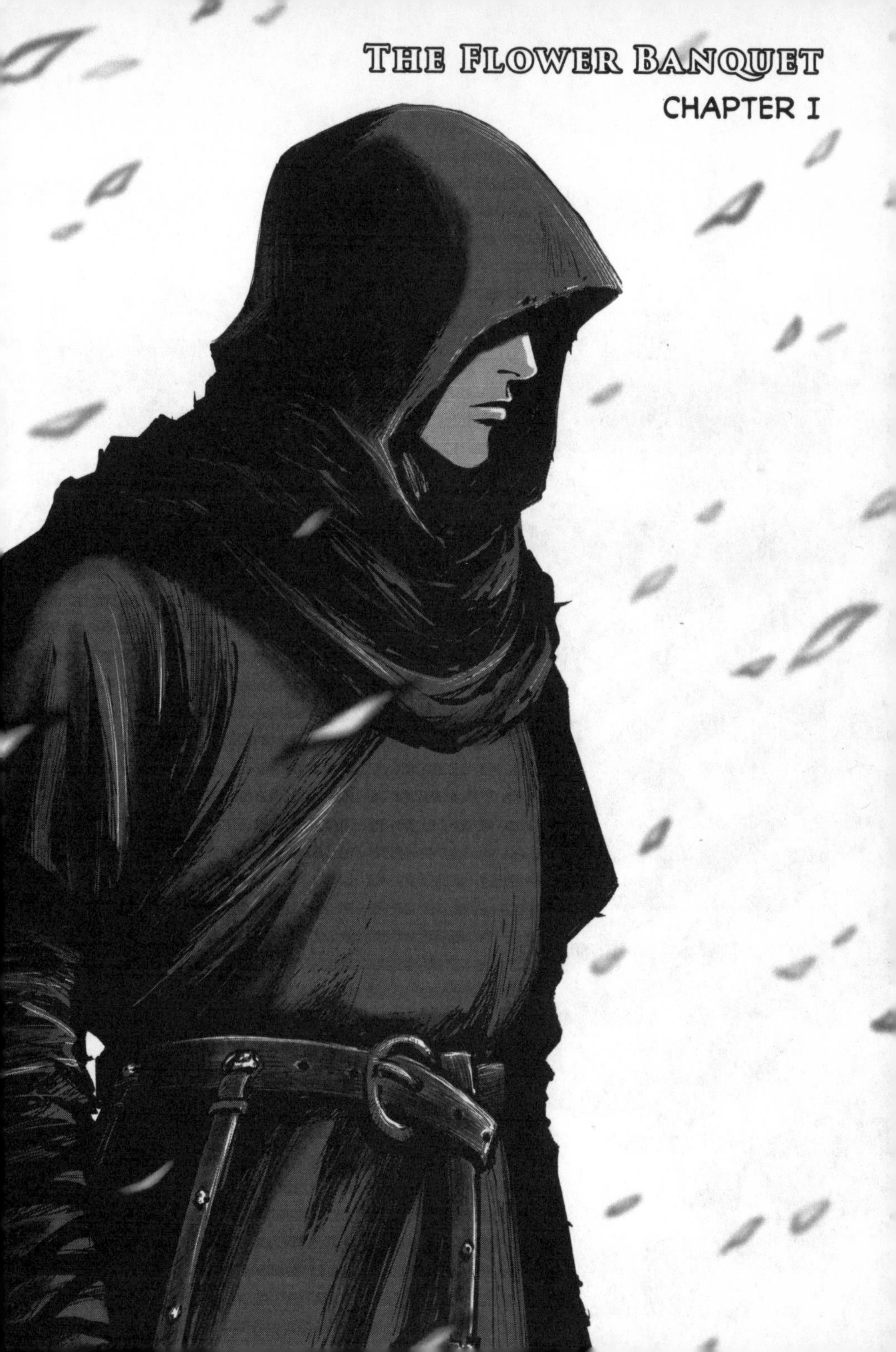

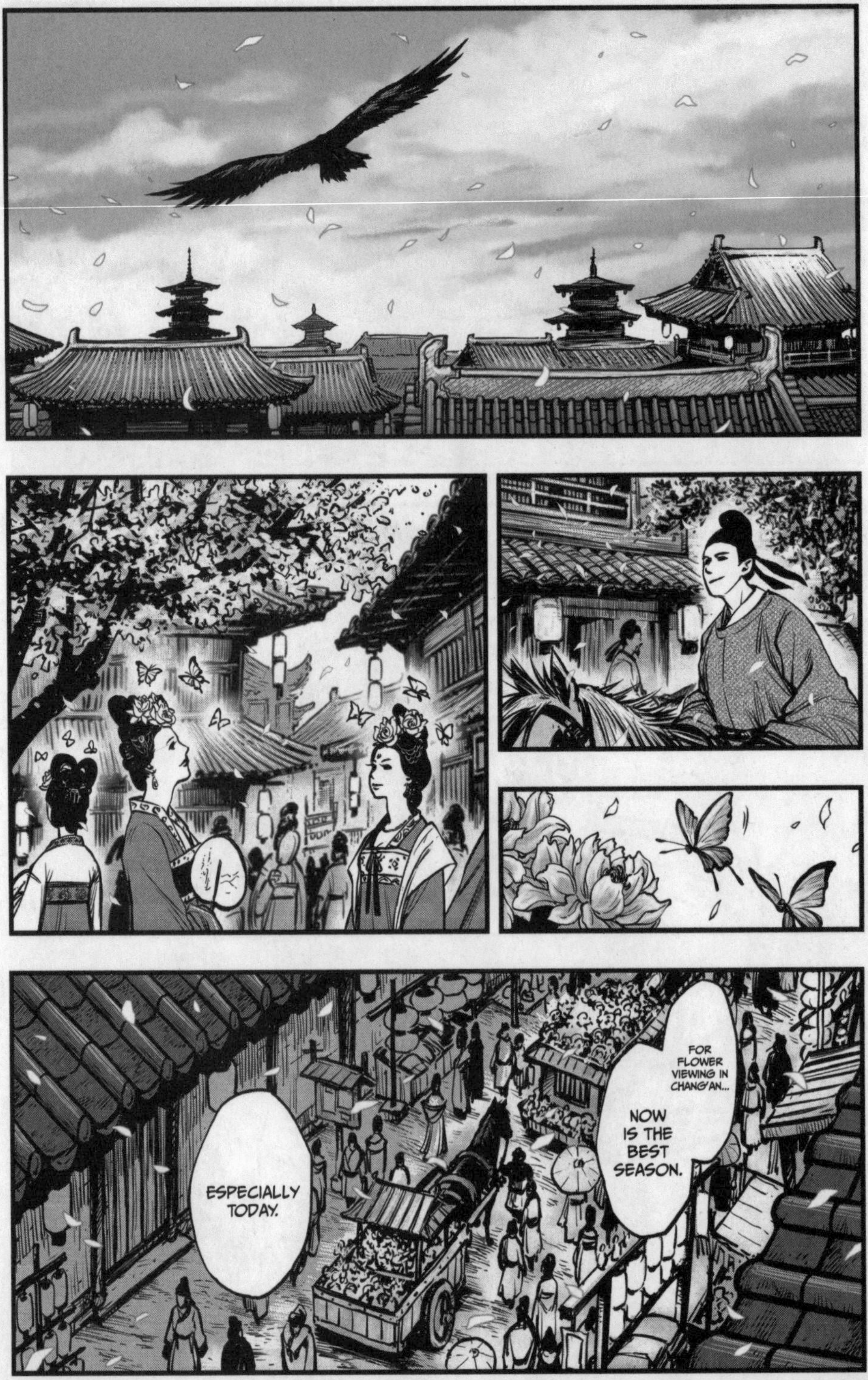
FOR FLOWER VIEWING IN CHANG'AN...
NOW IS THE BEST SEASON.
ESPECIALLY TODAY.

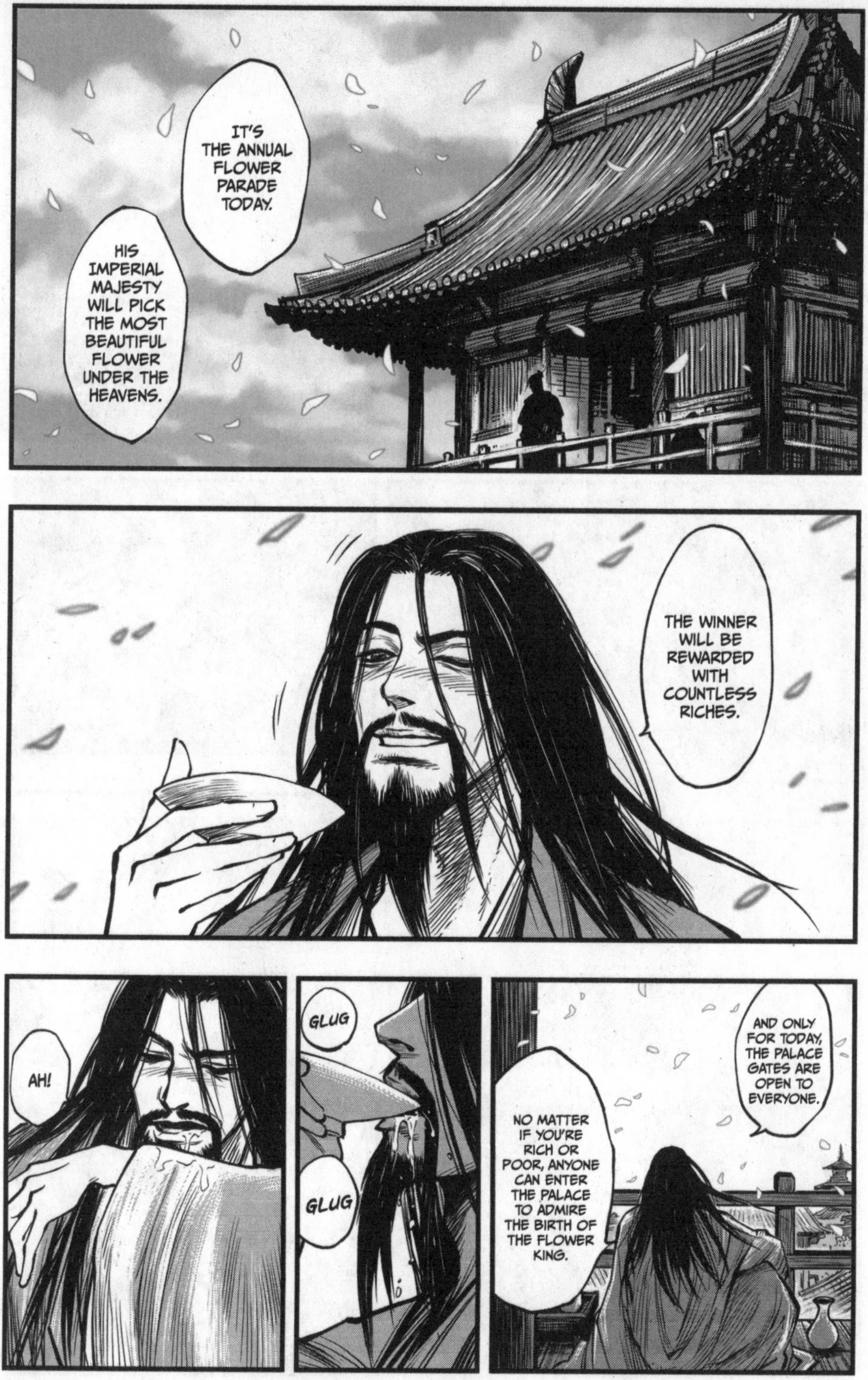
IT'S THE ANNUAL FLOWER PARADE TODAY.
HIS IMPERIAL MAJESTY WILL PICK THE MOST BEAUTIFUL FLOWER UNDER THE HEAVENS.
THE WINNER WILL BE REWARDED WITH COUNTLESS RICHES.
AND ONLY FOR TODAY, THE PALACE GATES ARE OPEN TO EVERYONE.
NO MATTER IF YOU'RE RICH OR POOR, ANYONE CAN ENTER THE PALACE TO ADMIRE THE BIRTH OF THE FLOWER KING.
GLUG
GLUG
AH!

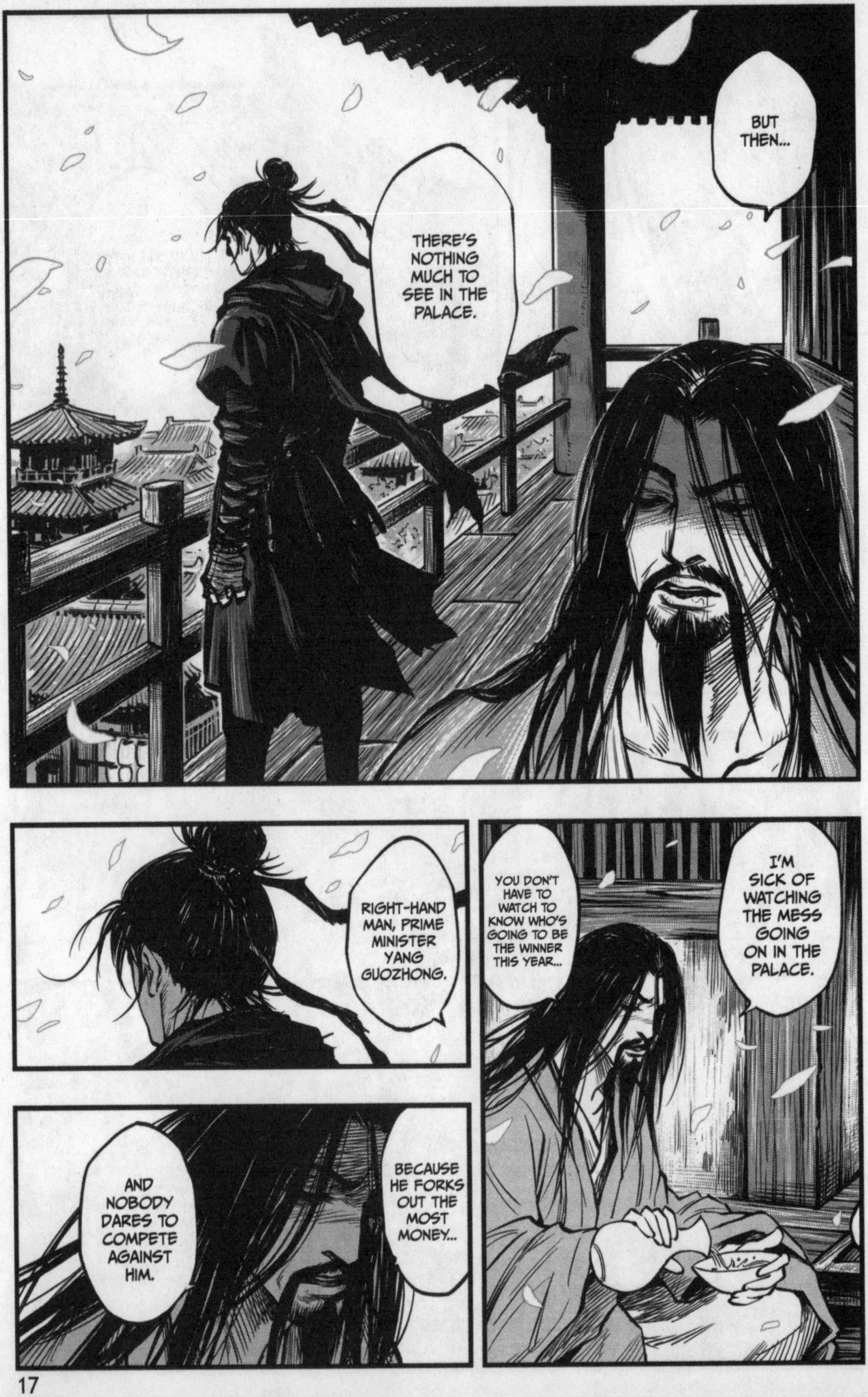
BUT THEN...
THERE'S NOTHING MUCH TO SEE IN THE PALACE.
I'M SICK OF WATCHING THE MESS GOING ON IN THE PALACE.
YOU DON'T HAVE TO WATCH TO KNOW WHO'S GOING TO BE THE WINNER THIS YEAR...
RIGHT-HAND MAN, PRIME MINISTER YANG GUOZHONG.
BECAUSE HE FORKS OUT THE MOST MONEY...
AND NOBODY DARES TO COMPETE AGAINST HIM.

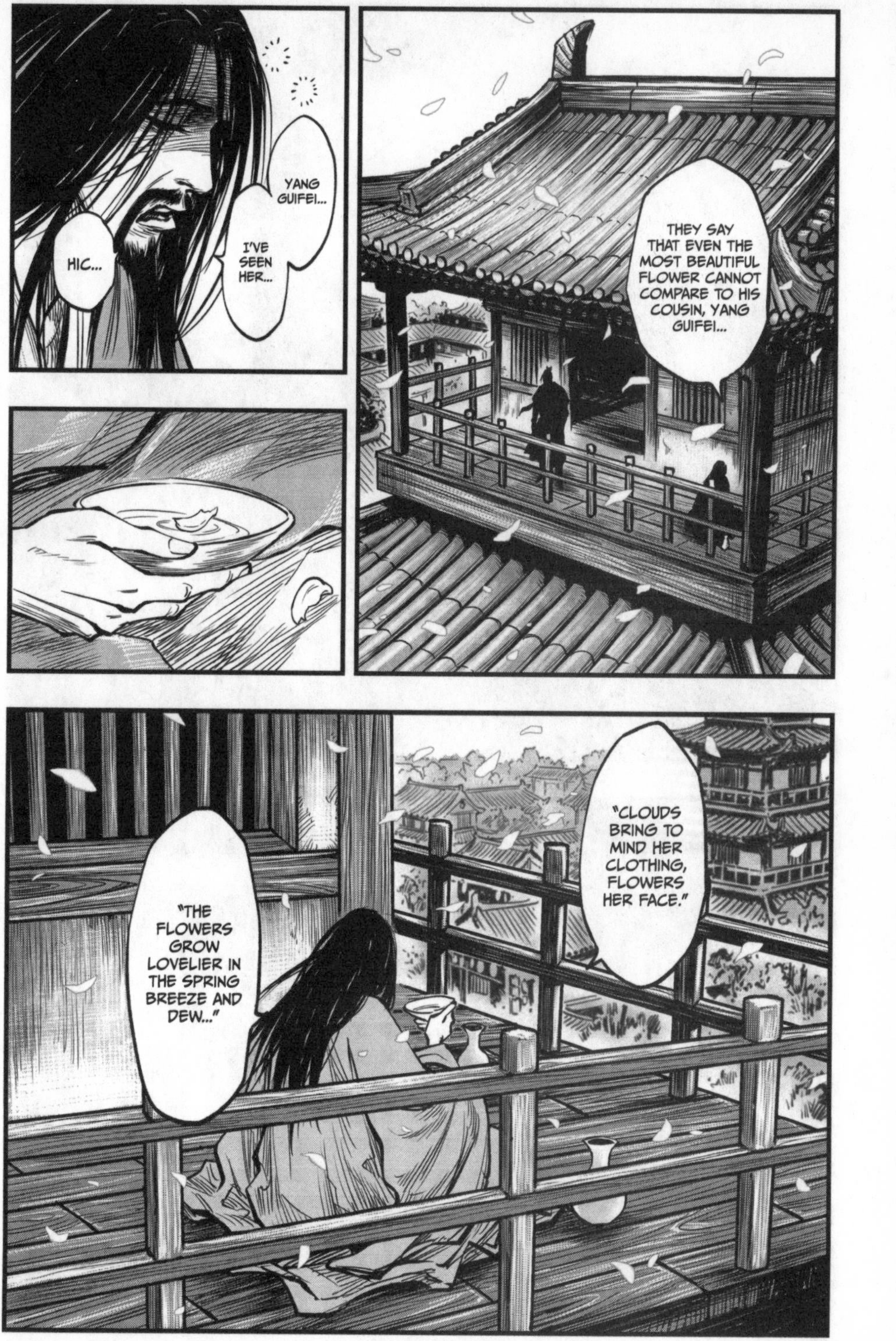
THEY SAY THAT EVEN THE MOST BEAUTIFUL FLOWER CANNOT COMPARE TO HIS COUSIN, YANG GUIFEI...
YANG GUIFEI...
I'VE SEEN HER...
HIC...
"CLOUDS BRING TO MIND HER CLOTHING, FLOWERS HER FACE."
"THE FLOWERS GROW LOVELIER IN THE SPRING BREEZE AND DEW..."

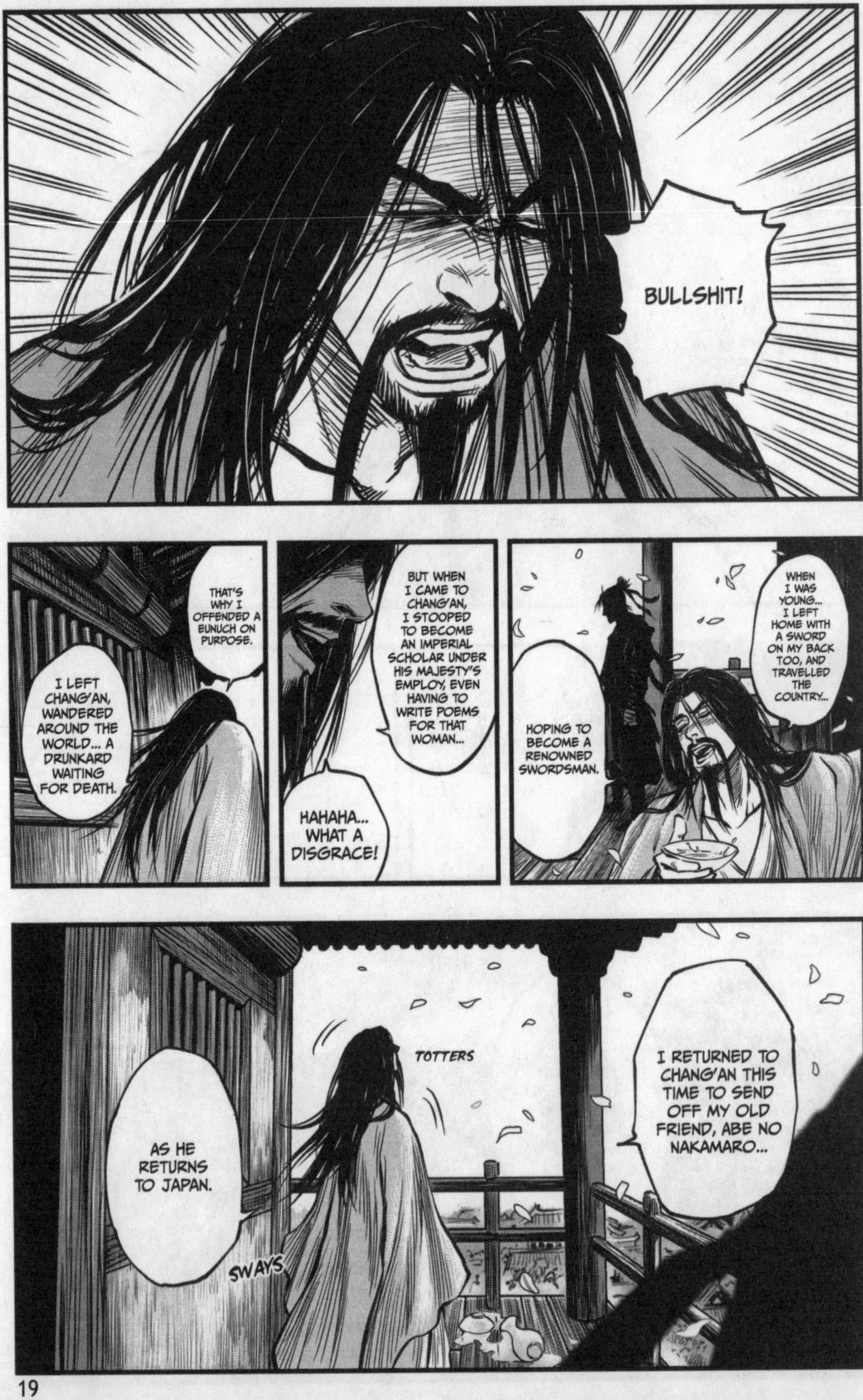
BULLSHIT!
WHEN I WAS YOUNG... I LEFT HOME WITH A SWORD ON MY BACK TOO, AND TRAVELLED THE COUNTRY...
HOPING TO BECOME A RENOWNED SWORDSMAN.
BUT WHEN I CAME TO CHANG'AN, I STOOPED TO BECOME AN IMPERIAL SCHOLAR UNDER HIS MAJESTY'S EMPLOY, EVEN HAVING TO WRITE POEMS FOR THAT WOMAN...
HAHAHA... WHAT A DISGRACE!
THAT'S WHY I OFFENDED A EUNUCH ON PURPOSE.
I LEFT CHANG'AN, WANDERED AROUND THE WORLD... A DRUNKARD WAITING FOR DEATH.
I RETURNED TO CHANG'AN THIS TIME TO SEND OFF MY OLD FRIEND, ABE NO NAKAMARO...
TOTTERS
AS HE RETURNS TO JAPAN.
SWAYS

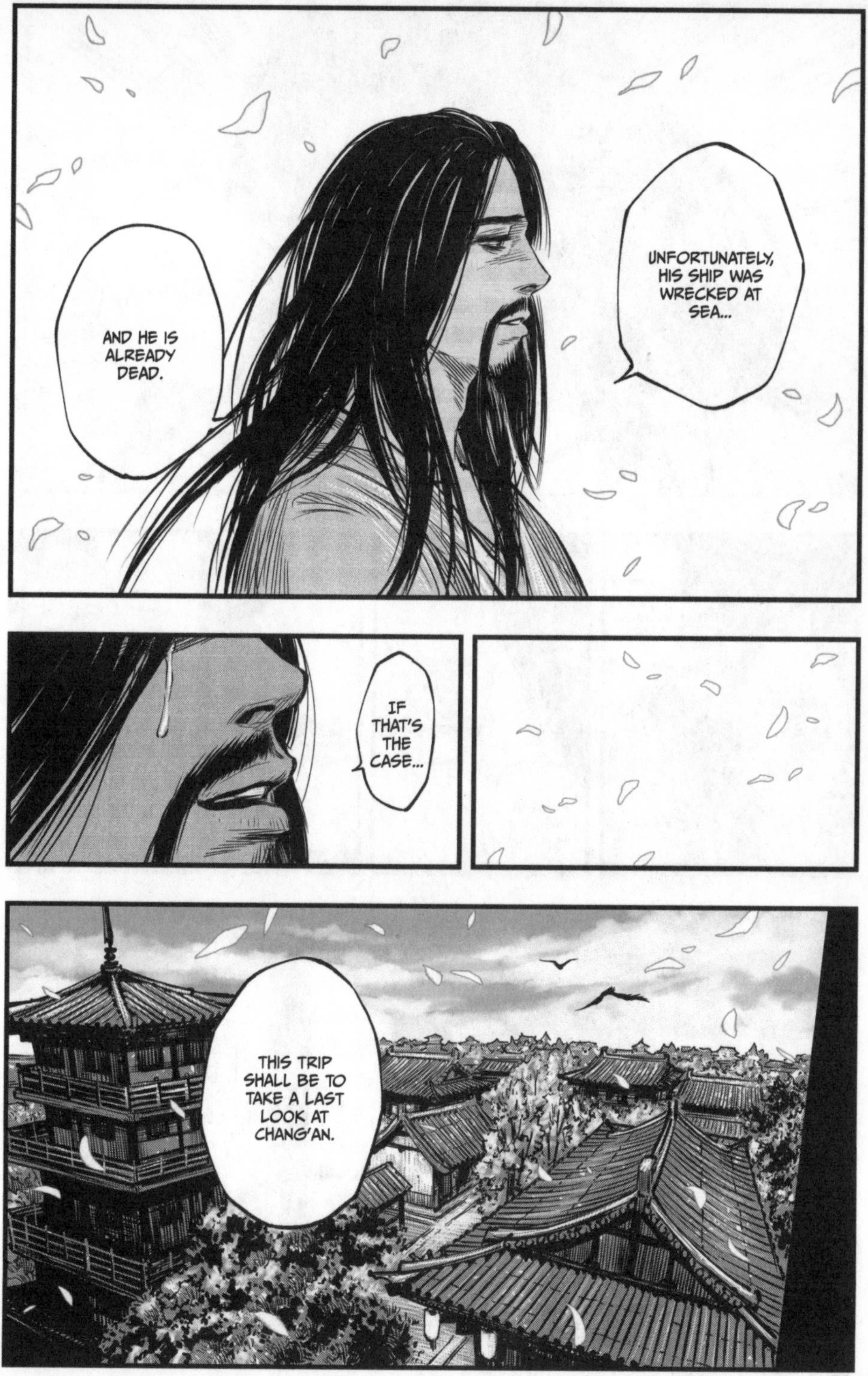
UNFORTUNATELY, HIS SHIP WAS WRECKED AT SEA...
AND HE IS ALREADY DEAD.
IF THAT'S THE CASE...
THIS TRIP SHALL BE TO TAKE A LAST LOOK AT CHANG'AN.

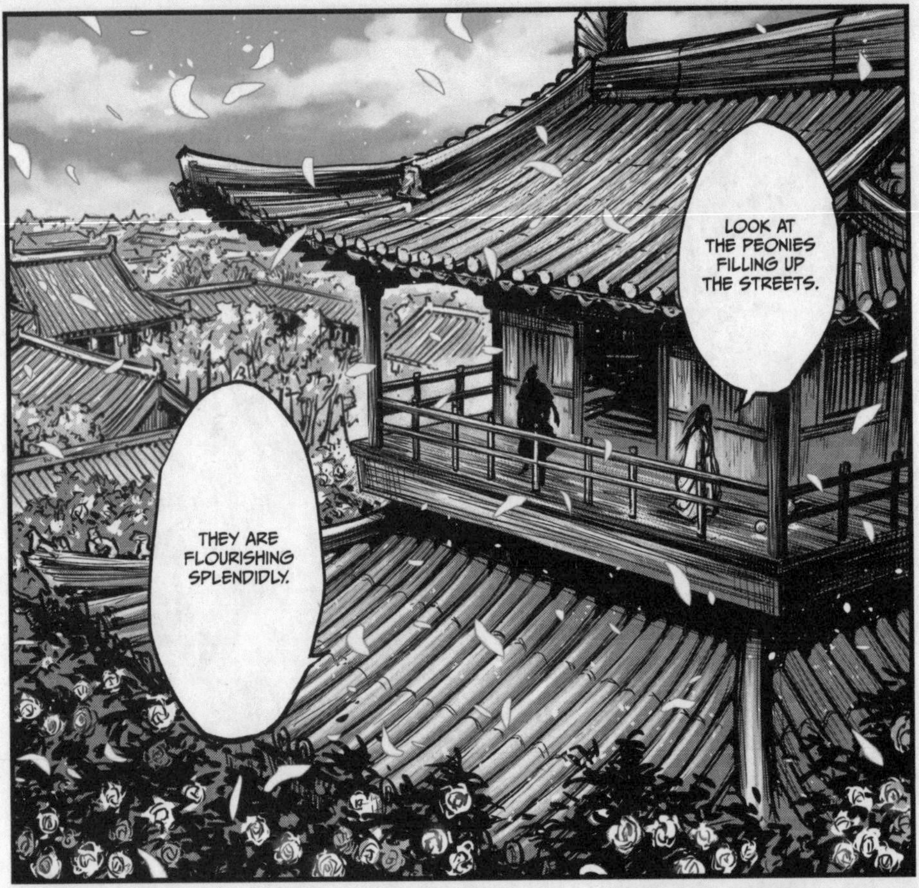
LOOK AT THE PEONIES FILLING UP THE STREETS.
THEY ARE FLOURISHING SPLENDIDLY.

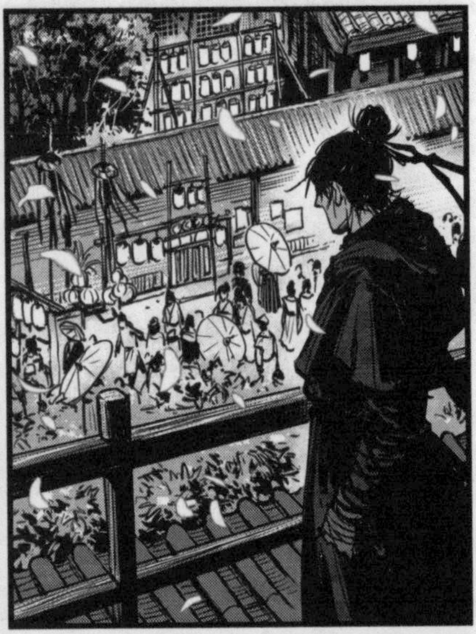

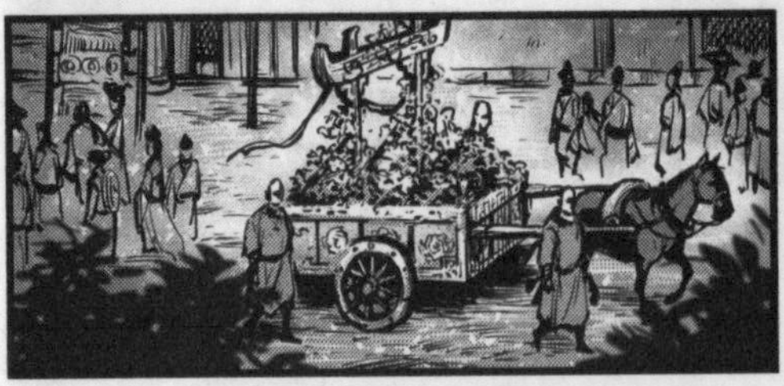

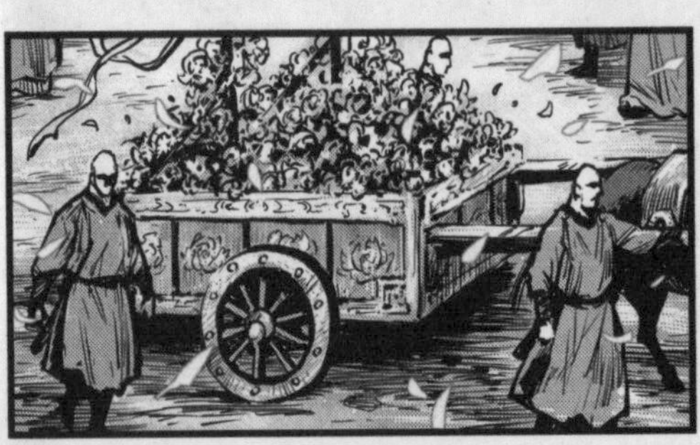

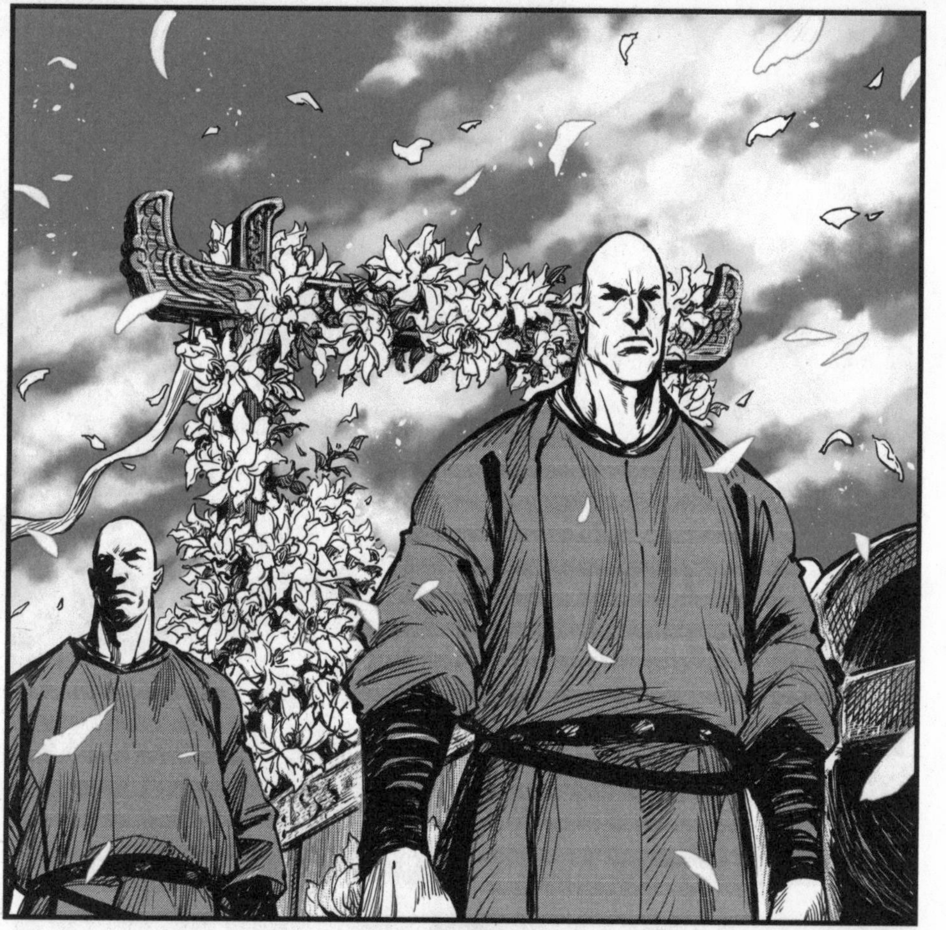

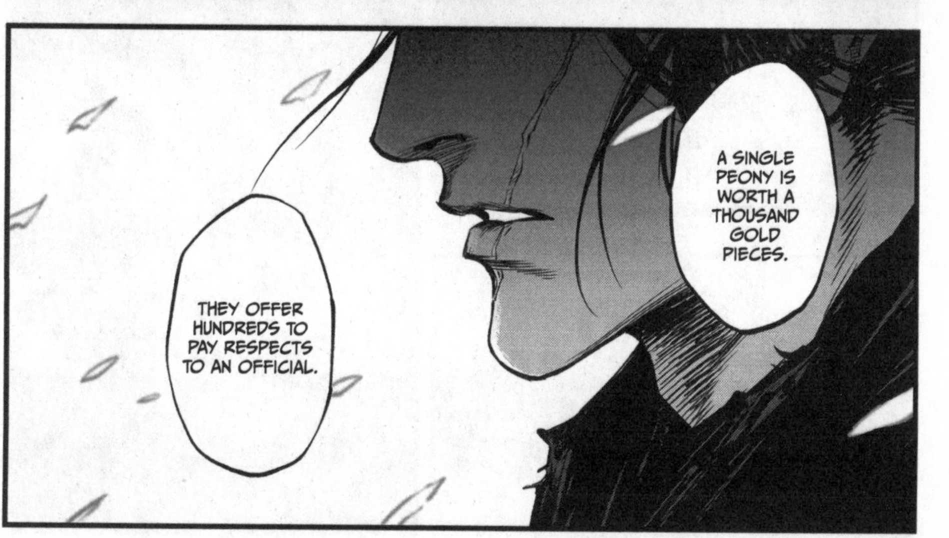
A SINGLE PEONY IS WORTH A THOUSAND GOLD PIECES.
THEY OFFER HUNDREDS TO PAY RESPECTS TO AN OFFICIAL.

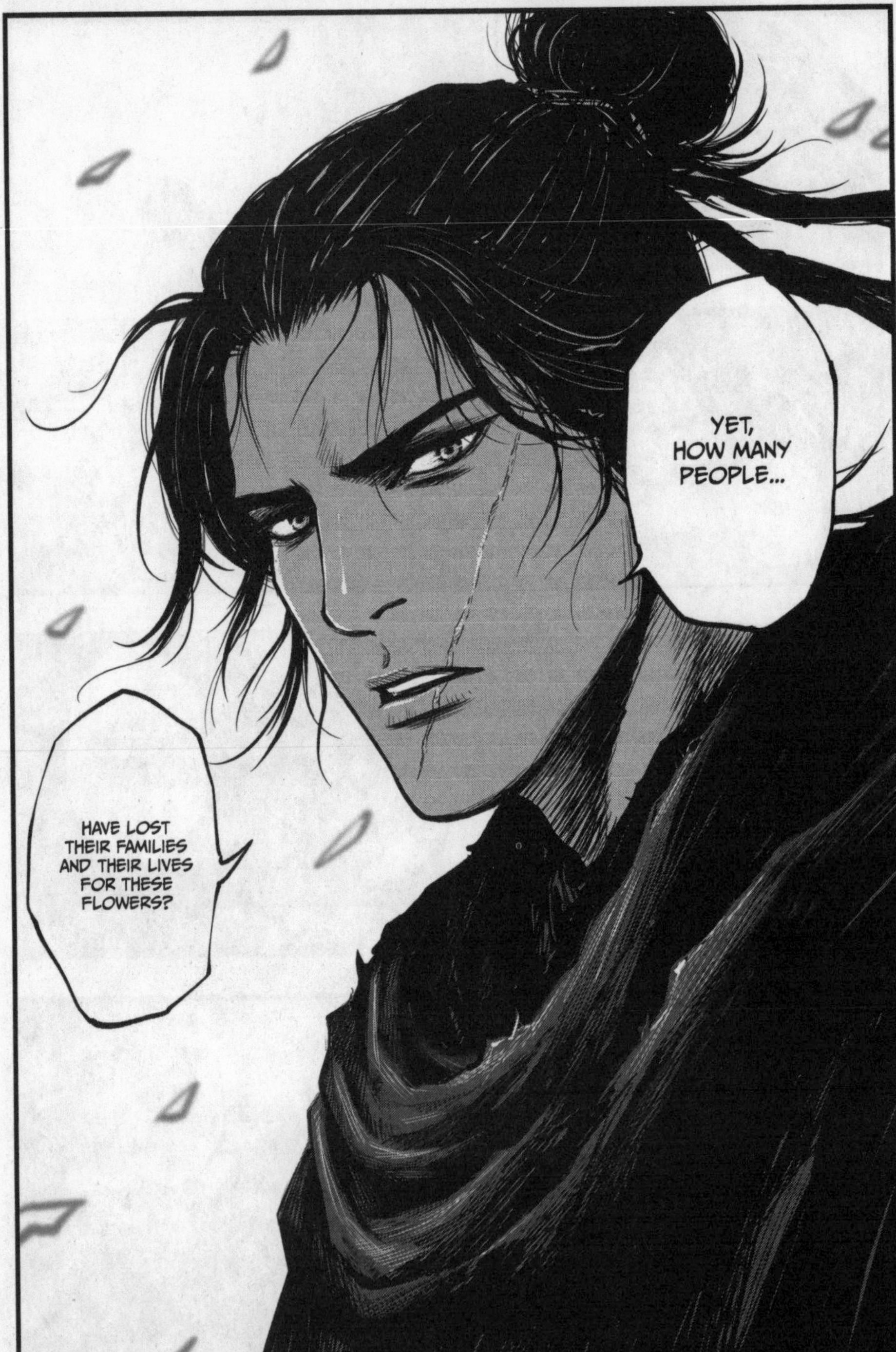
YET, HOW MANY PEOPLE...
HAVE LOST THEIR FAMILIES AND THEIR LIVES FOR THESE FLOWERS?

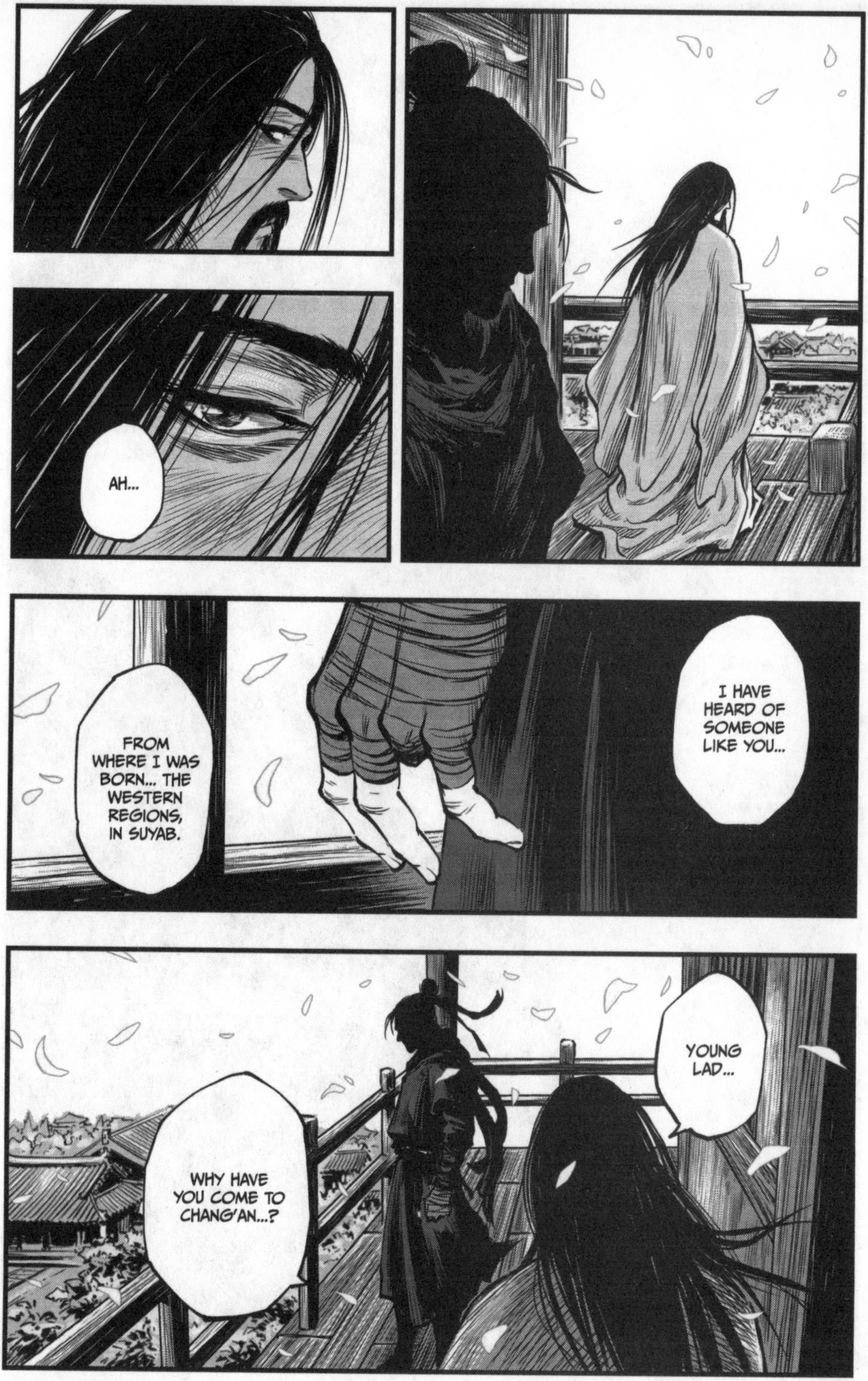
AH...
I HAVE HEARD OF SOMEONE LIKE YOU...
FROM WHERE I WAS BORN... THE WESTERN REGIONS, IN SUYAB.
YOUNG LAD...
WHY HAVE YOU COME TO CHANG'AN...?

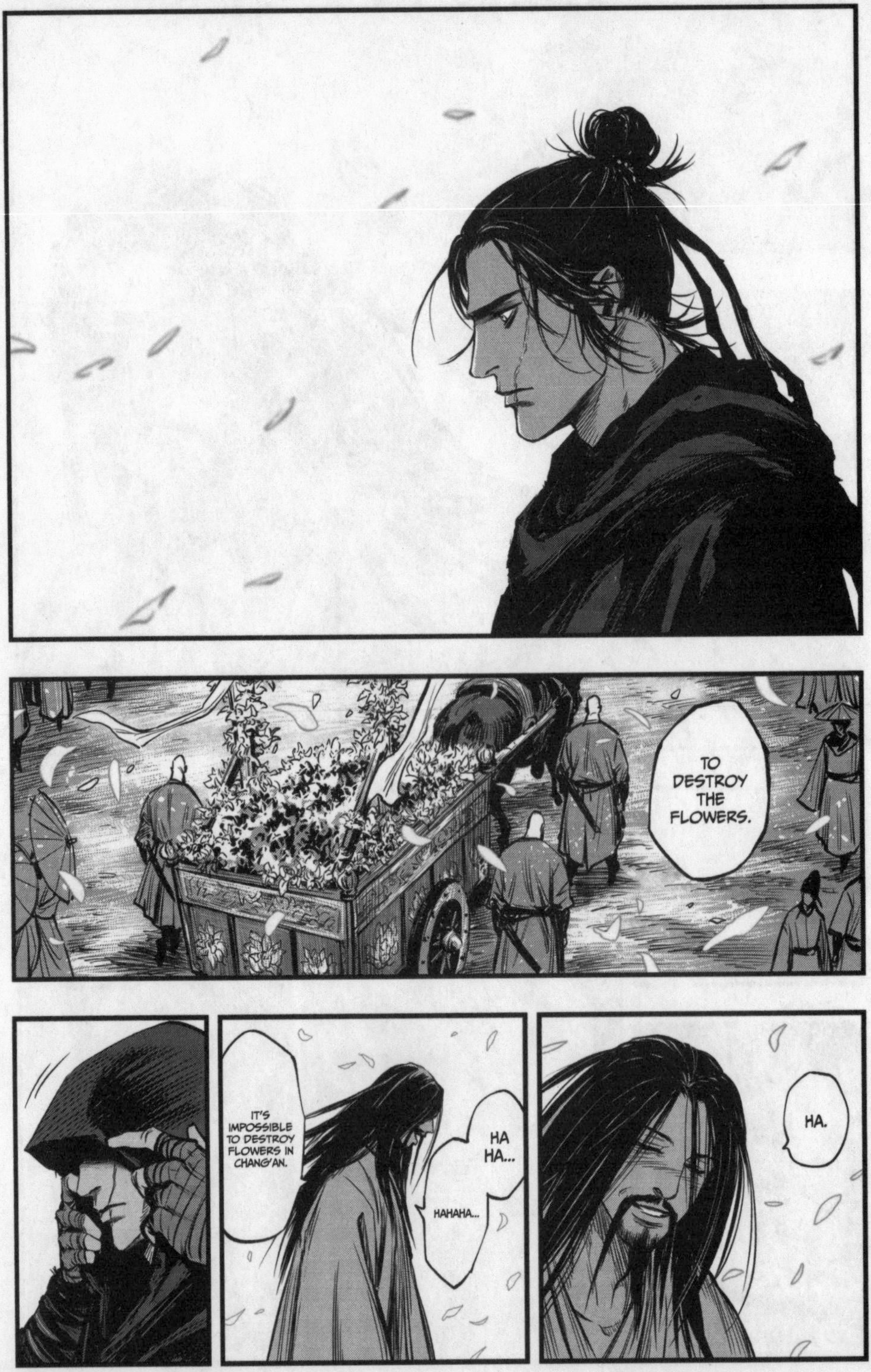
TO DESTROY THE FLOWERS.
HA.
IT'S IMPOSSIBLE TO DESTROY FLOWERS IN CHANG'AN.
HA HA...
HAHAHA...

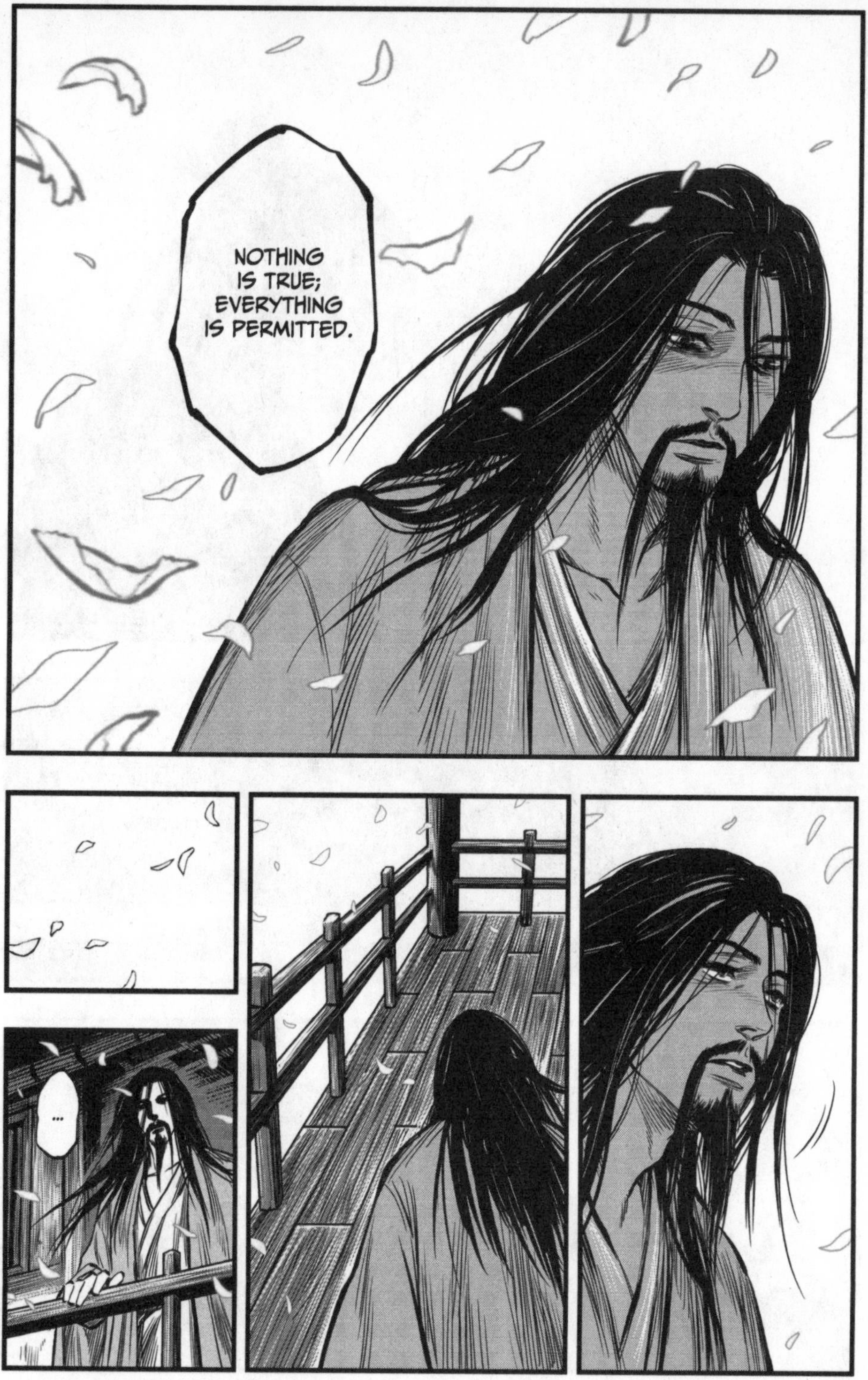
NOTHING IS TRUE; EVERYTHING IS PERMITTED.
...

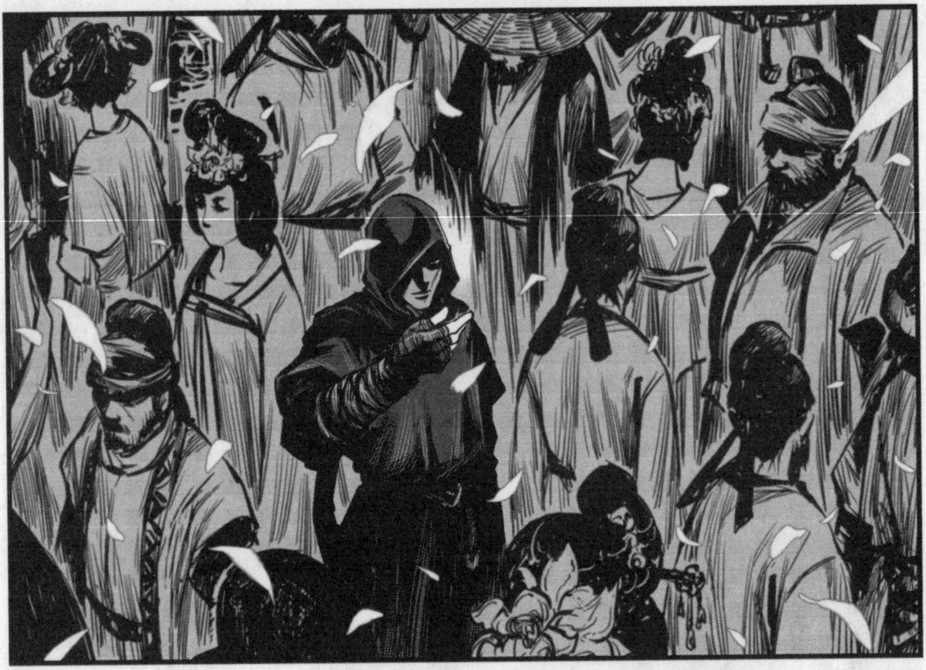
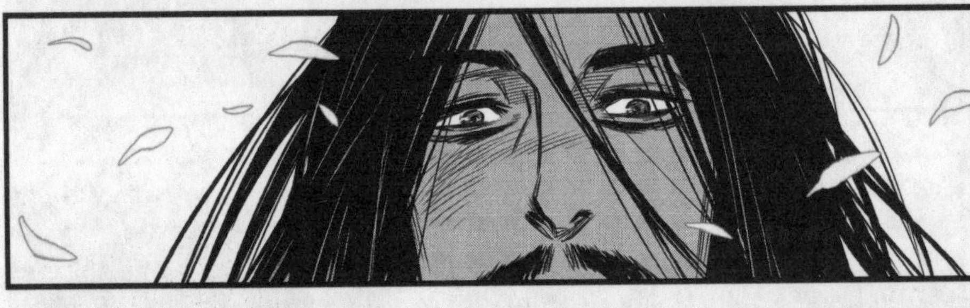
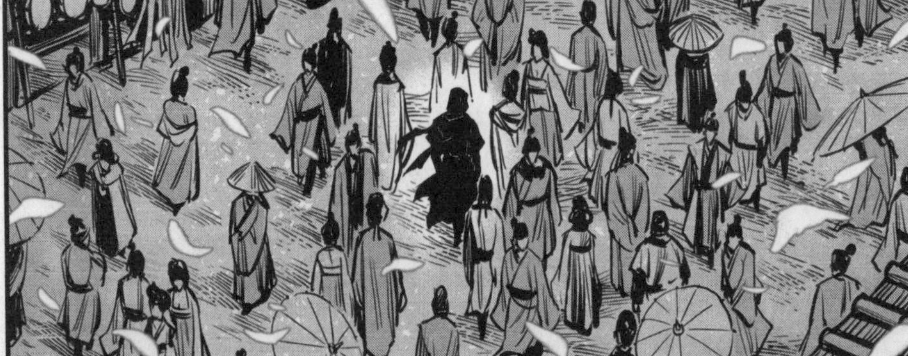

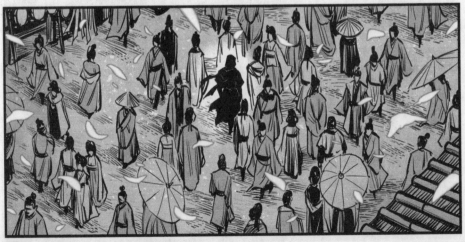

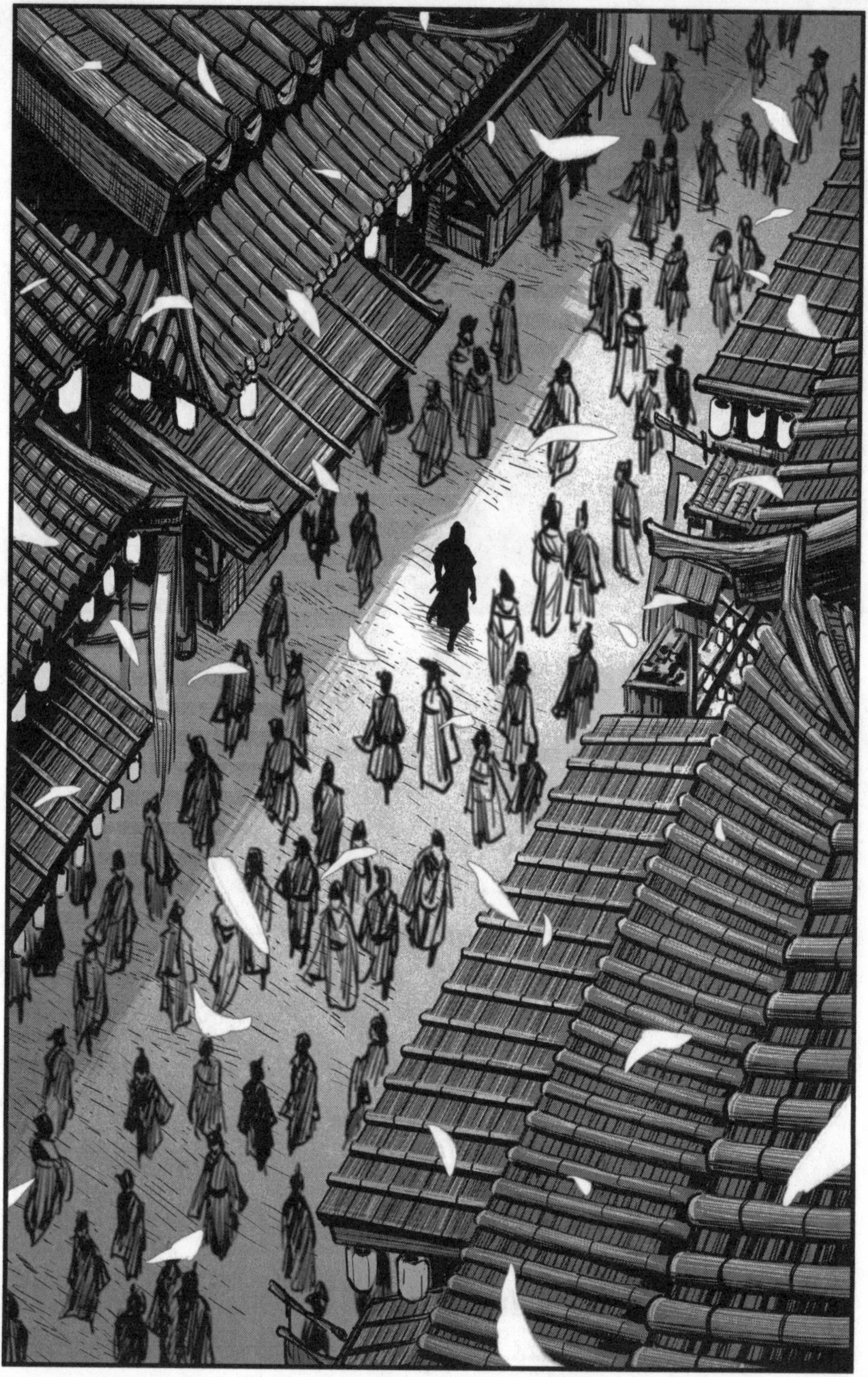

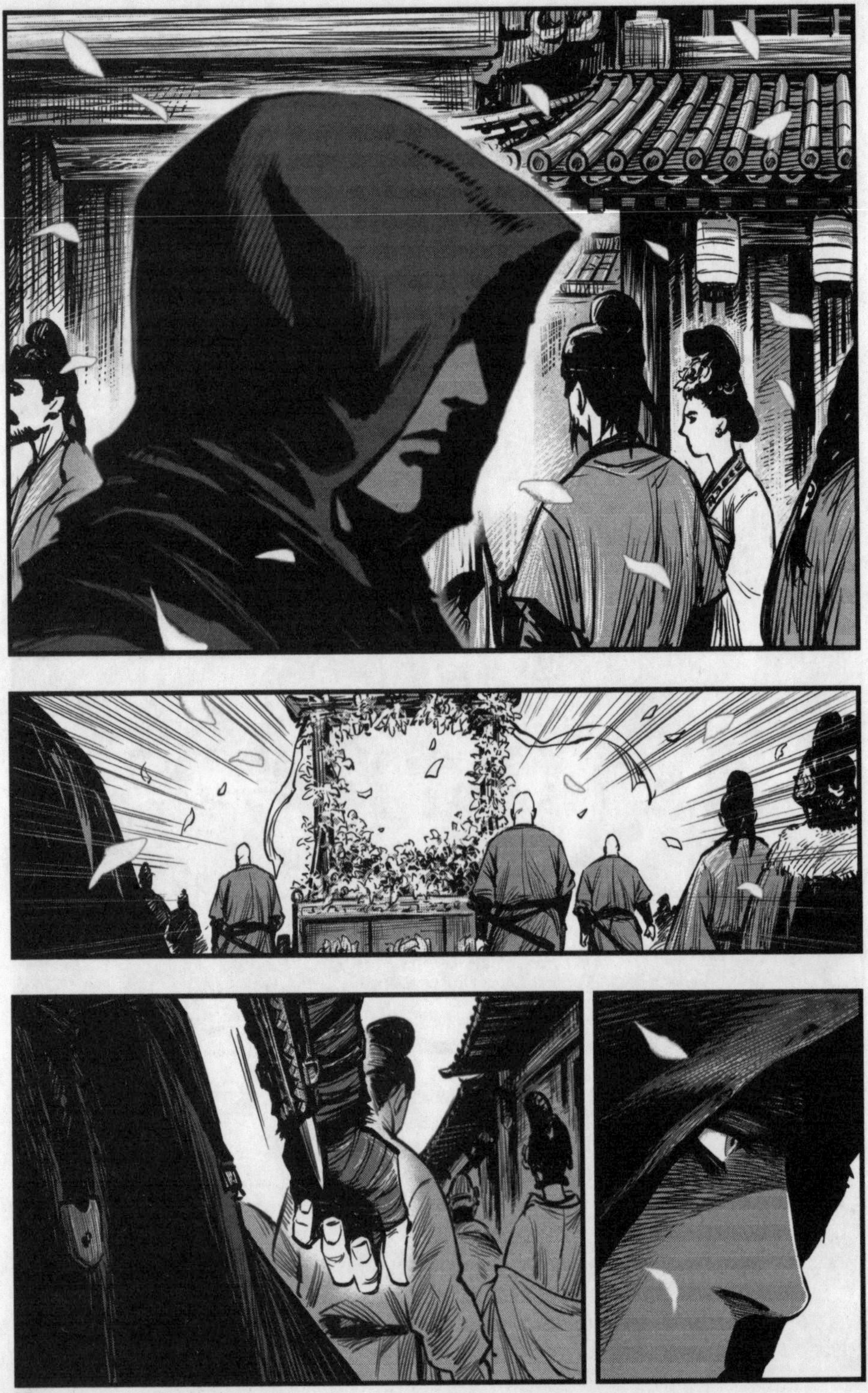

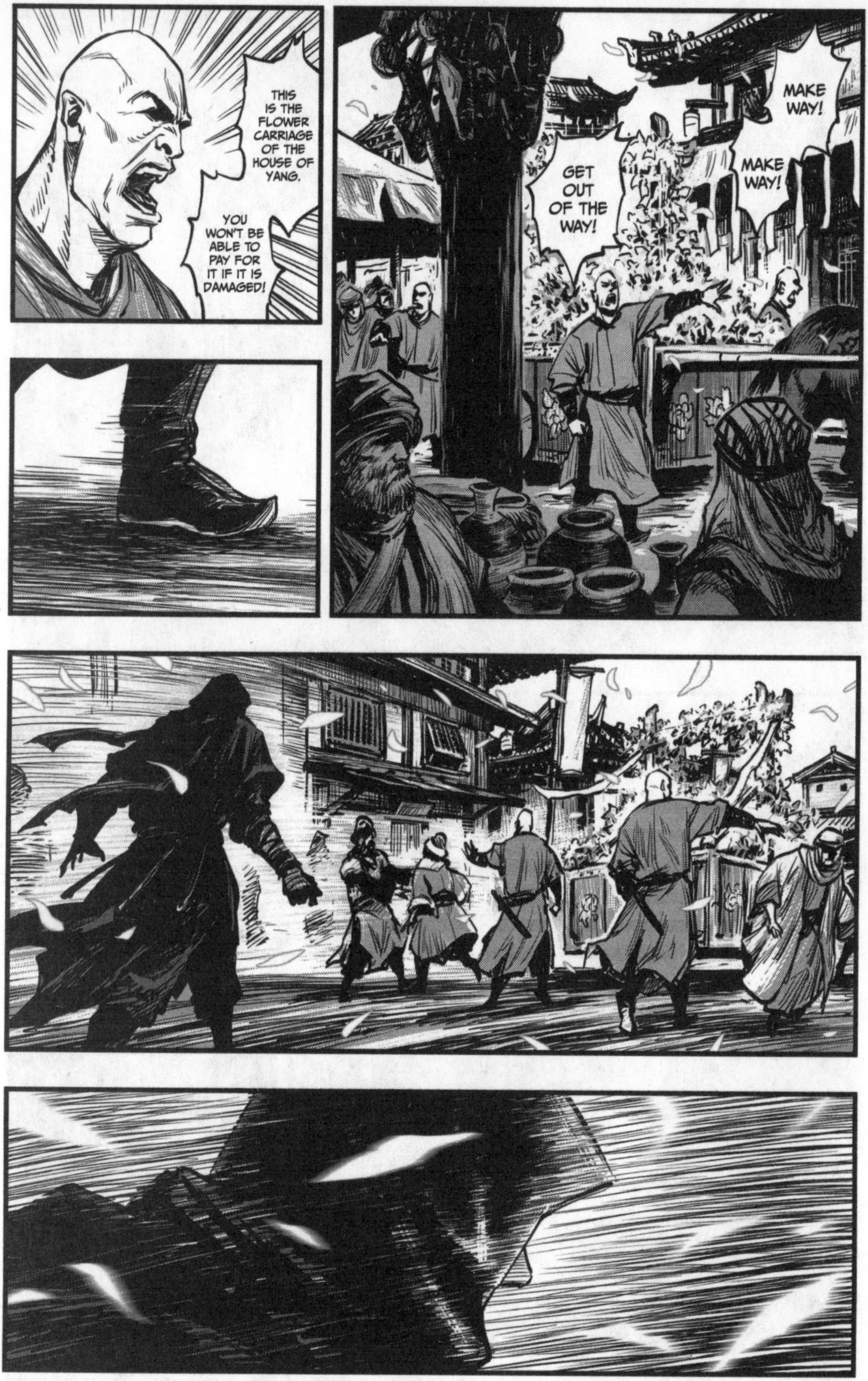
MAKE WAY!
MAKE WAY!
GET OUT OF THE WAY!
THIS IS THE FLOWER CARRIAGE OF THE HOUSE OF YANG.
YOU WON'T BE ABLE TO PAY FOR IT IF IT IS DAMAGED!

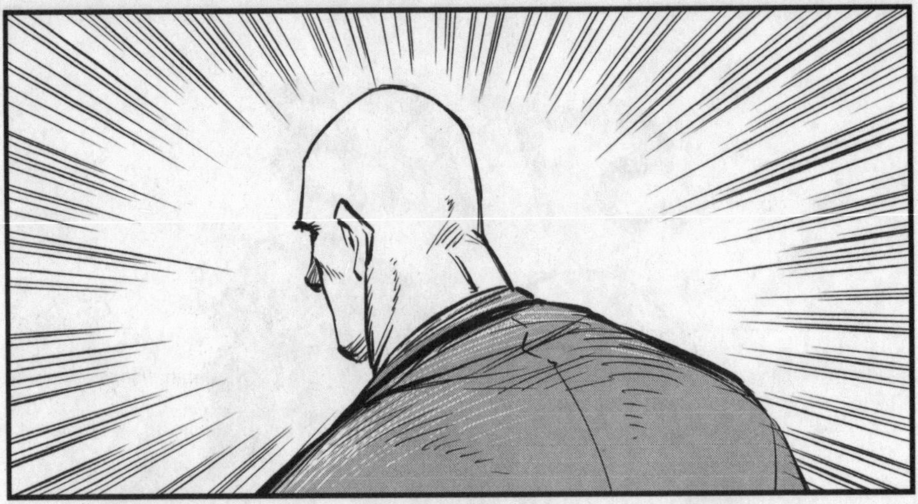

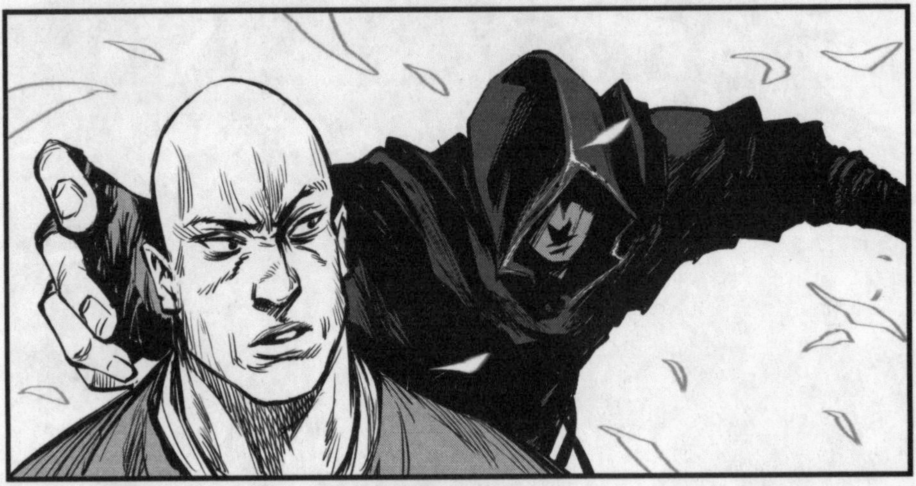

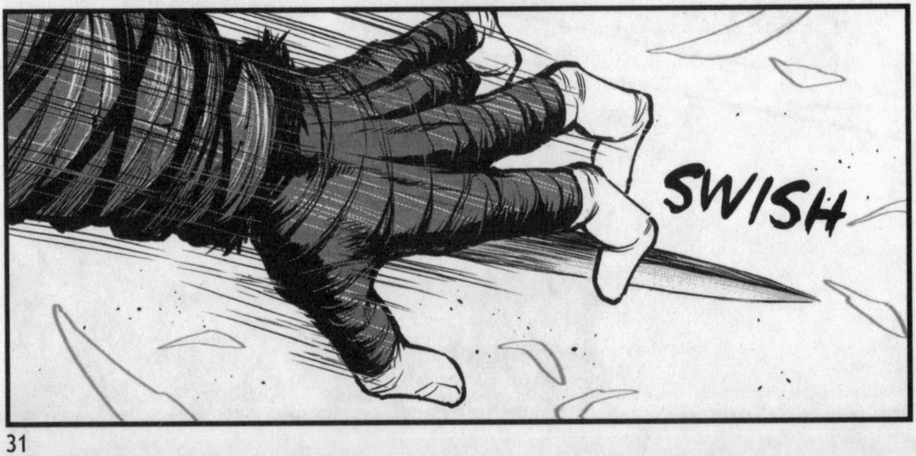
SWISH

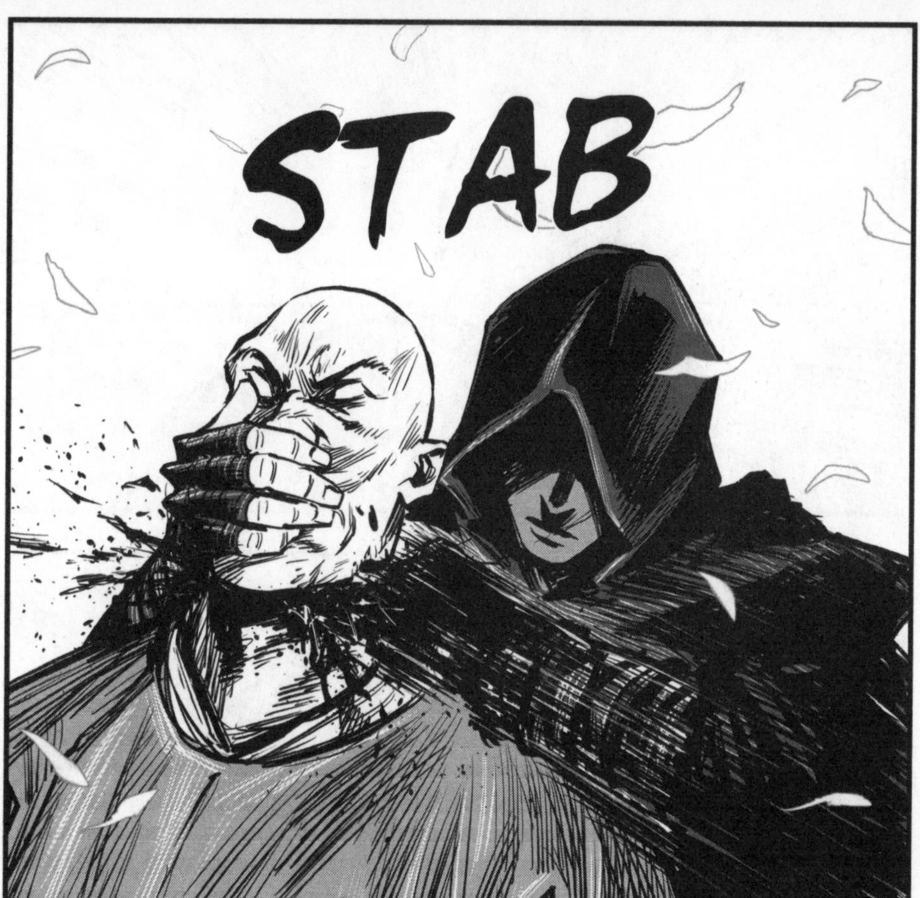
STAB
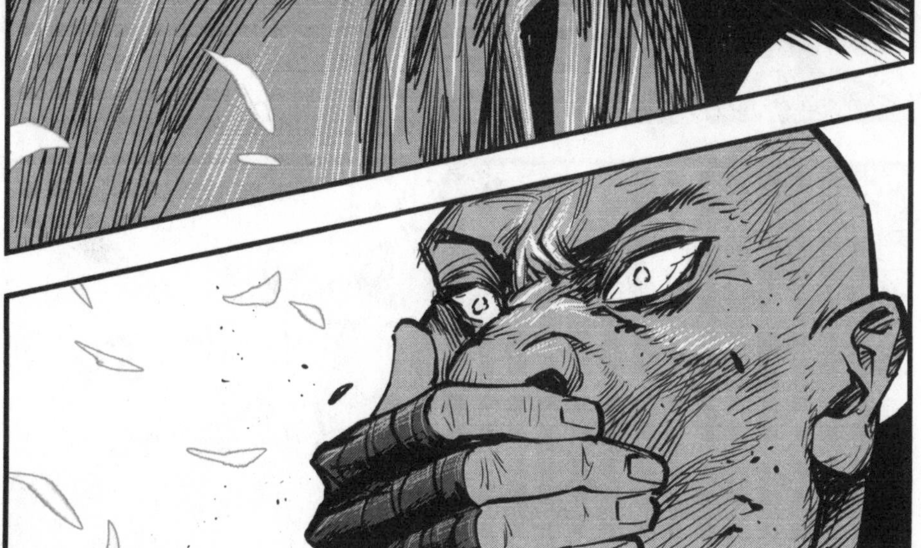

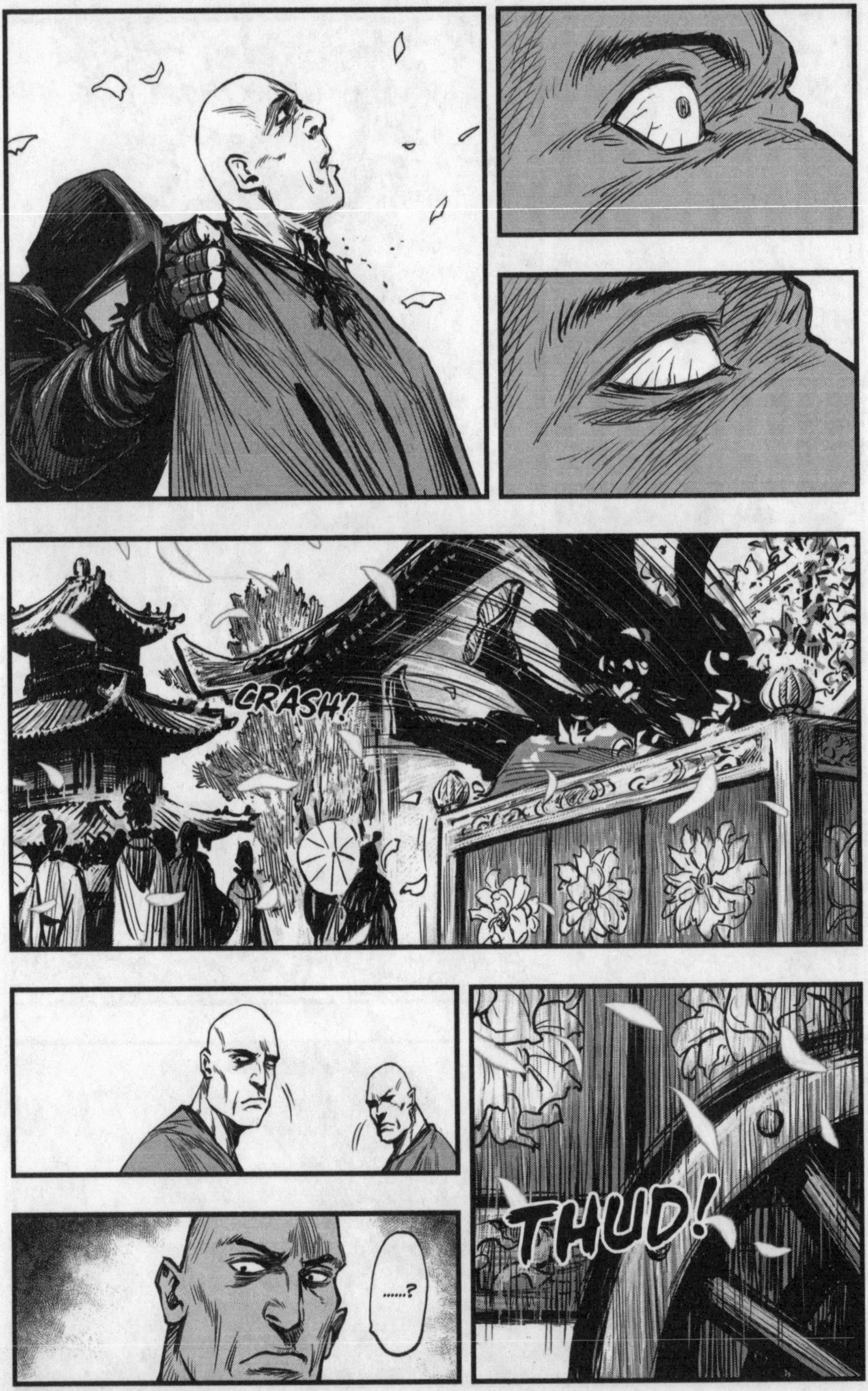
CRASH!
THUD!
......?

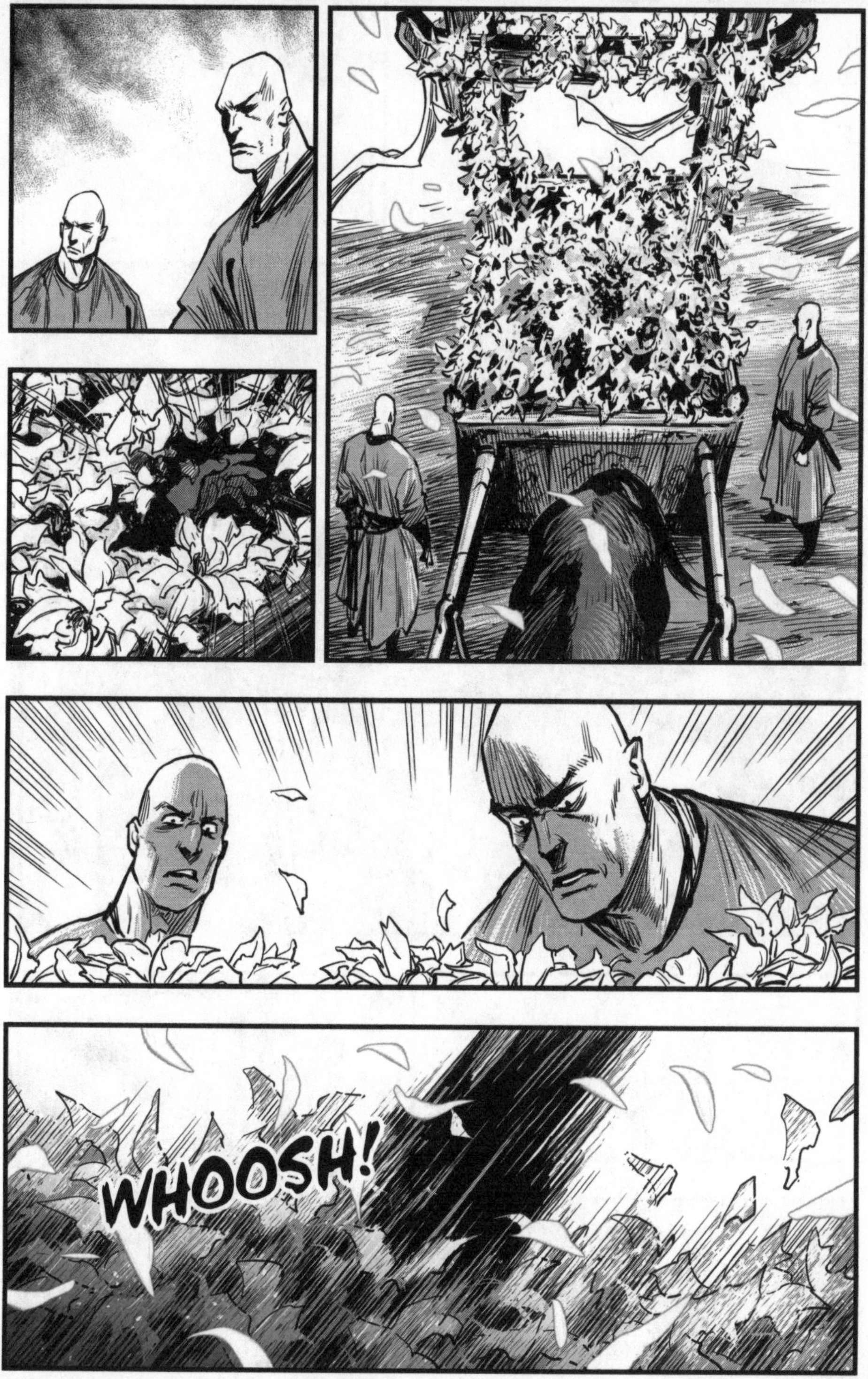
WHOOSH!

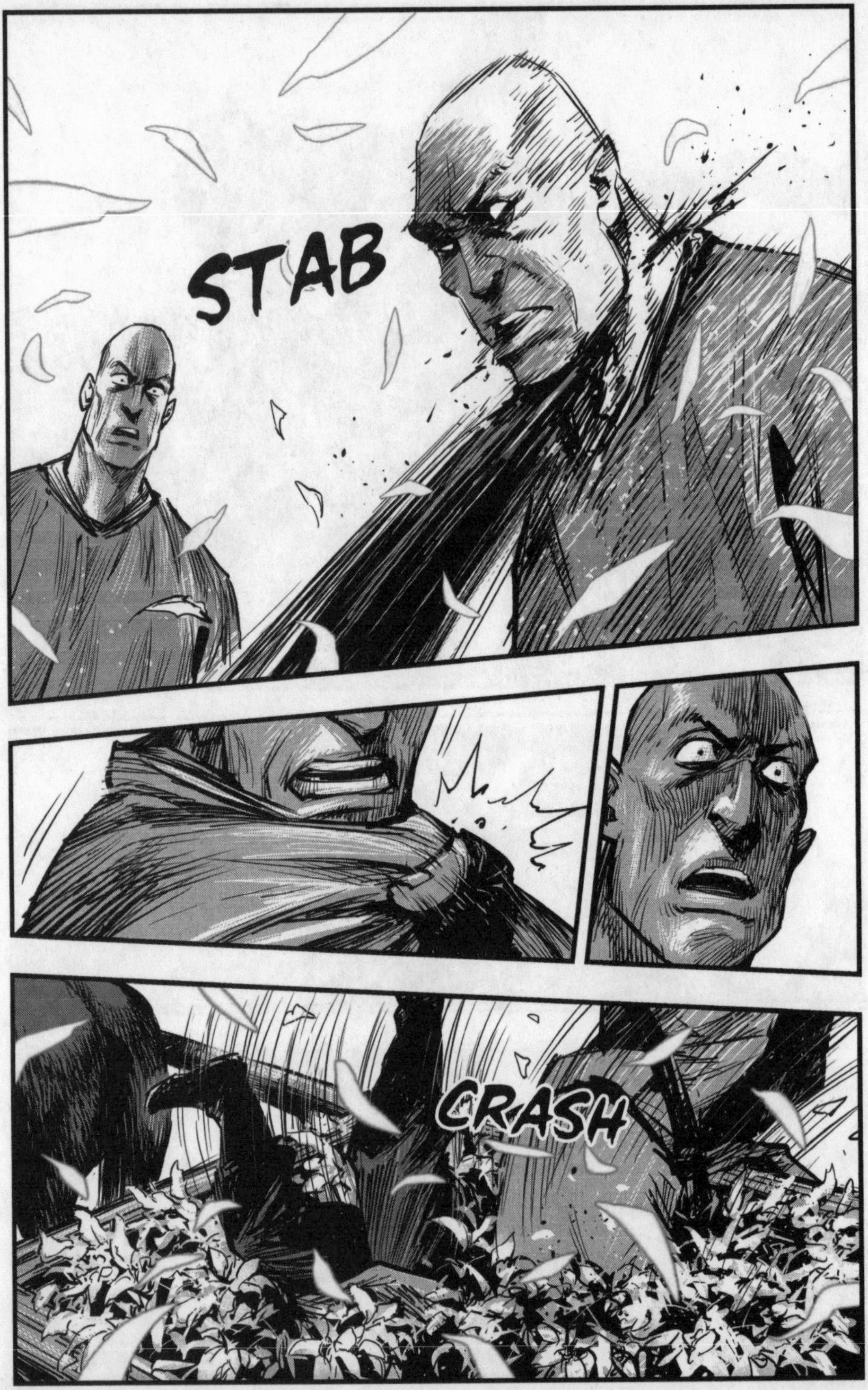
STAB
CRASH

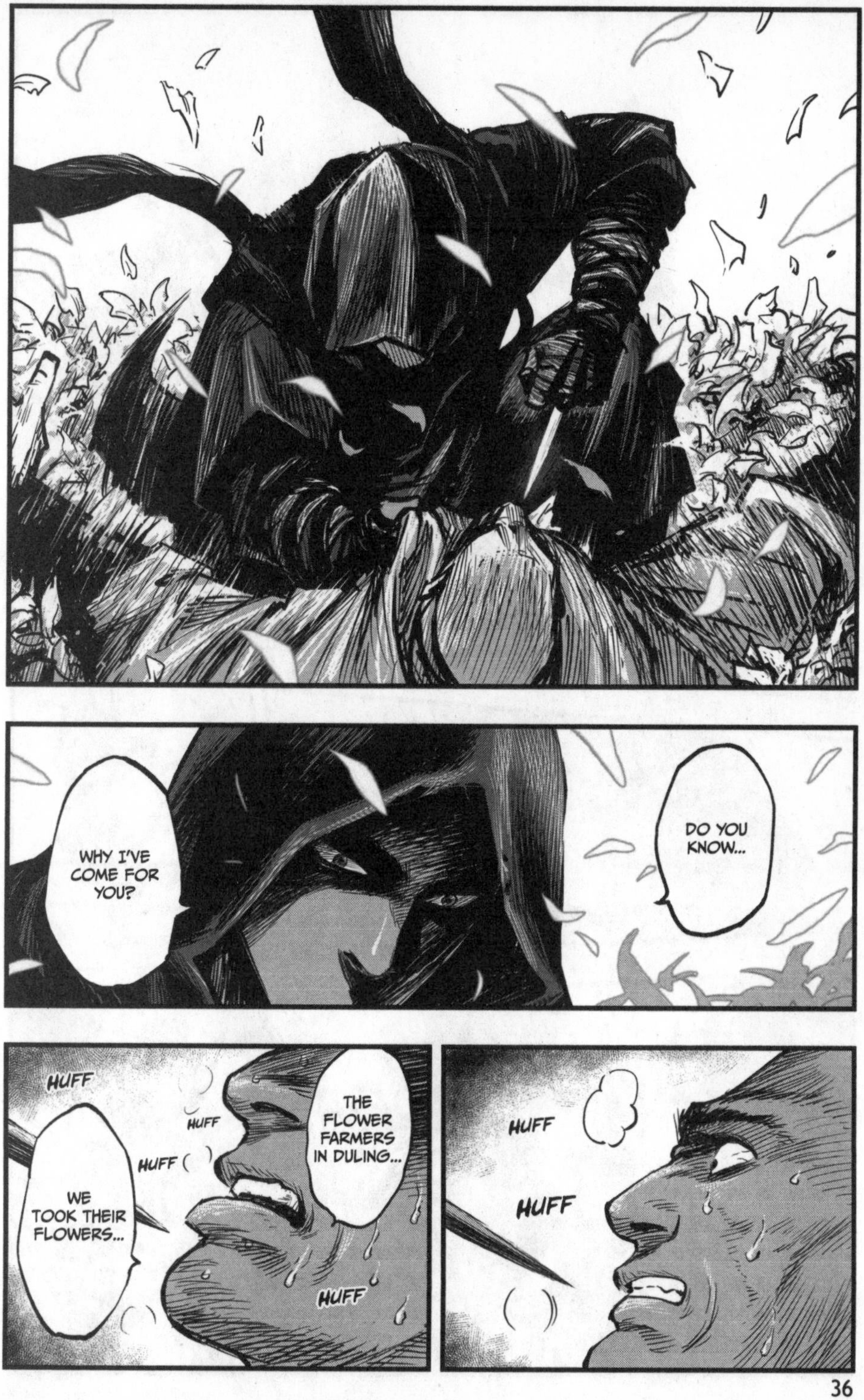
DO YOU KNOW...
WHY I'VE COME FOR YOU?
HUFF
HUFF
HUFF
THE FLOWER FARMERS IN DULING...
HUFF
HUFF
WE TOOK THEIR FLOWERS...
HUFF

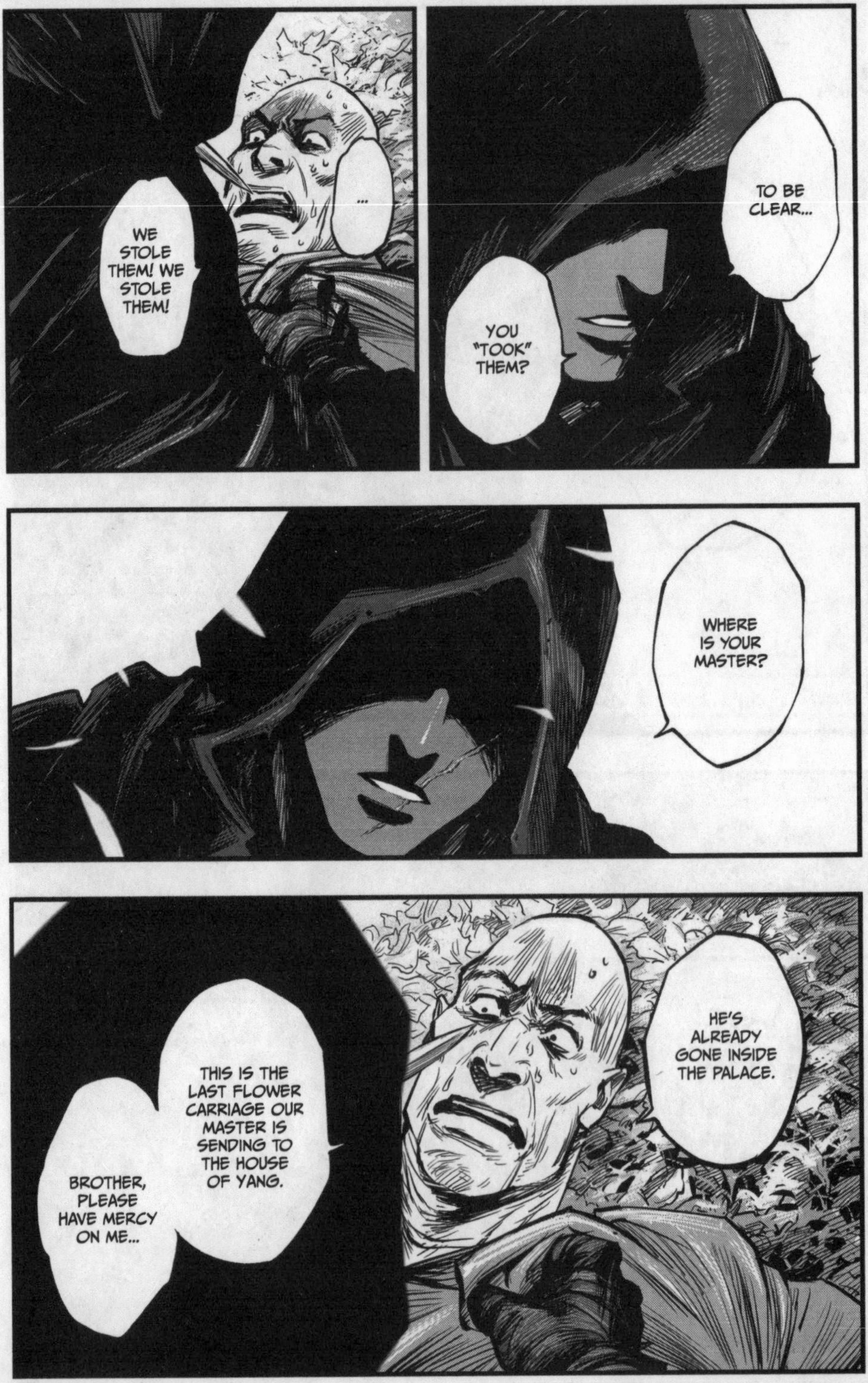
TO BE CLEAR...
YOU "TOOK" THEM?
...
WE STOLE THEM! WE STOLE THEM!
WHERE IS YOUR MASTER?
HE'S ALREADY GONE INSIDE THE PALACE.
THIS IS THE LAST FLOWER CARRIAGE OUR MASTER IS SENDING TO THE HOUSE OF YANG.
BROTHER, PLEASE HAVE MERCY ON ME...

YOU HAD
NO MERCY
FOR THEM.

SPLATTER!

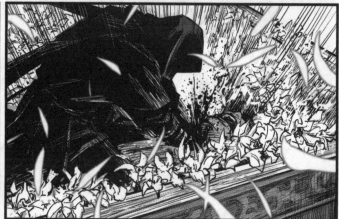

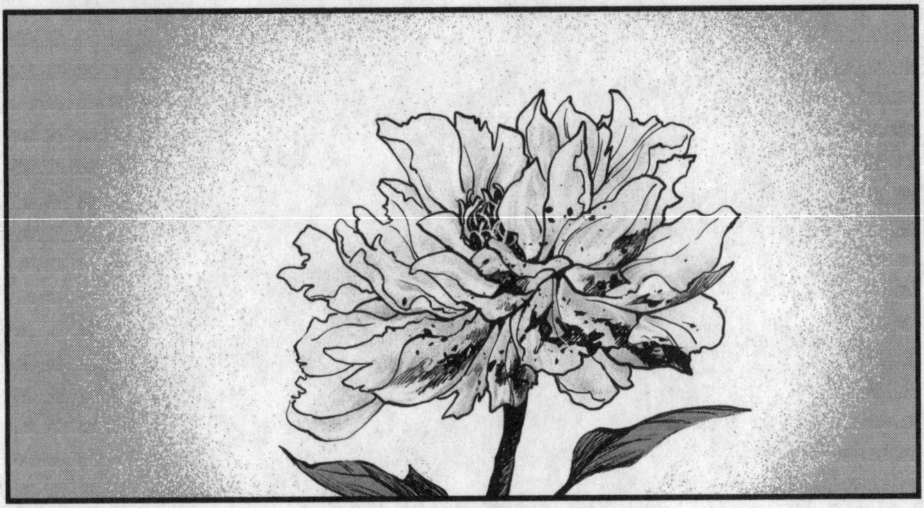

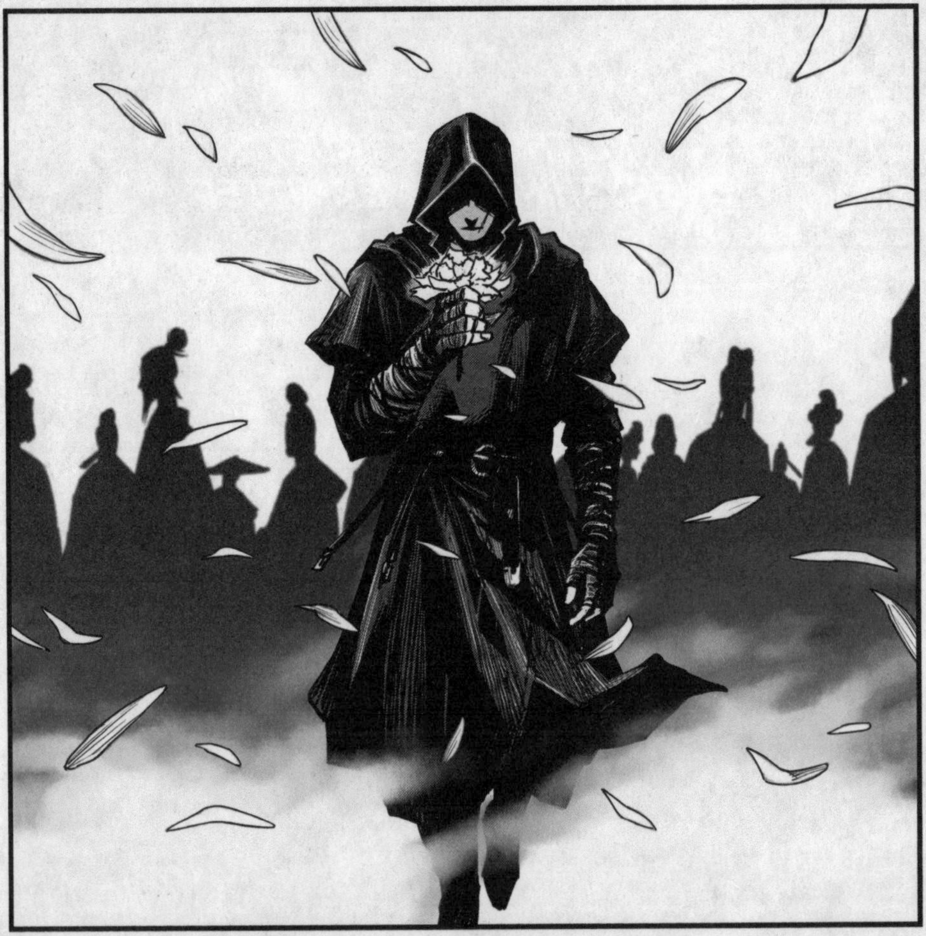

NOTHING IS TRUE;
EVERYTHING IS PERMITTED.

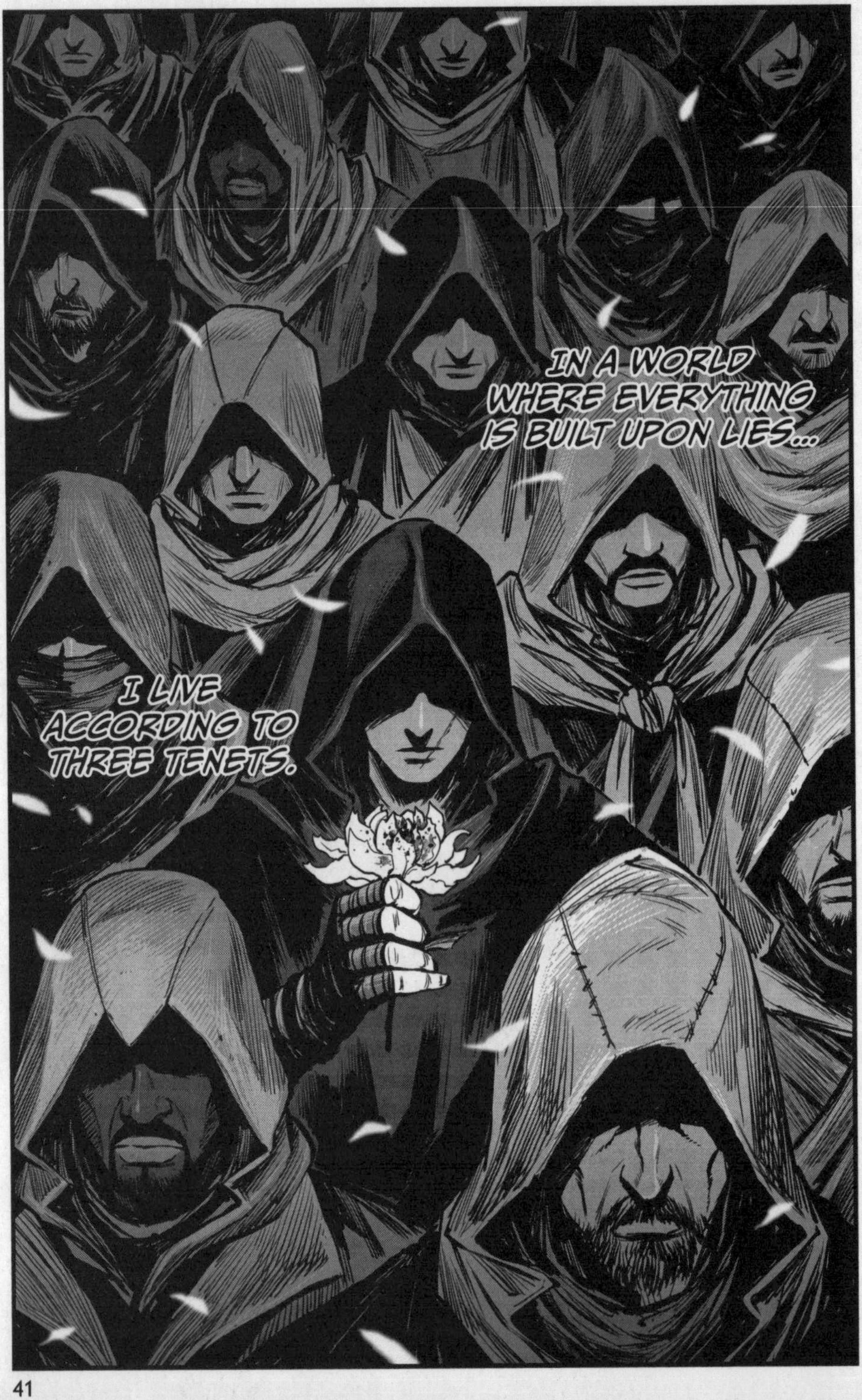
IN A WORLD WHERE EVERYTHING IS BUILT UPON LIES...
I LIVE ACCORDING TO THREE TENETS.

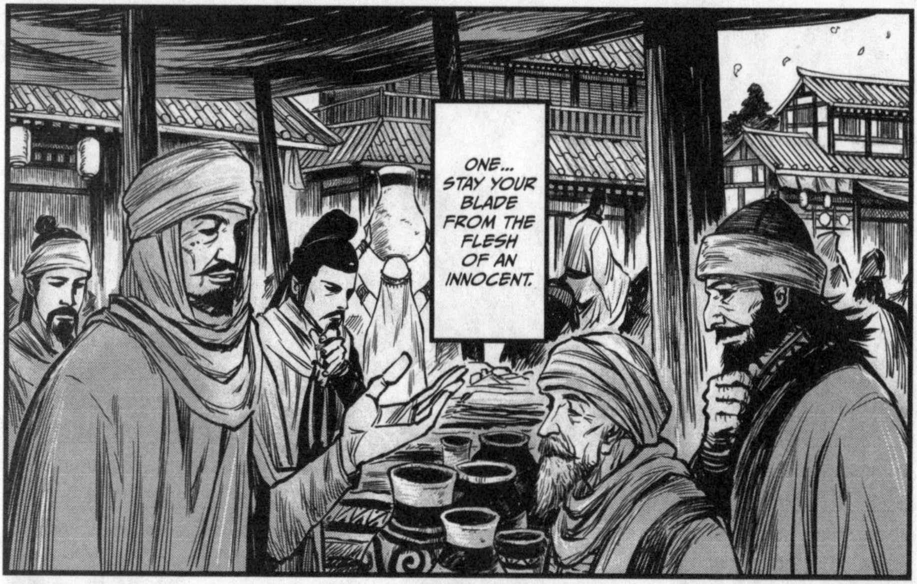
ONE... STAY YOUR BLADE FROM THE FLESH OF AN INNOCENT.

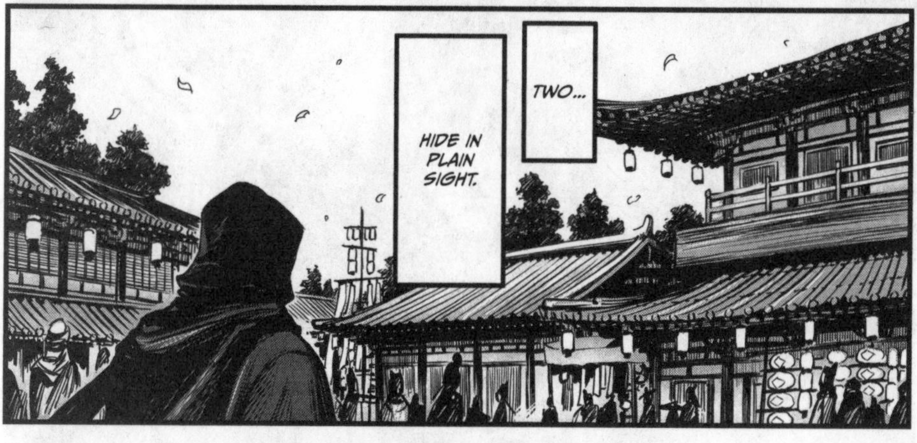
TWO...
HIDE IN PLAIN SIGHT.

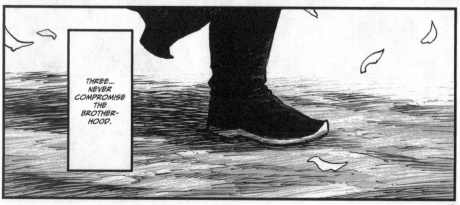

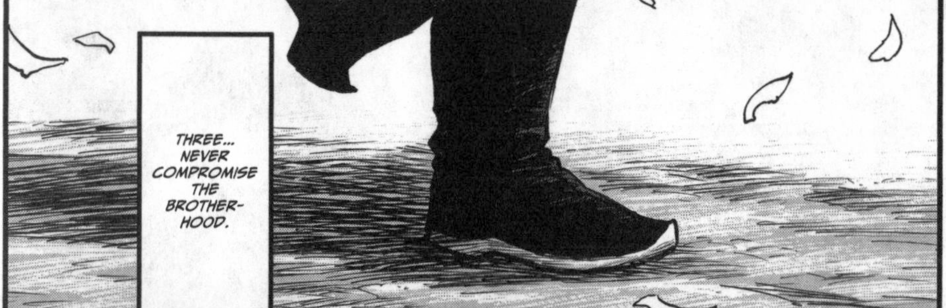
THREE... NEVER COMPROMISE THE BROTHER-HOOD.

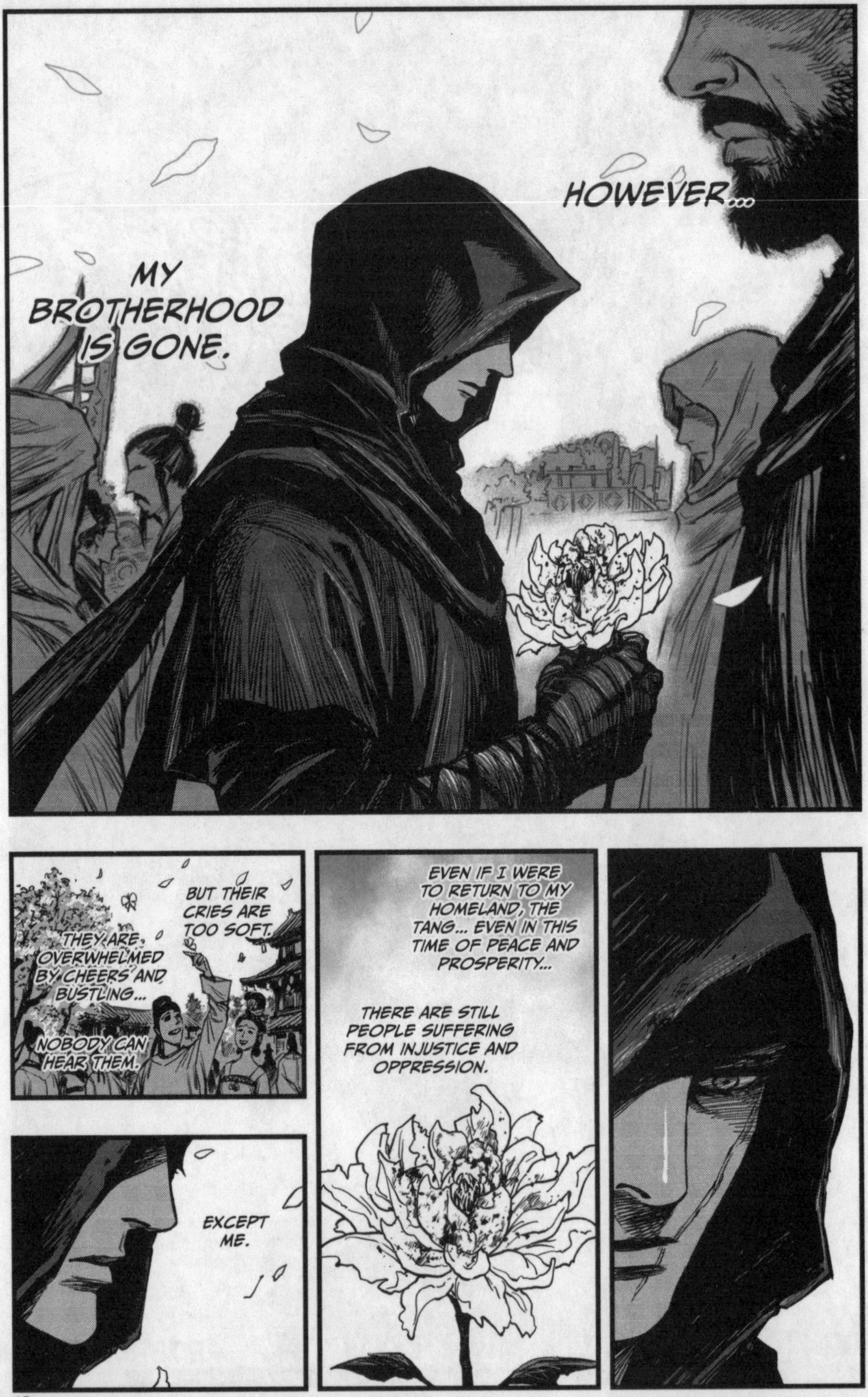
MY BROTHERHOOD IS GONE.
HOWEVER...
THEY ARE OVERWHELMED BY CHEERS AND BUSTLING...
BUT THEIR CRIES ARE TOO SOFT.
NOBODY CAN HEAR THEM.
EXCEPT ME.
EVEN IF I WERE TO RETURN TO MY HOMELAND, THE TANG... EVEN IN THIS TIME OF PEACE AND PROSPERITY...
THERE ARE STILL PEOPLE SUFFERING FROM INJUSTICE AND OPPRESSION.

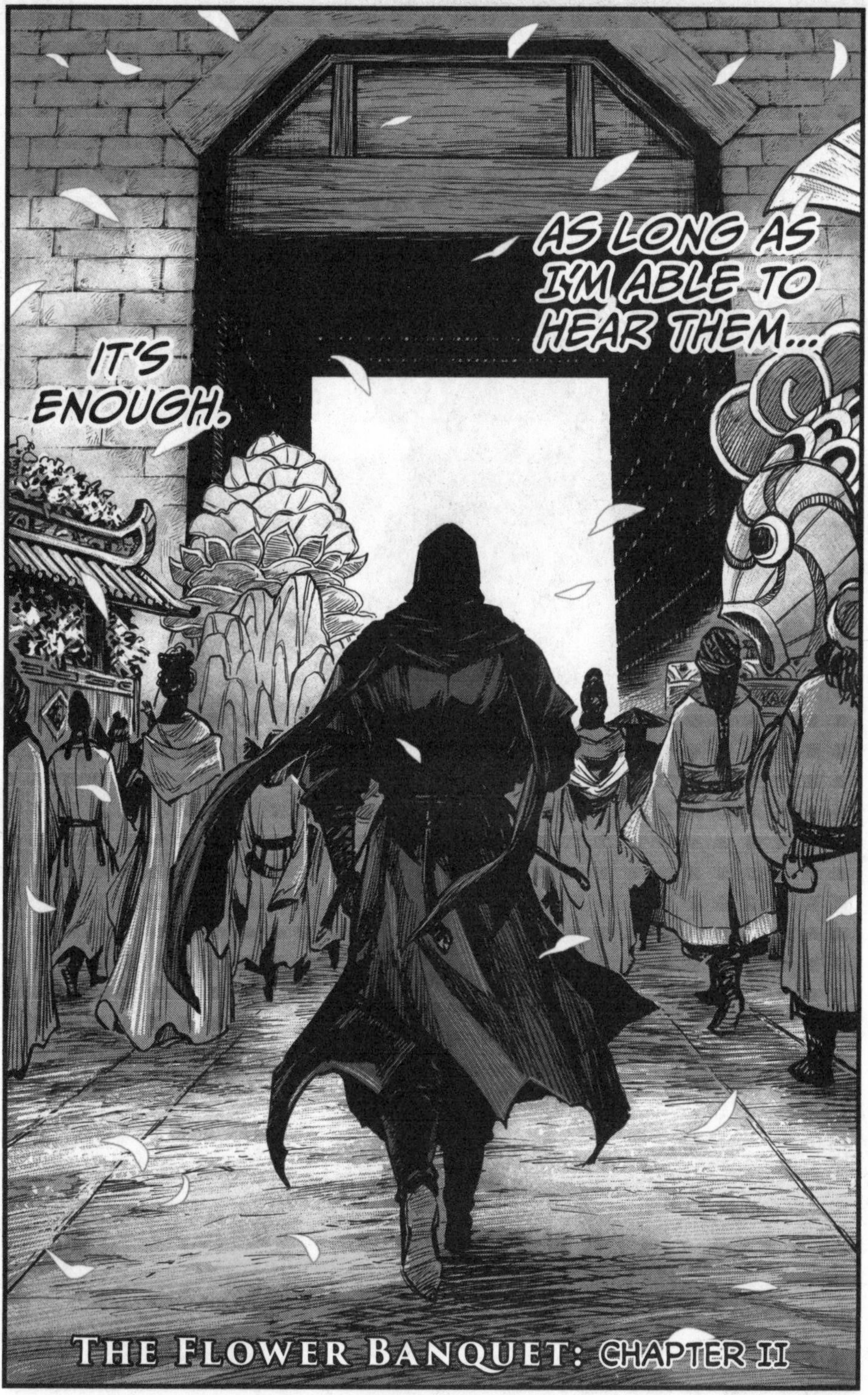
AS LONG AS I'M ABLE TO HEAR THEM...
IT'S ENOUGH.
THE FLOWER BANQUET: CHAPTER II

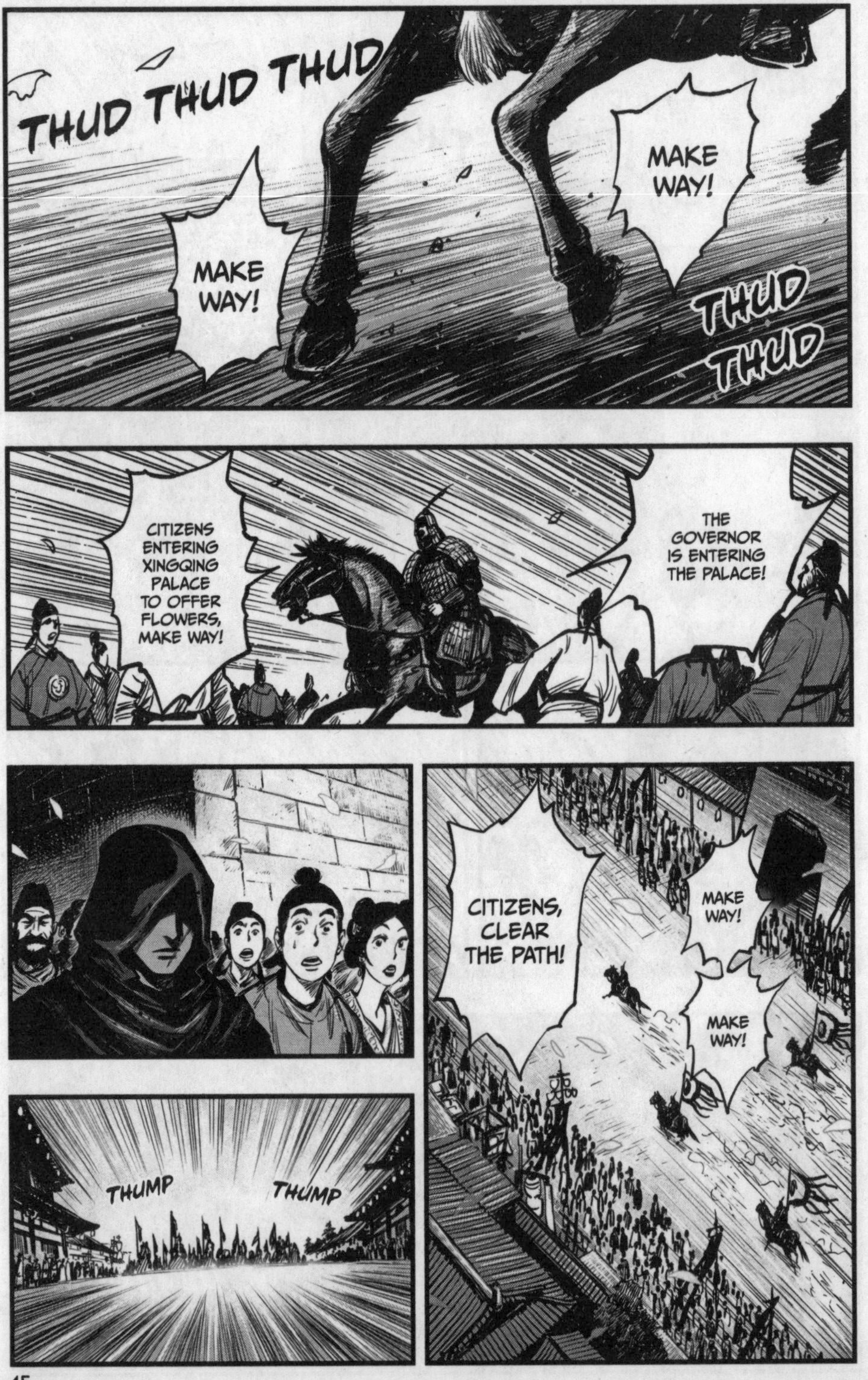
MAKE WAY!
THUD THUD THUD
THUD THUD
MAKE WAY!
THE GOVERNOR IS ENTERING THE PALACE!
CITIZENS ENTERING XINGQING PALACE TO OFFER FLOWERS, MAKE WAY!
MAKE WAY!
CITIZENS, CLEAR THE PATH!
MAKE WAY!
THUMP
THUMP

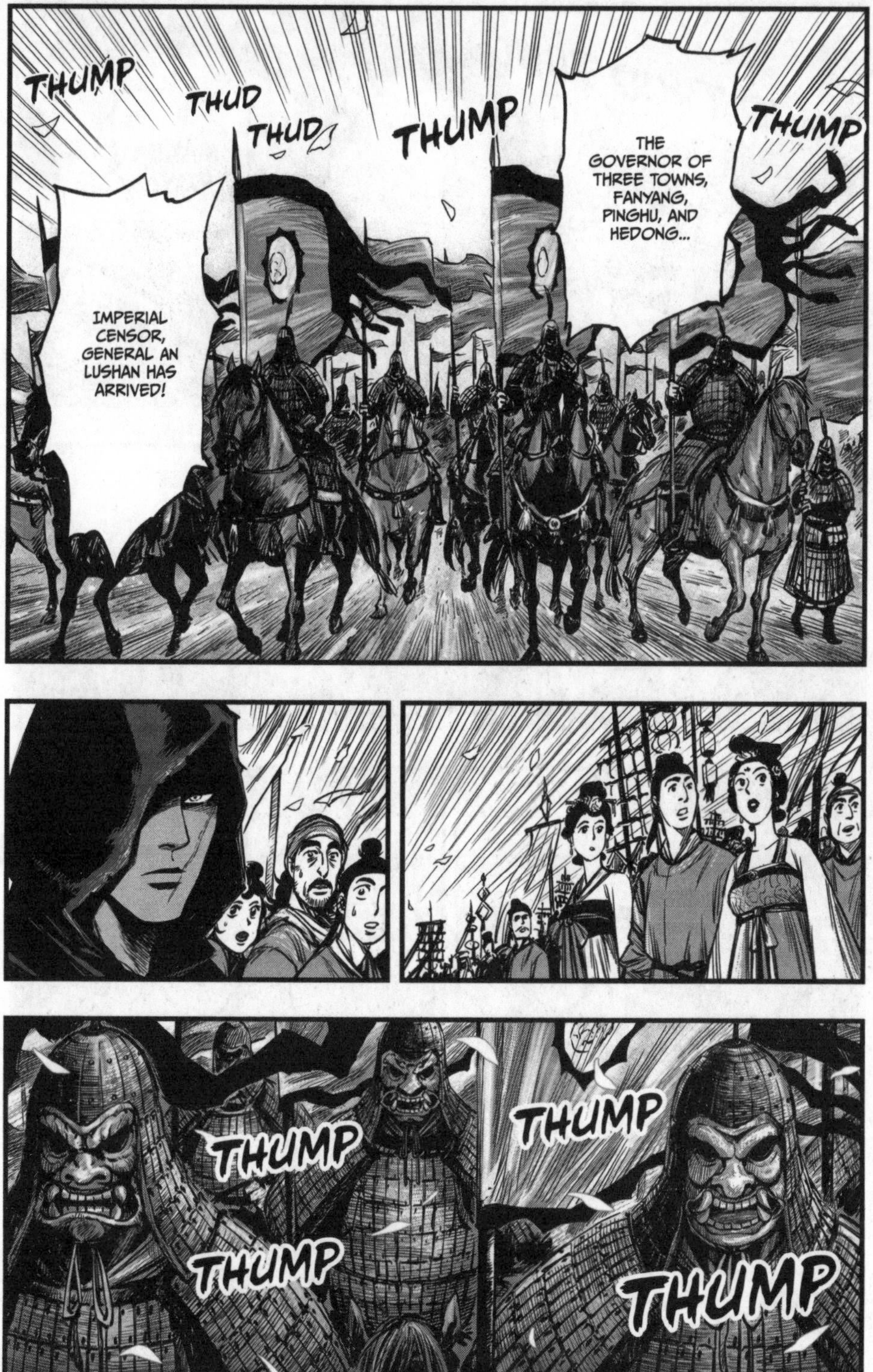
THUMP
THUD
THUD
THUMP
THUMP
IMPERIAL CENSOR, GENERAL AN LUSHAN HAS ARRIVED!
THE GOVERNOR OF THREE TOWNS, FANYANG, PINGHU, AND HEDONG...
THUMP
THUMP
THUMP
THUMP

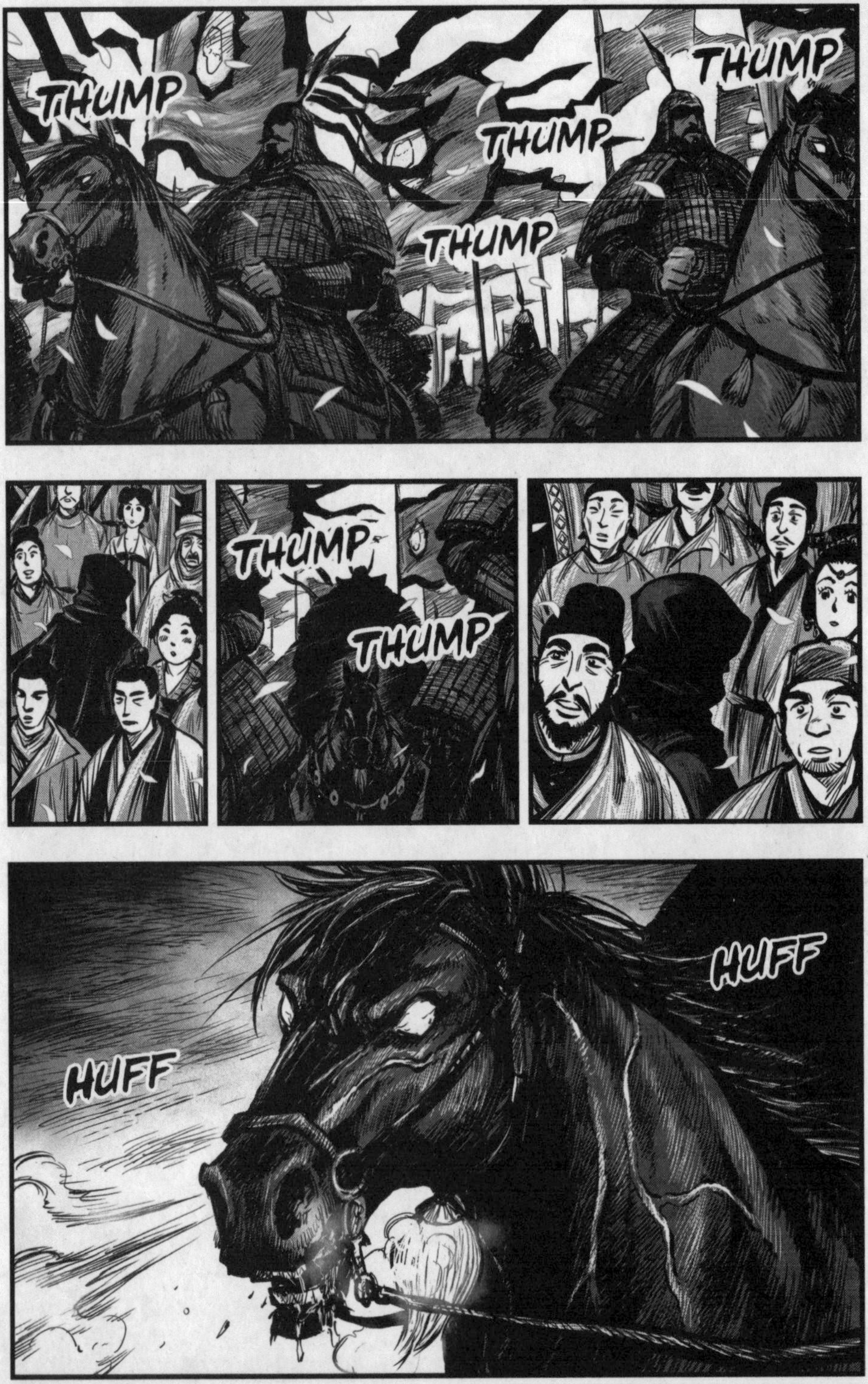
THUMP
THUMP
THUMP
THUMP
THUMP
THUMP
HUFF
HUFF

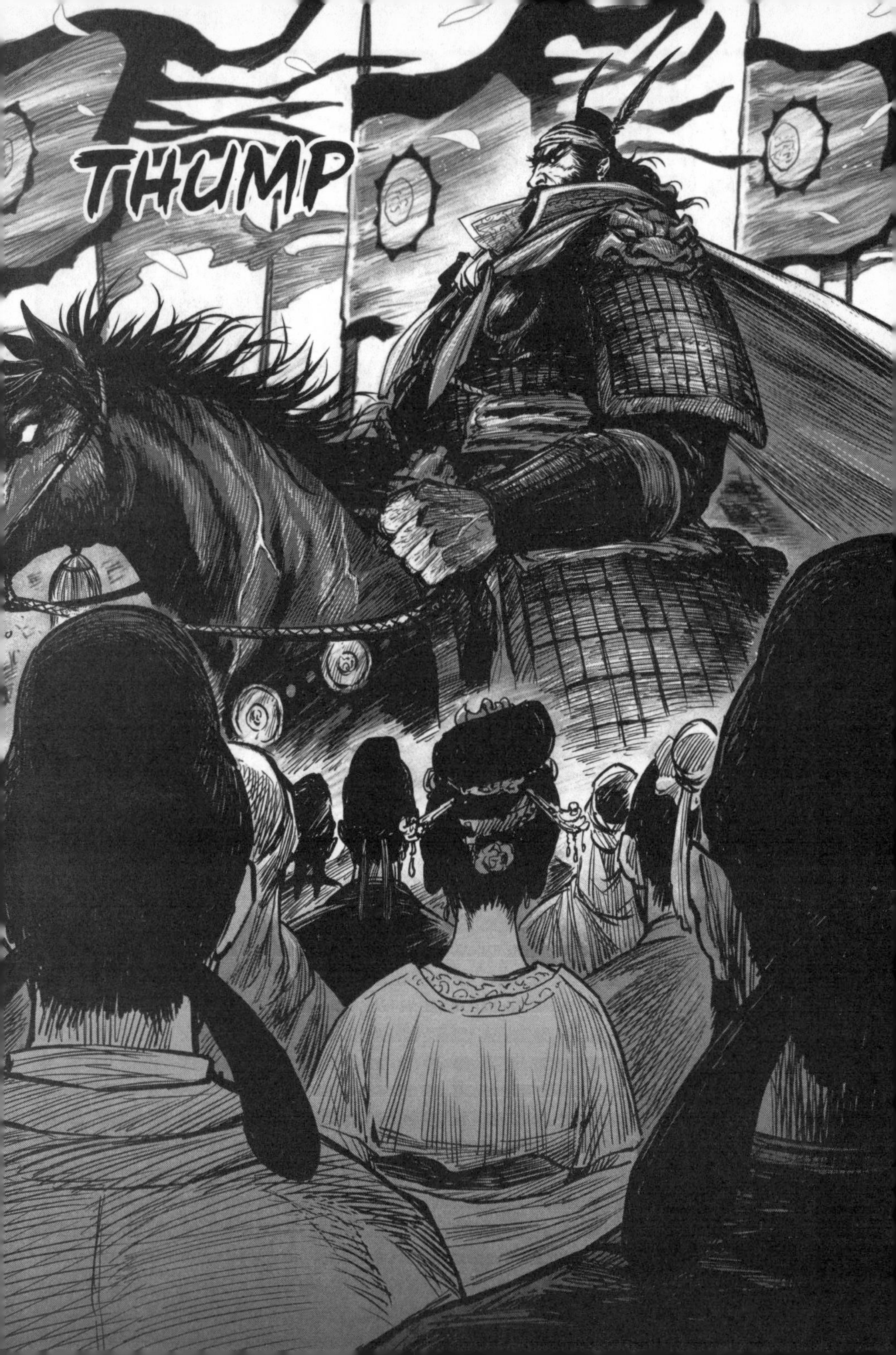
THUMP

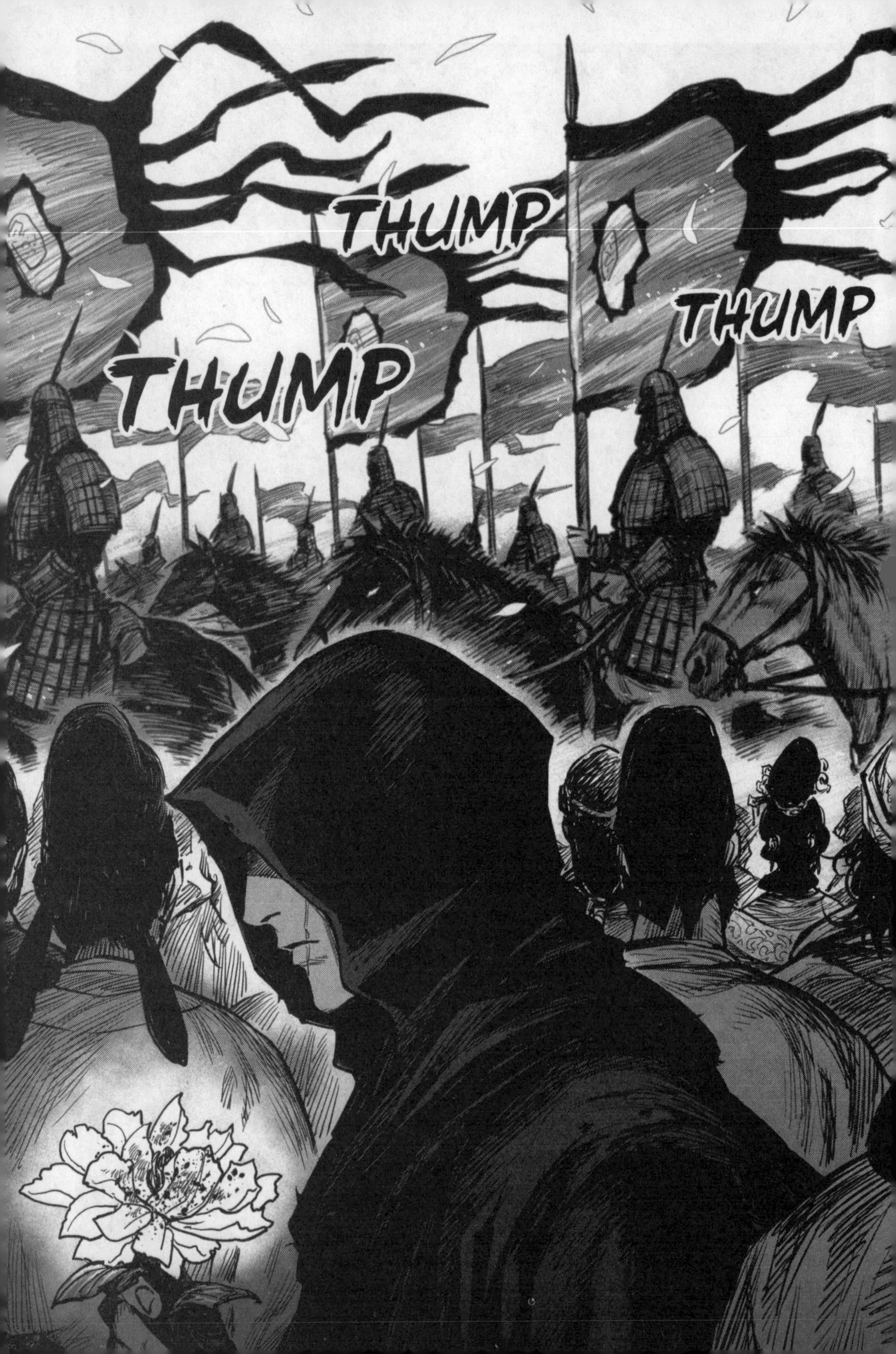
THUMP
THUMP
THUMP

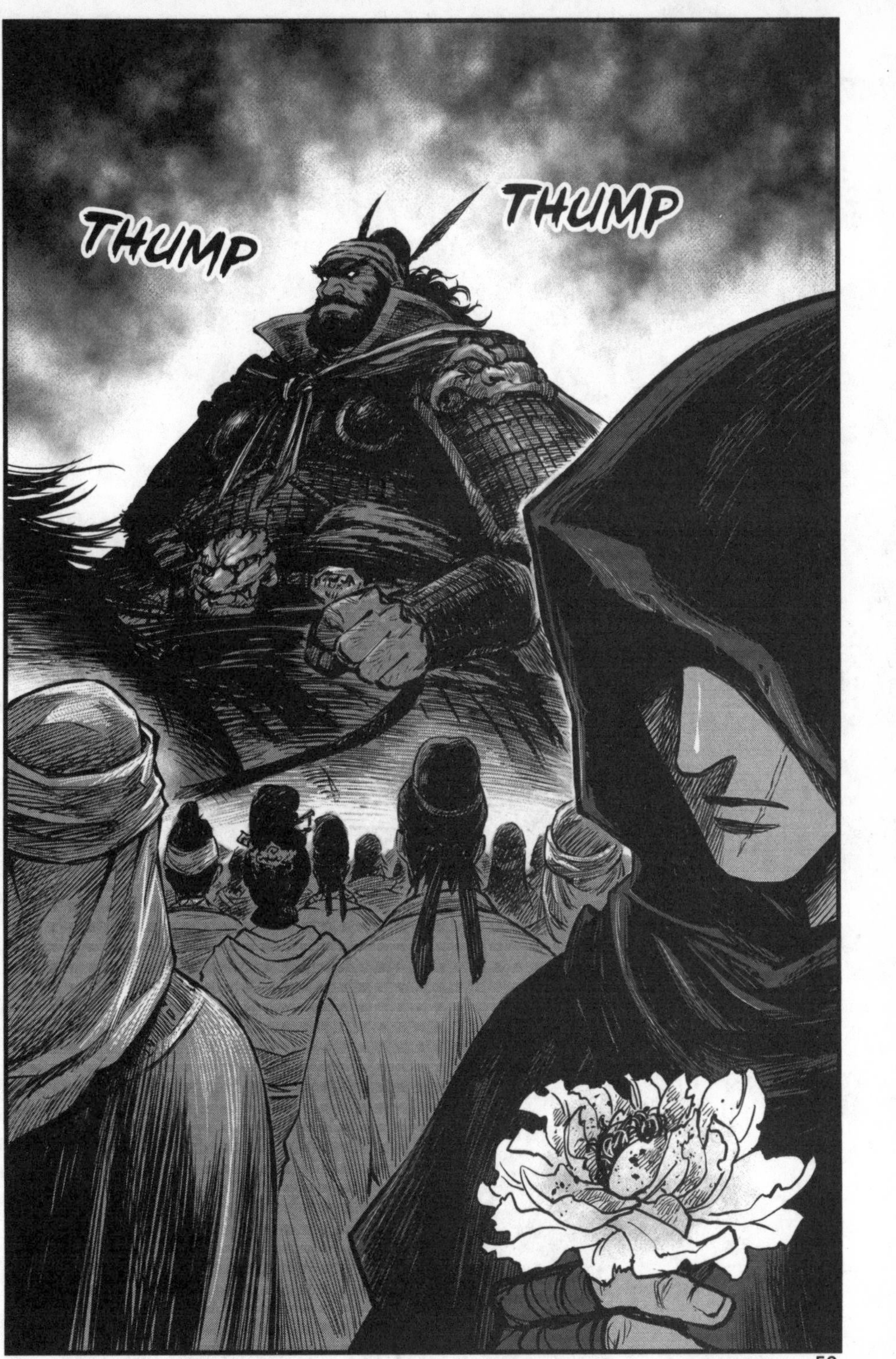
THUMP
THUMP

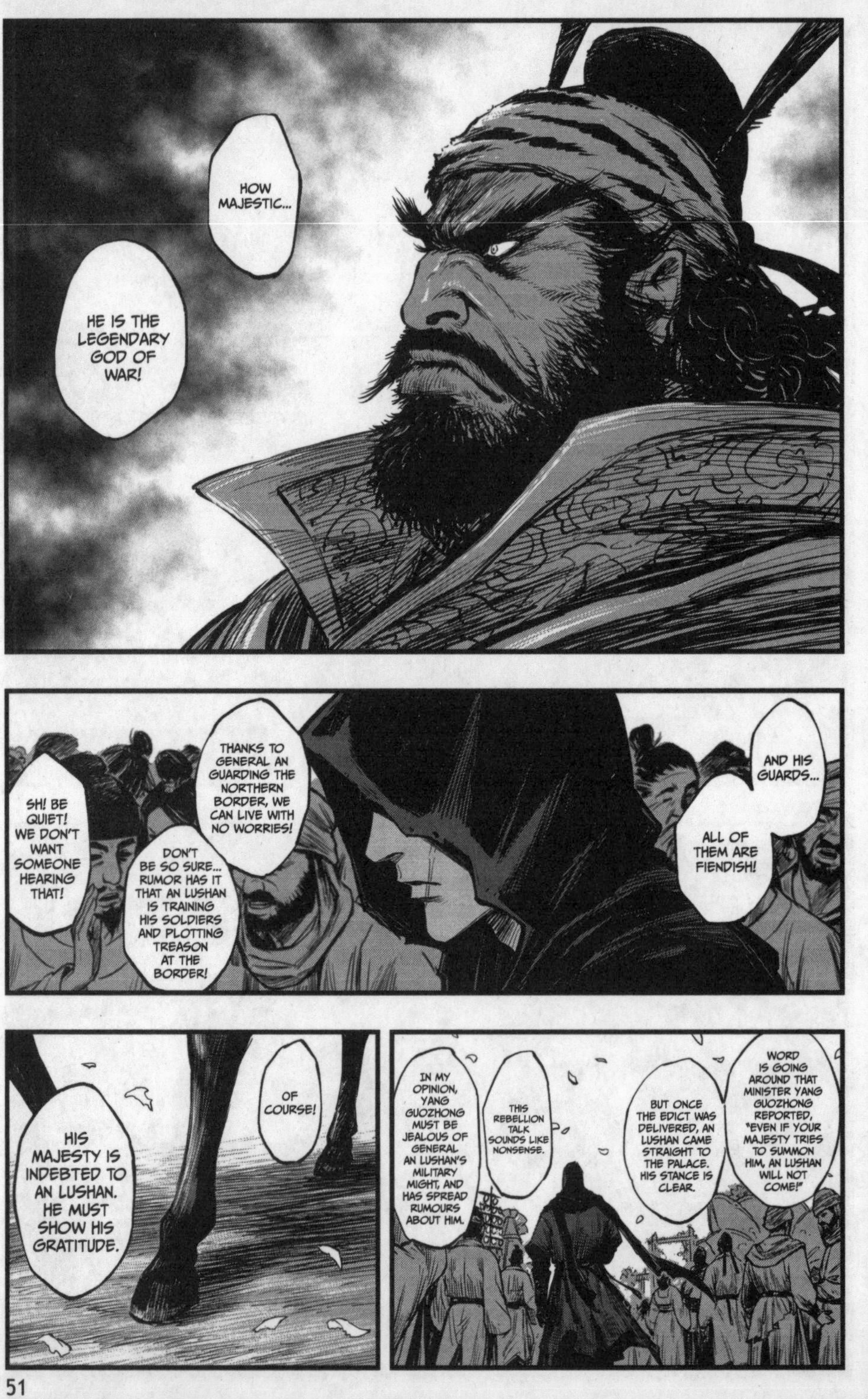
HOW MAJESTIC...
HE IS THE LEGENDARY GOD OF WAR!
AND HIS GUARDS...
ALL OF THEM ARE FIENDISH!
THANKS TO GENERAL AN GUARDING THE NORTHERN BORDER, WE CAN LIVE WITH NO WORRIES!
DON'T BE SO SURE... RUMOR HAS IT THAT AN LUSHAN IS TRAINING HIS SOLDIERS AND PLOTTING TREASON AT THE BORDER!
SH! BE QUIET! WE DON'T WANT SOMEONE HEARING THAT!
WORD IS GOING AROUND THAT MINISTER YANG GUOZHONG REPORTED, "EVEN IF YOUR MAJESTY TRIES TO SUMMON HIM, AN LUSHAN WILL NOT COME!"
BUT ONCE THE EDICT WAS DELIVERED, AN LUSHAN CAME STRAIGHT TO THE PALACE. HIS STANCE IS CLEAR.
THIS REBELLION TALK SOUNDS LIKE NONSENSE.
IN MY OPINION, YANG GUOZHONG MUST BE JEALOUS OF GENERAL AN LUSHAN'S MILITARY MIGHT, AND HAS SPREAD RUMOURS ABOUT HIM.
OF COURSE!
HIS MAJESTY IS INDEBTED TO AN LUSHAN. HE MUST SHOW HIS GRATITUDE.

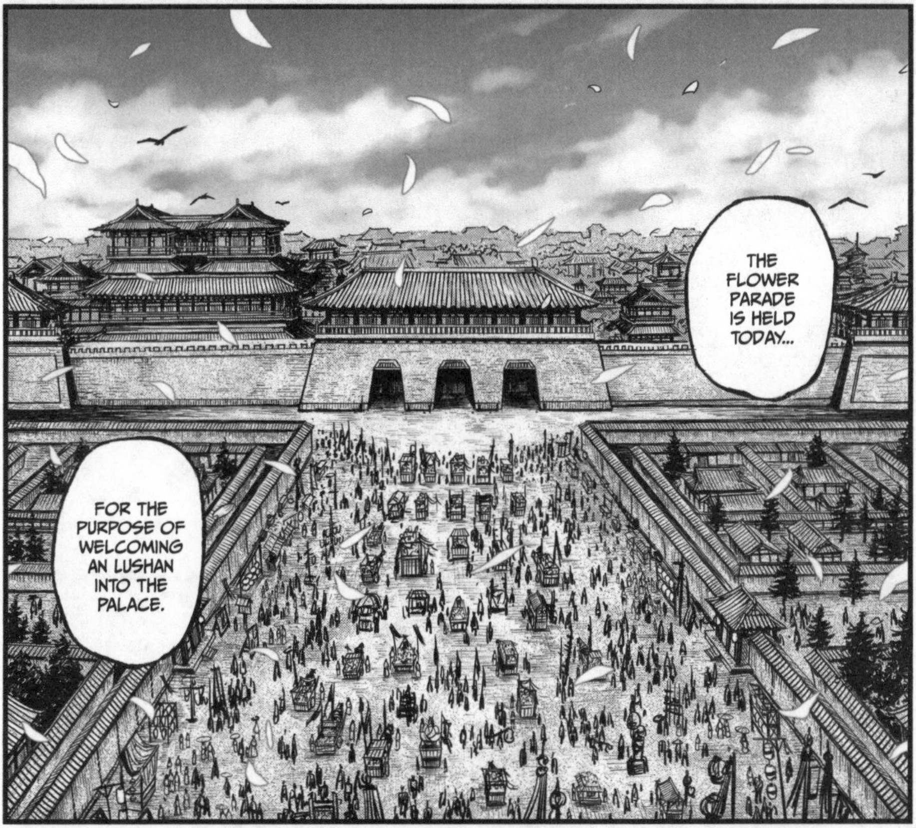
THE FLOWER PARADE IS HELD TODAY...
FOR THE PURPOSE OF WELCOMING AN LUSHAN INTO THE PALACE.
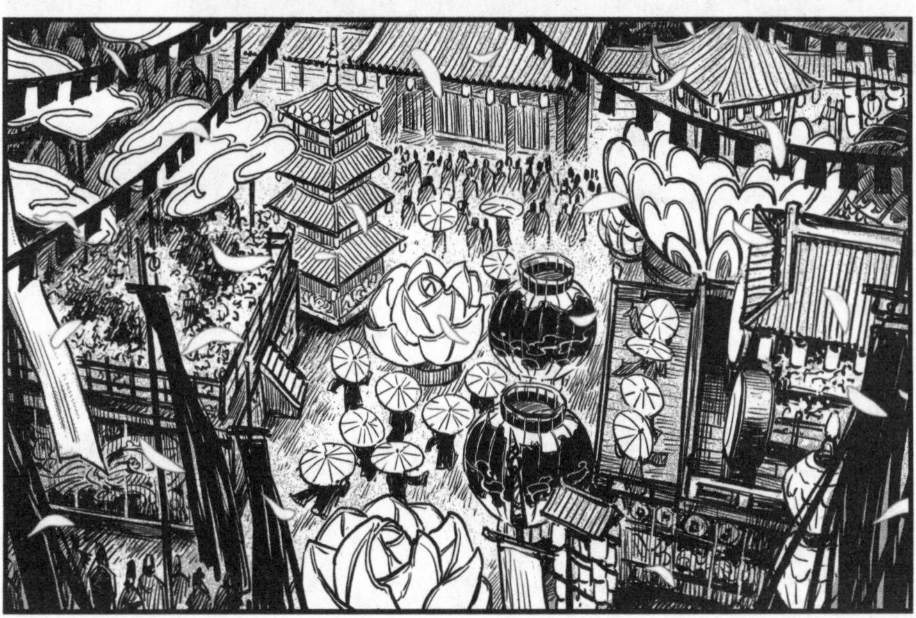

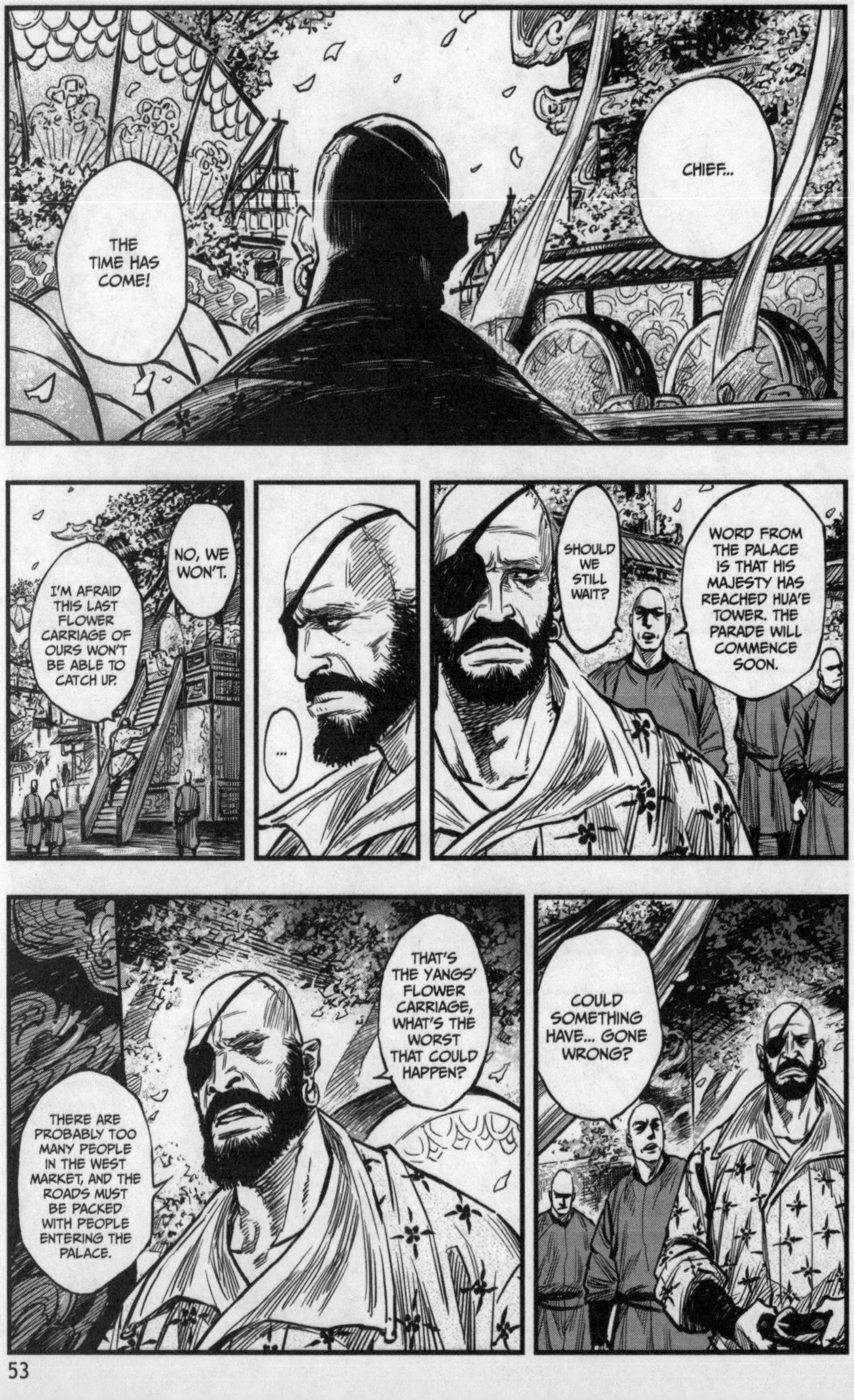
CHIEF...
THE TIME HAS COME!
WORD FROM THE PALACE IS THAT HIS MAJESTY HAS REACHED HUA'E TOWER. THE PARADE WILL COMMENCE SOON.
SHOULD WE STILL WAIT?
...
NO, WE WON'T.
I'M AFRAID THIS LAST FLOWER CARRIAGE OF OURS WON'T BE ABLE TO CATCH UP.
COULD SOMETHING HAVE... GONE WRONG?
THAT'S THE YANGS' FLOWER CARRIAGE, WHAT'S THE WORST THAT COULD HAPPEN?
THERE ARE PROBABLY TOO MANY PEOPLE IN THE WEST MARKET, AND THE ROADS MUST BE PACKED WITH PEOPLE ENTERING THE PALACE.

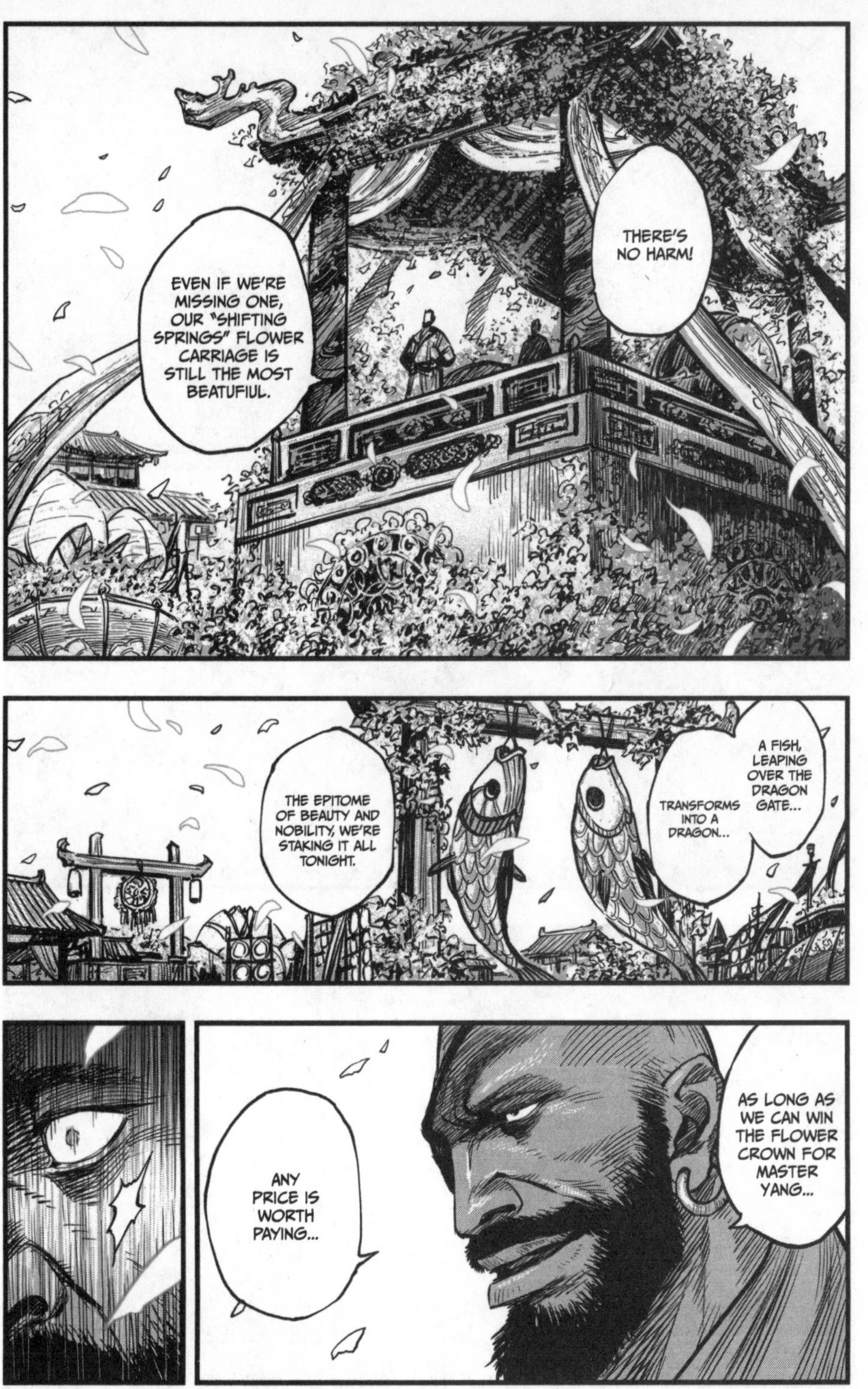
THERE'S NO HARM!
EVEN IF WE'RE MISSING ONE, OUR "SHIFTING SPRINGS" FLOWER CARRIAGE IS STILL THE MOST BEATUFIUL.
A FISH, LEAPING OVER THE DRAGON GATE...
TRANSFORMS INTO A DRAGON...
THE EPITOME OF BEAUTY AND NOBILITY, WE'RE STAKING IT ALL TONIGHT.
AS LONG AS WE CAN WIN THE FLOWER CROWN FOR MASTER YANG...
ANY PRICE IS WORTH PAYING...

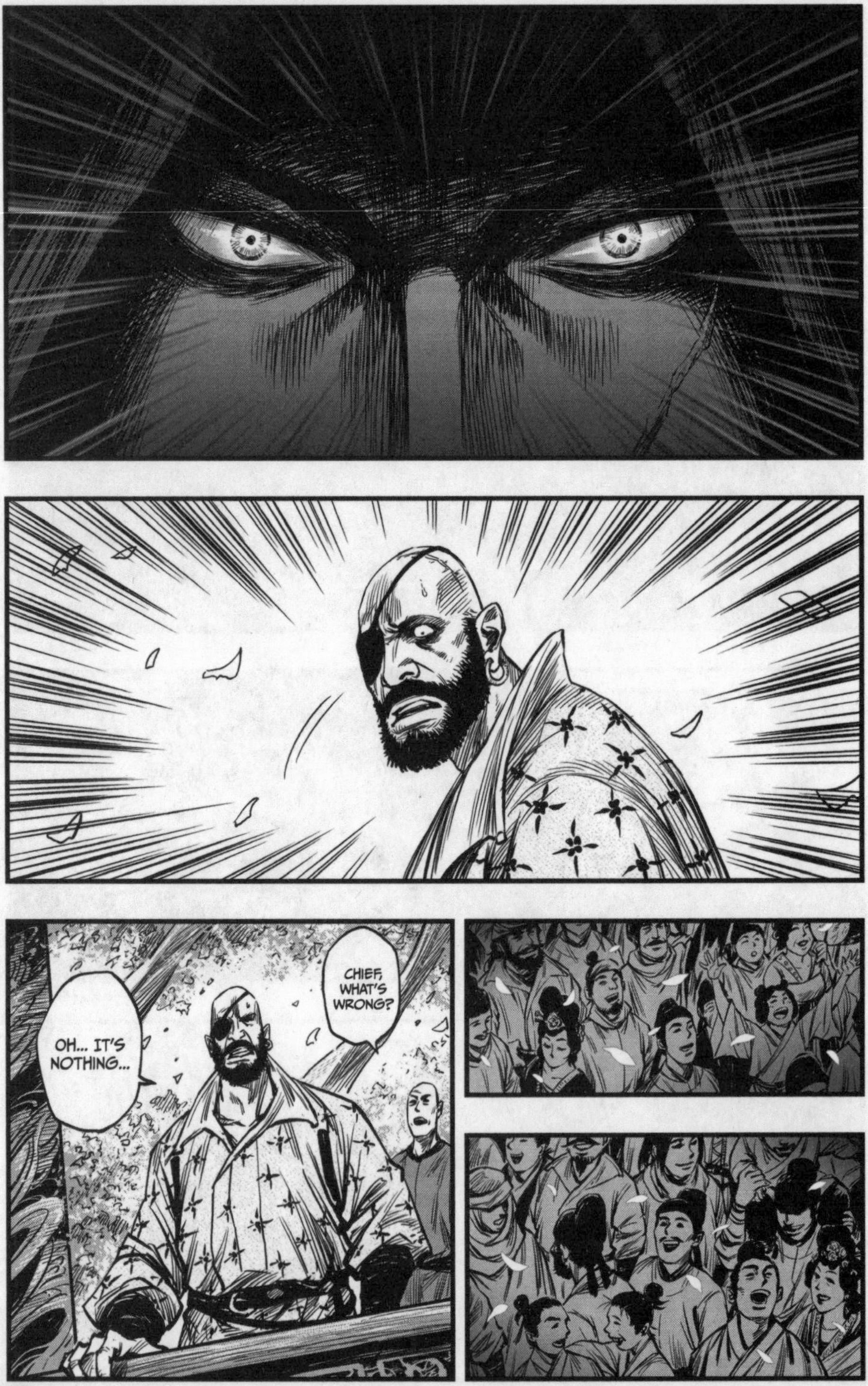
CHIEF, WHAT'S WRONG?
OH... IT'S NOTHING...

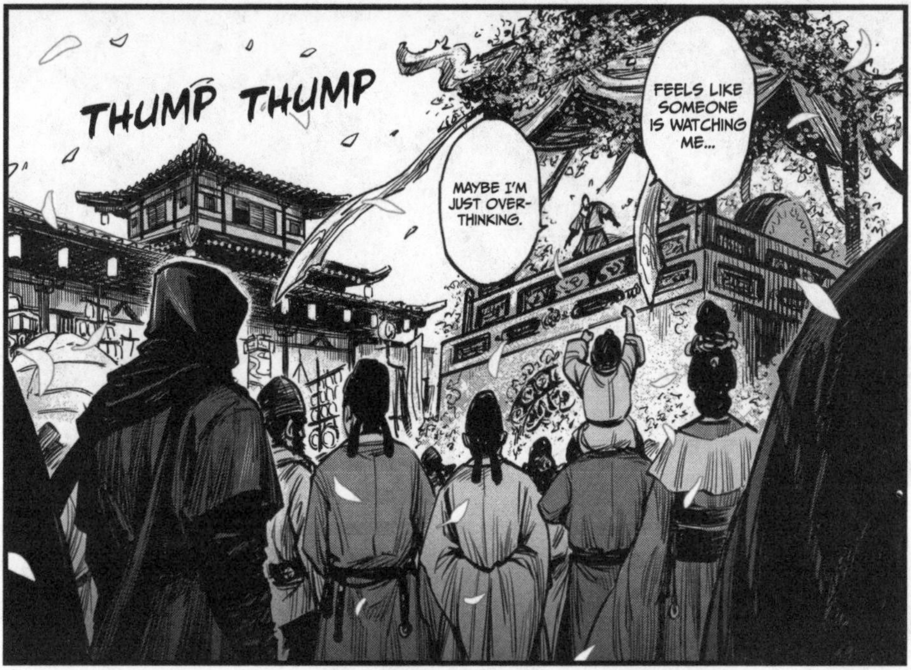
FEELS LIKE SOMEONE IS WATCHING ME...
MAYBE I'M JUST OVER-THINKING.
THUMP THUMP

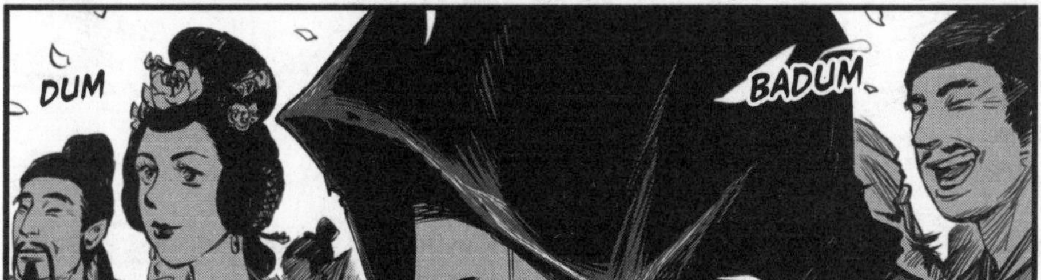
BADUM
DUM
DUM

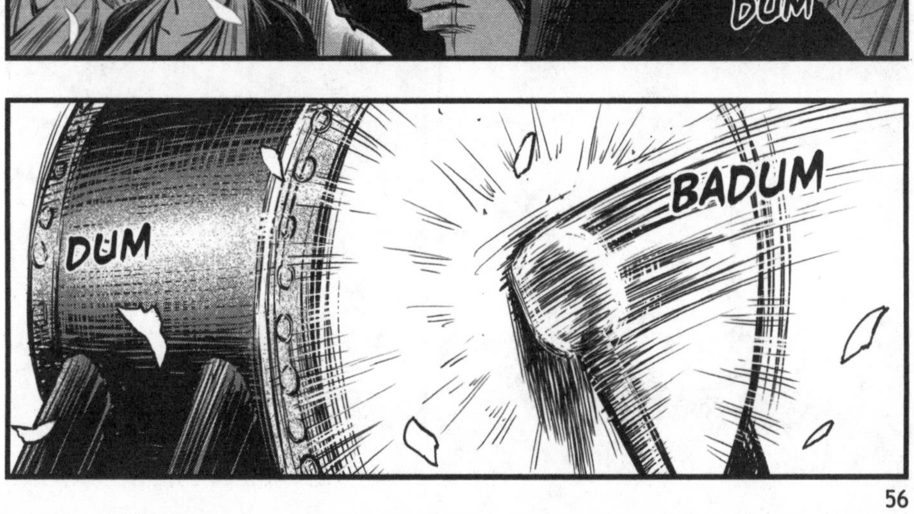
BADUM
DUM

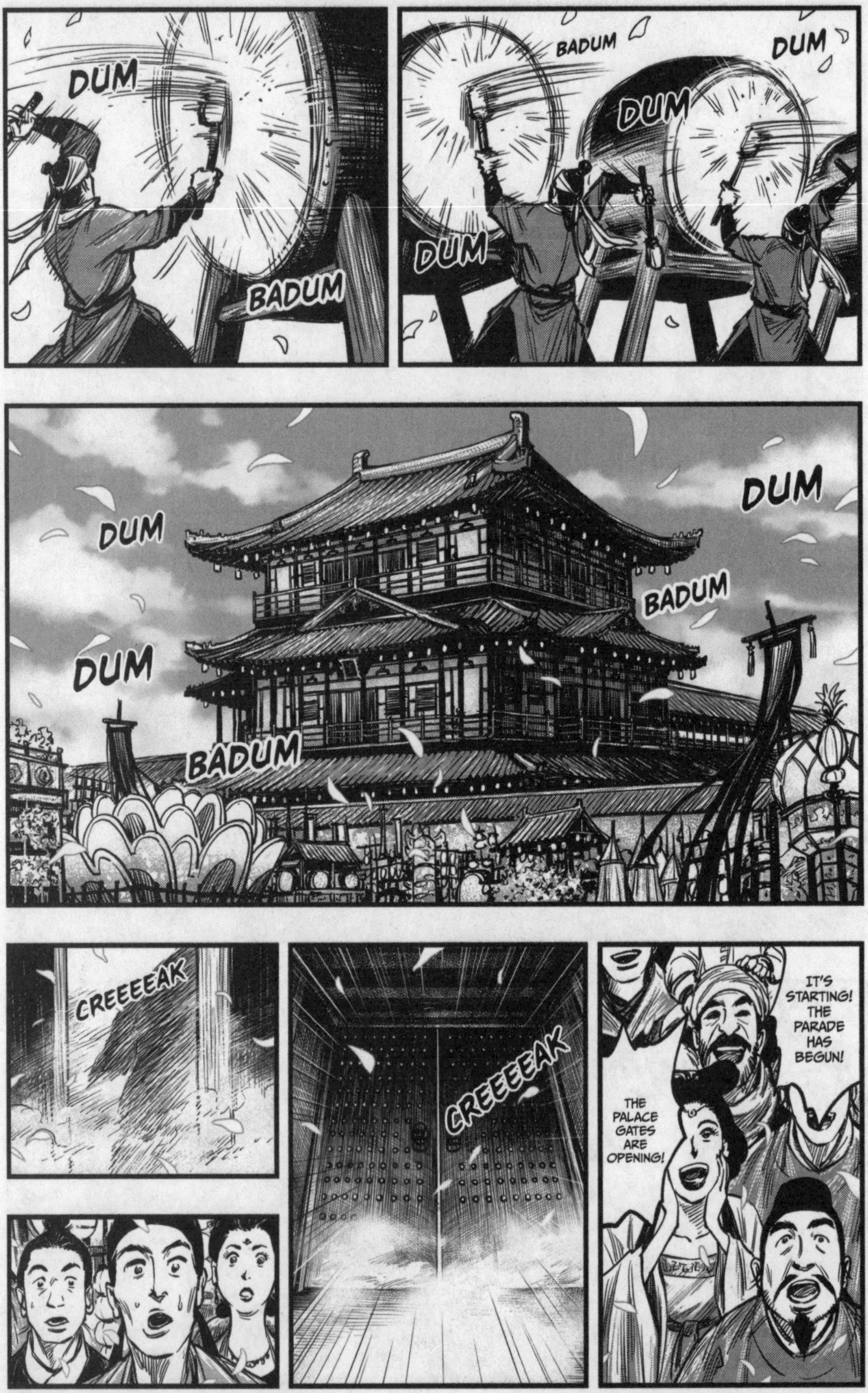
DUM
BADUM
DUM
DUM
DUM
DUM
BADUM
DUM
BADUM
DUM
DUM
BADUM
IT'S STARTING! THE PARADE HAS BEGUN!
THE PALACE GATES ARE OPENING!
CREEEEAK
CREEEEAK

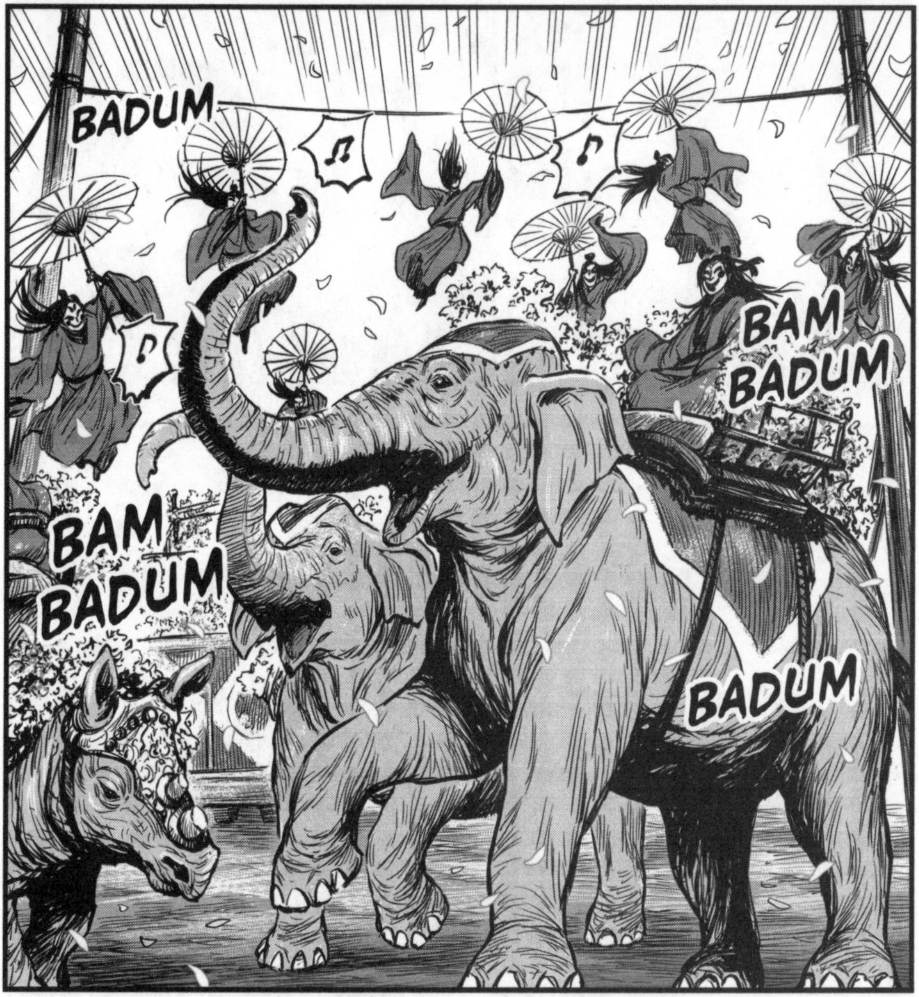
BADUM
BAM BADUM
BAM BADUM
BADUM

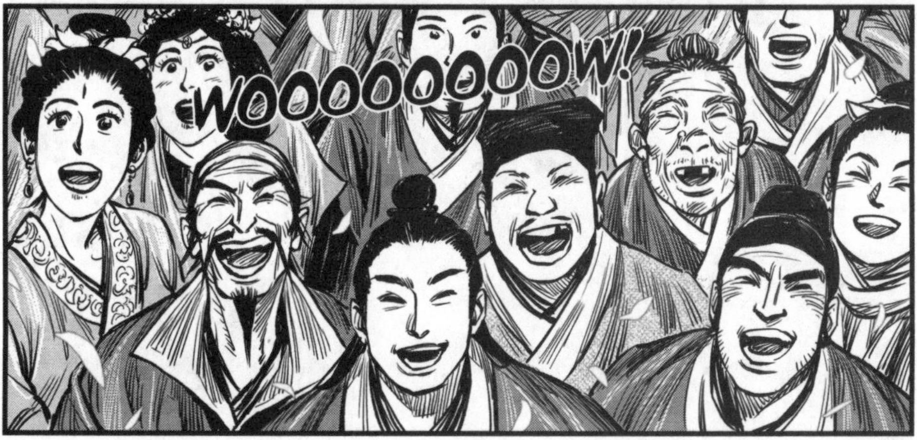
WOOOOOOOOOW!

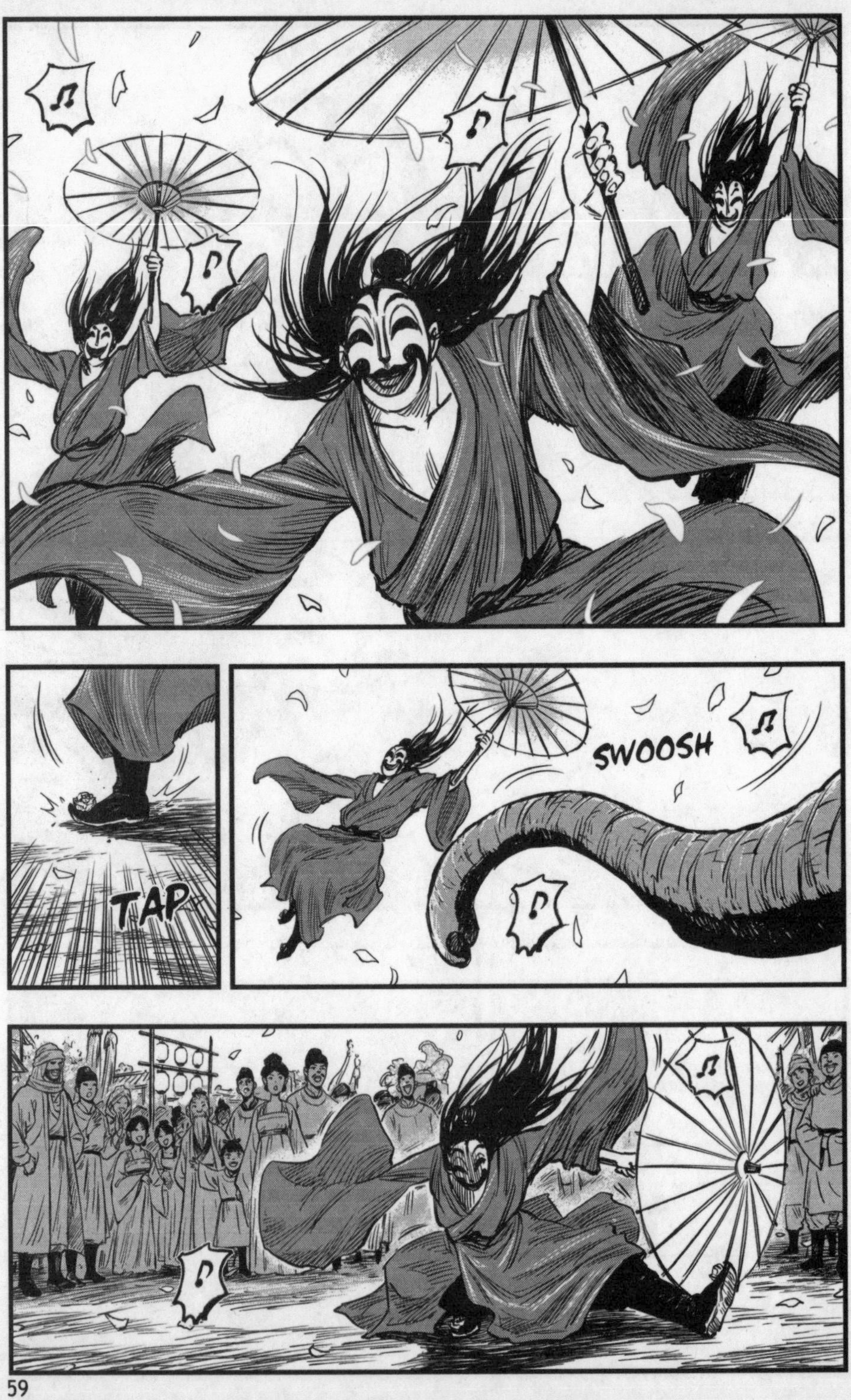
SWOOSH
TAP

FUU

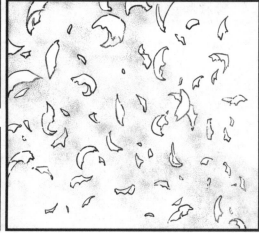

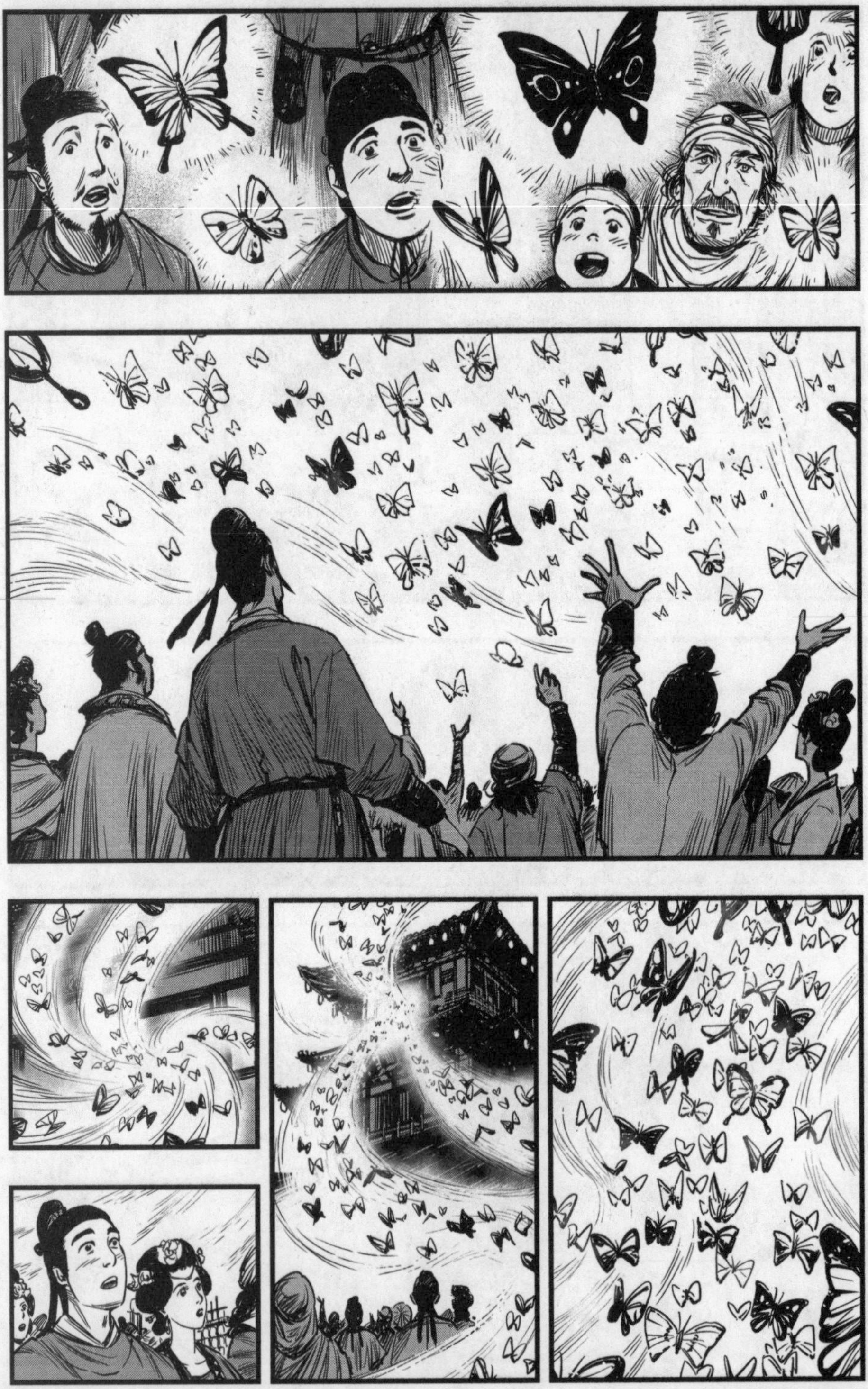

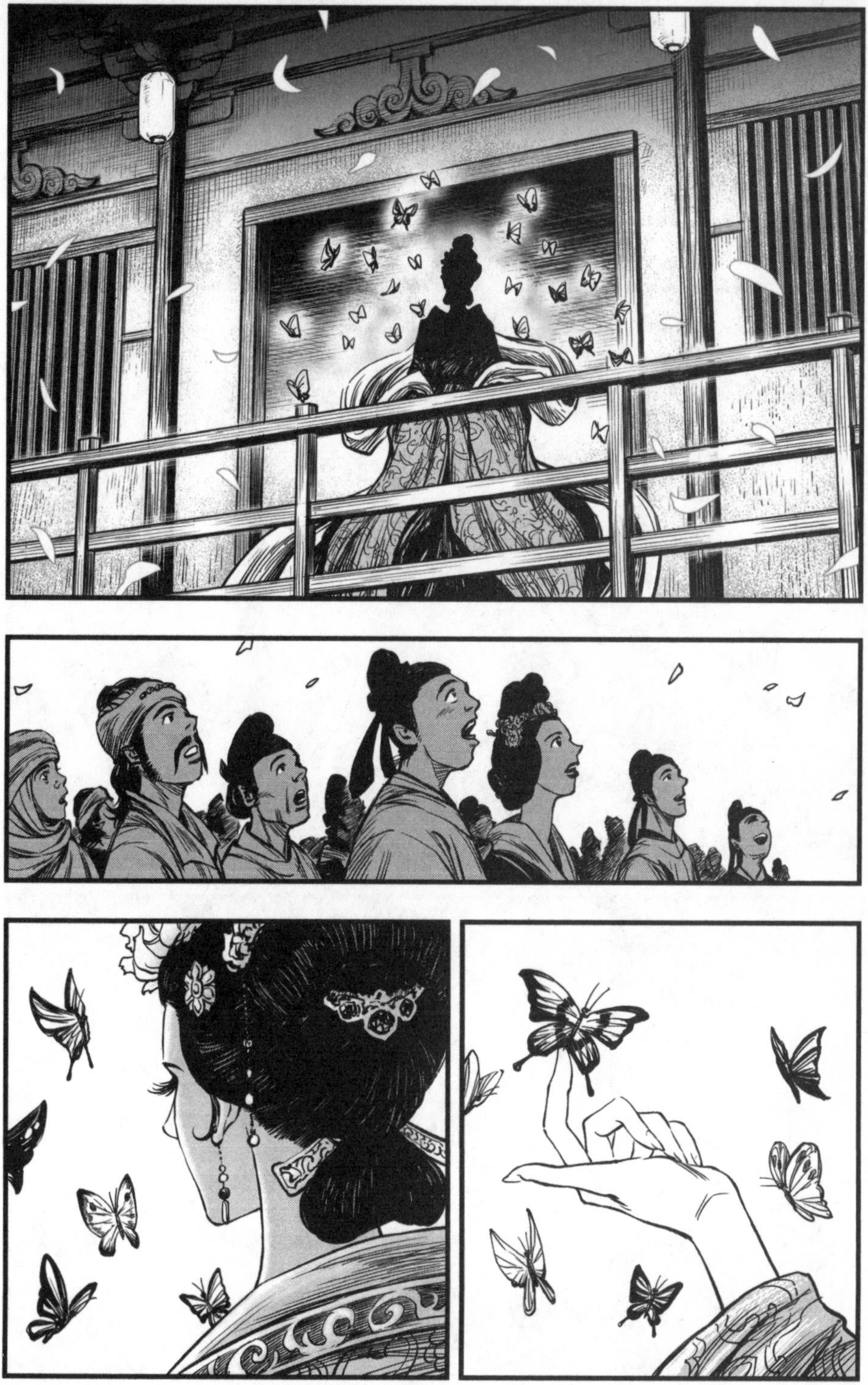

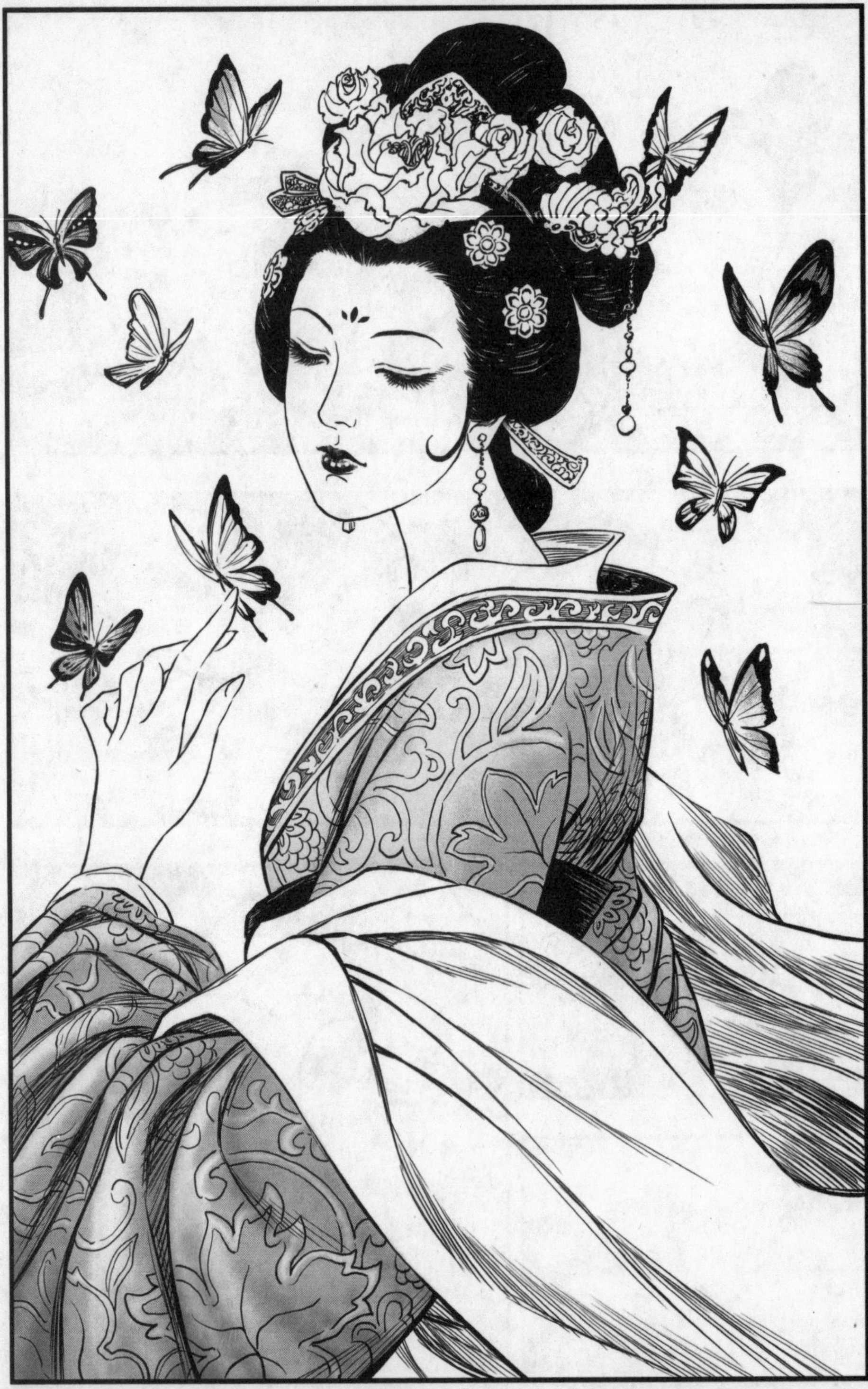

LADY GUIFEI...

IT'S LADY GUIFEI!

YOUR HIGHNESS!

YOUR HIGHNESS!

YOUR HIGHNESS!

YOUR HIGHNESS!

YOUR HIGHNESS!

YOUR HIGHNESS!

YOUR HIGHNESS!

YOUR HIGHNESS!

YOUR HIGHNESS!

YOUR HIGHNESS!

YOUR HIGHNESS!

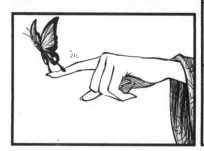

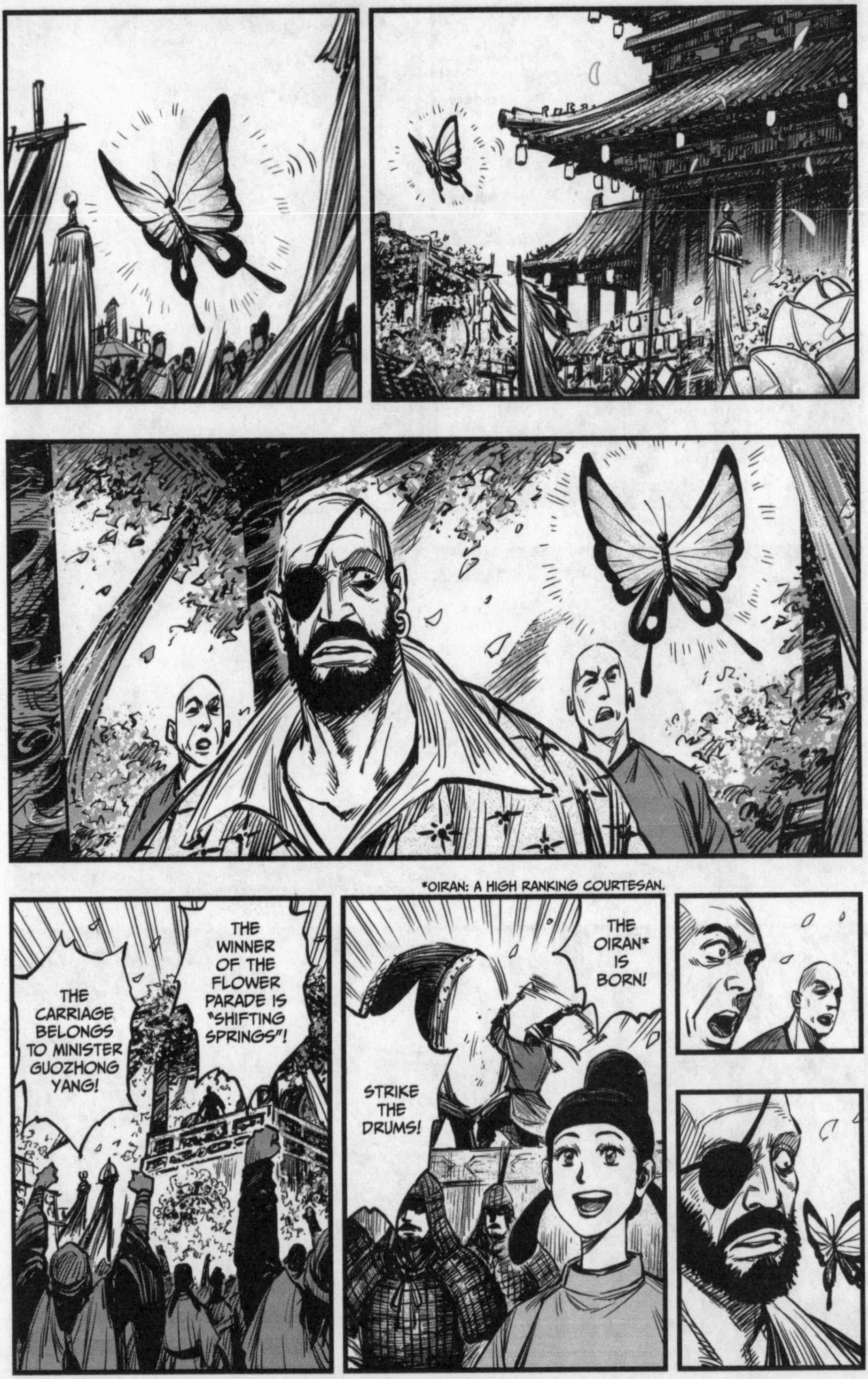
THE WINNER OF THE FLOWER PARADE IS "SHIFTING SPRINGS"!
THE CARRIAGE BELONGS TO MINISTER GUOZHONG YANG!
THE OIRAN* IS BORN!
STRIKE THE DRUMS!

*OIRAN: A HIGH RANKING COURTESAN.

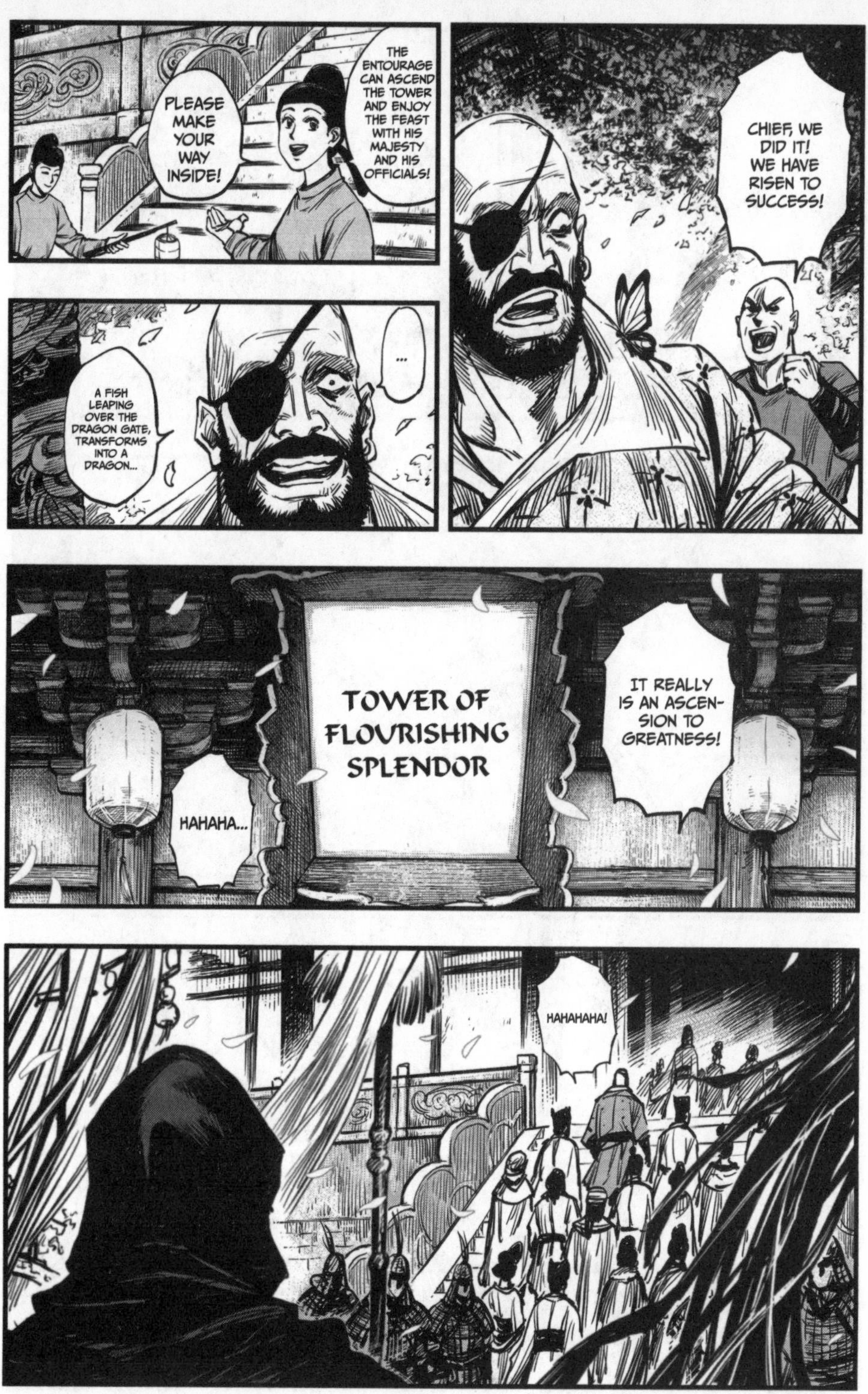
PLEASE MAKE YOUR WAY INSIDE!
THE ENTOURAGE CAN ASCEND THE TOWER AND ENJOY THE FEAST WITH HIS MAJESTY AND HIS OFFICIALS!
CHIEF, WE DID IT! WE HAVE RISEN TO SUCCESS!
...
A FISH LEAPING OVER THE DRAGON GATE, TRANSFORMS INTO A DRAGON...
TOWER OF FLOURISHING SPLENDOR
HAHAHA...
IT REALLY IS AN ASCENSION TO GREATNESS!
HAHAHAHA!

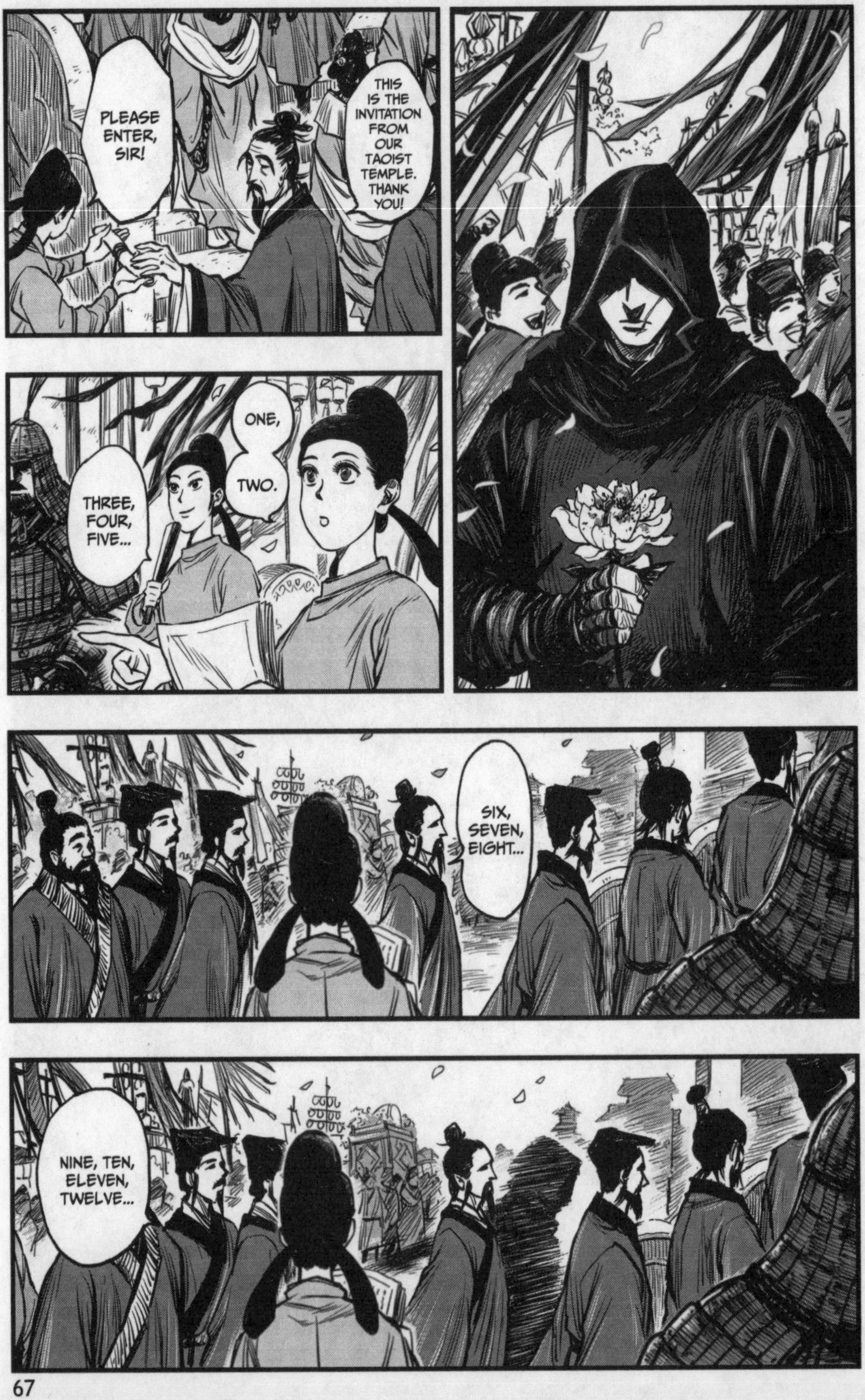
THIS IS THE INVITATION FROM OUR TAOIST TEMPLE. THANK YOU!
PLEASE ENTER, SIR!
ONE,
TWO.
THREE, FOUR, FIVE...
SIX, SEVEN, EIGHT...
NINE, TEN, ELEVEN, TWELVE...

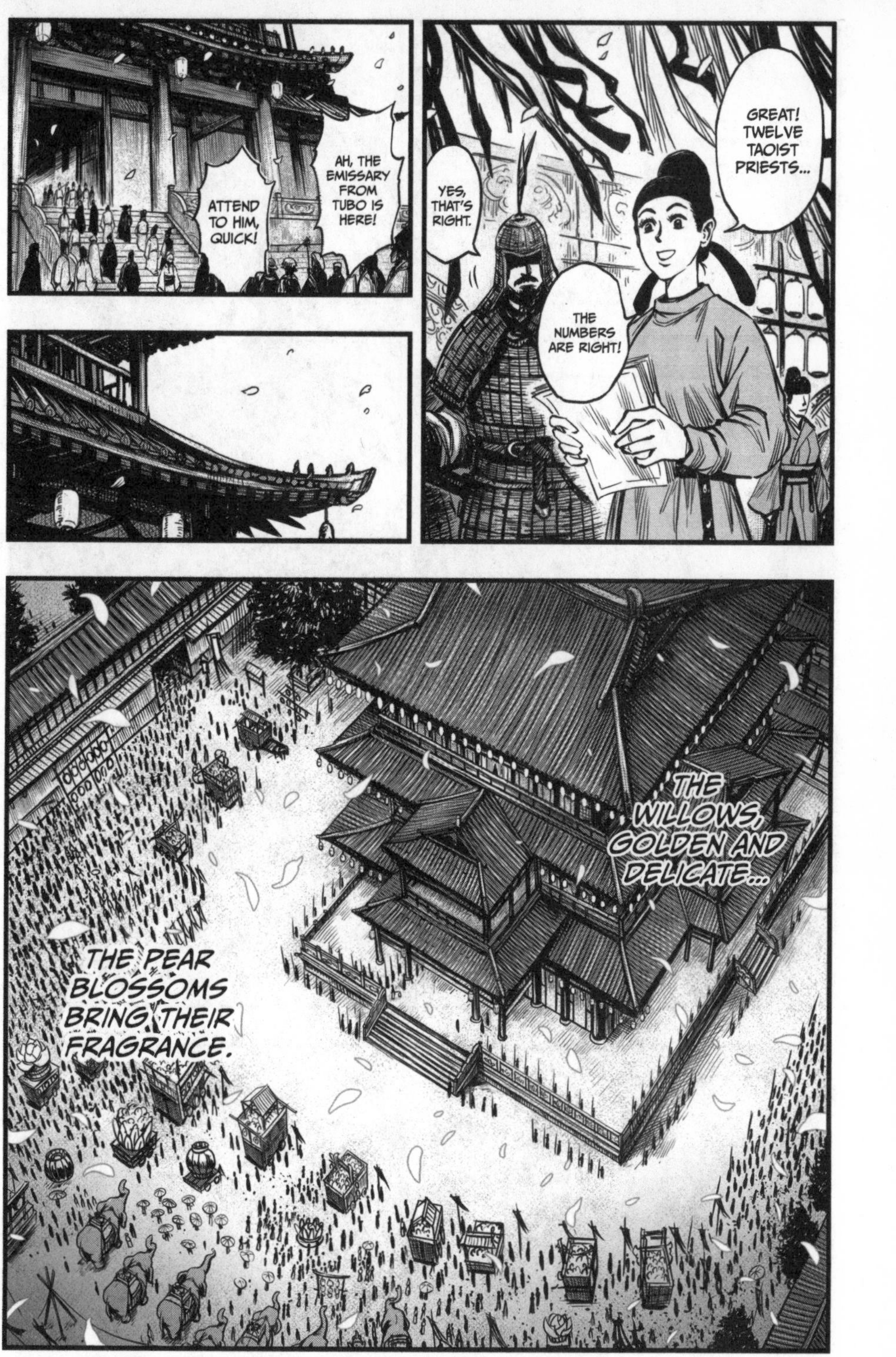
GREAT! TWELVE TAOIST PRIESTS...
YES, THAT'S RIGHT.
THE NUMBERS ARE RIGHT!
AH, THE EMISSARY FROM TUBO IS HERE!
ATTEND TO HIM, QUICK!
THE WILLOWS, GOLDEN AND DELICATE...
THE PEAR BLOSSOMS BRING THEIR FRAGRANCE.

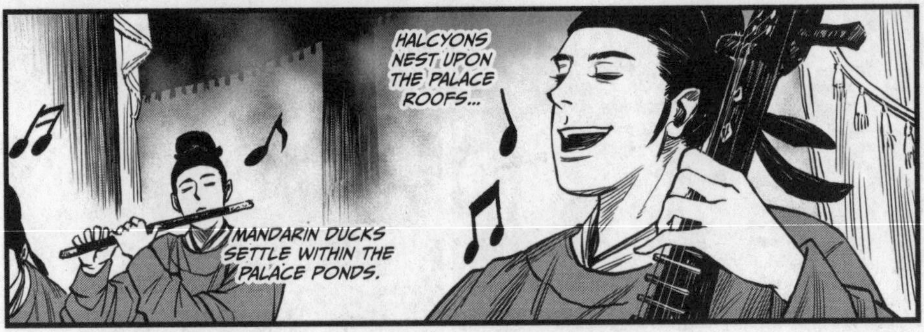
HALCYONS NEST UPON THE PALACE ROOFS...
MANDARIN DUCKS SETTLE WITHIN THE PALACE PONDS.

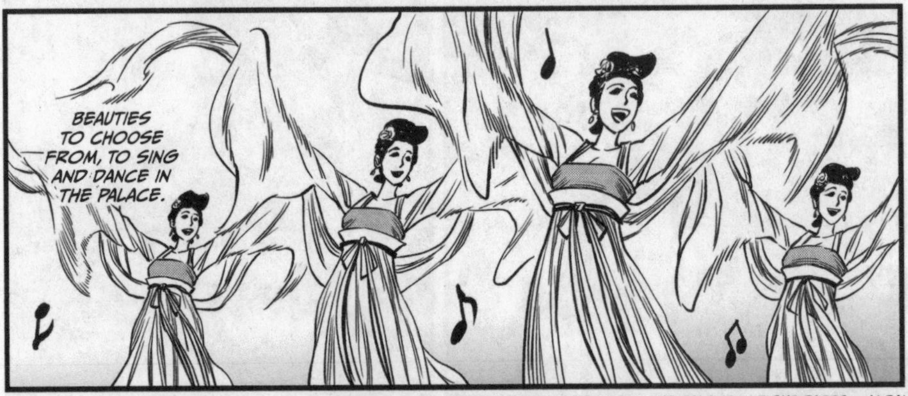
BEAUTIES TO CHOOSE FROM, TO SING AND DANCE IN THE PALACE.

* LYRICS FOR WANDERING IN THE PALACE IN EIGHT PARTS — LI BAI

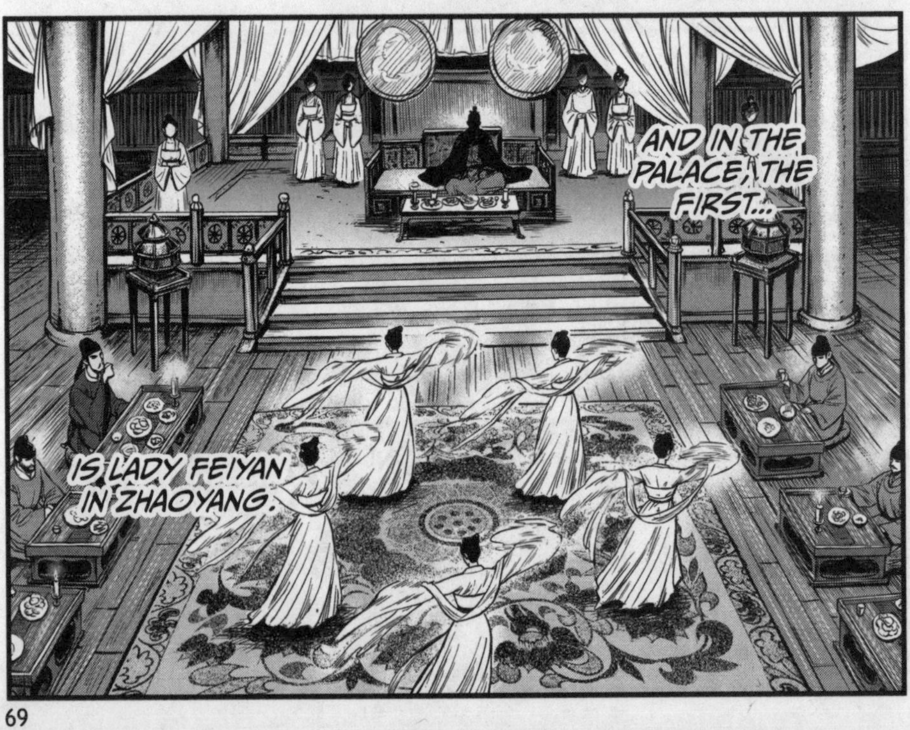
AND IN THE PALACE, THE FIRST...
IS LADY FEIYAN IN ZHAOYANG.

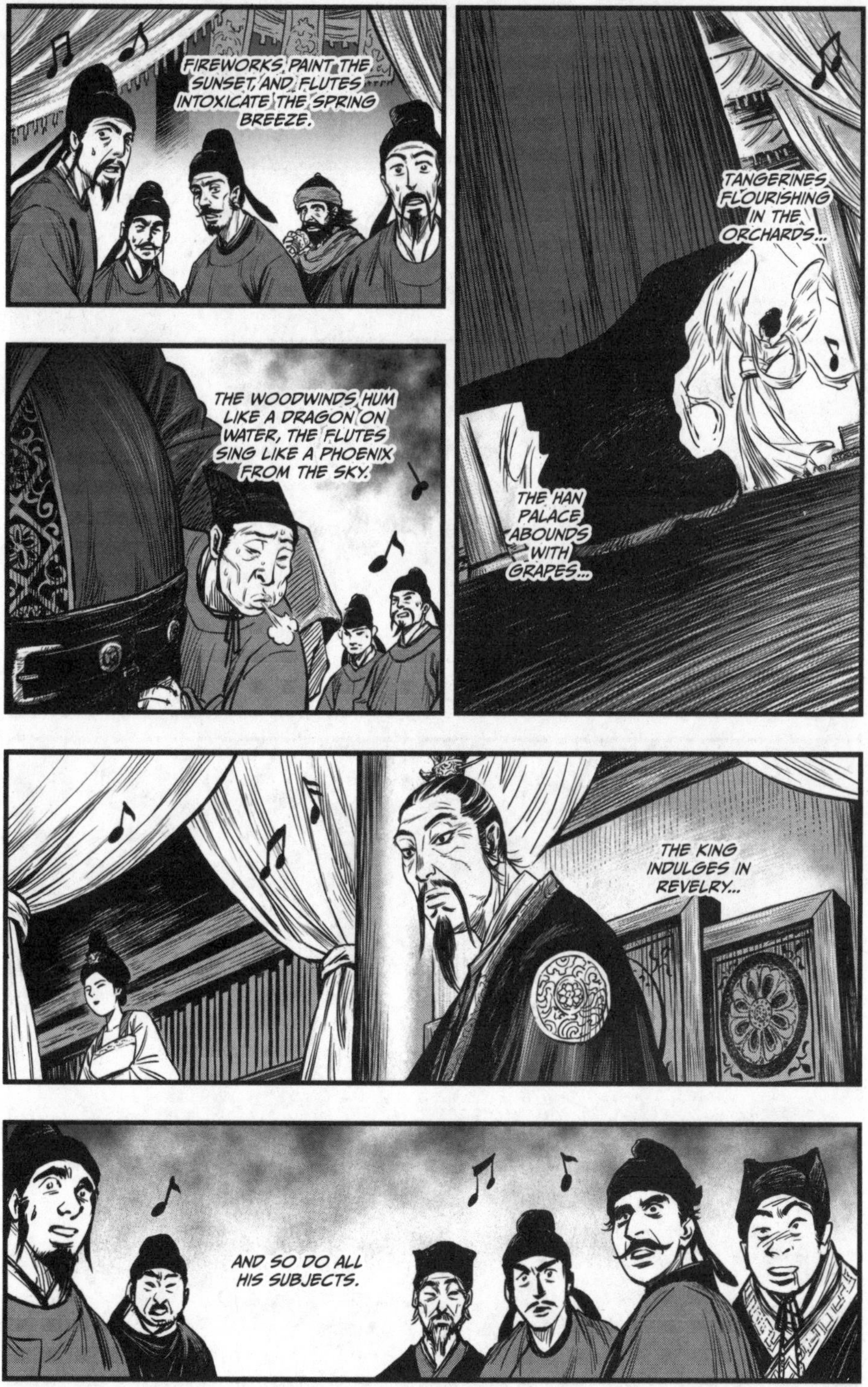
FIREWORKS PAINT THE SUNSET, AND FLUTES INTOXICATE THE SPRING BREEZE.
TANGERINES FLOURISHING IN THE ORCHARDS...
THE HAN PALACE ABOUNDS WITH GRAPES...
THE WOODWINDS HUM LIKE A DRAGON ON WATER, THE FLUTES SING LIKE A PHOENIX FROM THE SKY.
THE KING INDULGES IN REVELRY...
AND SO DO ALL HIS SUBJECTS.

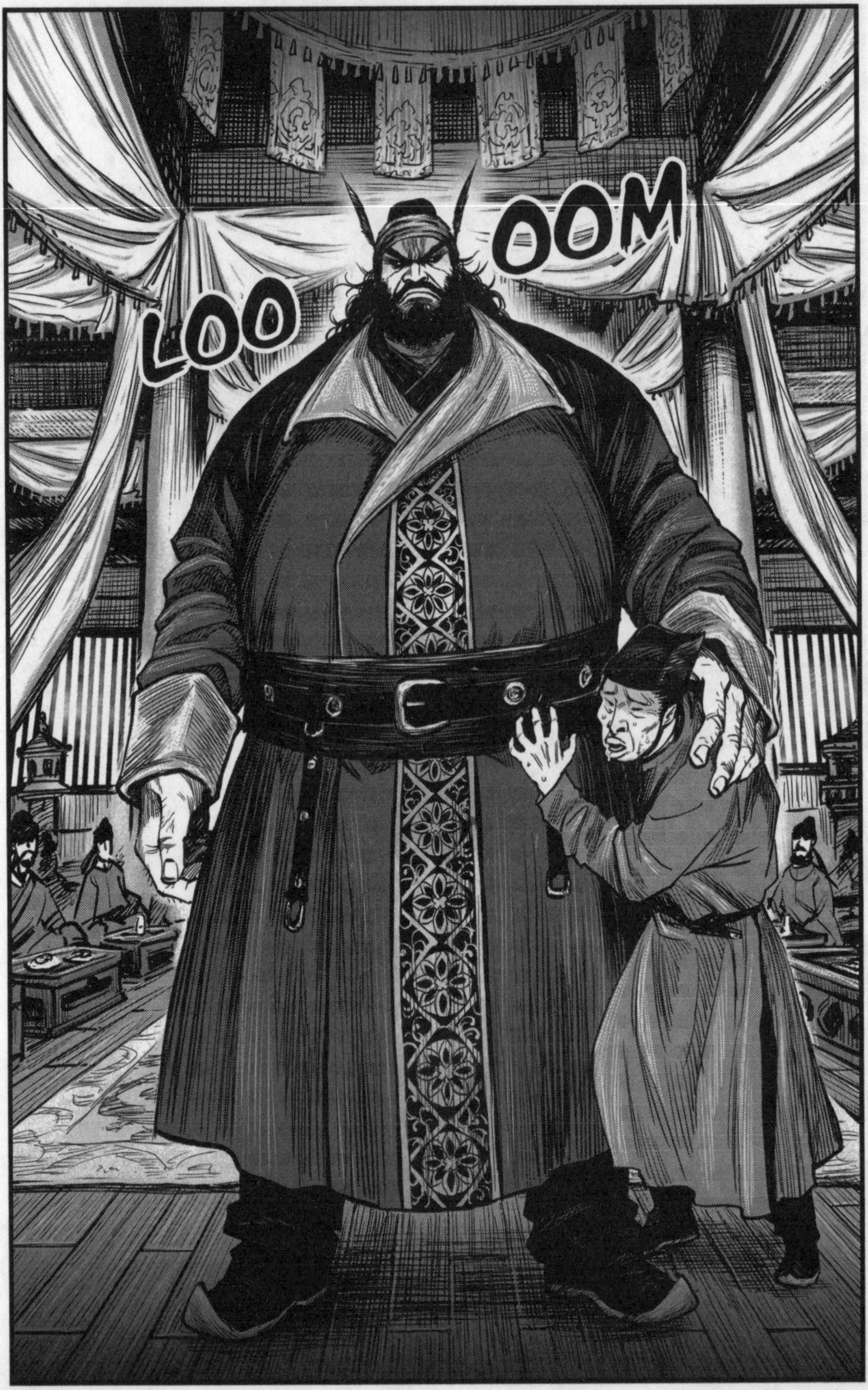
LOO
OOM

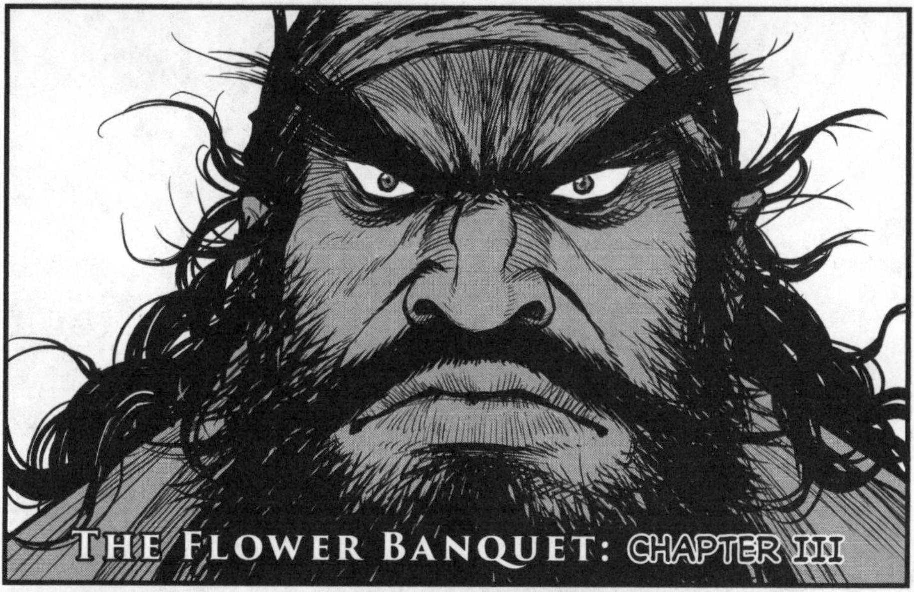
THE FLOWER BANQUET: CHAPTER III

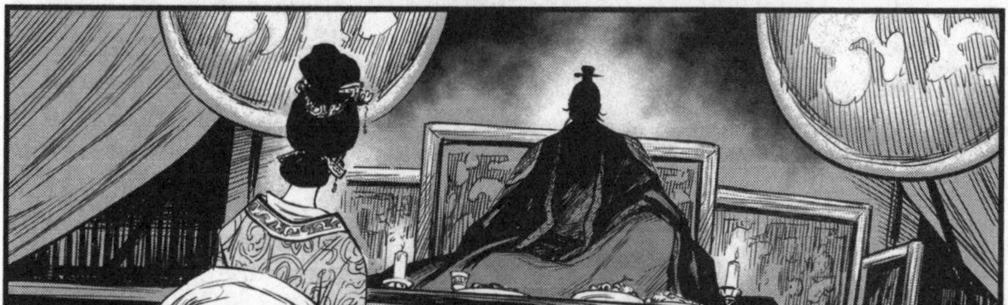

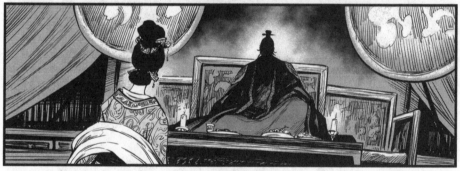

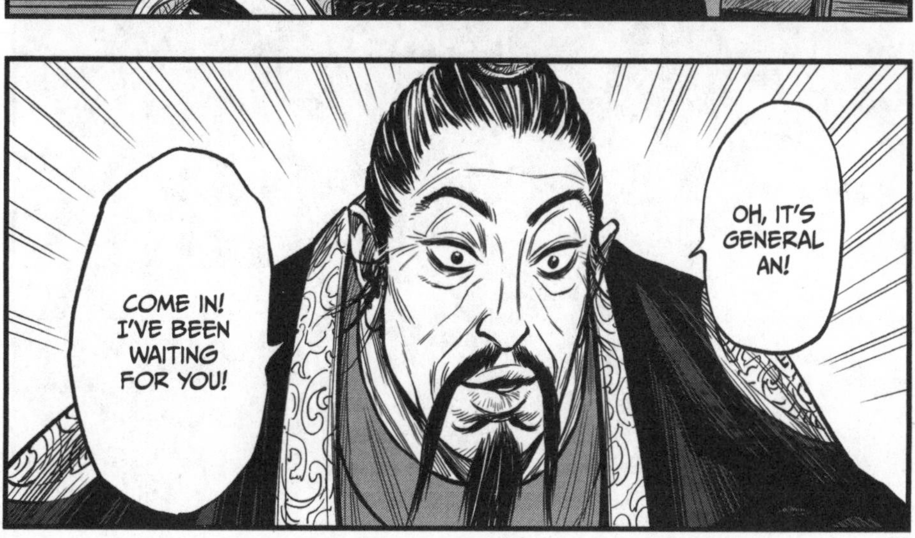
OH, IT'S GENERAL AN!
COME IN! I'VE BEEN WAITING FOR YOU!

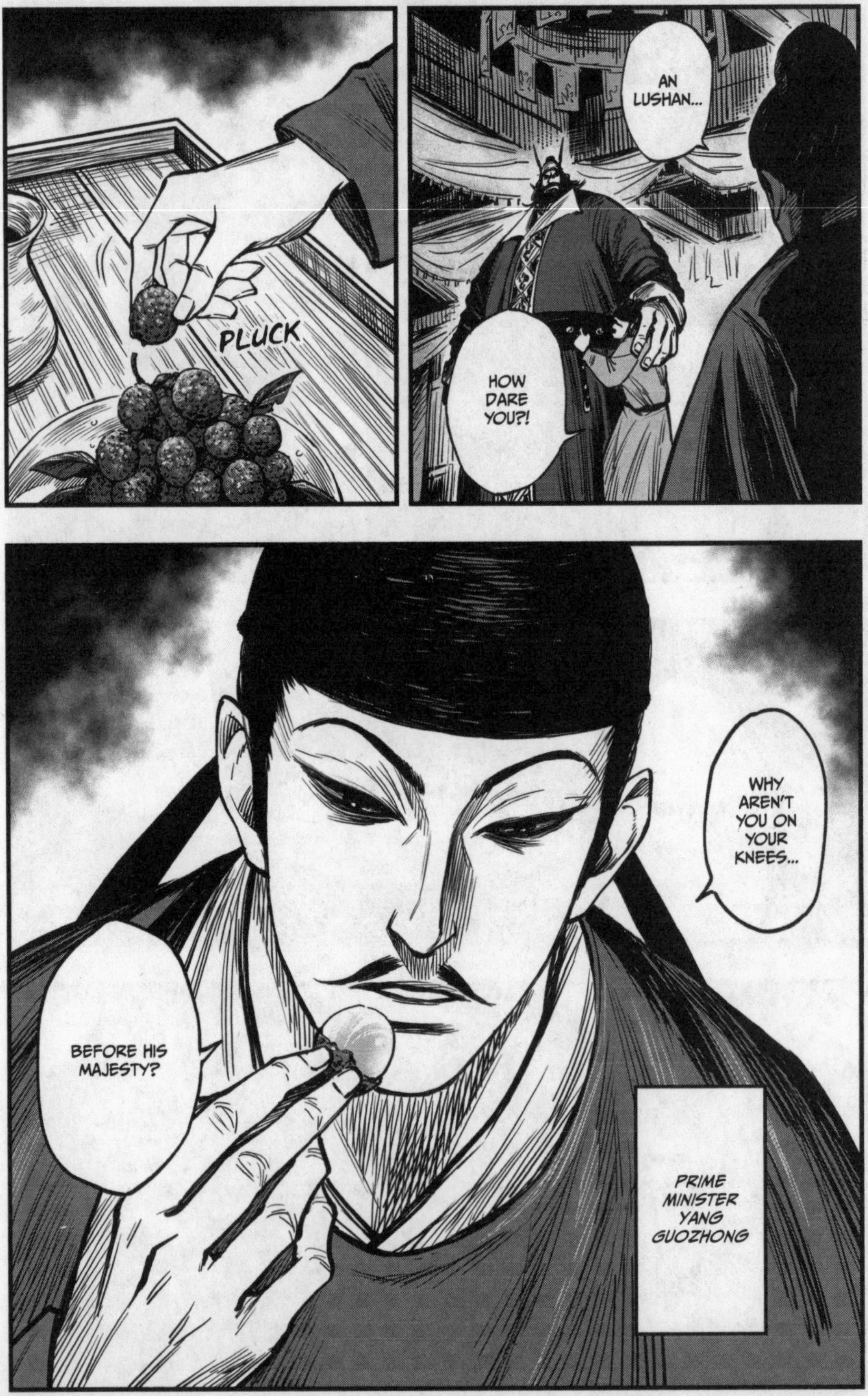
AN LUSHAN...
HOW DARE YOU?!
PLUCK
WHY AREN'T YOU ON YOUR KNEES...
BEFORE HIS MAJESTY?
PRIME MINISTER YANG GUOZHONG

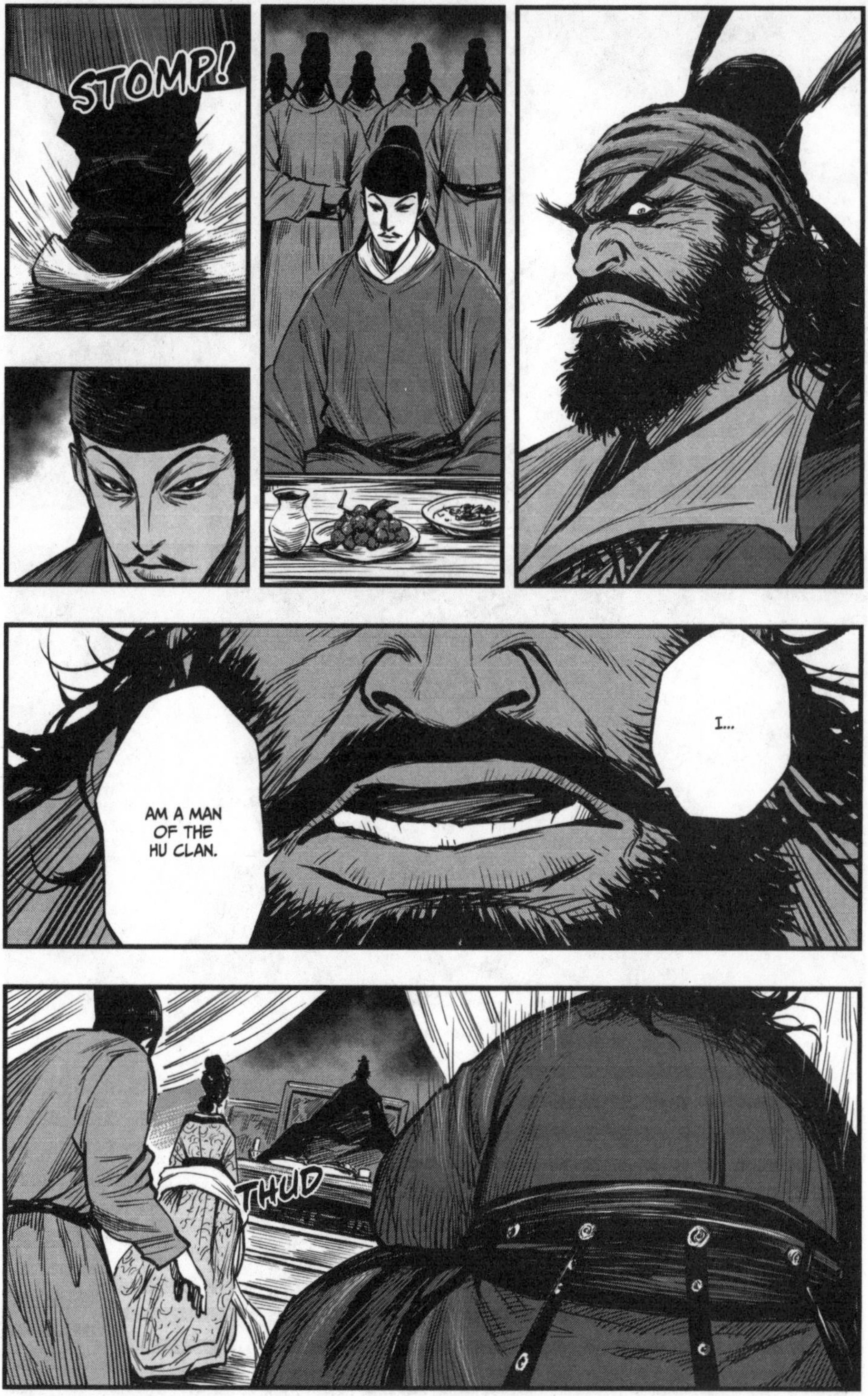
STOMP!
I...
AM A MAN OF THE HU CLAN.
THUD

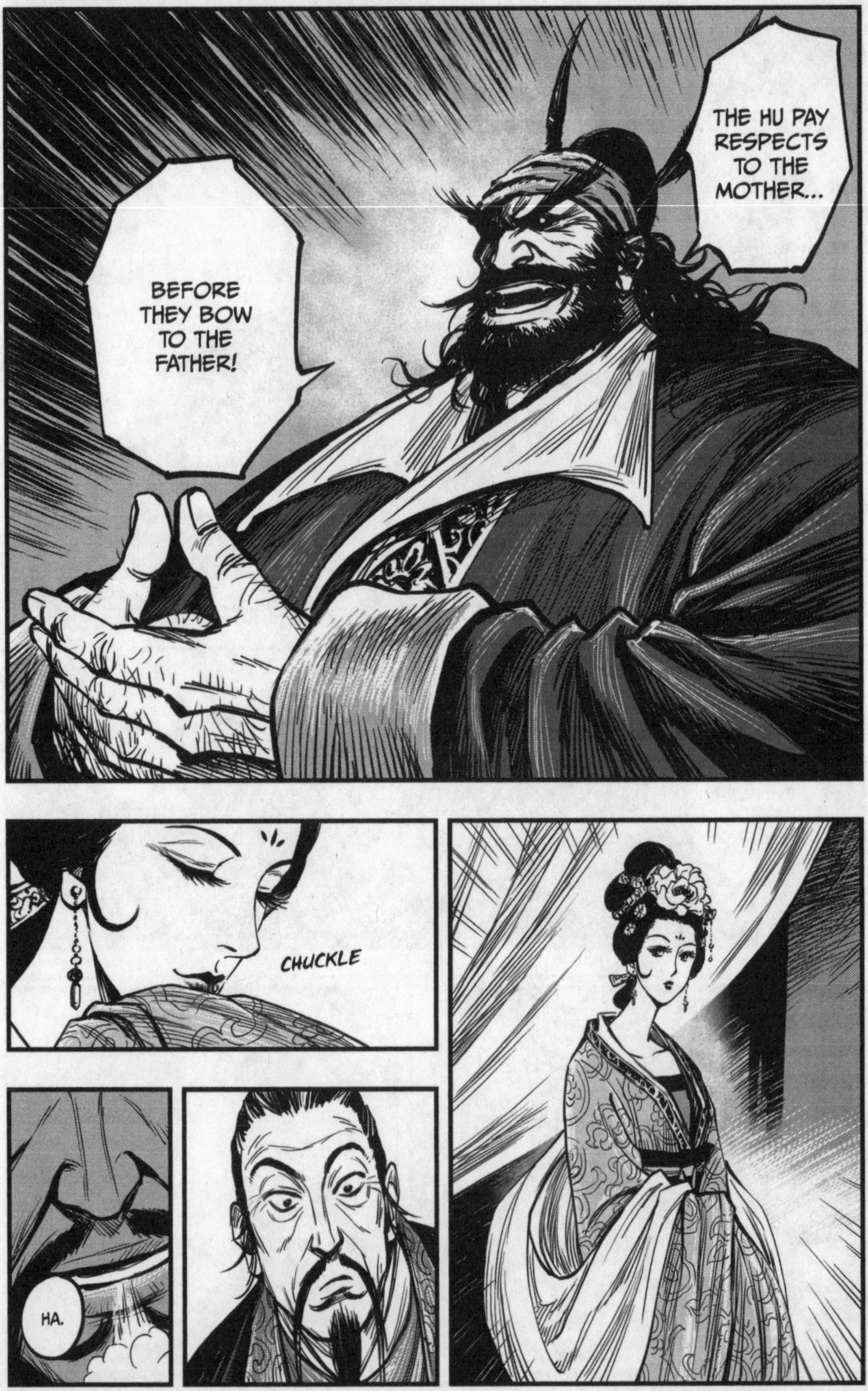
THE HU PAY RESPECTS TO THE MOTHER...
BEFORE THEY BOW TO THE FATHER!
CHUCKLE
HA.

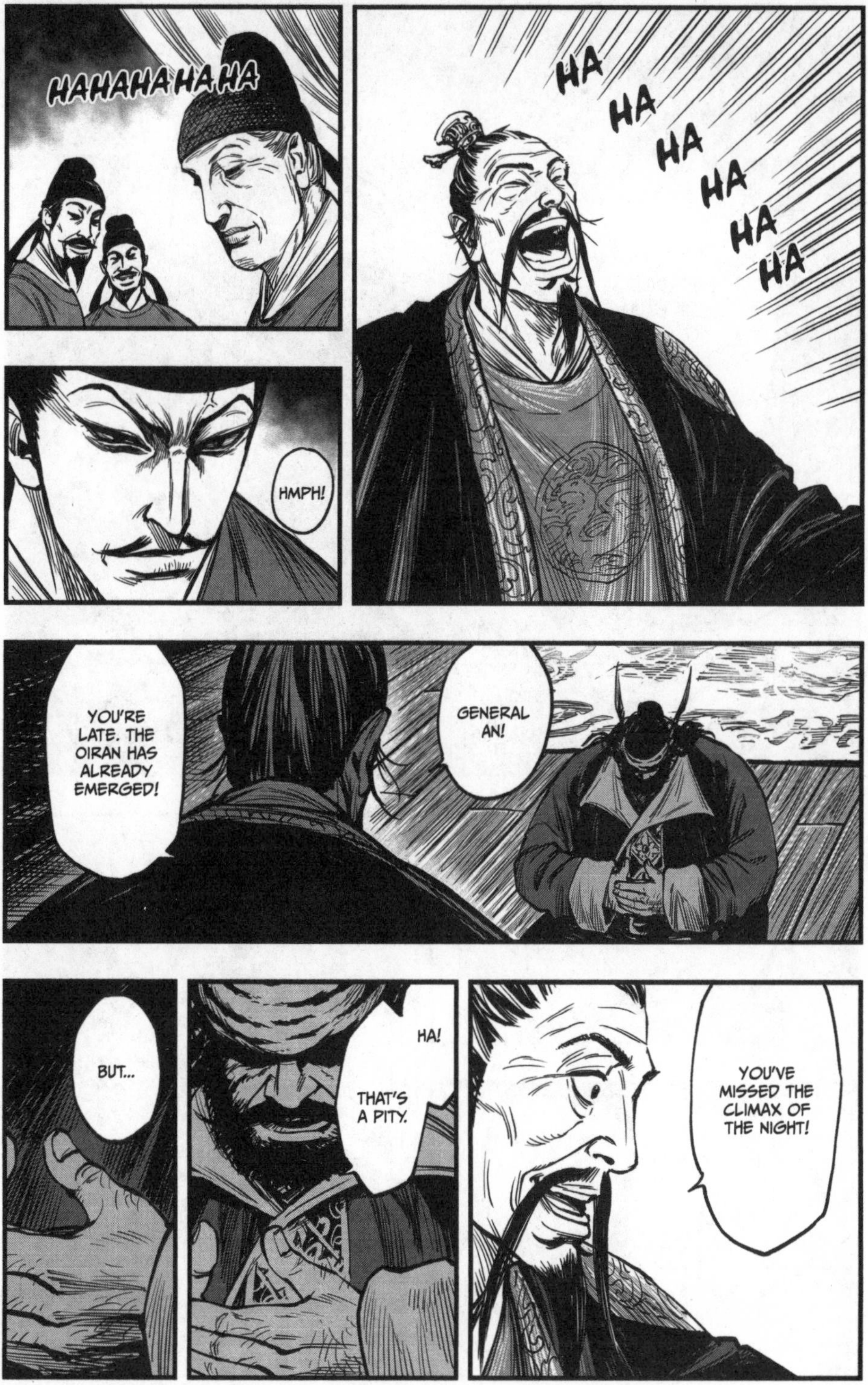
HA HA HA HA HA HA
HAHAHAHAHAHA
HMPH!
GENERAL AN!
YOU'RE LATE. THE OIRAN HAS ALREADY EMERGED!
YOU'VE MISSED THE CLIMAX OF THE NIGHT!
HA!
THAT'S A PITY.
BUT...

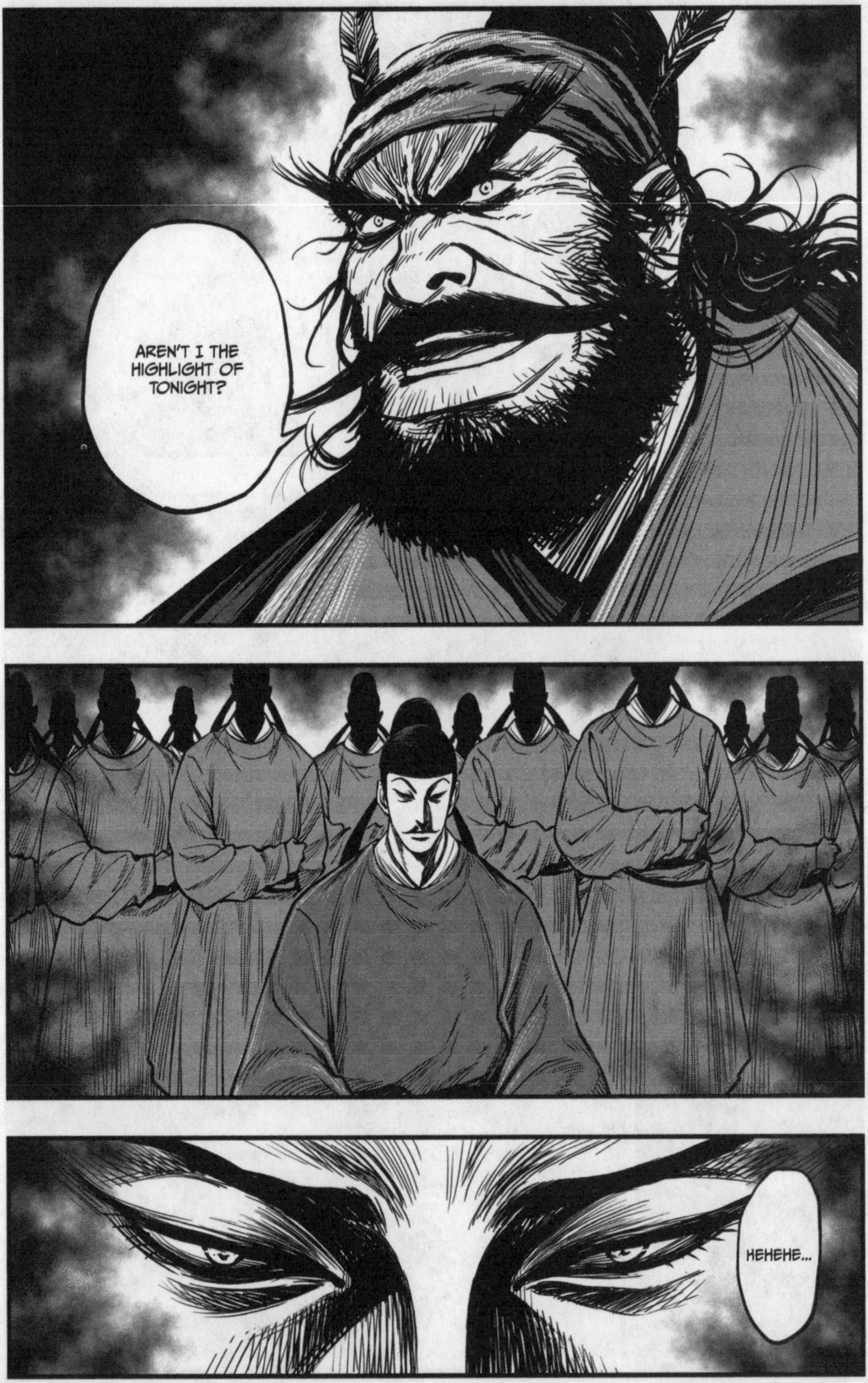
AREN'T I THE HIGHLIGHT OF TONIGHT?
HEHEHE...

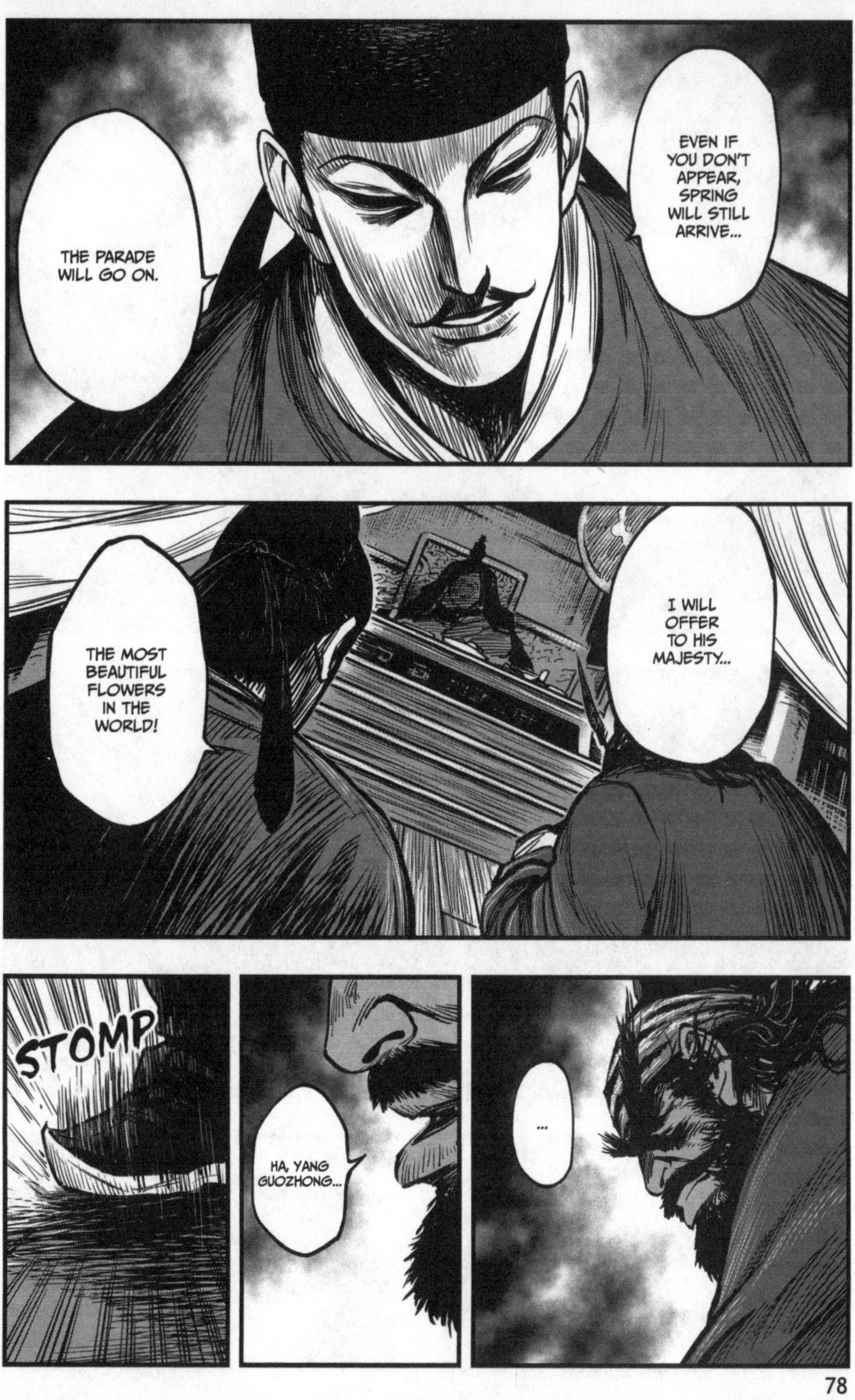
EVEN IF YOU DON'T APPEAR, SPRING WILL STILL ARRIVE...
THE PARADE WILL GO ON.
I WILL OFFER TO HIS MAJESTY...
THE MOST BEAUTIFUL FLOWERS IN THE WORLD!
...
HA, YANG GUOZHONG...
STOMP

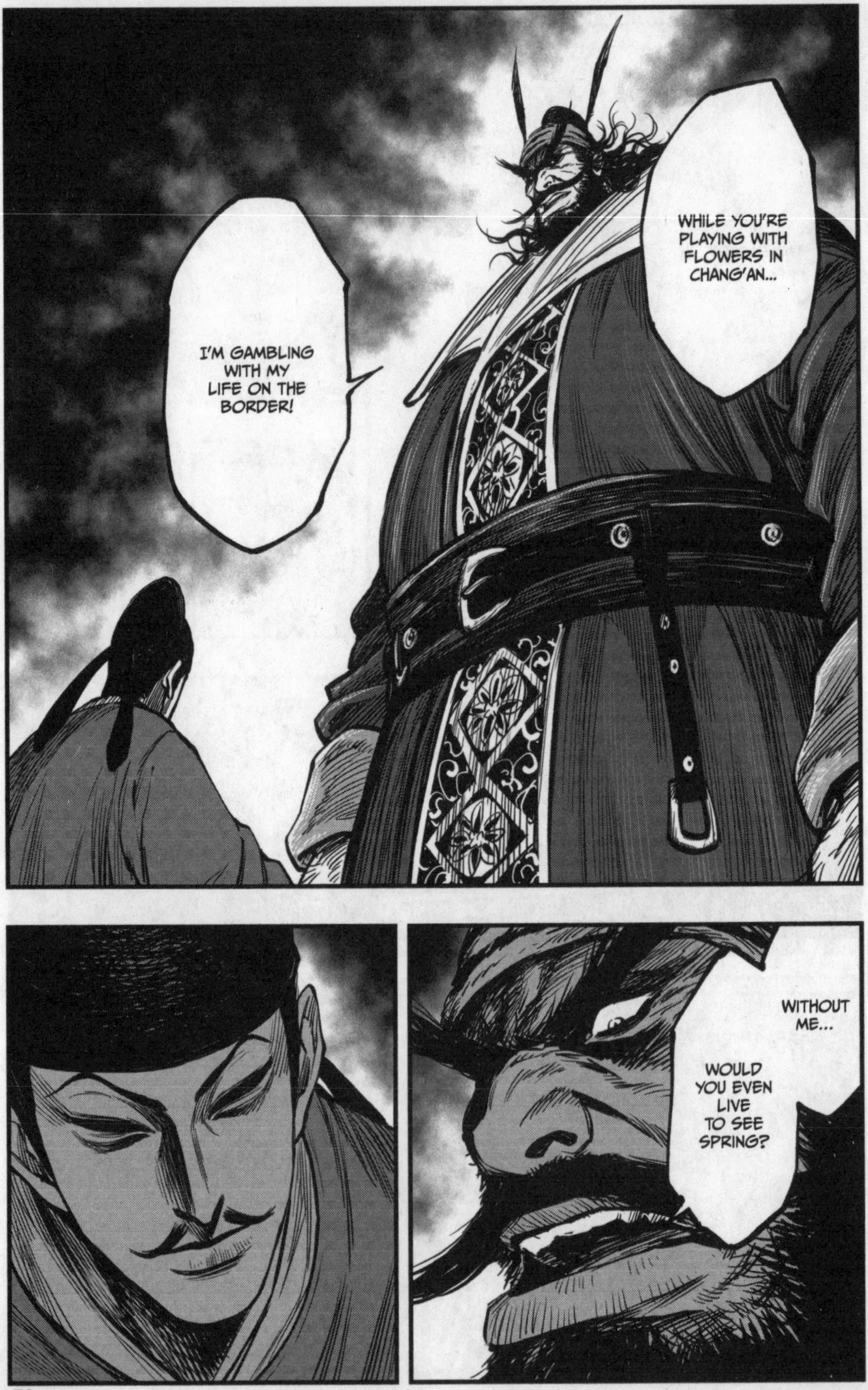
WHILE YOU'RE PLAYING WITH FLOWERS IN CHANG'AN...
I'M GAMBLING WITH MY LIFE ON THE BORDER!
WITHOUT ME...
WOULD YOU EVEN LIVE TO SEE SPRING?

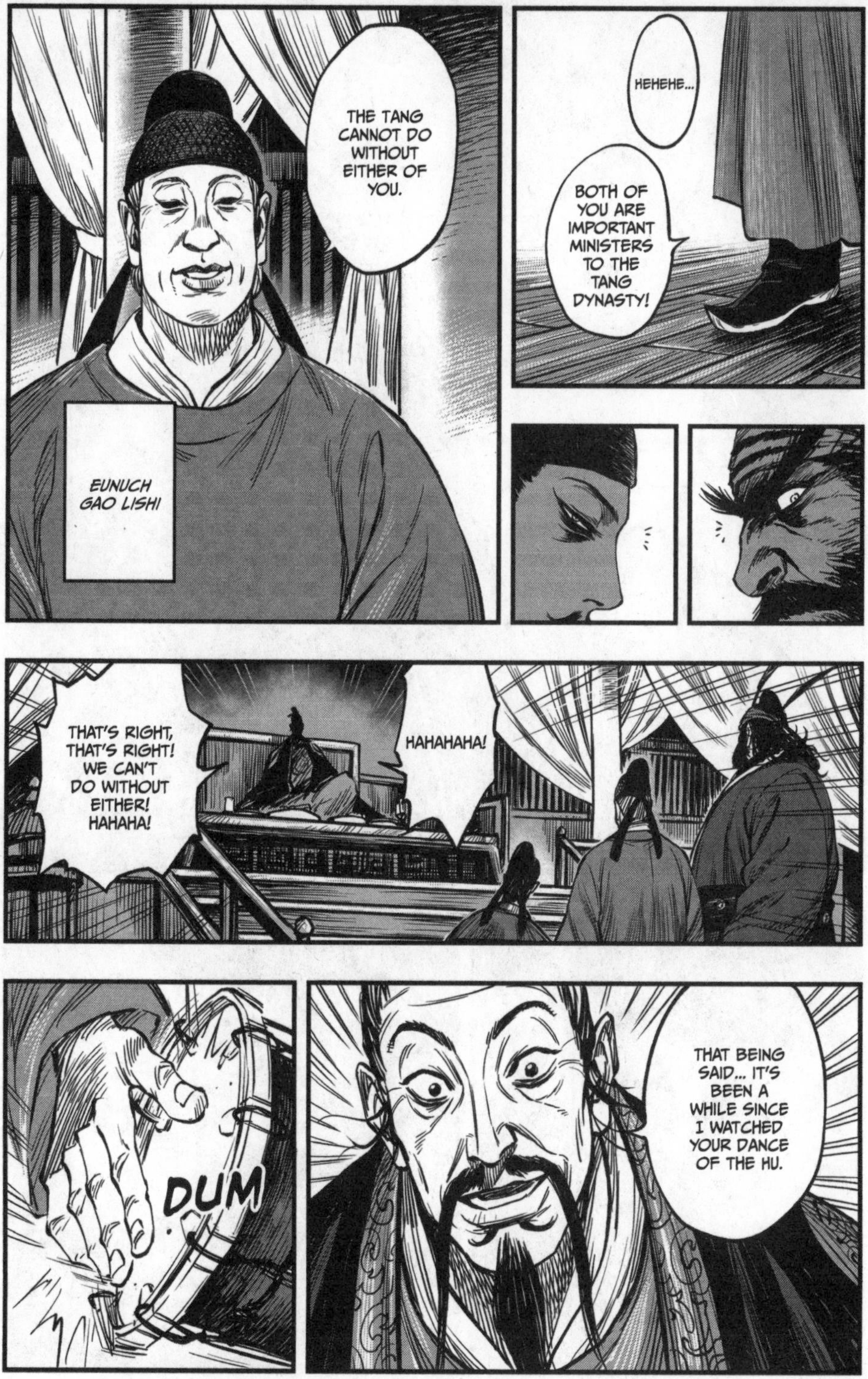
THE TANG CANNOT DO WITHOUT EITHER OF YOU.
EUNUCH GAO LISHI
HEHEHE...
BOTH OF YOU ARE IMPORTANT MINISTERS TO THE TANG DYNASTY!
THAT'S RIGHT, THAT'S RIGHT! WE CAN'T DO WITHOUT EITHER! HAHAHA!
HAHAHAHA!
DUM
THAT BEING SAID... IT'S BEEN A WHILE SINCE I WATCHED YOUR DANCE OF THE HU.

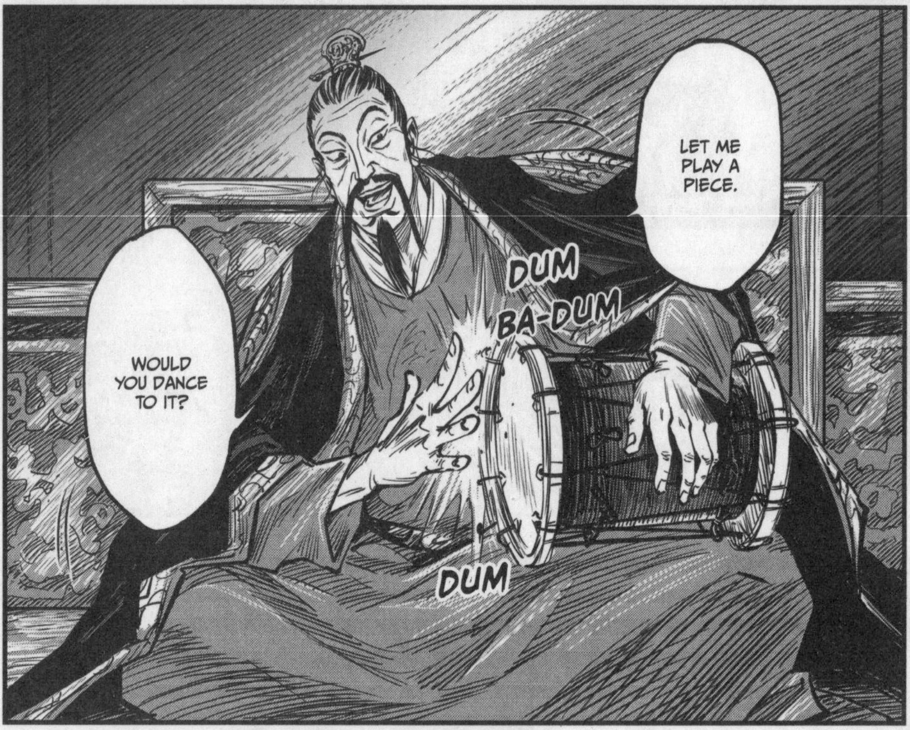
LET ME PLAY A PIECE.
DUM
BA-DUM
WOULD YOU DANCE TO IT?
DUM

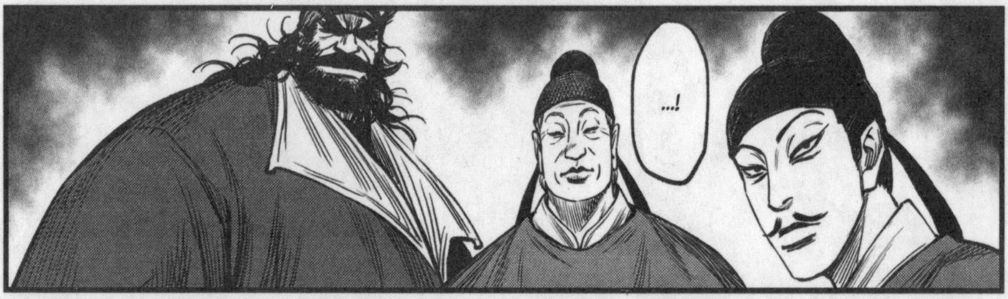
...!

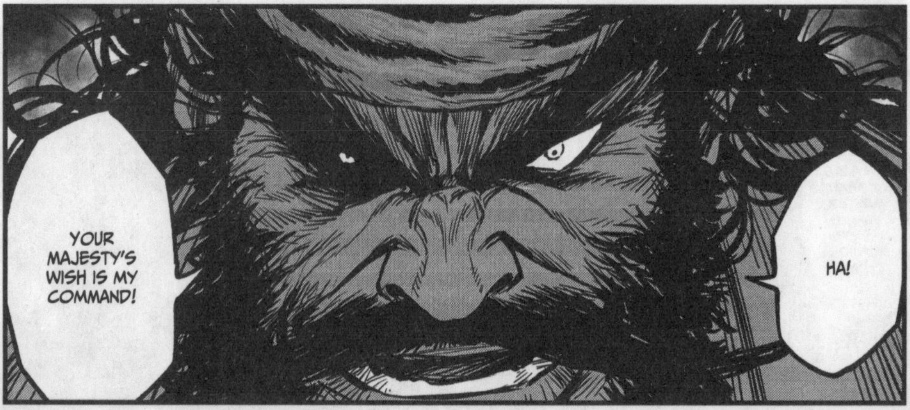
HA!
YOUR MAJESTY'S WISH IS MY COMMAND!

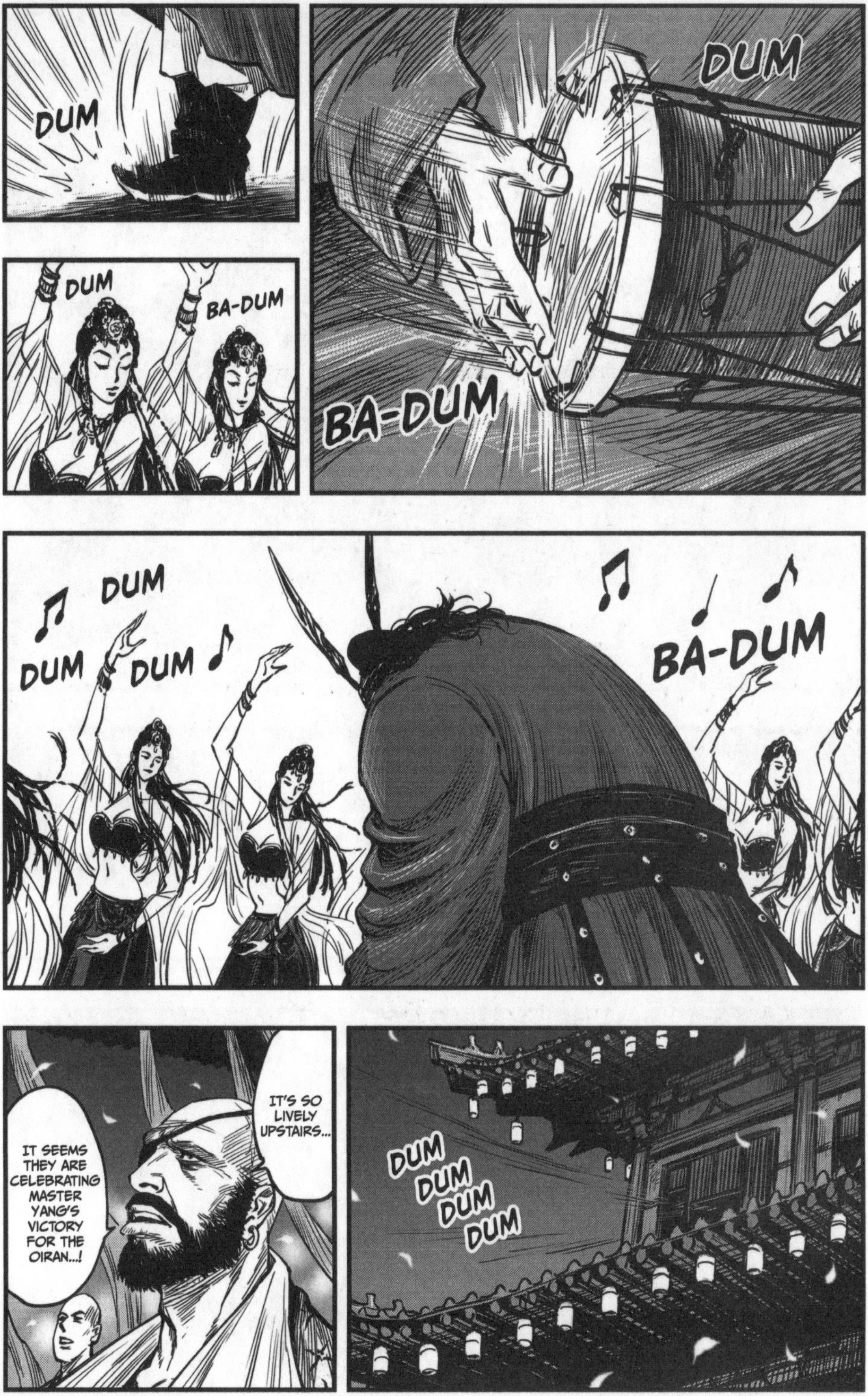
DUM
BA-DUM
DUM
DUM
BA-DUM
BA-DUM
DUM
DUM
DUM
DUM DUM DUM DUM
IT'S SO LIVELY UPSTAIRS...
IT SEEMS THEY ARE CELEBRATING MASTER YANG'S VICTORY FOR THE OIRAN...!

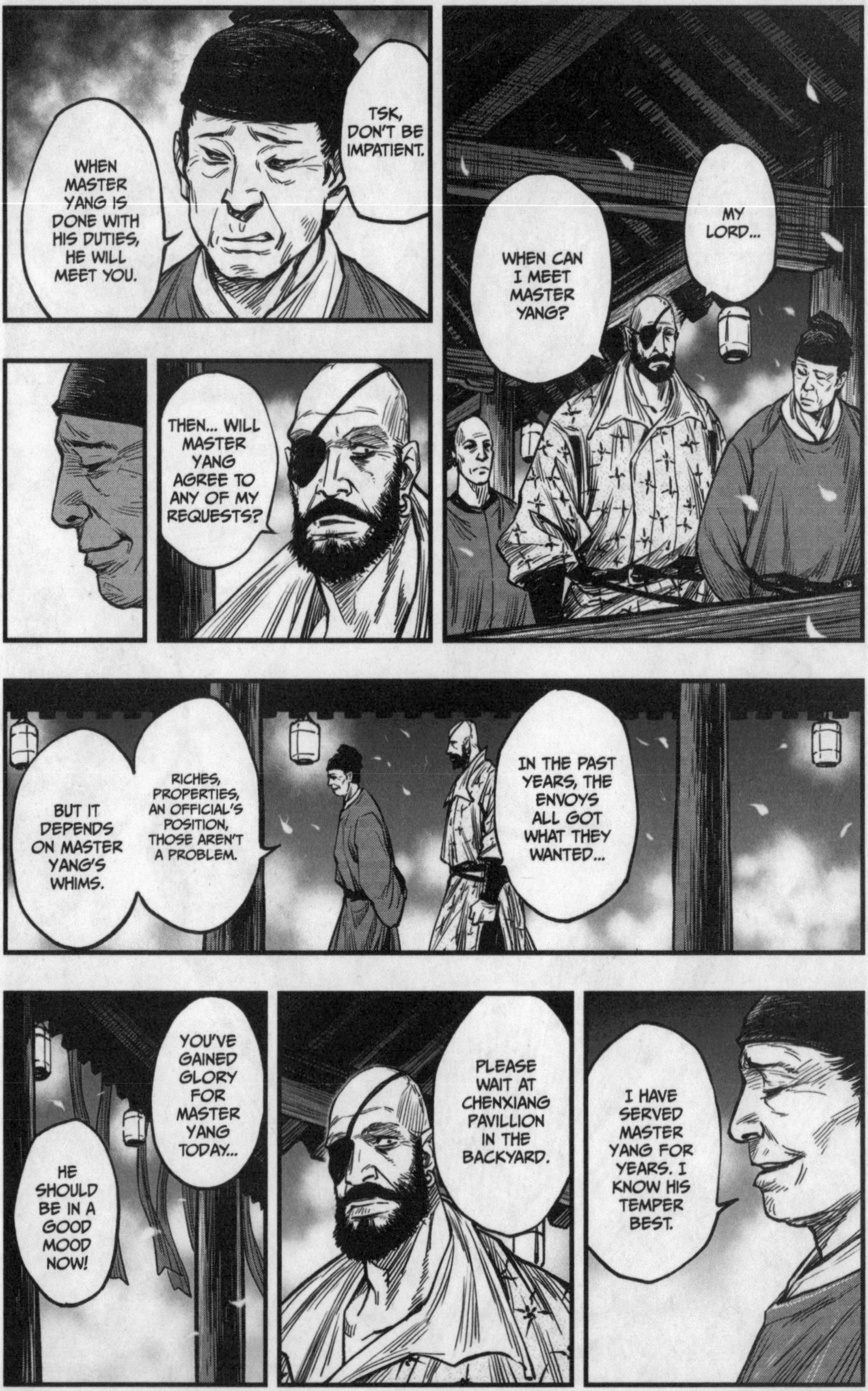
MY LORD...
WHEN CAN I MEET MASTER YANG?
TSK, DON'T BE IMPATIENT.
WHEN MASTER YANG IS DONE WITH HIS DUTIES, HE WILL MEET YOU.
THEN... WILL MASTER YANG AGREE TO ANY OF MY REQUESTS?
IN THE PAST YEARS, THE ENVOYS ALL GOT WHAT THEY WANTED...
RICHES, PROPERTIES, AN OFFICIAL'S POSITION, THOSE AREN'T A PROBLEM.
BUT IT DEPENDS ON MASTER YANG'S WHIMS.
I HAVE SERVED MASTER YANG FOR YEARS. I KNOW HIS TEMPER BEST.
PLEASE WAIT AT CHENXIANG PAVILLION IN THE BACKYARD.
YOU'VE GAINED GLORY FOR MASTER YANG TODAY...
HE SHOULD BE IN A GOOD MOOD NOW!

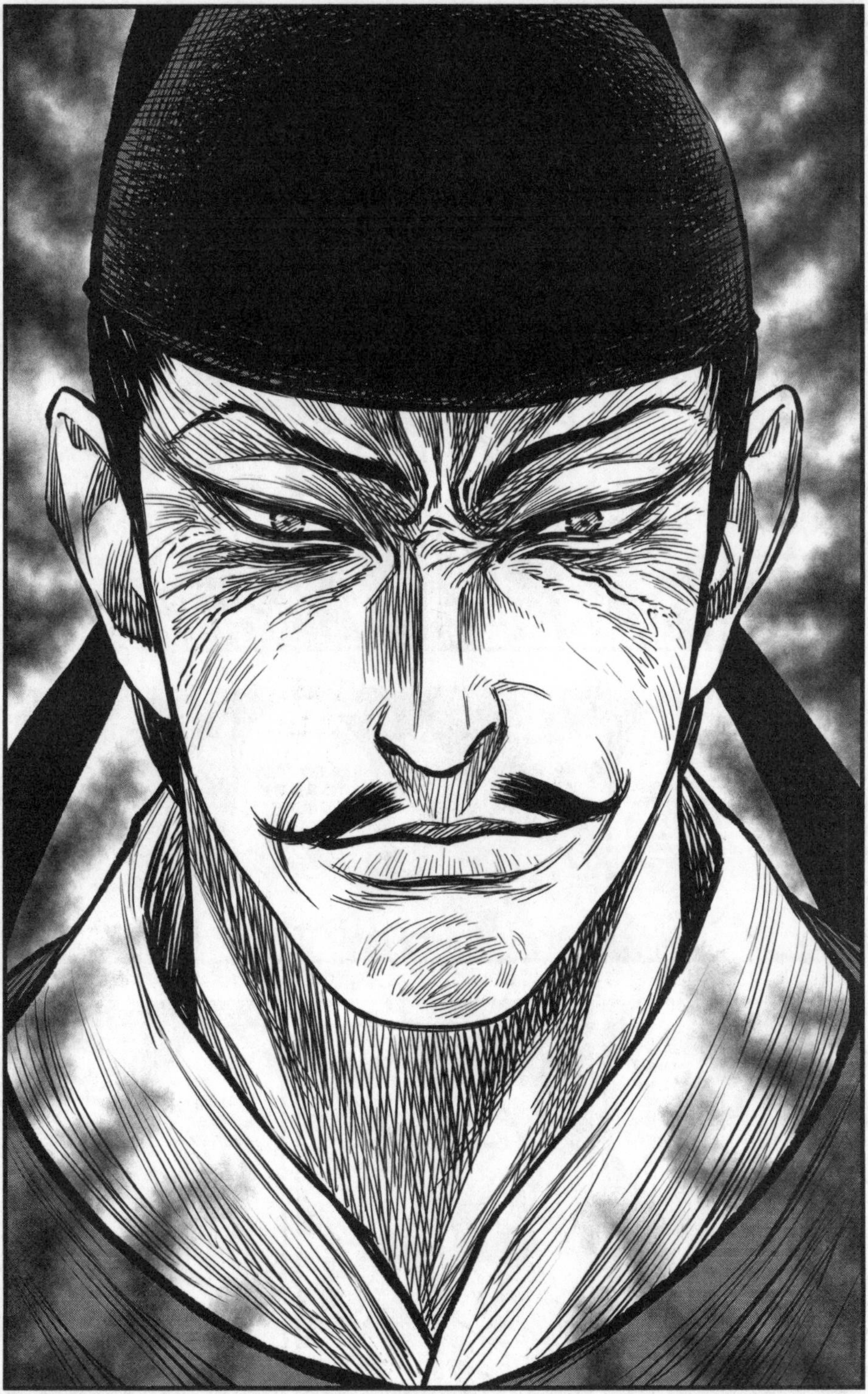

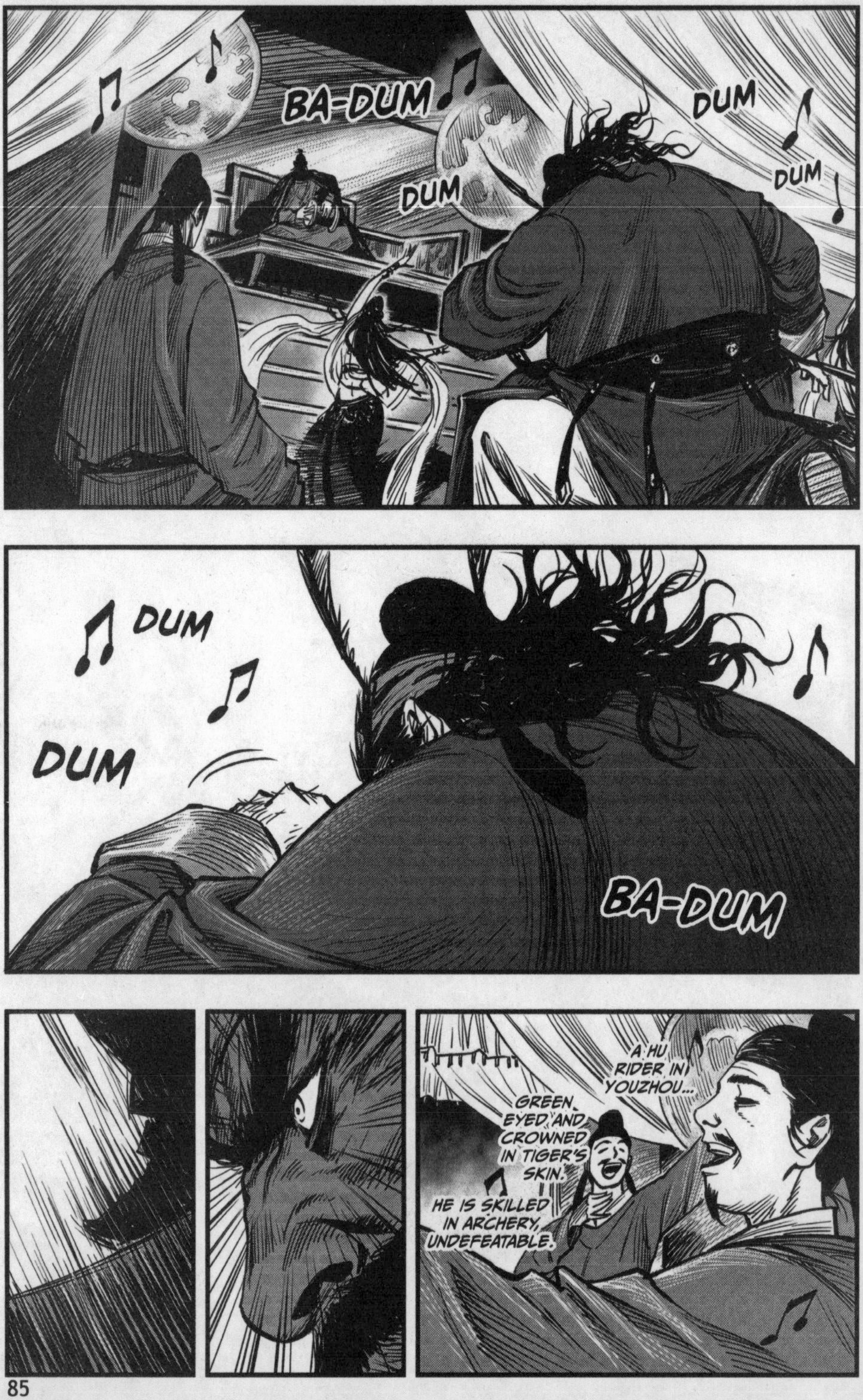
DUM
DUM
BA-DUM
DUM
DUM
DUM
BA-DUM
A HU RIDER IN YOUZHOU...
GREEN-EYED AND CROWNED IN TIGER'S SKIN.
HE IS SKILLED IN ARCHERY, UNDEFEATABLE.

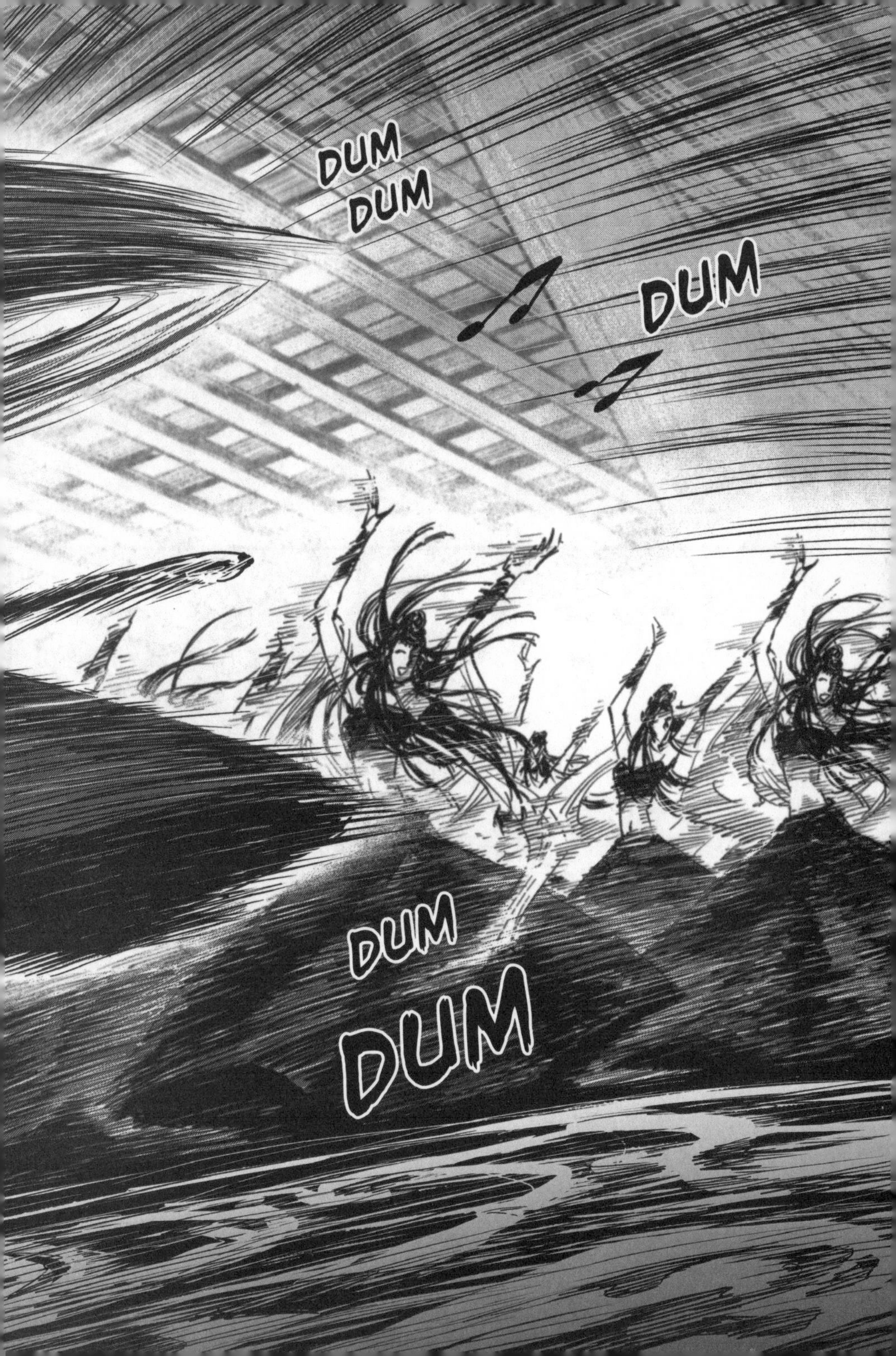
DUM
DUM DUM
DUM
DUM DUM

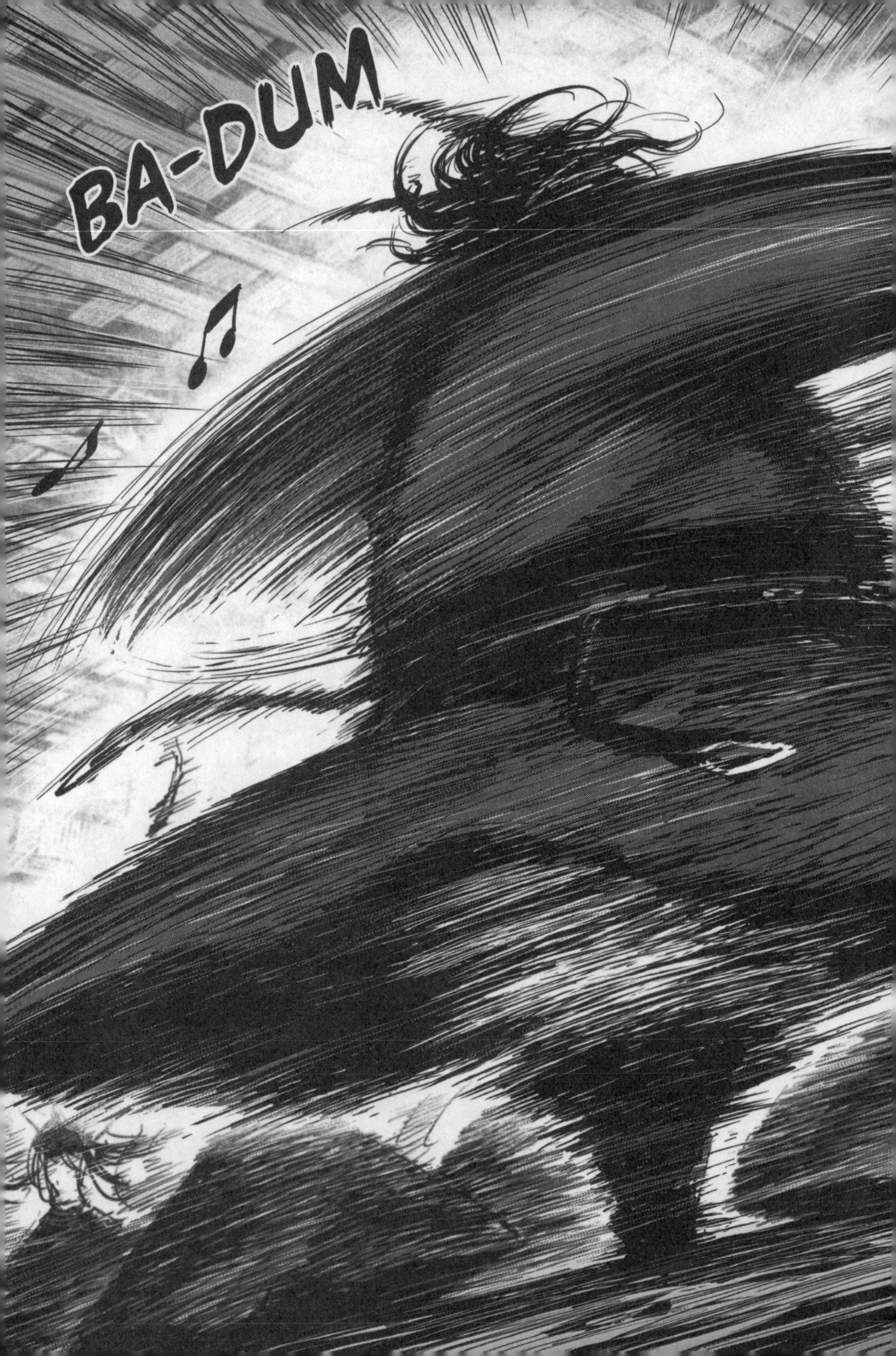
BA-DUM

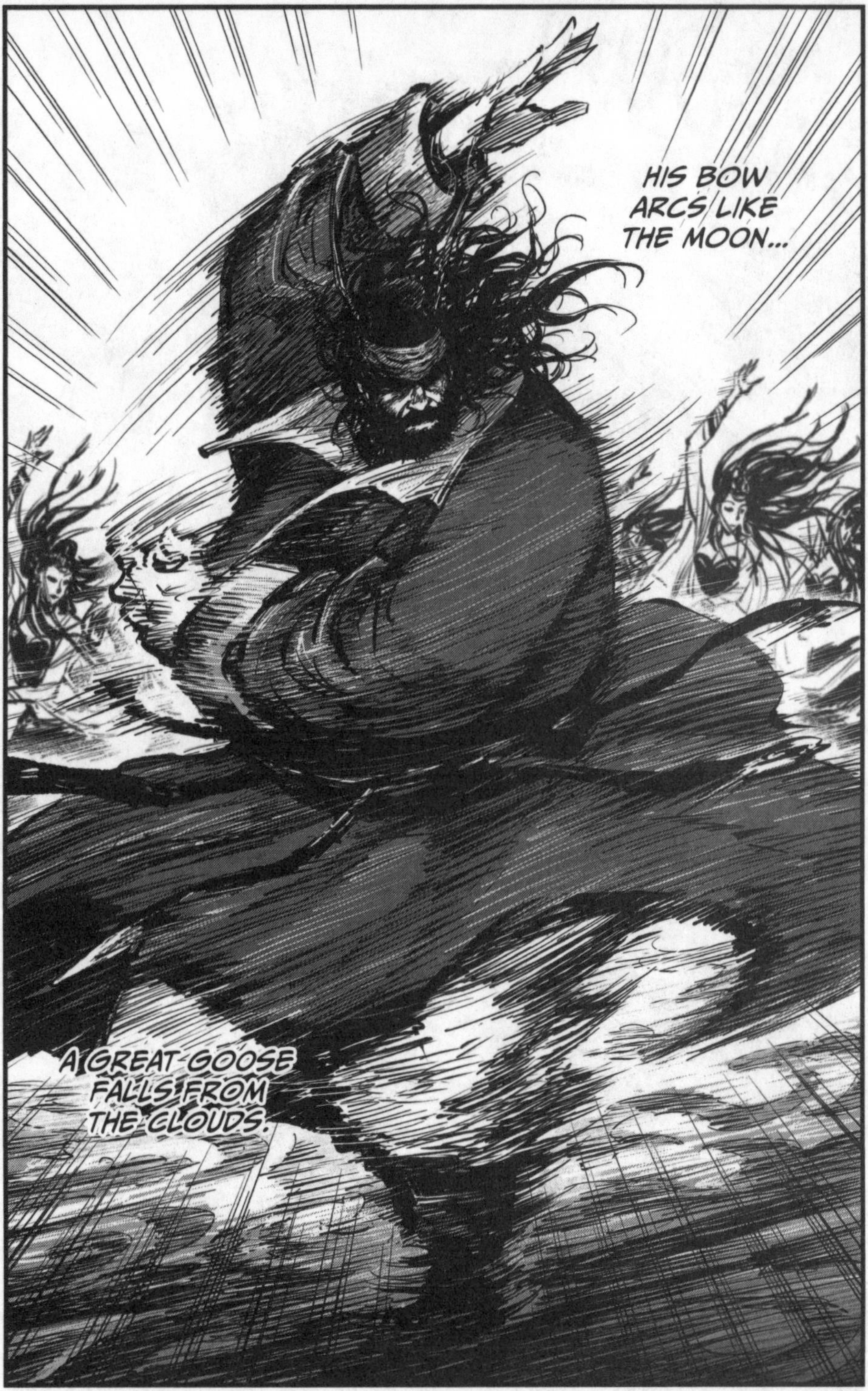
HIS BOW
ARCS LIKE
THE MOON...
A GREAT GOOSE
FALLS FROM
THE CLOUDS.

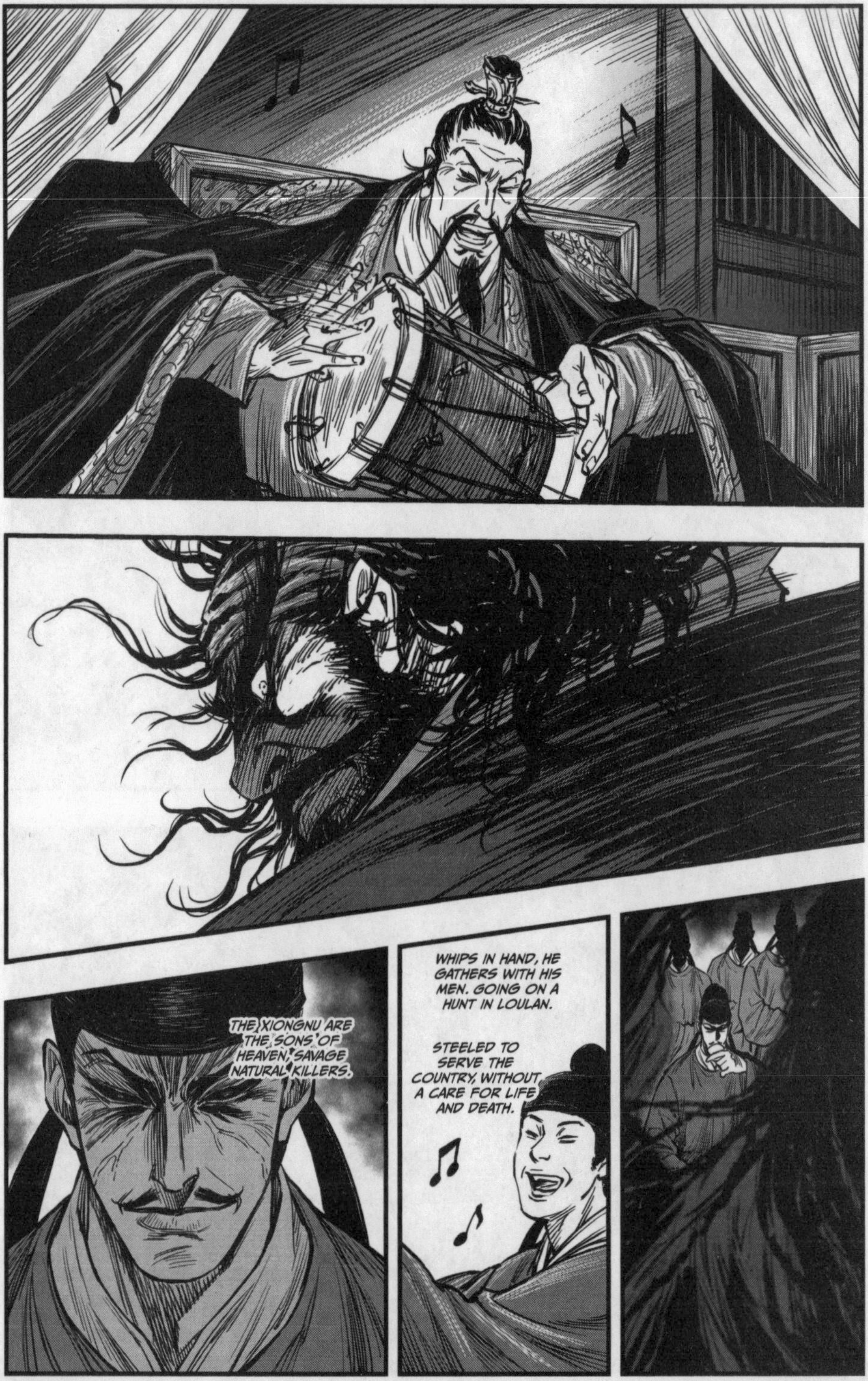
WHIPS IN HAND, HE GATHERS WITH HIS MEN. GOING ON A HUNT IN LOULAN.
STEELED TO SERVE THE COUNTRY, WITHOUT A CARE FOR LIFE AND DEATH.
THE XIONGNU ARE THE SONS OF HEAVEN, SAVAGE NATURAL KILLERS.

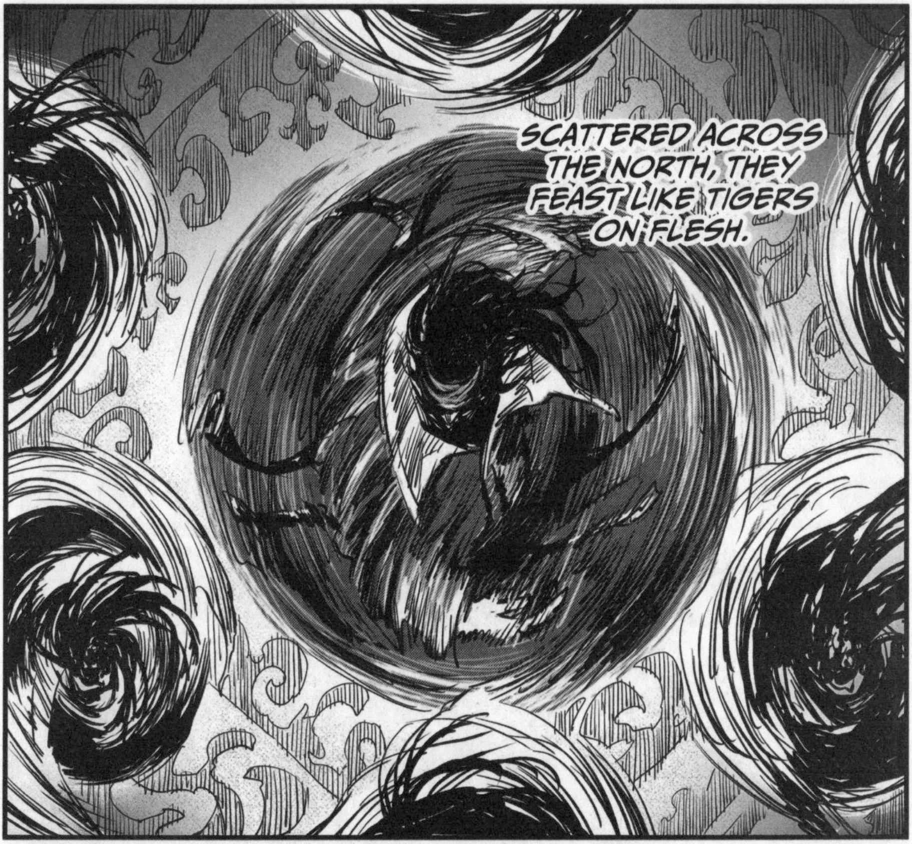
SCATTERED ACROSS THE NORTH, THEY FEAST LIKE TIGERS ON FLESH.

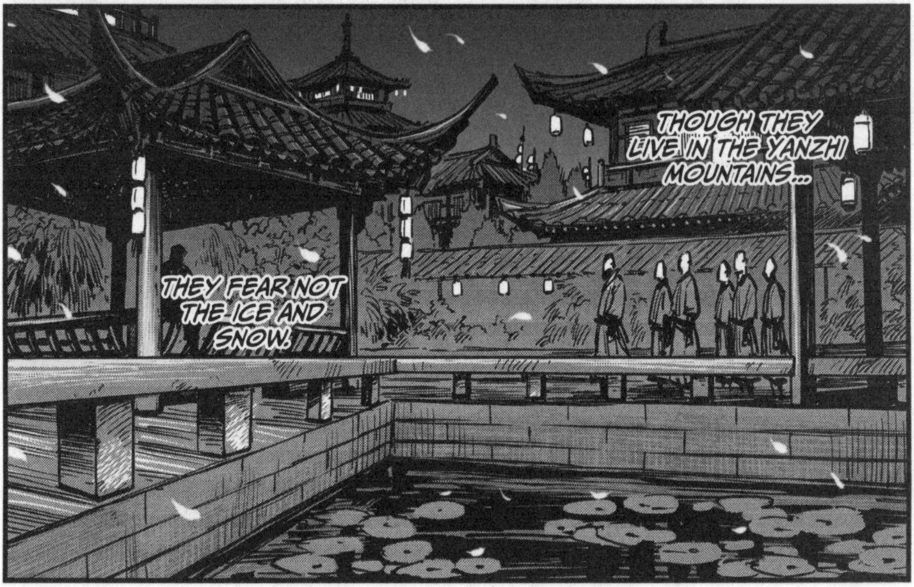
THOUGH THEY LIVE IN THE YANZHI MOUNTAINS...
THEY FEAR NOT THE ICE AND SNOW.

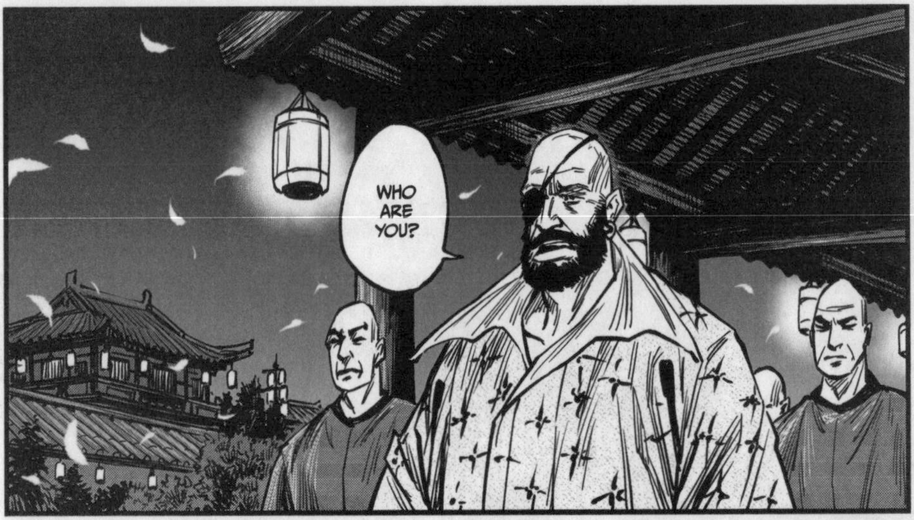
WHO ARE YOU?
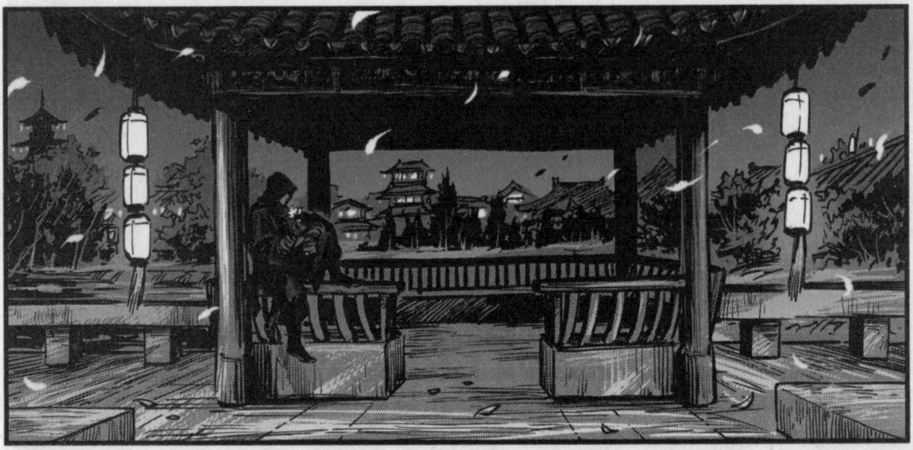
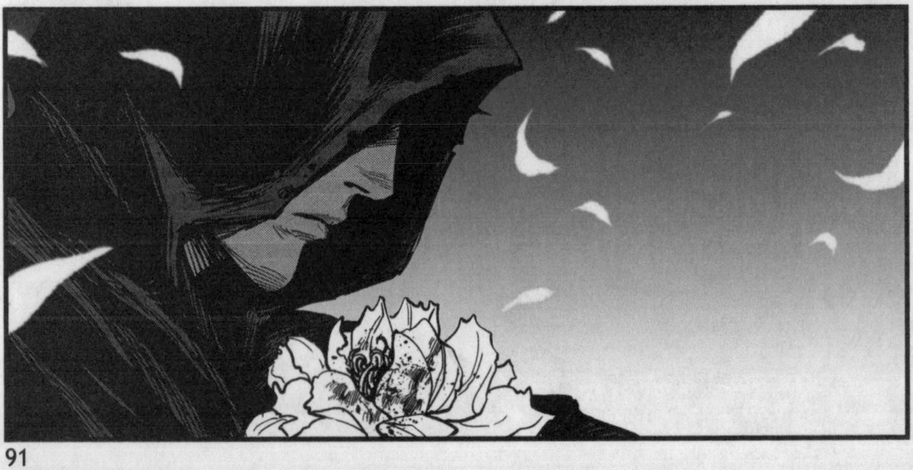

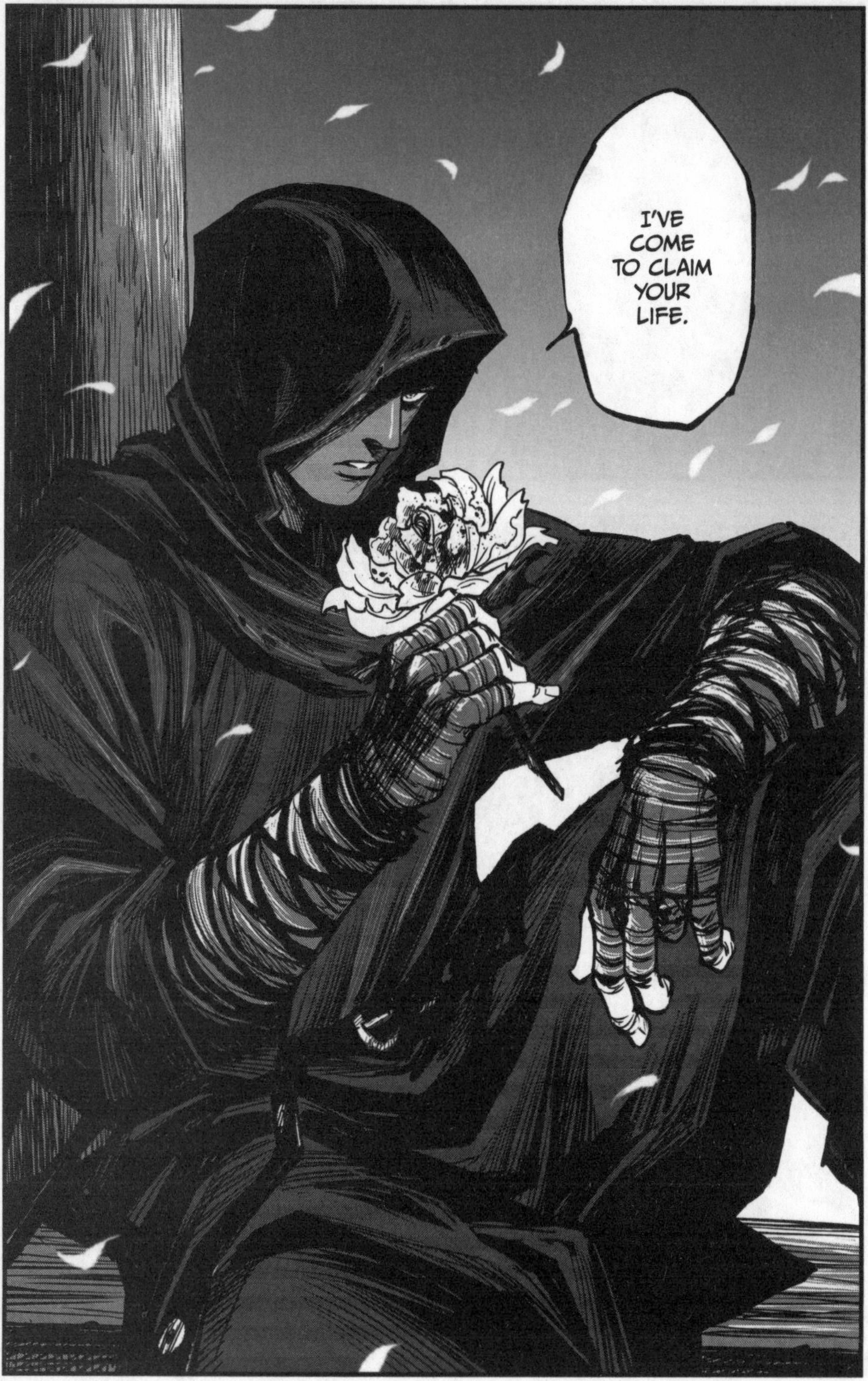
I'VE COME TO CLAIM YOUR LIFE.

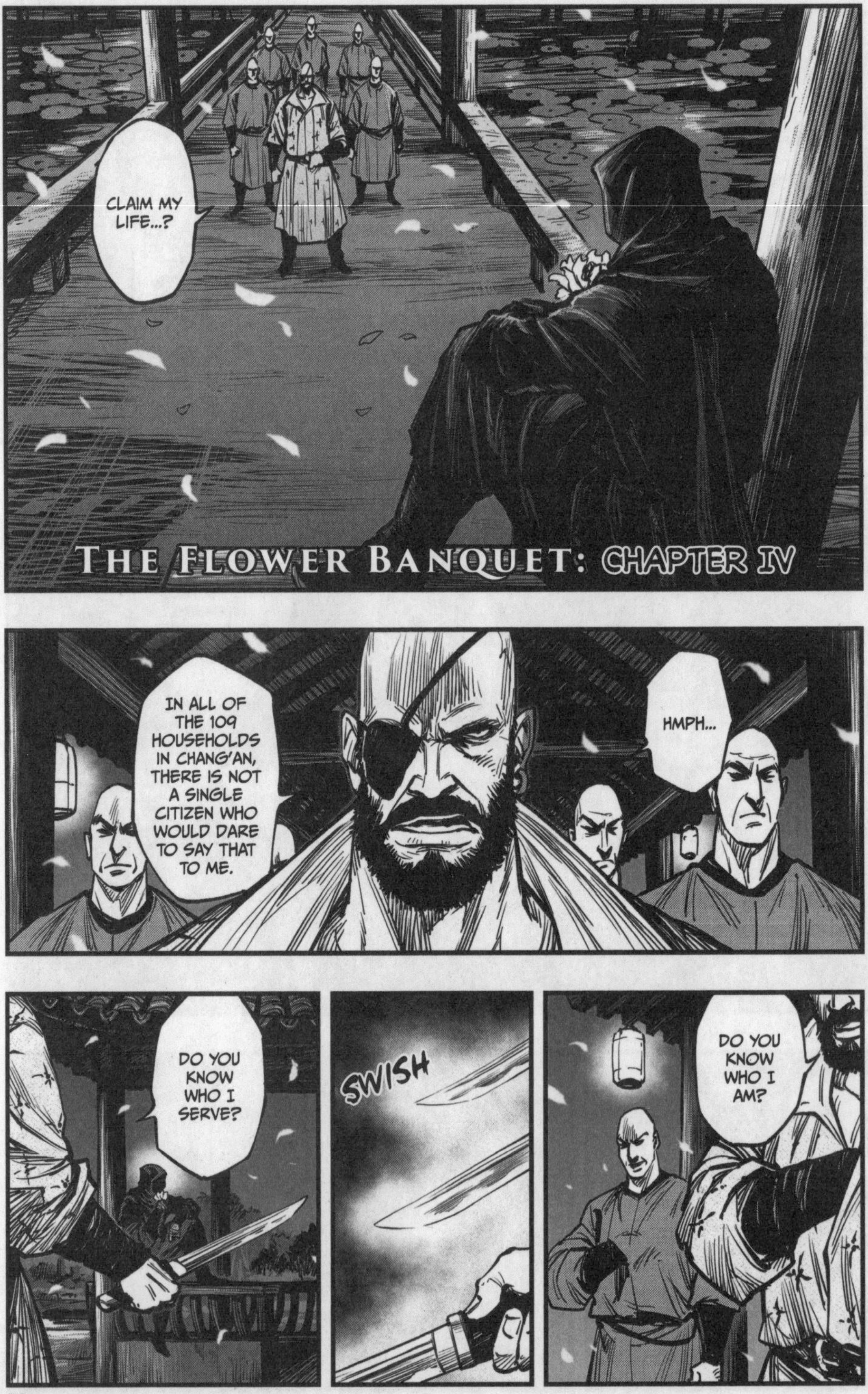
CLAIM MY LIFE...?
THE FLOWER BANQUET: CHAPTER IV
IN ALL OF THE 109 HOUSEHOLDS IN CHANG'AN, THERE IS NOT A SINGLE CITIZEN WHO WOULD DARE TO SAY THAT TO ME.
HMPH...
DO YOU KNOW WHO I SERVE?
SWISH
DO YOU KNOW WHO I AM?

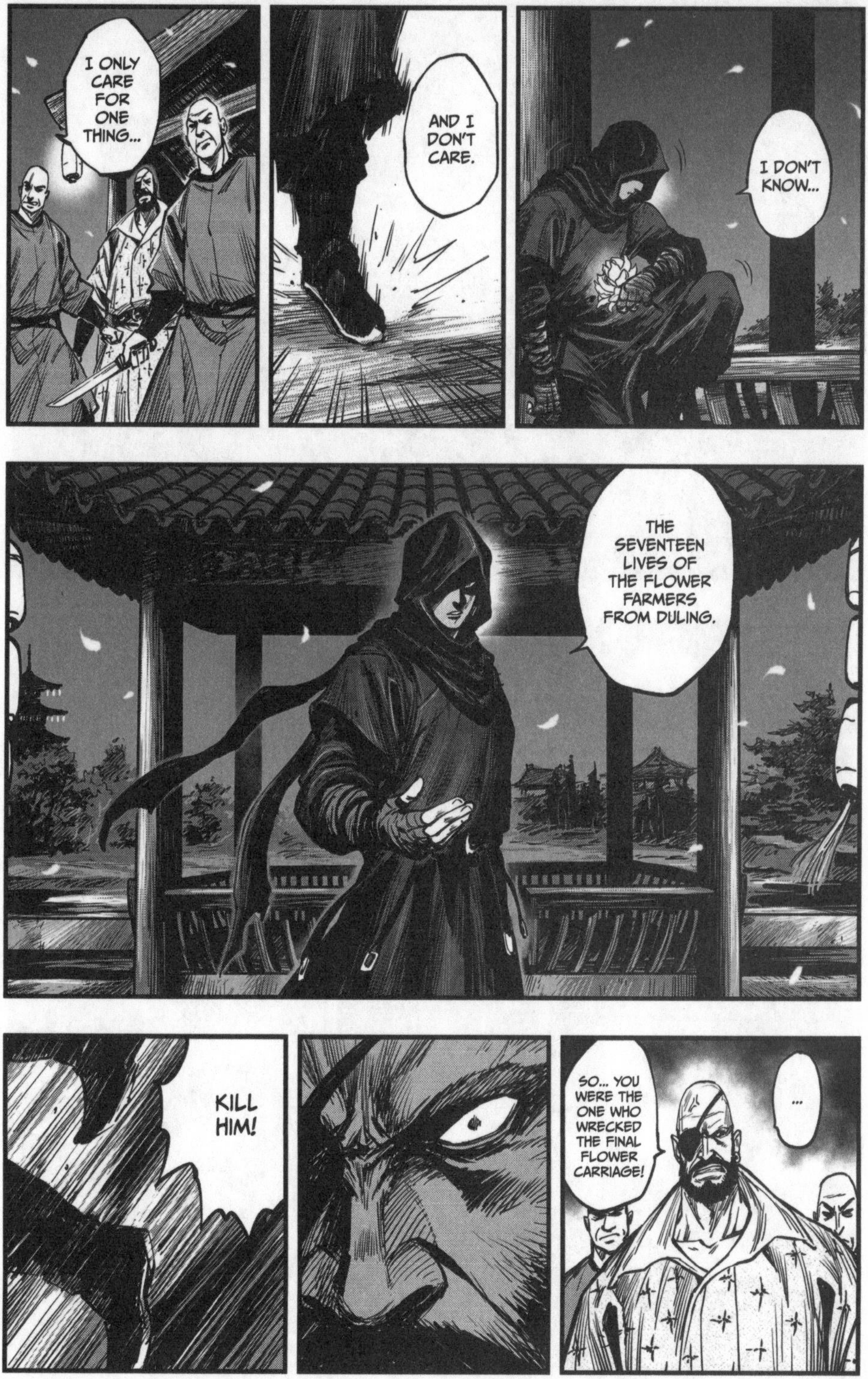
I DON'T KNOW...
AND I DON'T CARE.
I ONLY CARE FOR ONE THING...
THE SEVENTEEN LIVES OF THE FLOWER FARMERS FROM DULING.
...
SO... YOU WERE THE ONE WHO WRECKED THE FINAL FLOWER CARRIAGE!
KILL HIM!

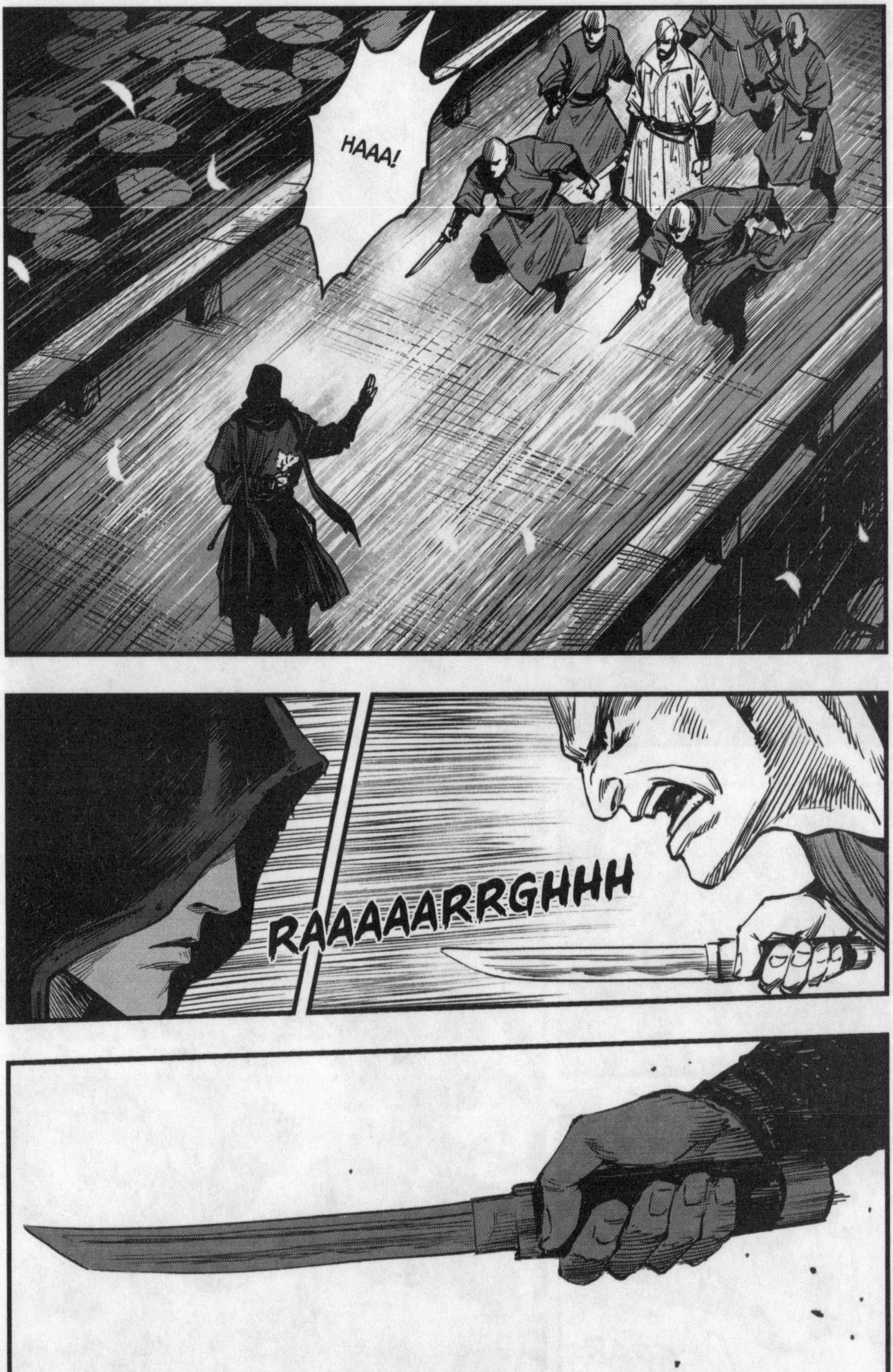
HAAA!
RAAAAARRGHHH

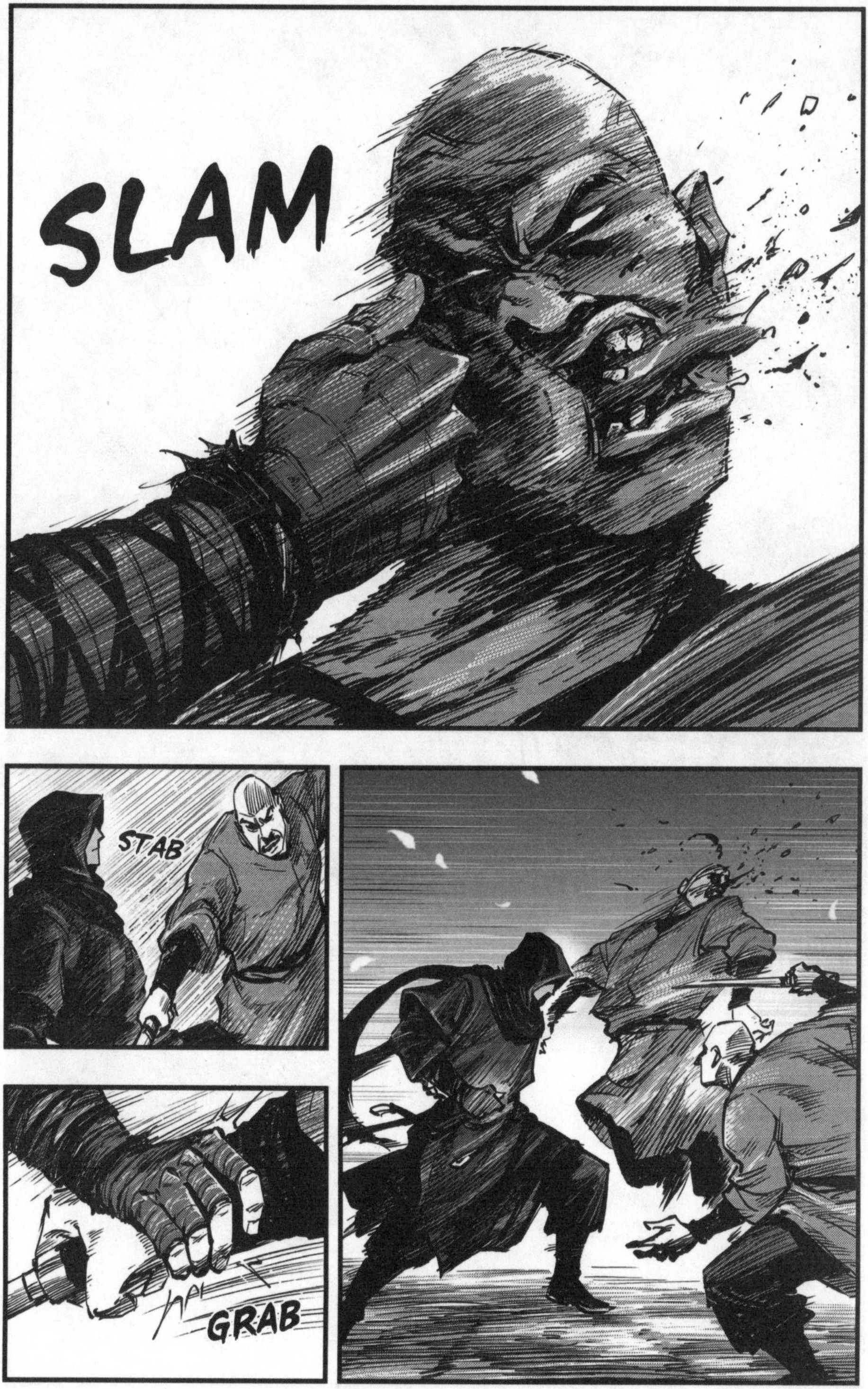
SLAM
STAB
GRAB

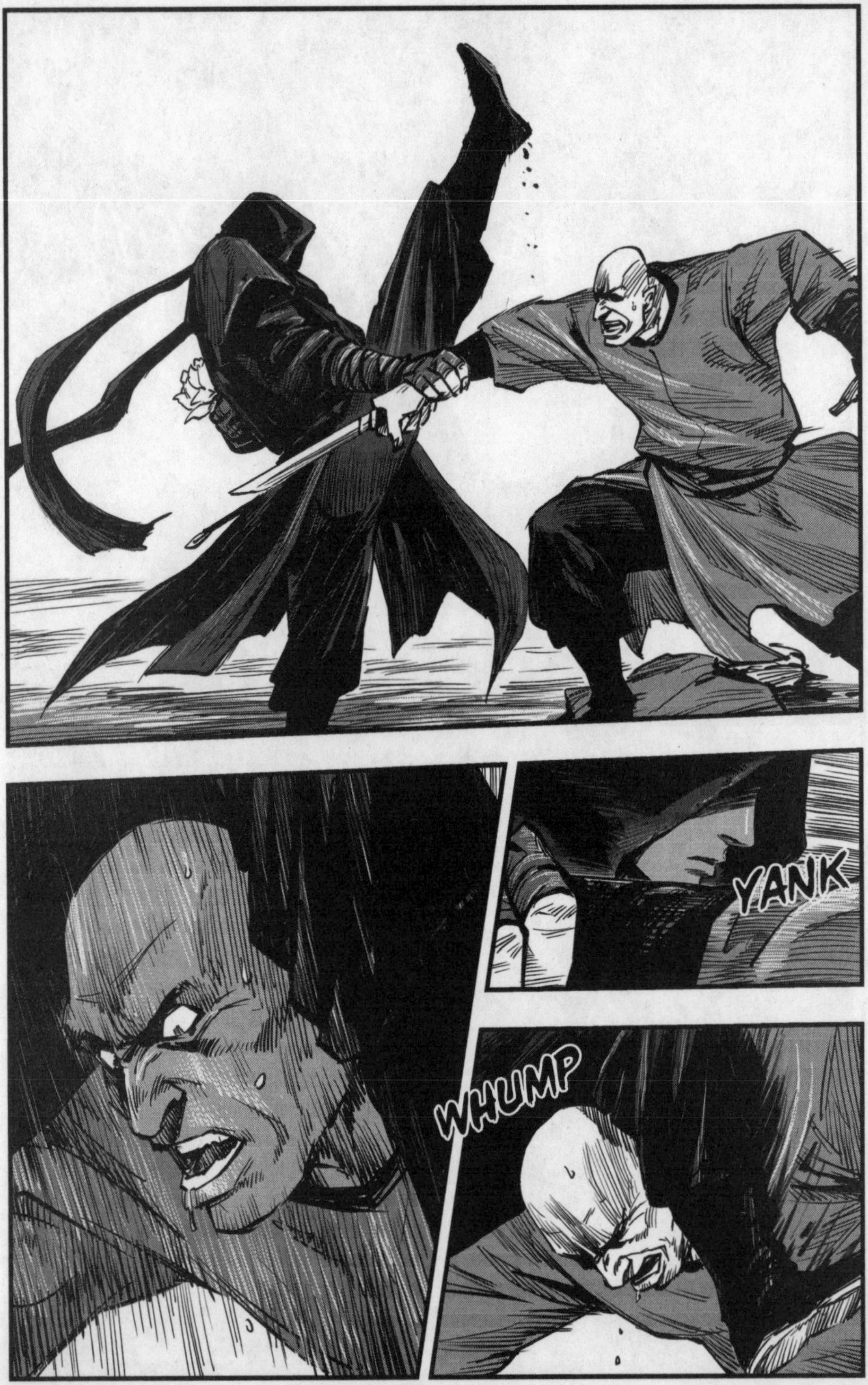
YANK
WHUMP

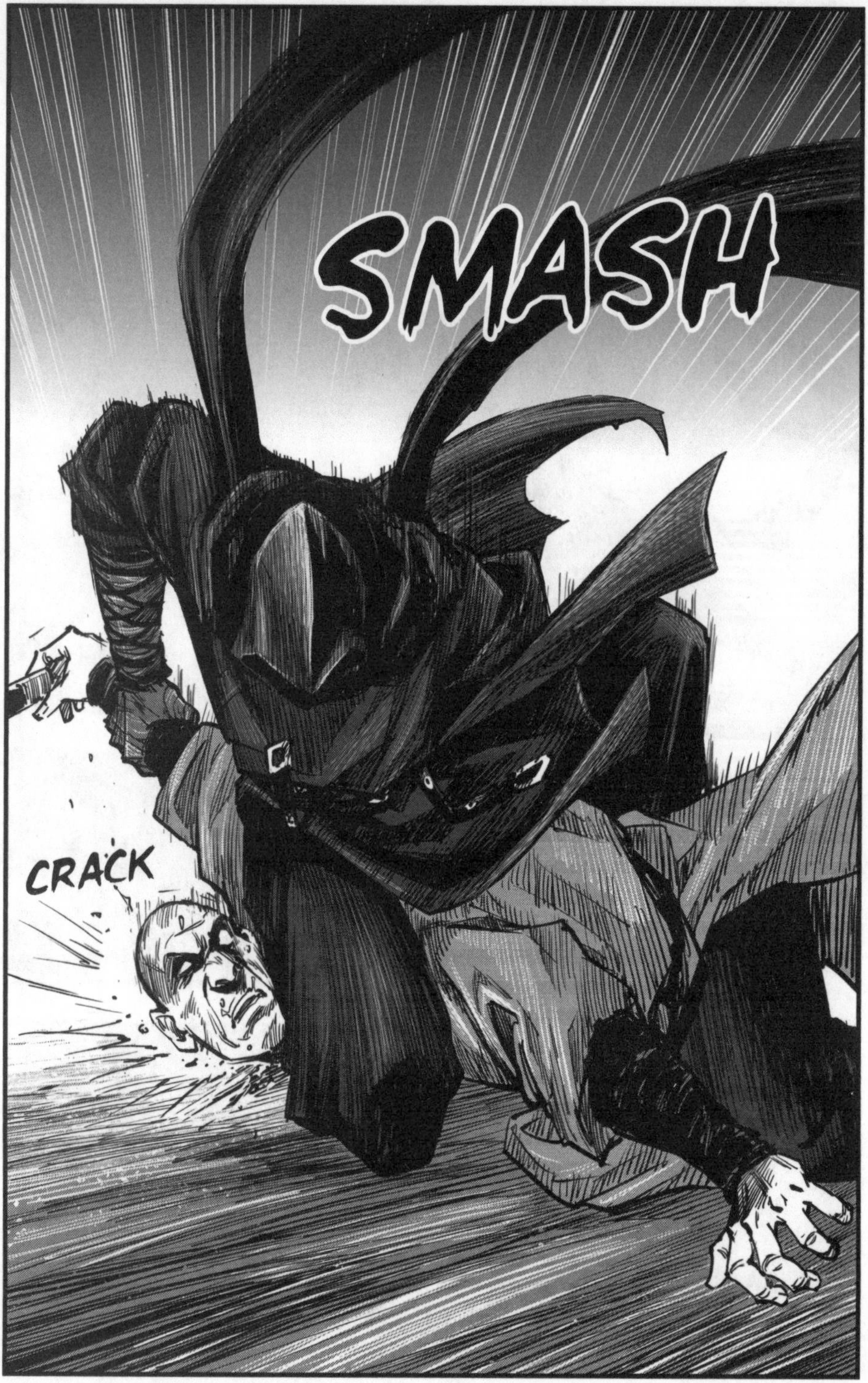
SMASH
CRACK

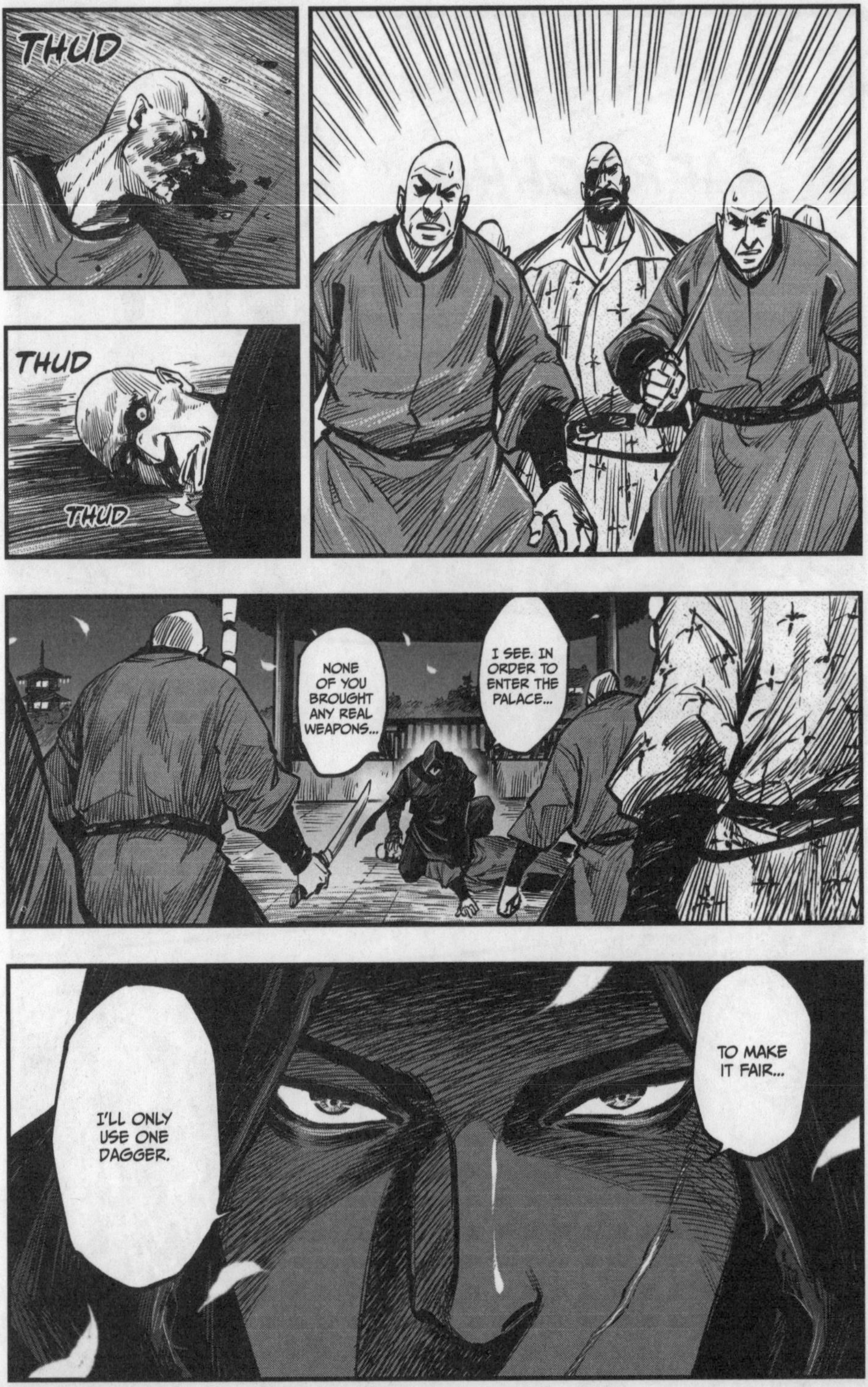
THUD
THUD
THUD
I SEE. IN ORDER TO ENTER THE PALACE...
NONE OF YOU BROUGHT ANY REAL WEAPONS...
TO MAKE IT FAIR...
I'LL ONLY USE ONE DAGGER.

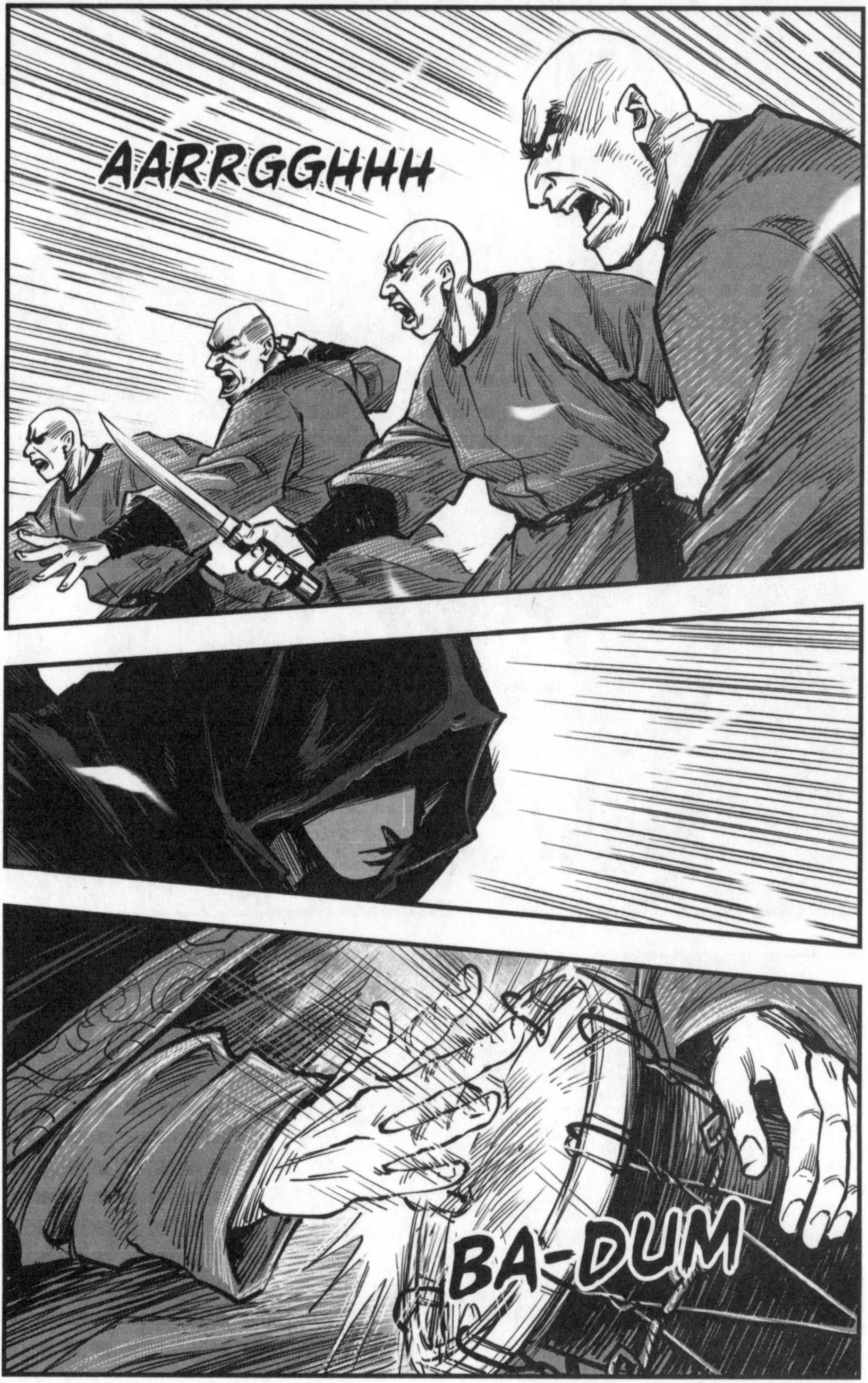
AARRGGHHH
BA-DUM

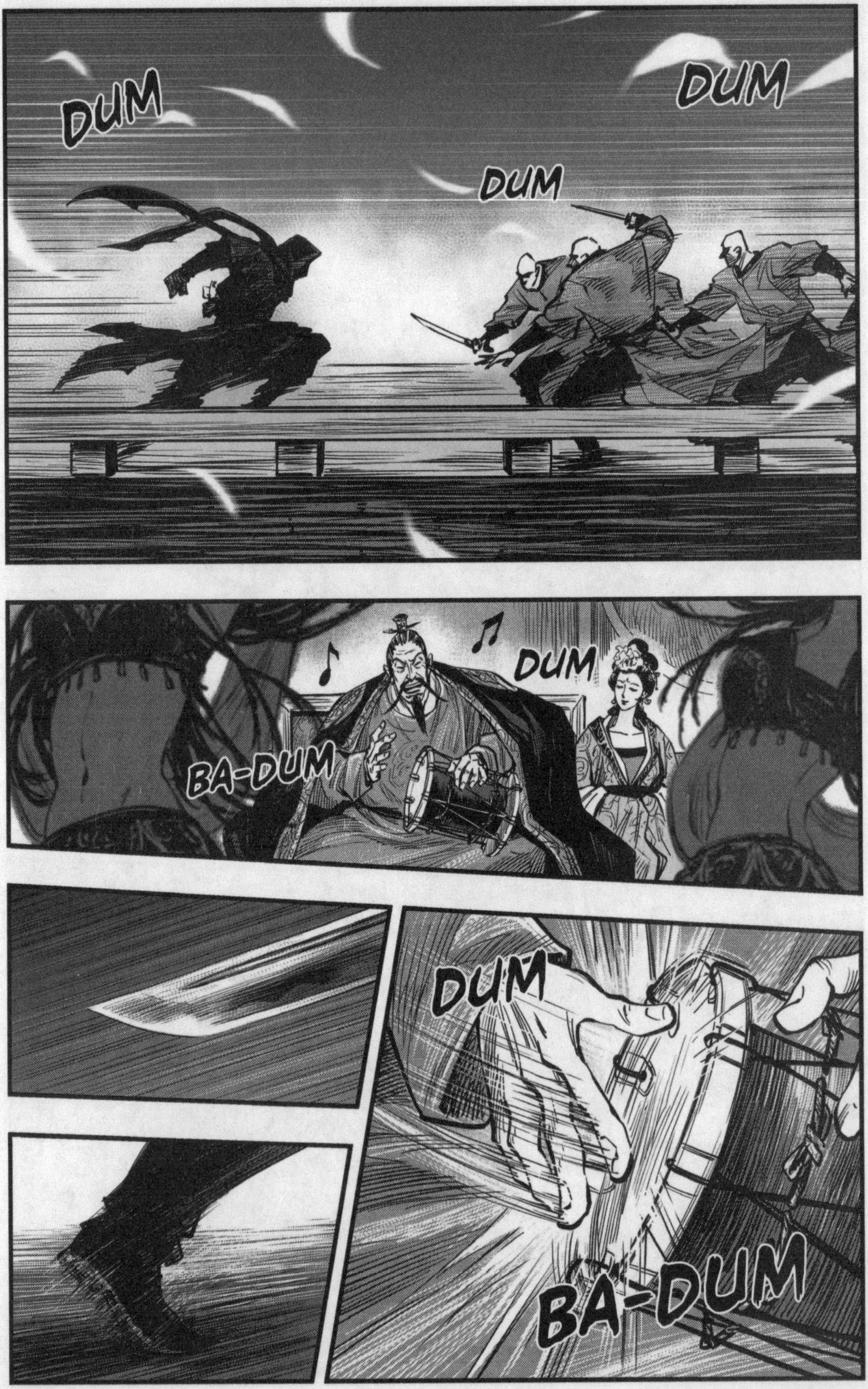
DUM
DUM
DUM
DUM
BA-DUM
DUM
BA-DUM

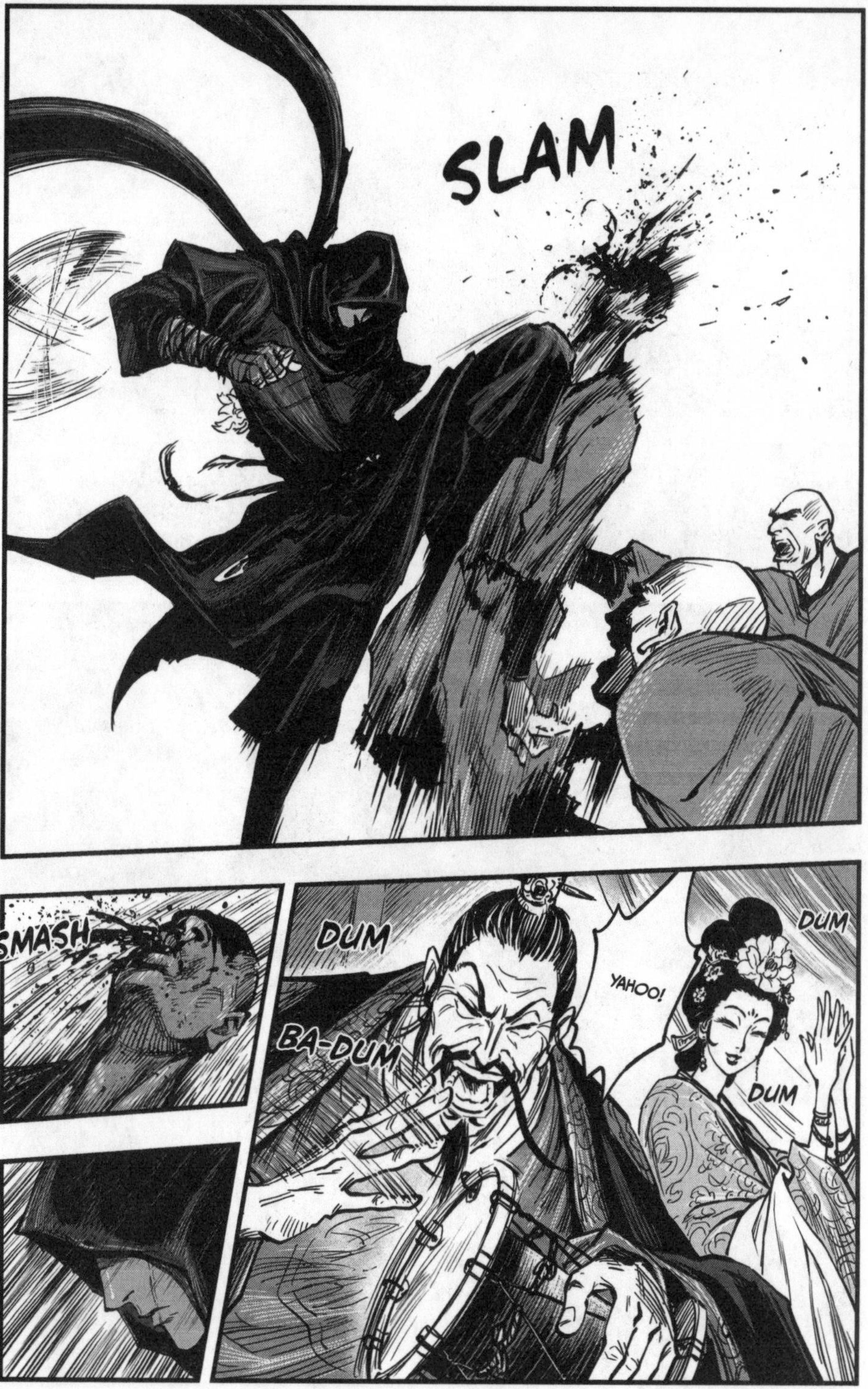
SLAM
DUM
YAHOO!
DUM
DUM
BA-DUM
SMASH

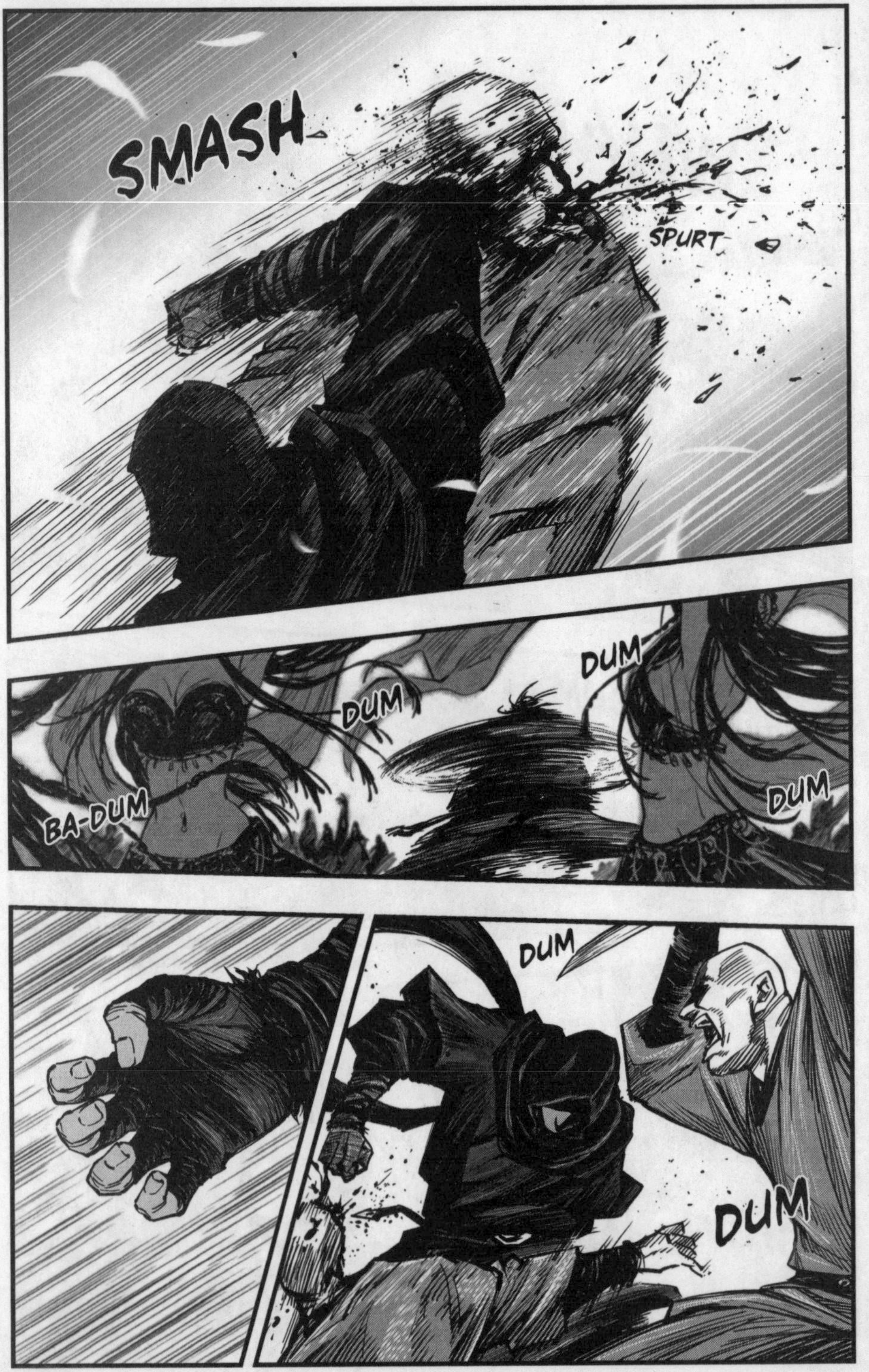
SMASH
SPURT
DUM
DUM
DUM
BA-DUM
DUM
DUM

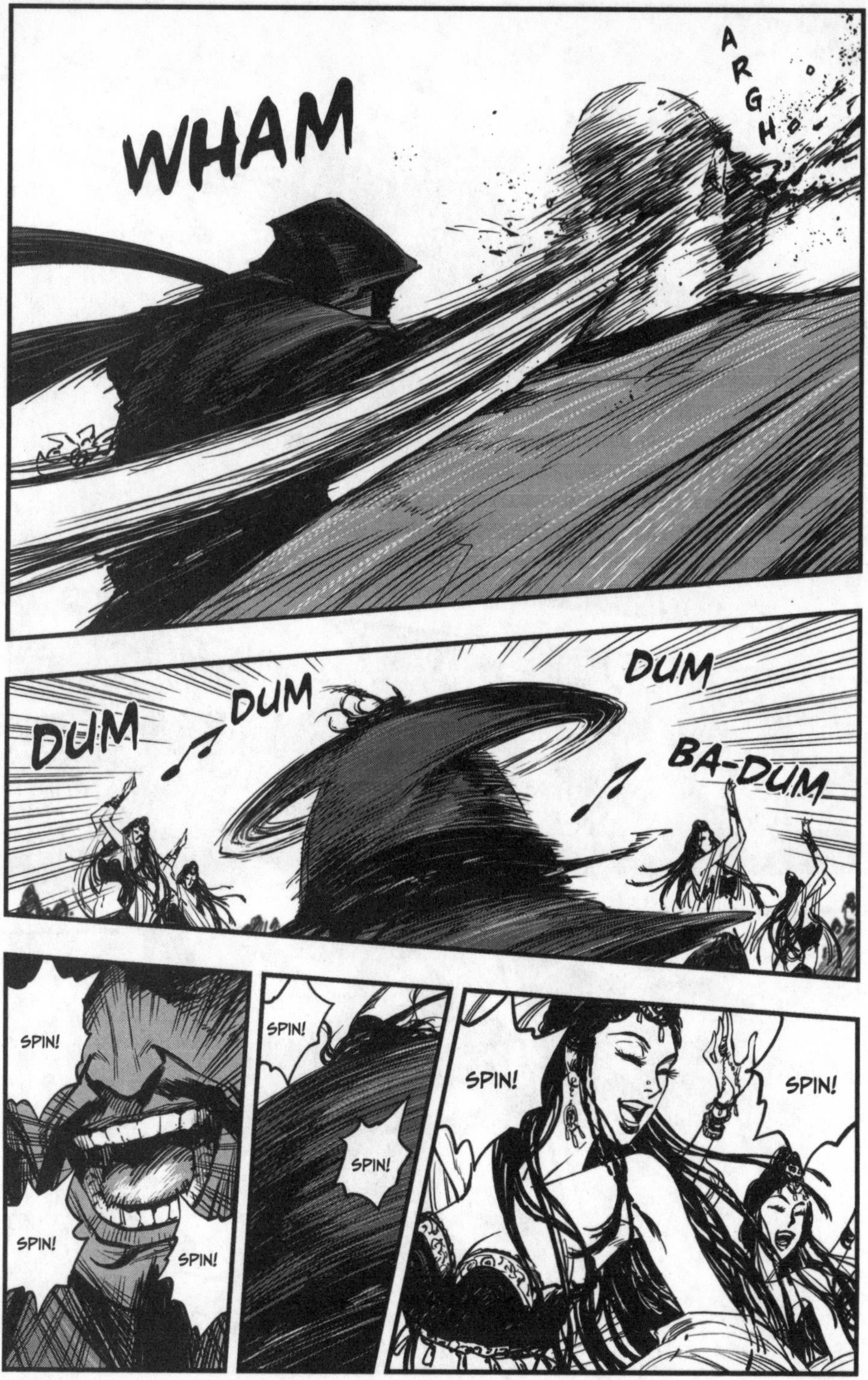
ARGH
WHAM
DUM
BA-DUM
DUM
DUM
SPIN!
SPIN!
SPIN!
SPIN!
SPIN!
SPIN!
SPIN!

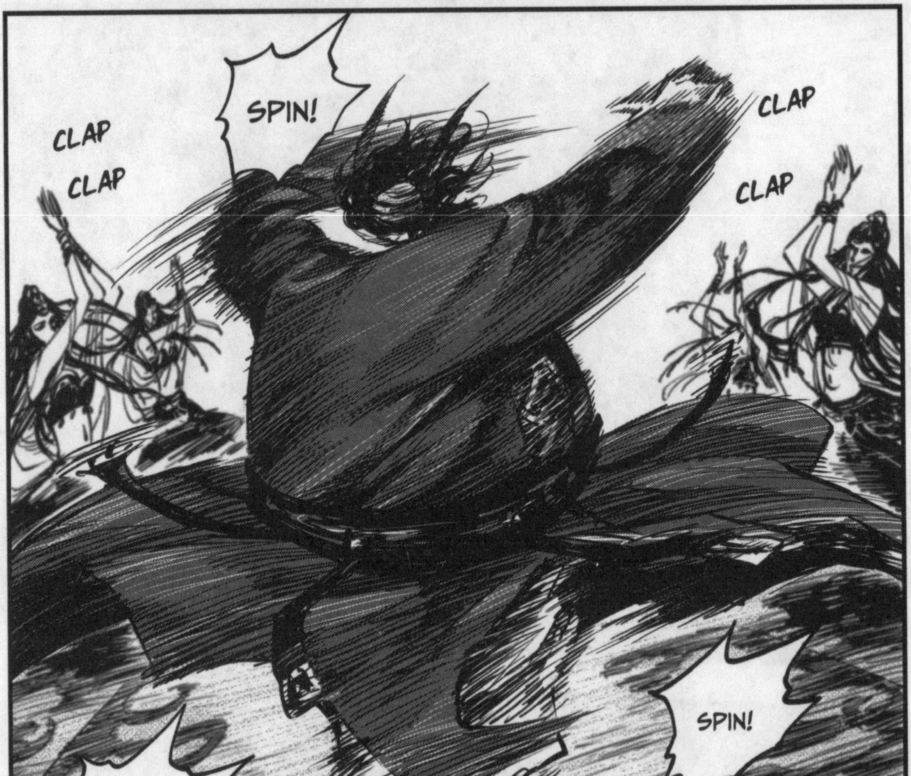
CLAP
CLAP
SPIN!
CLAP
CLAP
SPIN!
SPIN!
SPIN!

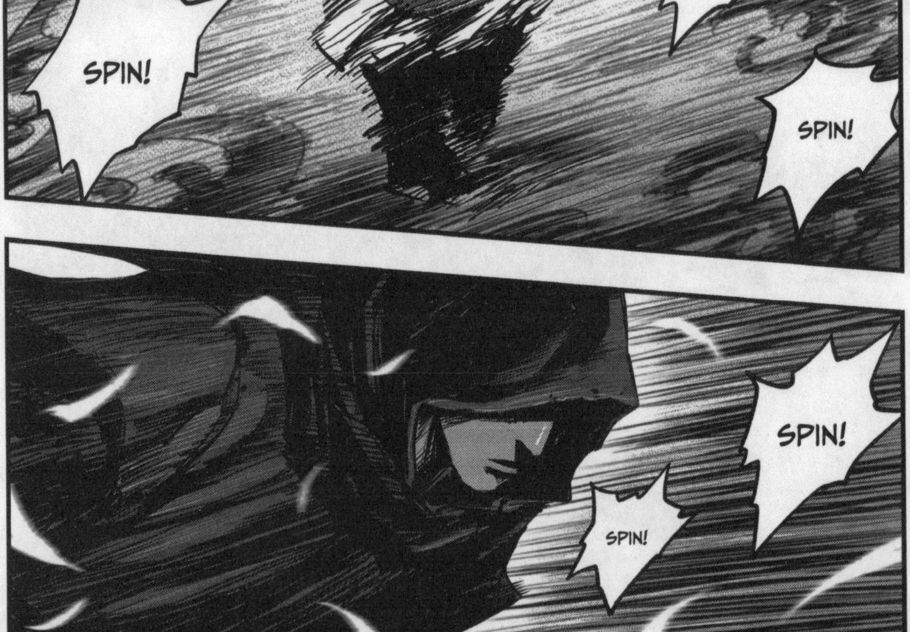
SPIN!
SPIN!

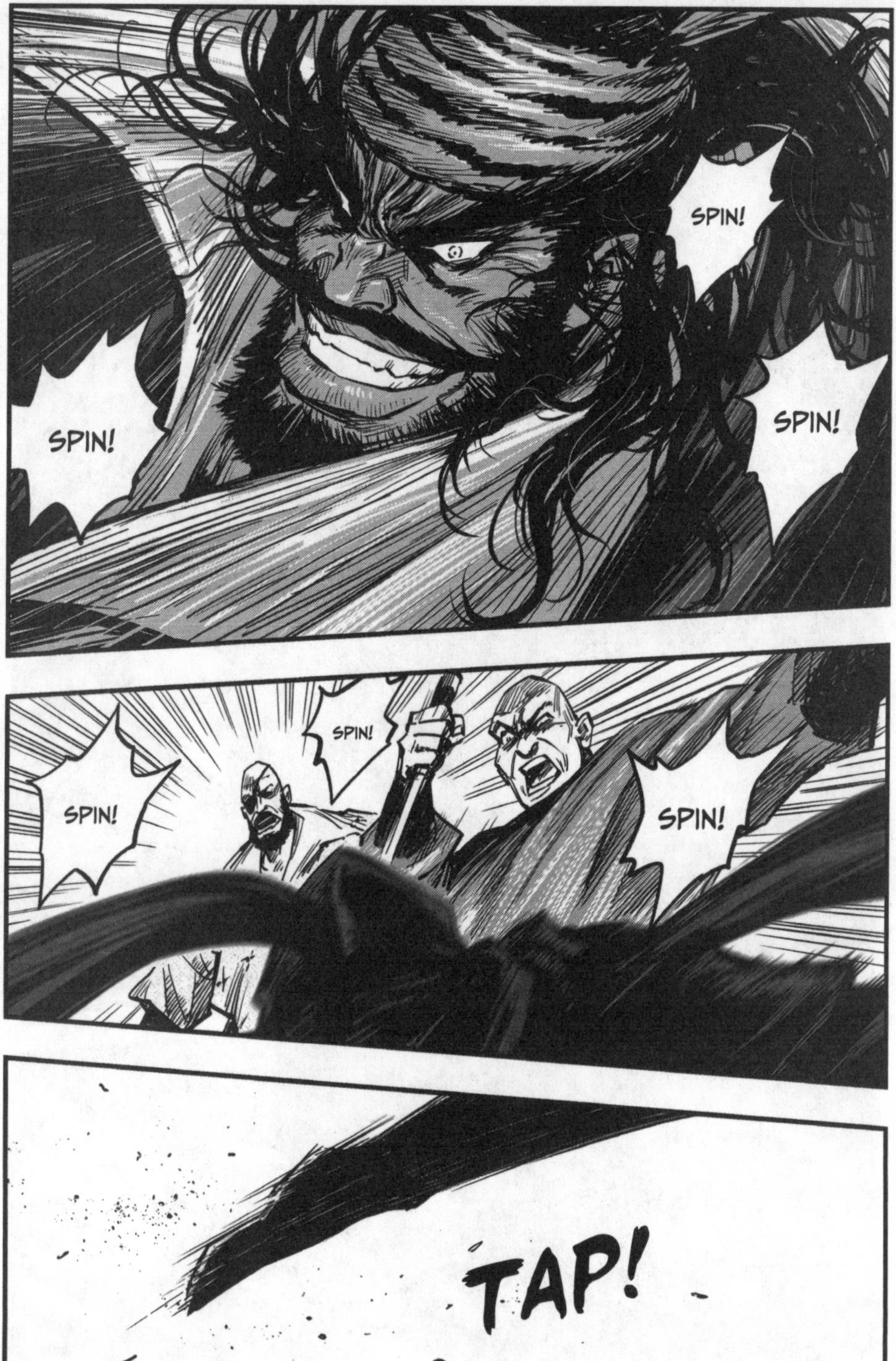
SPIN!
SPIN!
SPIN!
SPIN!
SPIN!
SPIN!
TAP!

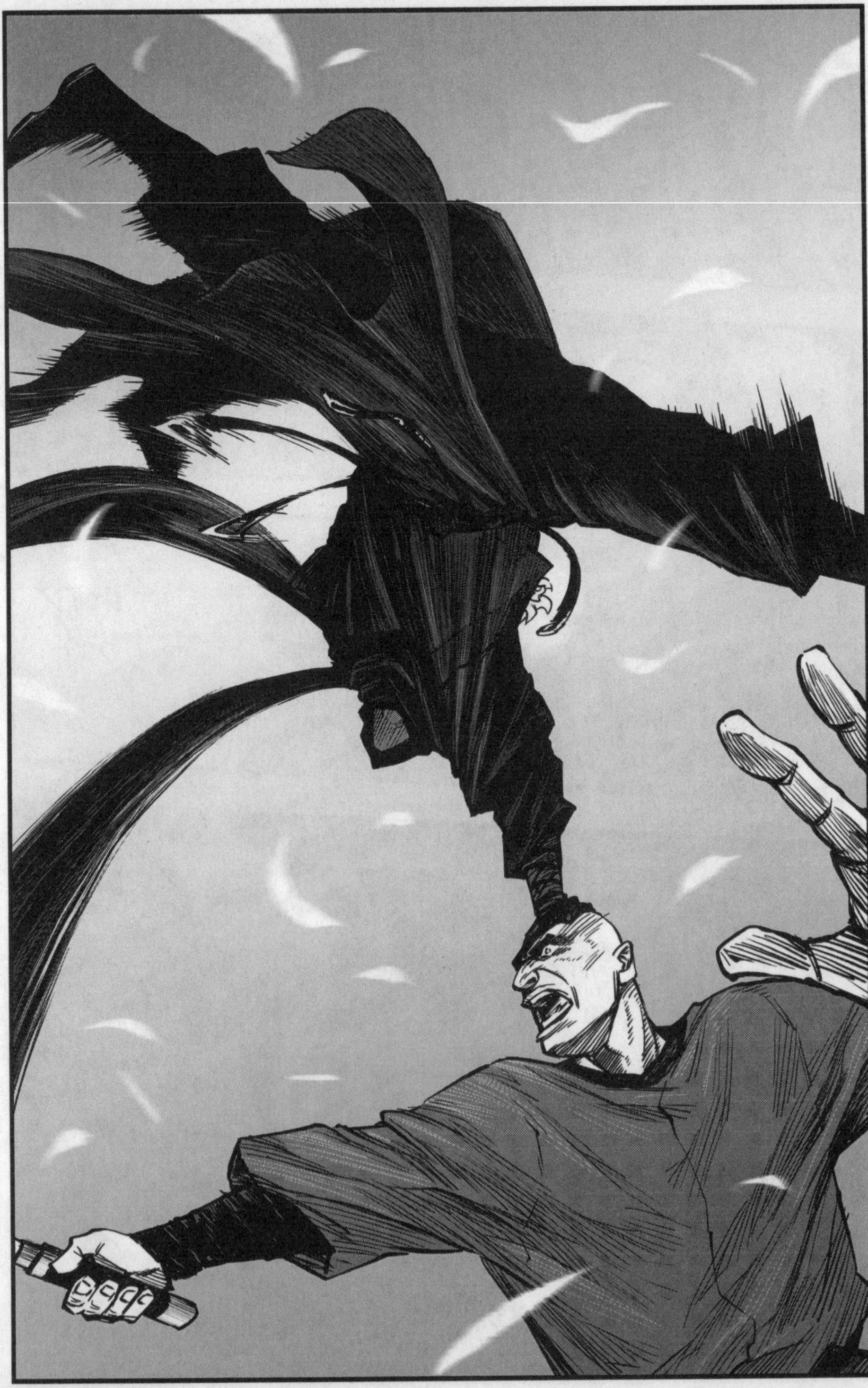

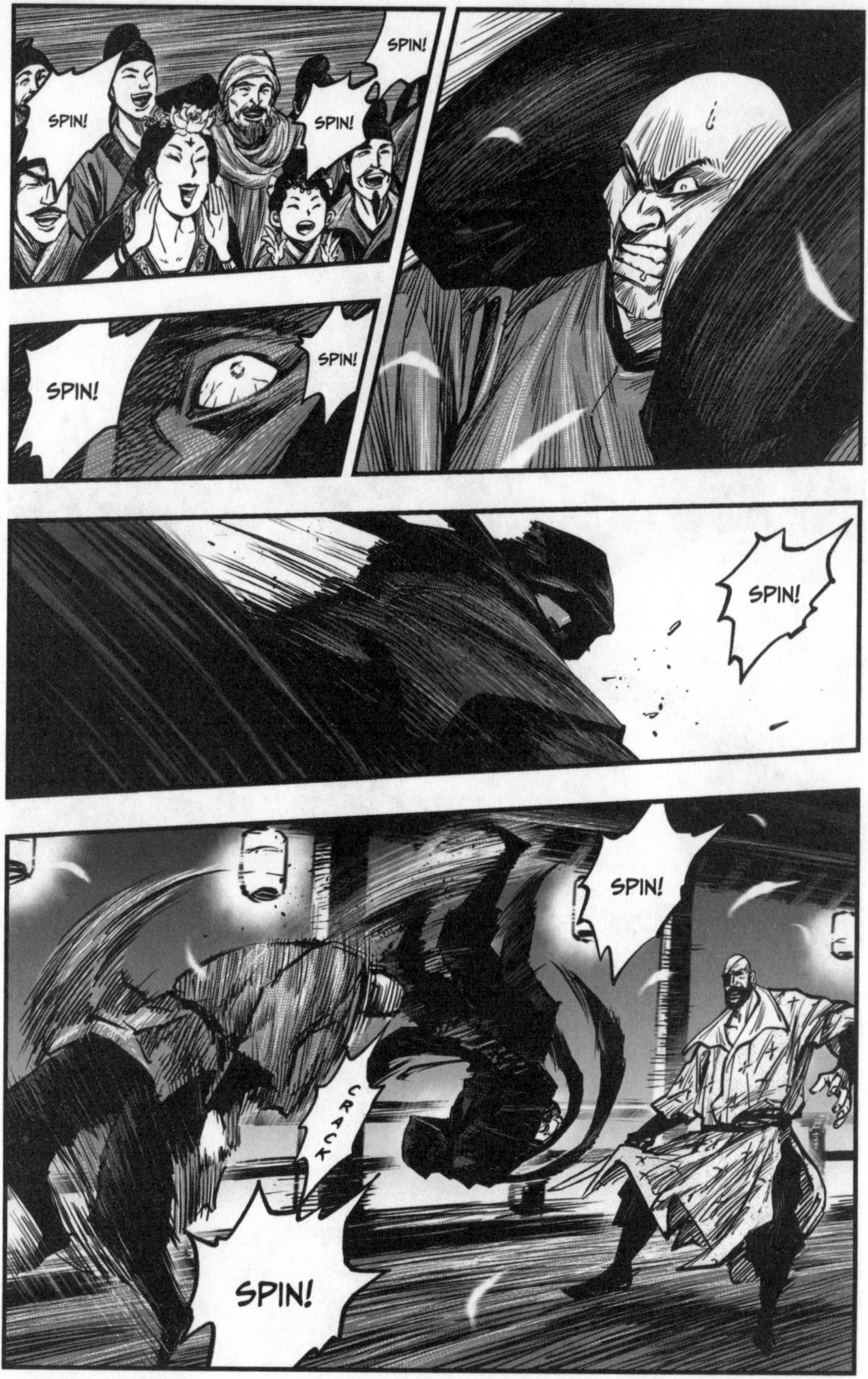
SPIN!
SPIN!
SPIN!
SPIN!
SPIN!
SPIN!
SPIN!
CRACK
SPIN!

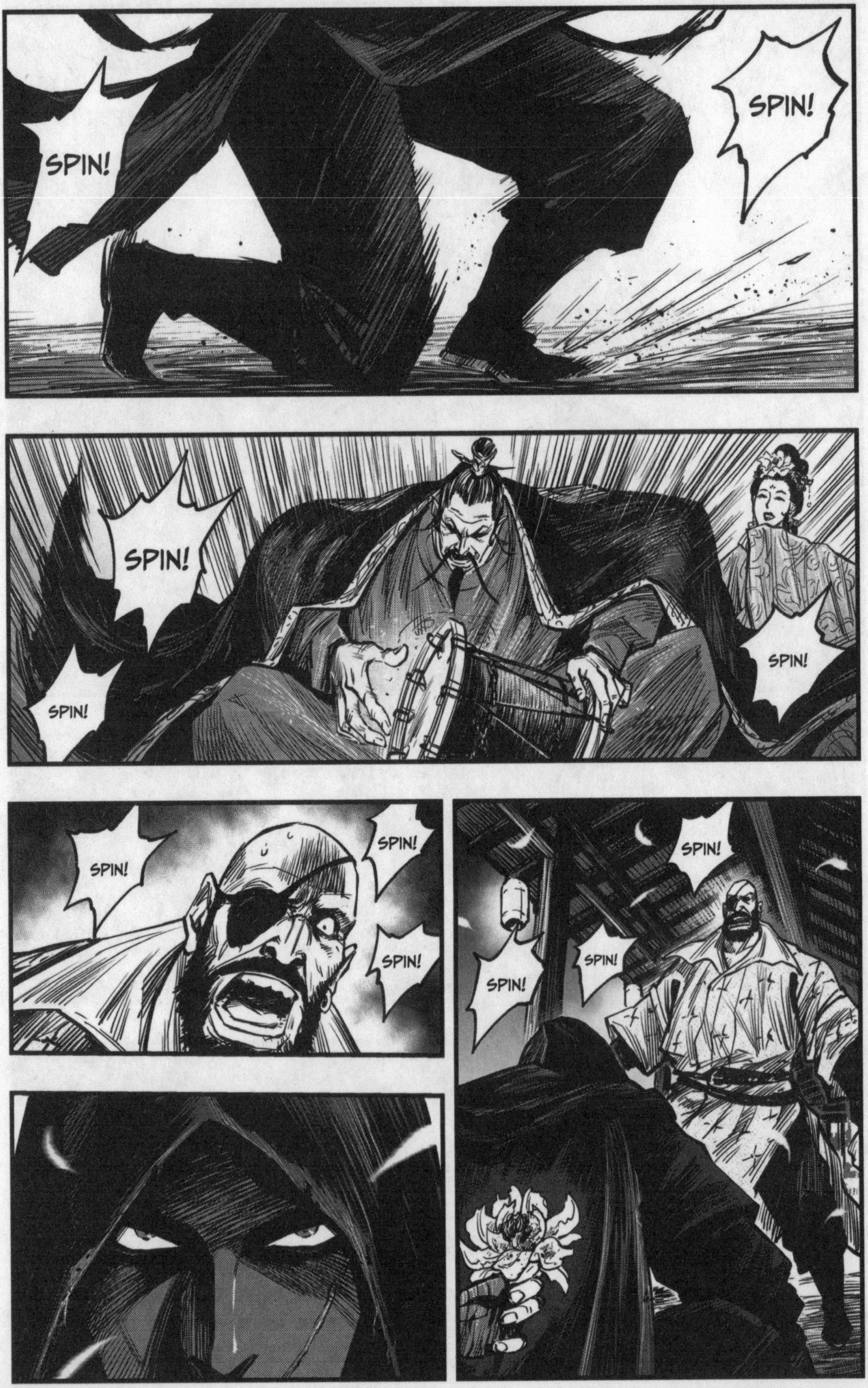
SPIN!
SPIN!
SPIN!
SPIN!
SPIN!
SPIN!
SPIN!
SPIN!
SPIN!
SPIN!
SPIN!
SPIN!

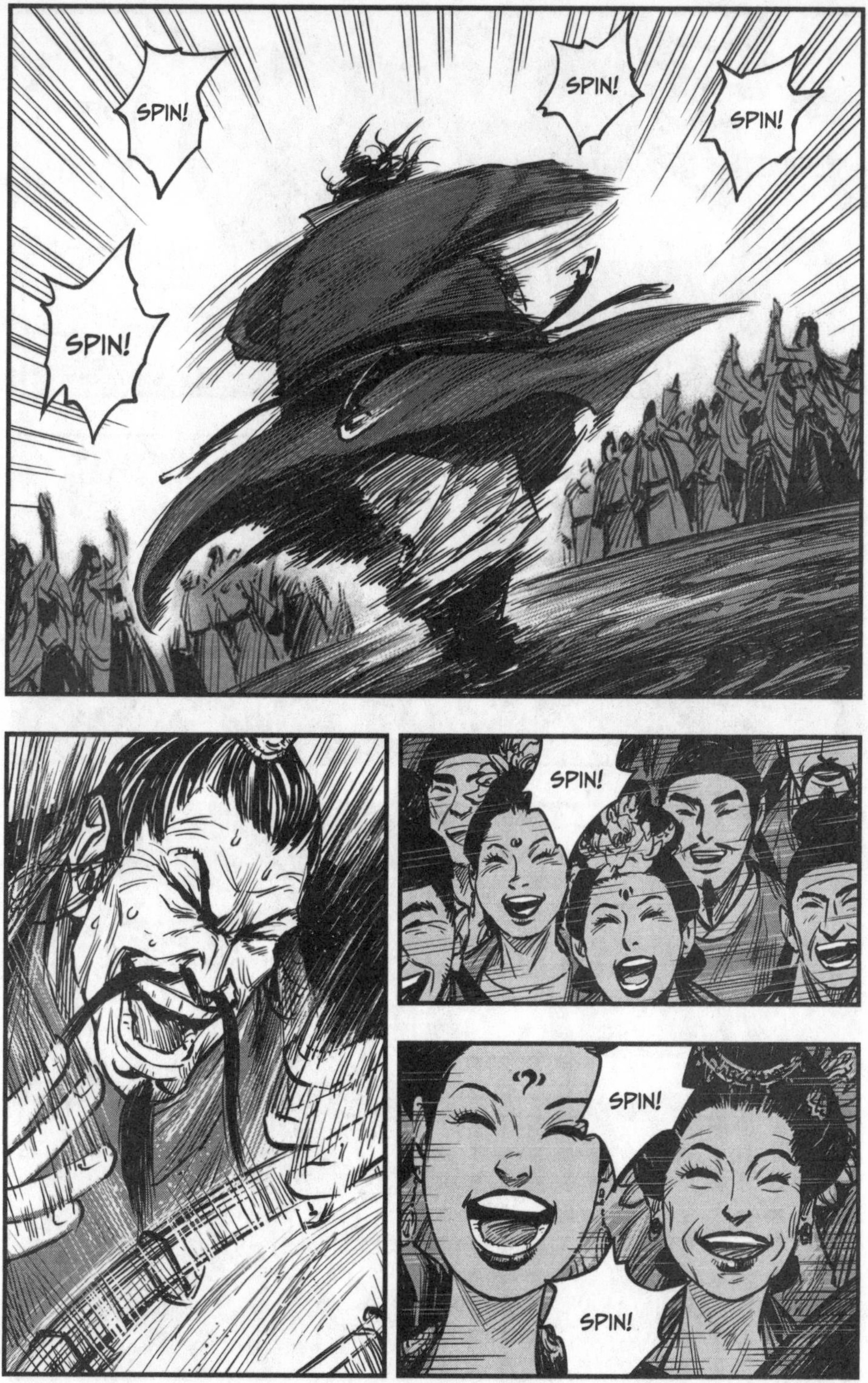
SPIN!
SPIN!
SPIN!
SPIN!
SPIN!
SPIN!
SPIN!

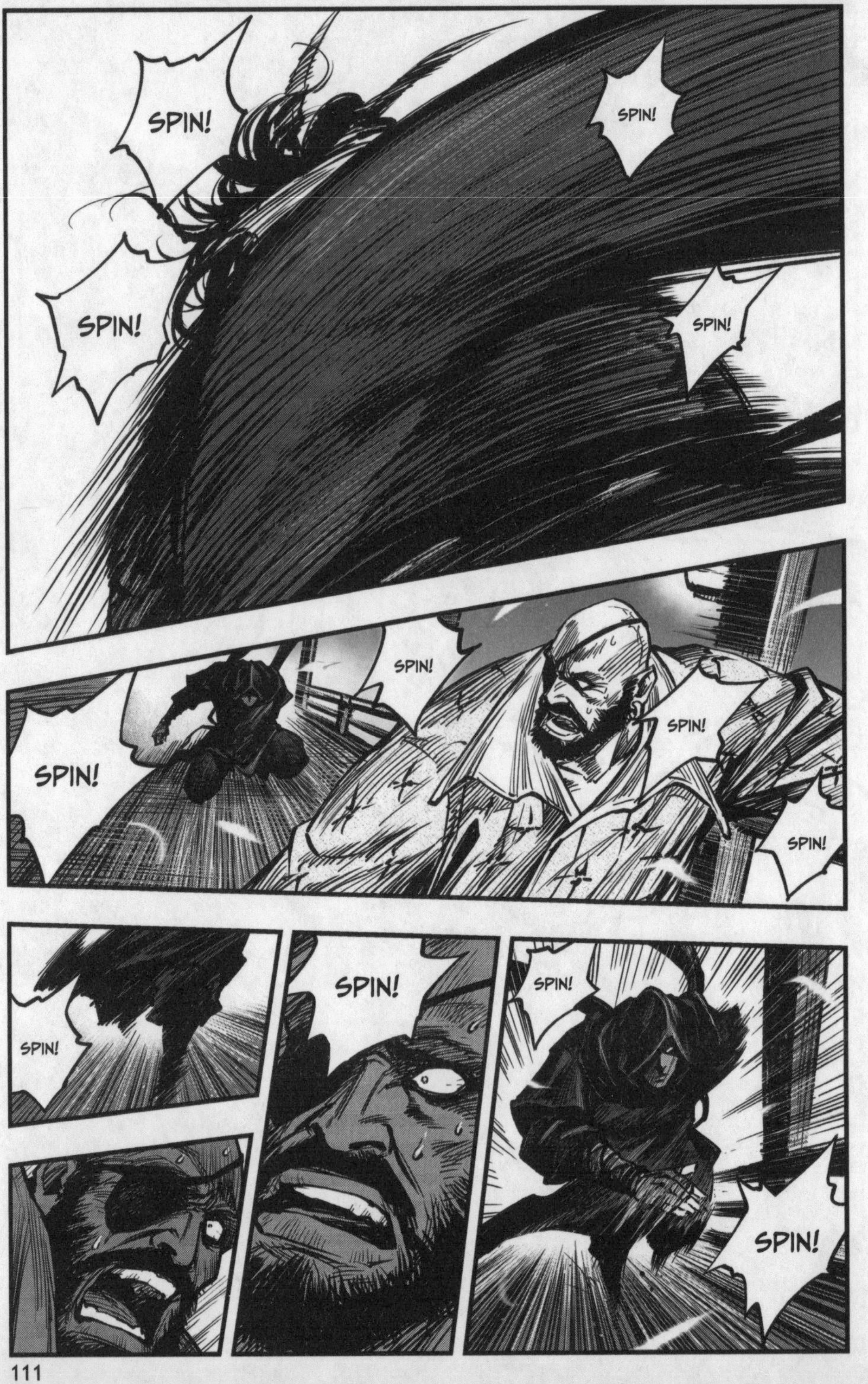
SPIN!
SPIN!
SPIN!
SPIN!
SPIN!
SPIN!
SPIN!
SPIN!
SPIN!
SPIN!
SPIN!
SPIN!

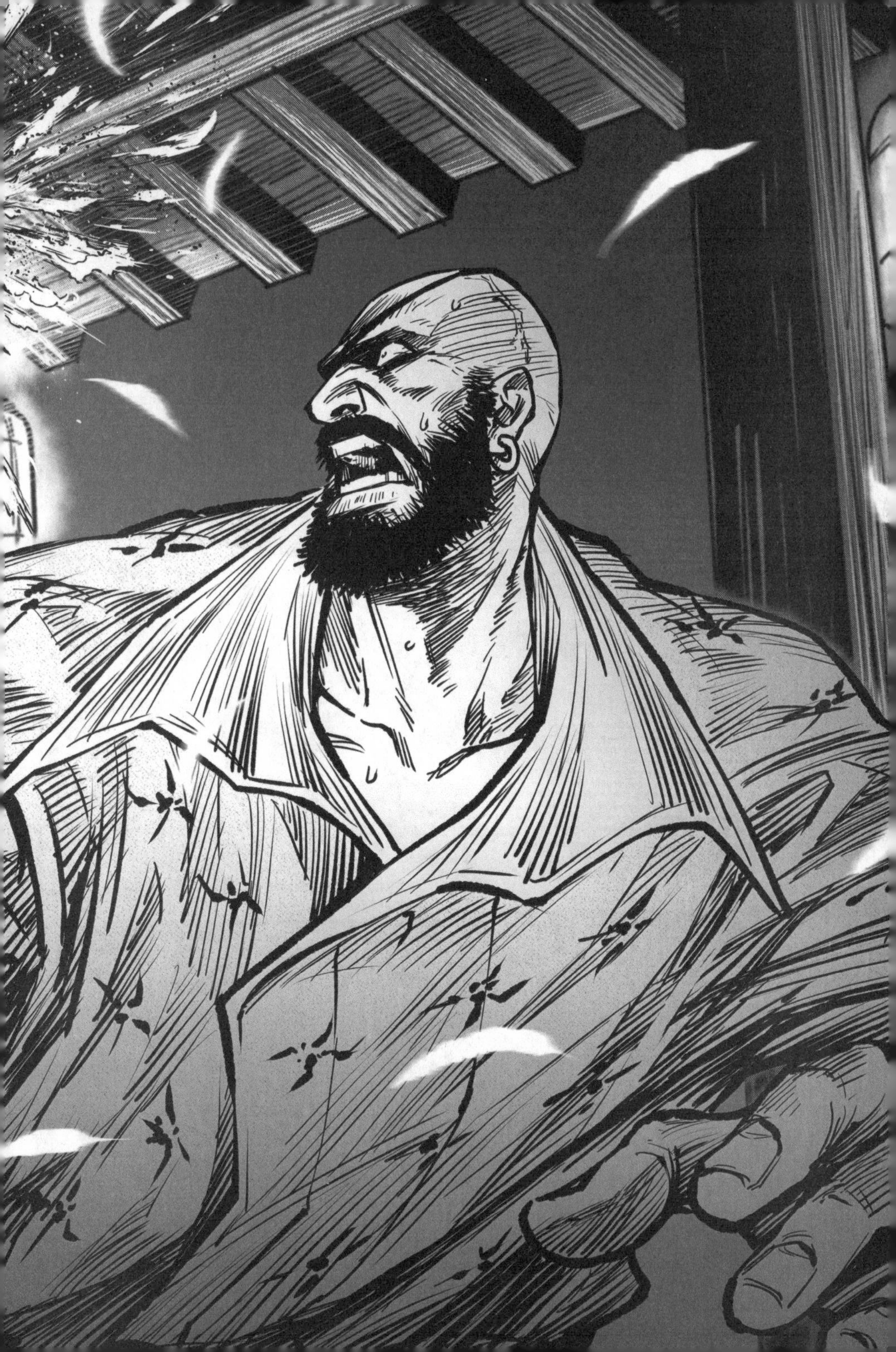

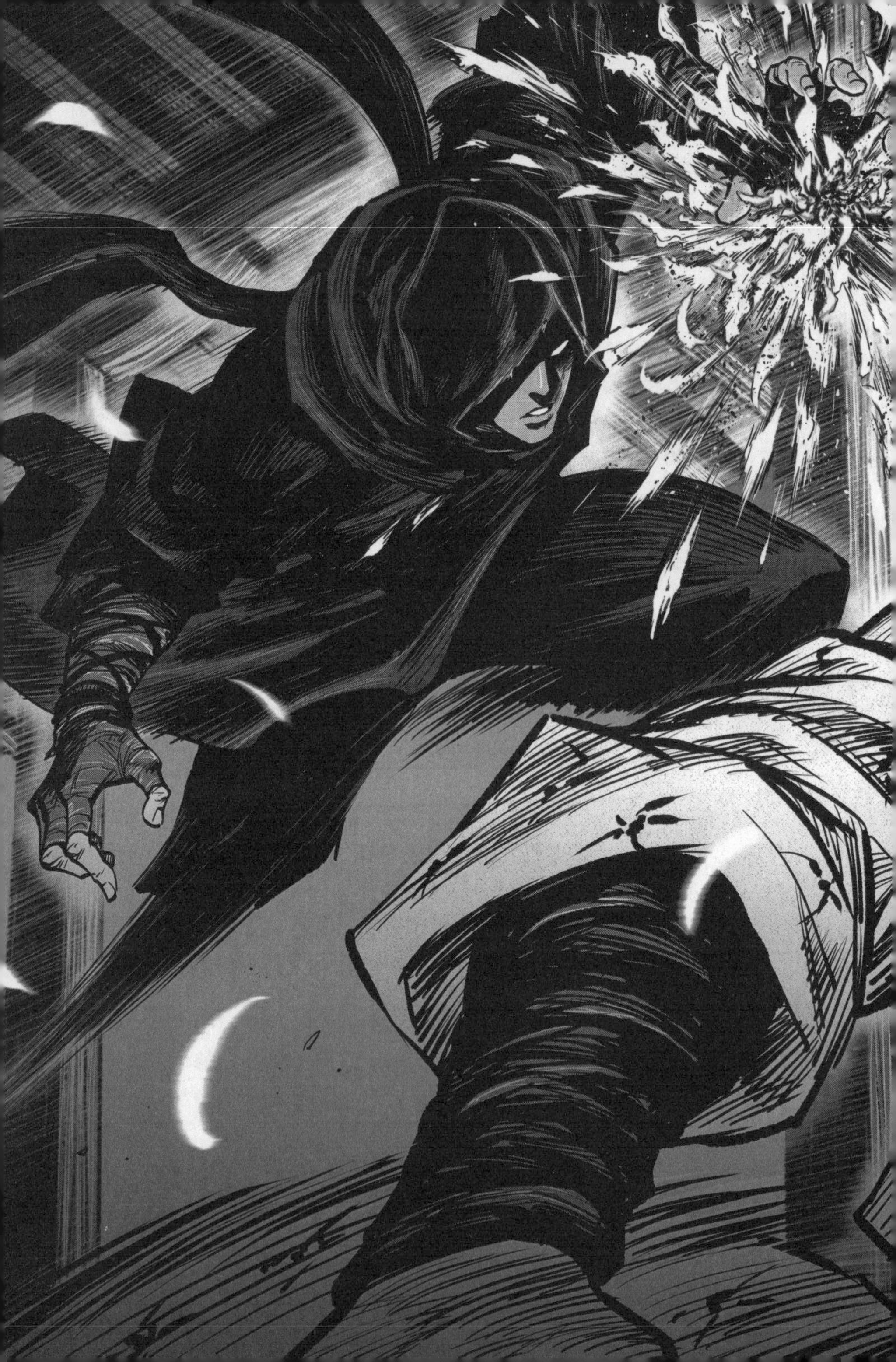

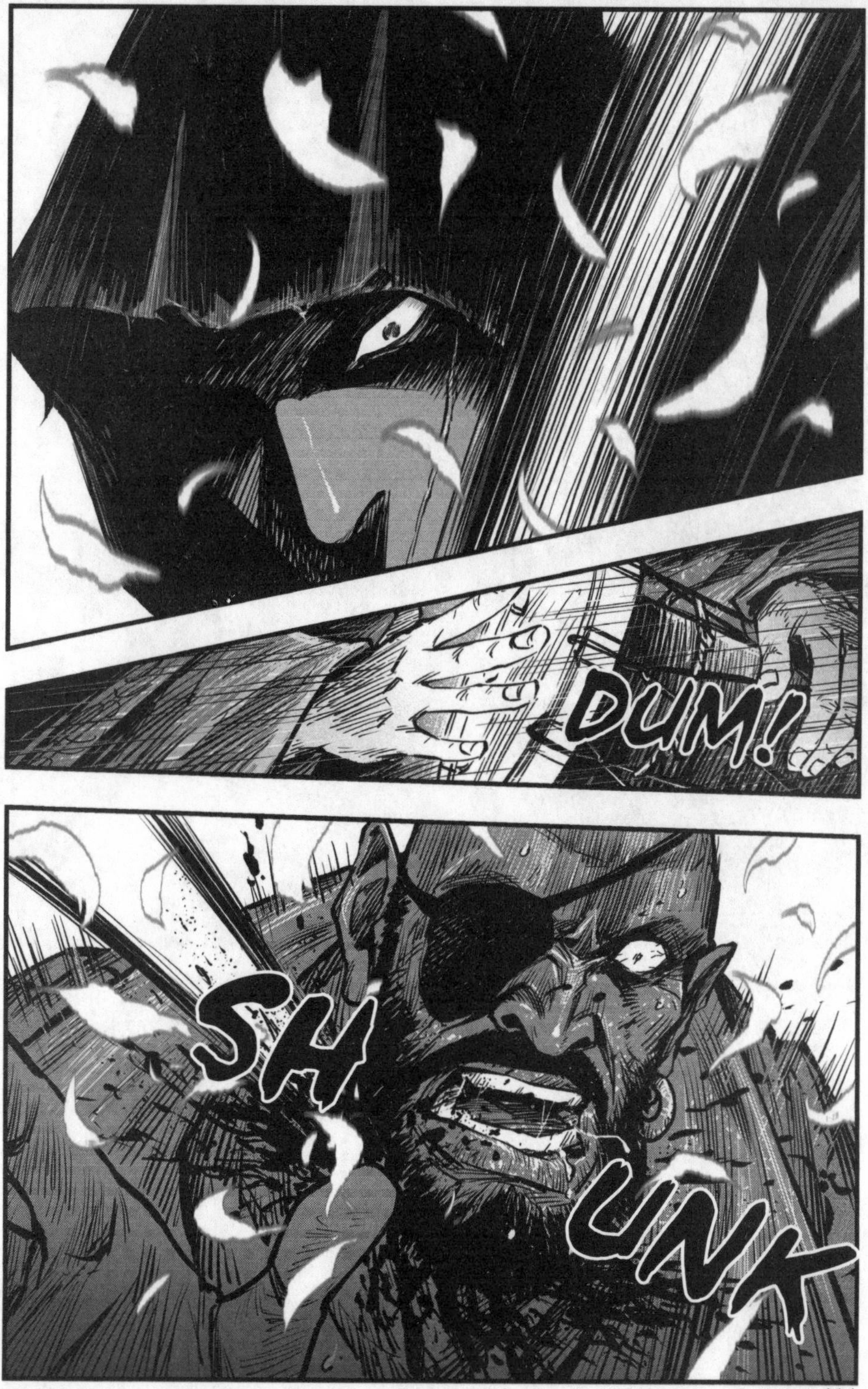
DUM!
SH
UNK

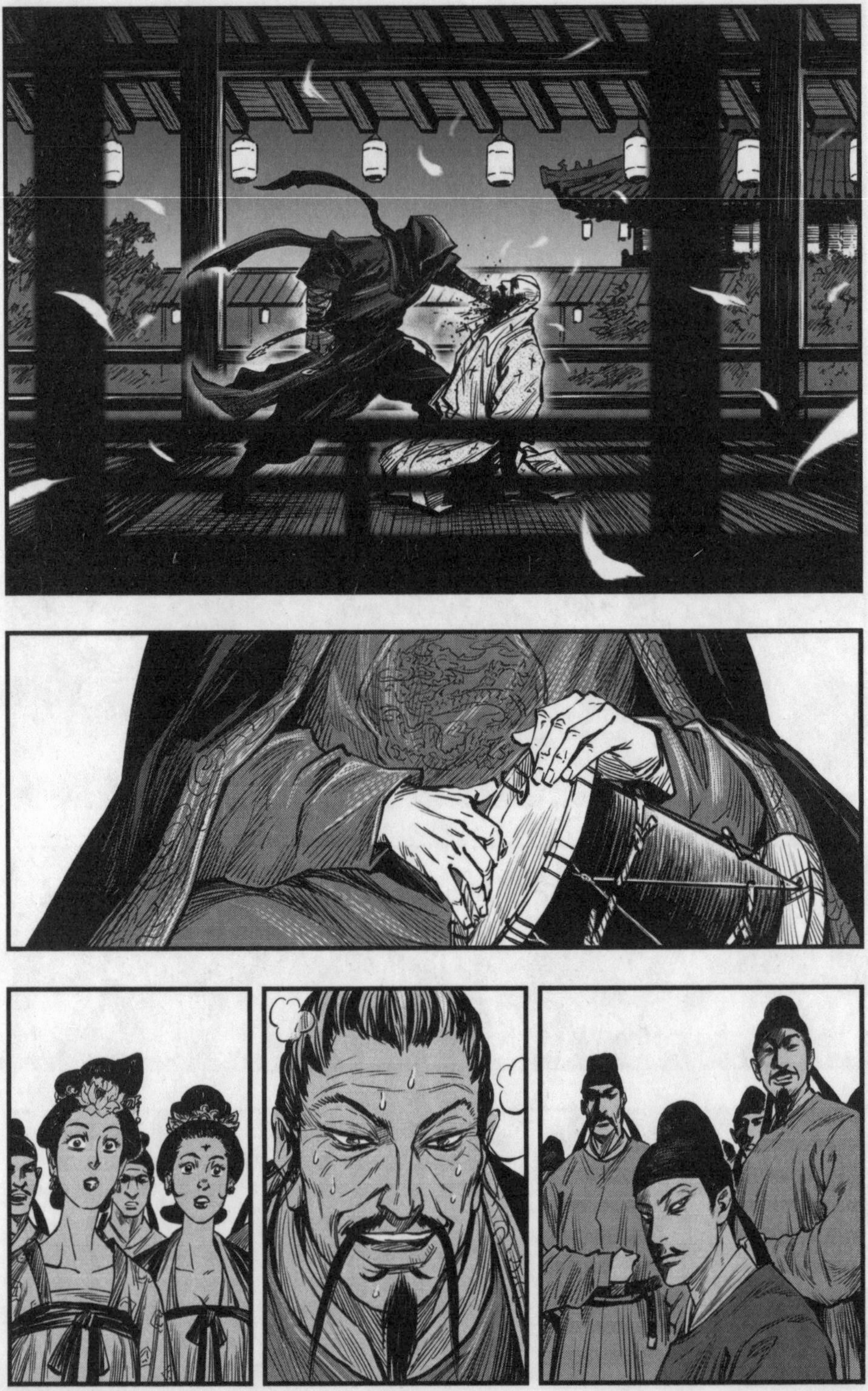

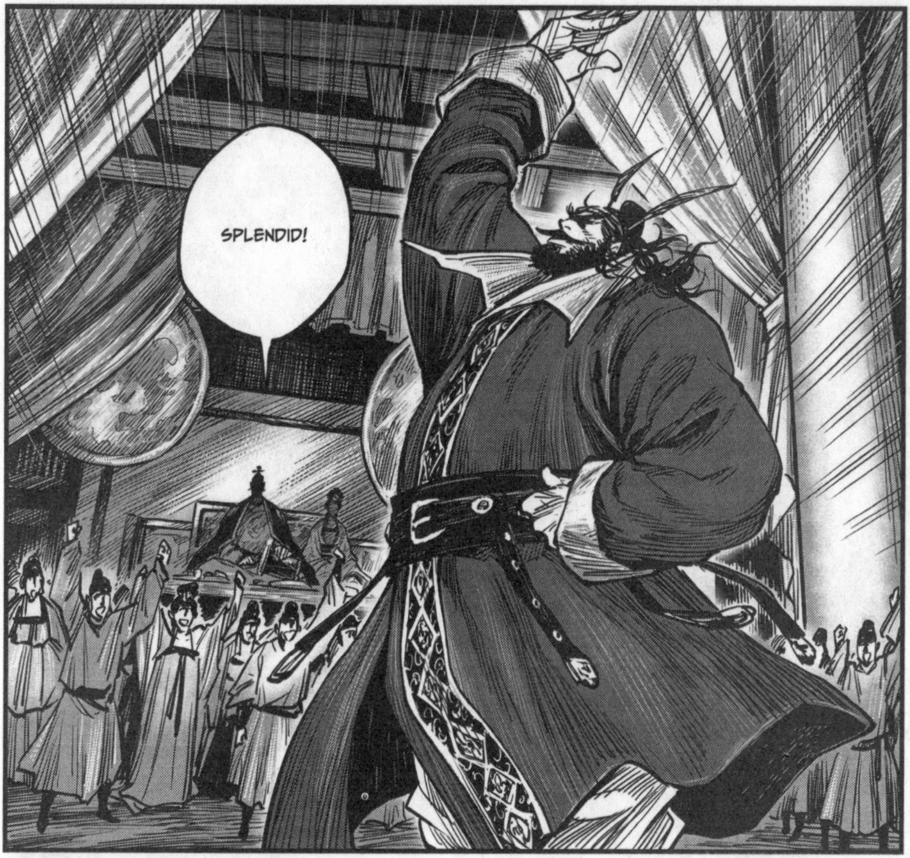
SPLENDID!
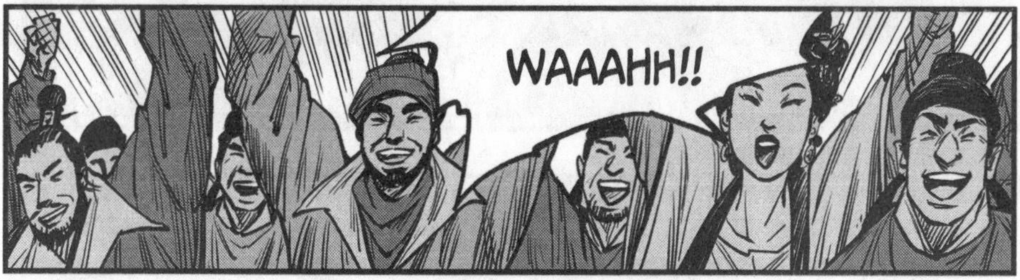
WAAAHH!!
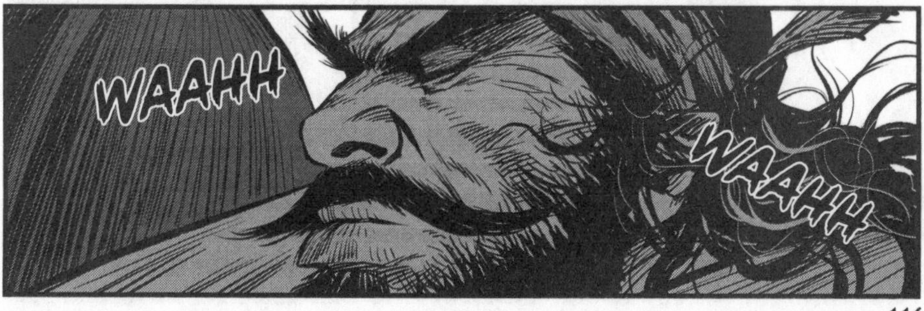
WAAHH
WAAHH

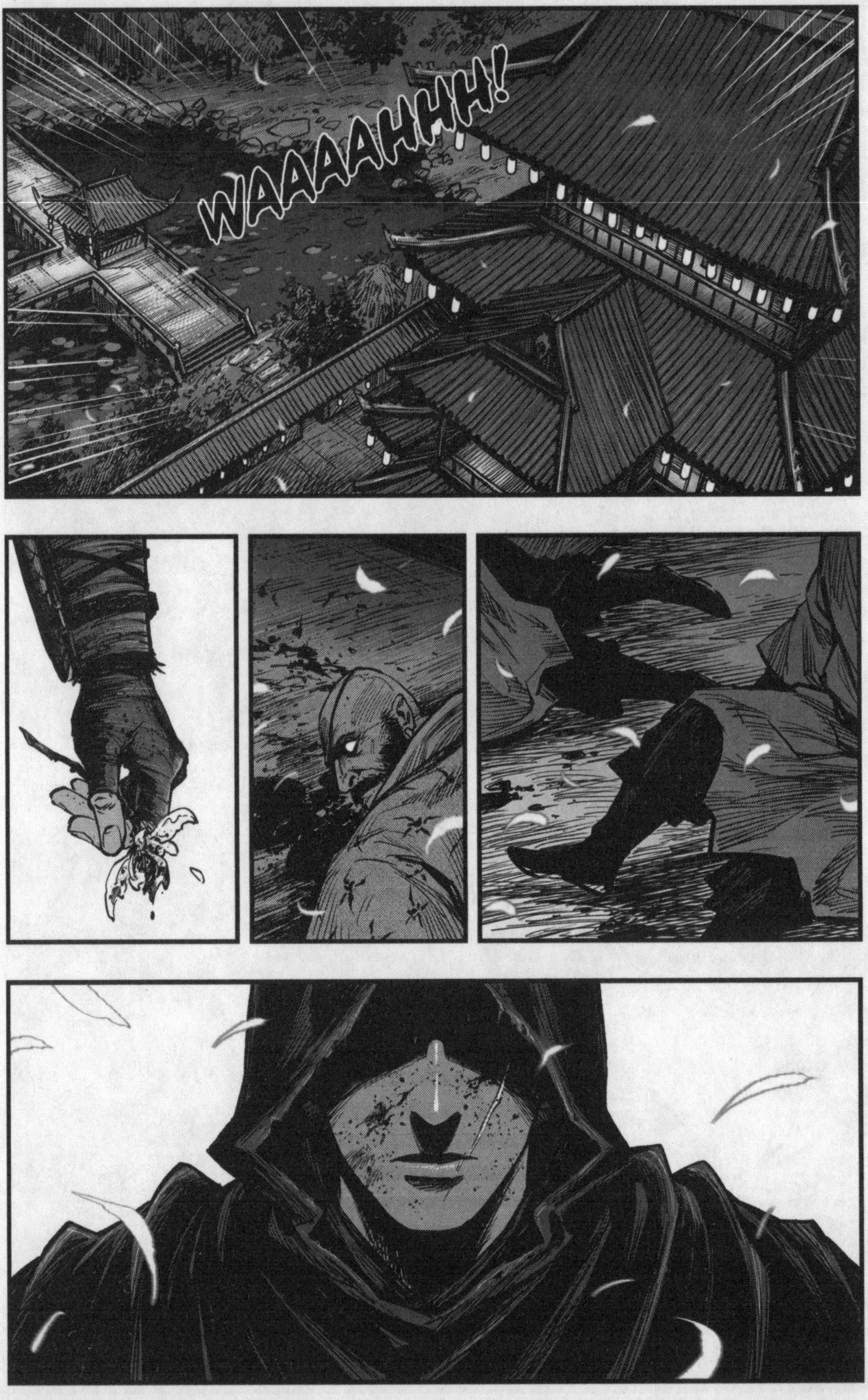
WAAAAHHH!

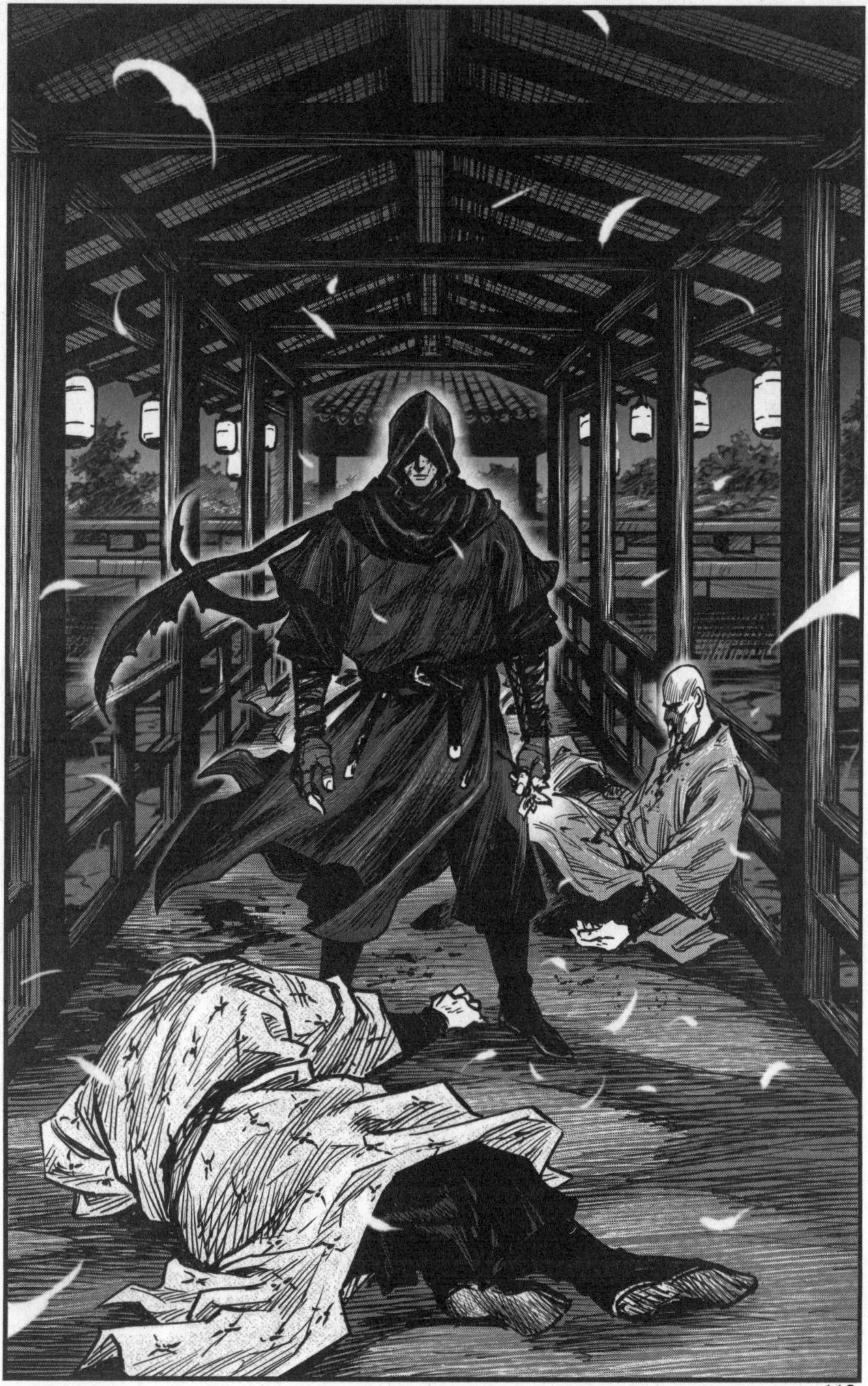

SHUFFLE

SHUFFLE

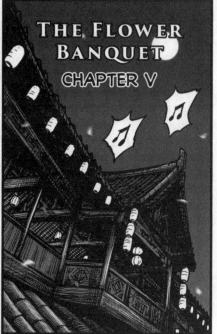

THE FLOWER BANQUET
CHAPTER V

SHUFFLE

SHUFFLE

SHUFFLE

SHUFFLE

SHUFFLE

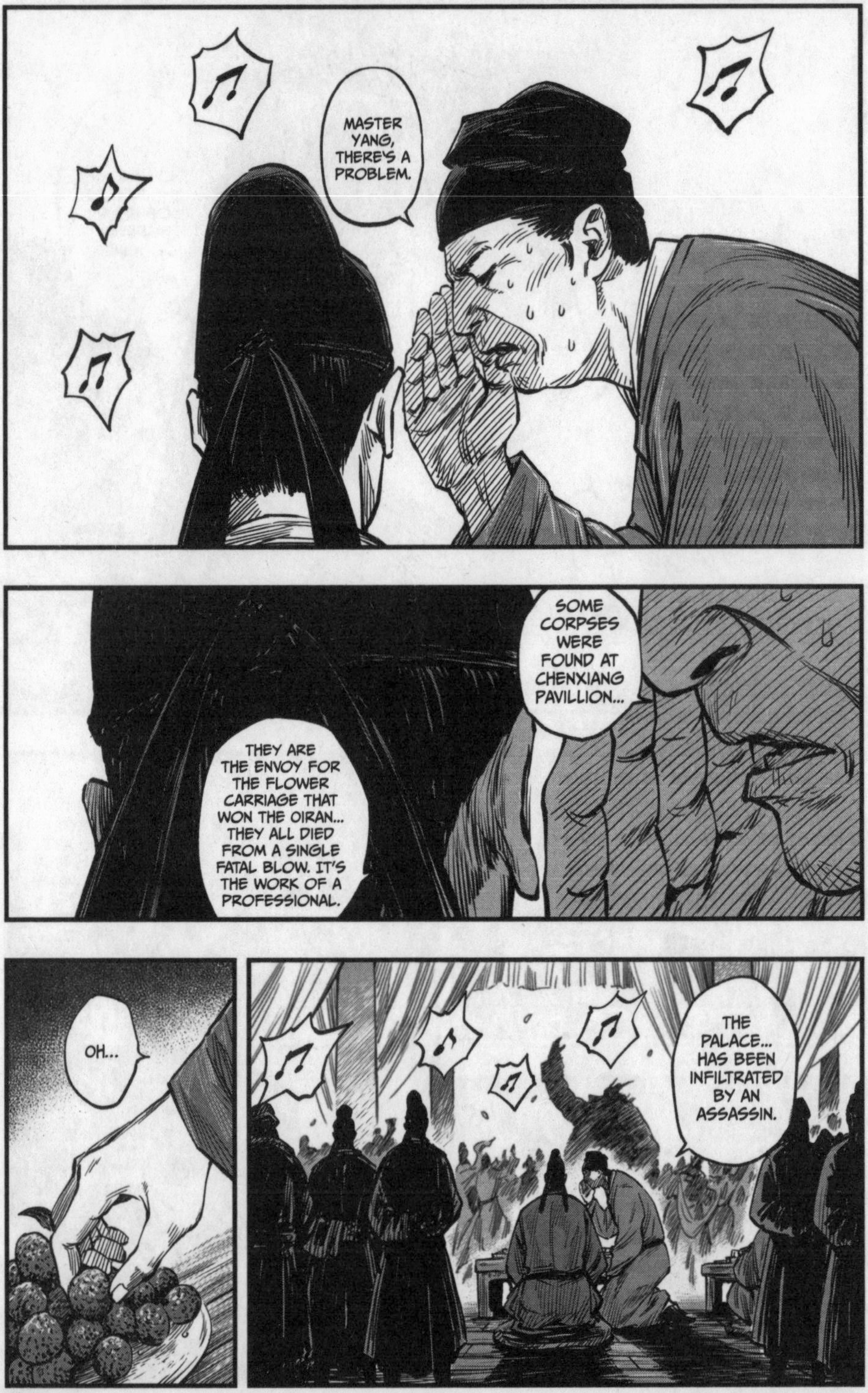
MASTER YANG, THERE'S A PROBLEM.
SOME CORPSES WERE FOUND AT CHENXIANG PAVILLION...
THEY ARE THE ENVOY FOR THE FLOWER CARRIAGE THAT WON THE OIRAN... THEY ALL DIED FROM A SINGLE FATAL BLOW. IT'S THE WORK OF A PROFESSIONAL.
THE PALACE... HAS BEEN INFILTRATED BY AN ASSASSIN.
OH...

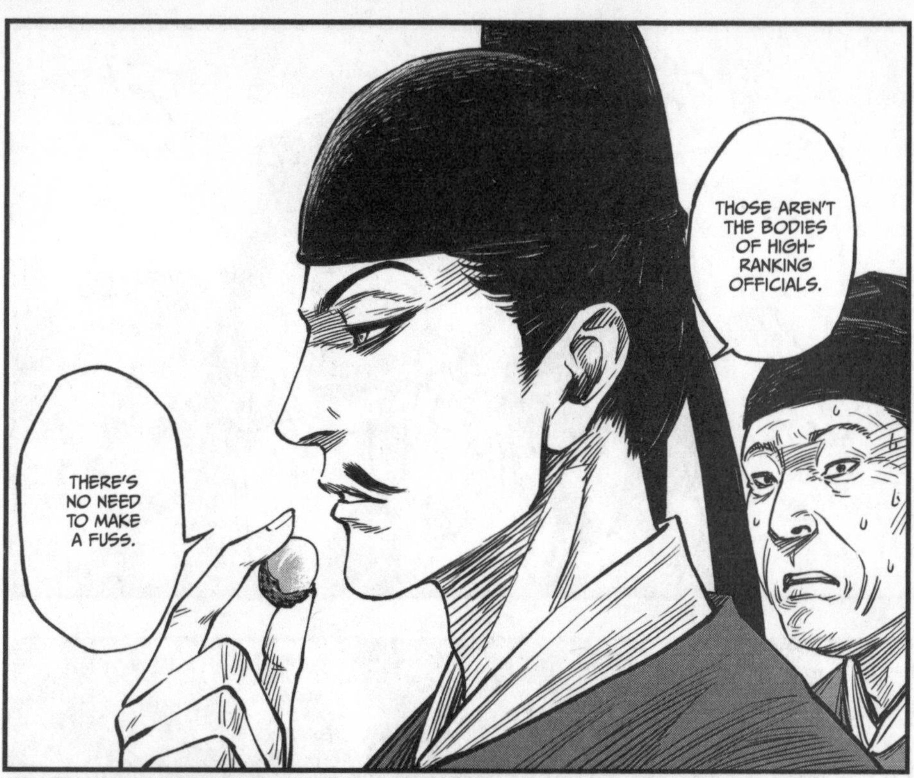
THOSE AREN'T THE BODIES OF HIGH-RANKING OFFICIALS.
THERE'S NO NEED TO MAKE A FUSS.

*YULIN: IMPERIAL GUARDS SERVING IN THE PALACE. THE YULIN IMPERIAL GUARDS AND LONGWU GUARDS FLANKING RIGHT AND LEFT RESPECTIVELY ARE TERMED THE "FOUR GUARDS OF BEIMEN."

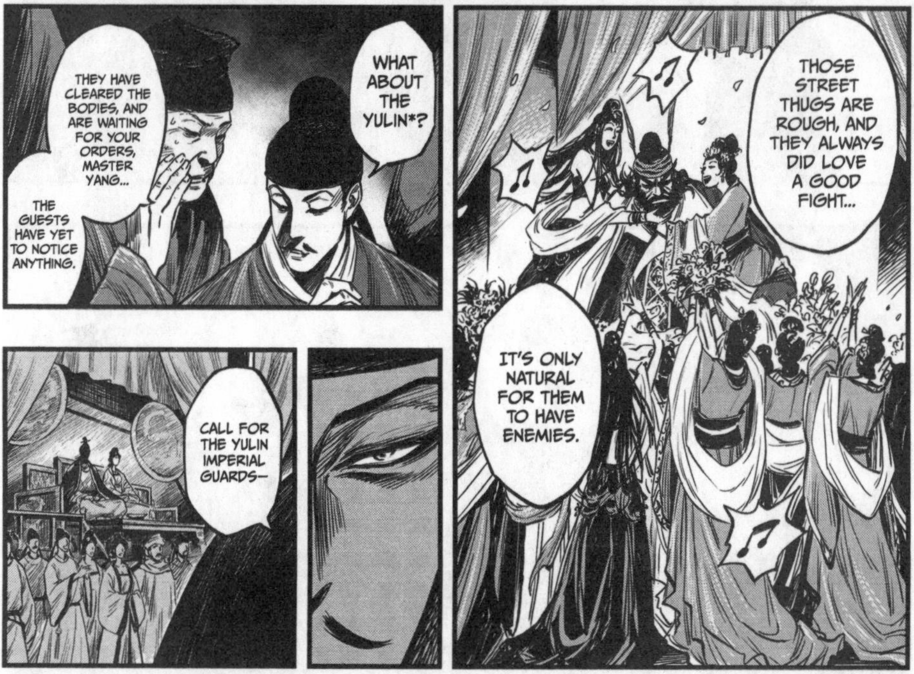
WHAT ABOUT THE YULIN*?
THEY HAVE CLEARED THE BODIES, AND ARE WAITING FOR YOUR ORDERS, MASTER YANG...
THE GUESTS HAVE YET TO NOTICE ANYTHING.
CALL FOR THE YULIN IMPERIAL GUARDS—
THOSE STREET THUGS ARE ROUGH, AND THEY ALWAYS DID LOVE A GOOD FIGHT...
IT'S ONLY NATURAL FOR THEM TO HAVE ENEMIES.

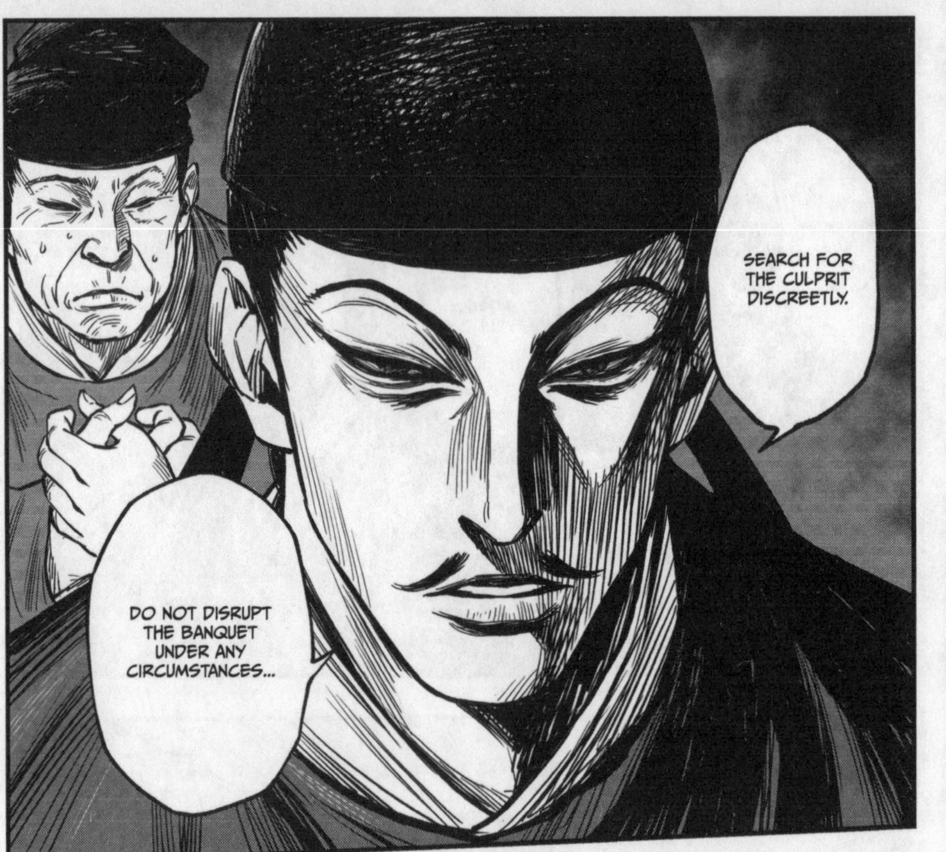
SEARCH FOR THE CULPRIT DISCREETLY.
DO NOT DISRUPT THE BANQUET UNDER ANY CIRCUMSTANCES...
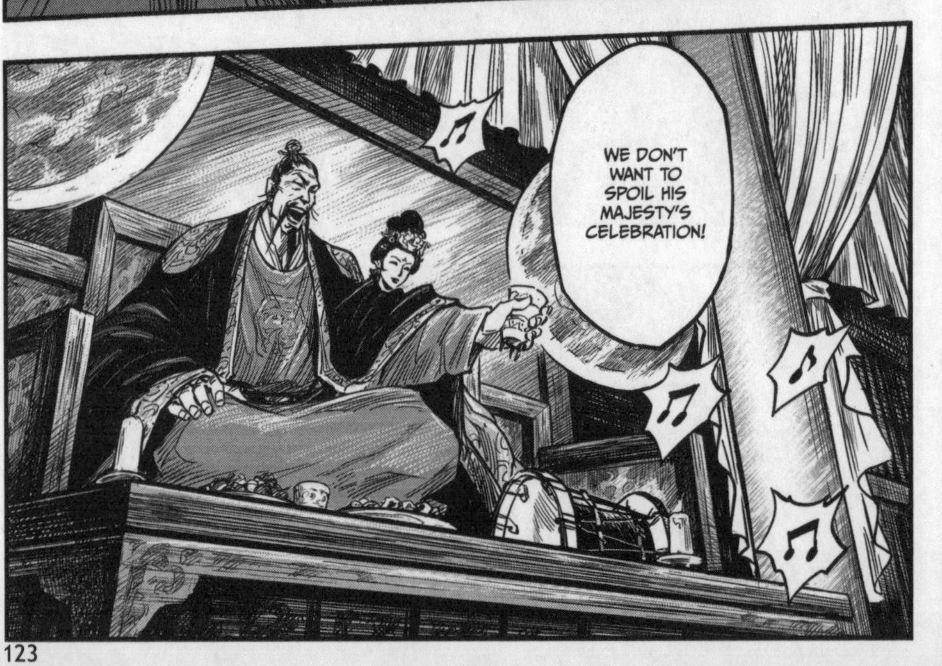
WE DON'T WANT TO SPOIL HIS MAJESTY'S CELEBRATION!
♪
♪
♪
♪

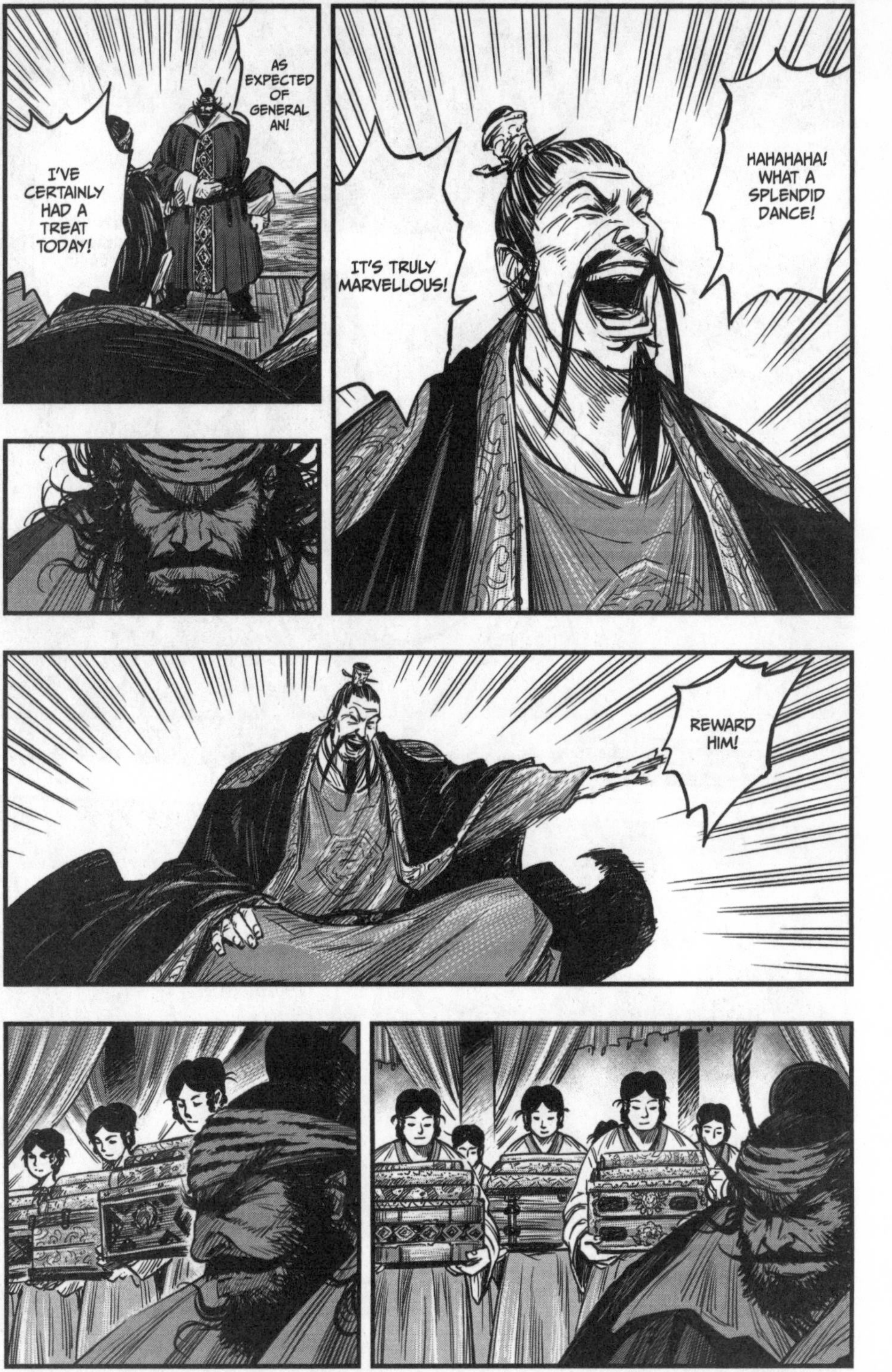
HAHAHAHA! WHAT A SPLENDID DANCE!
IT'S TRULY MARVELLOUS!
AS EXPECTED OF GENERAL AN!
I'VE CERTAINLY HAD A TREAT TODAY!
REWARD HIM!

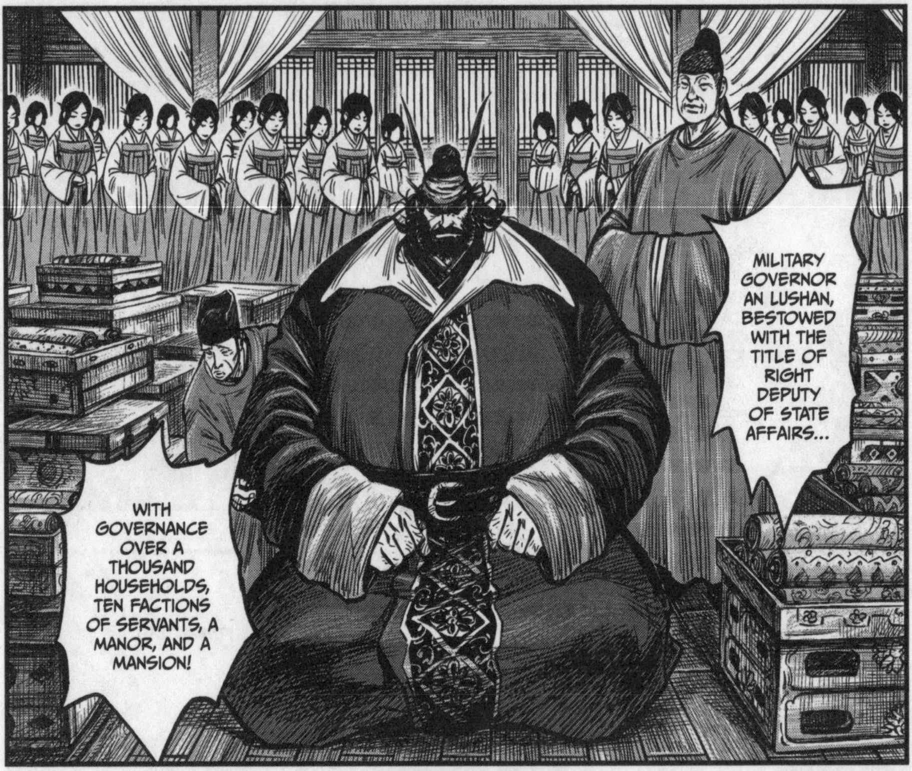
MILITARY GOVERNOR AN LUSHAN, BESTOWED WITH THE TITLE OF RIGHT DEPUTY OF STATE AFFAIRS...
WITH GOVERNANCE OVER A THOUSAND HOUSEHOLDS, TEN FACTIONS OF SERVANTS, A MANOR, AND A MANSION!

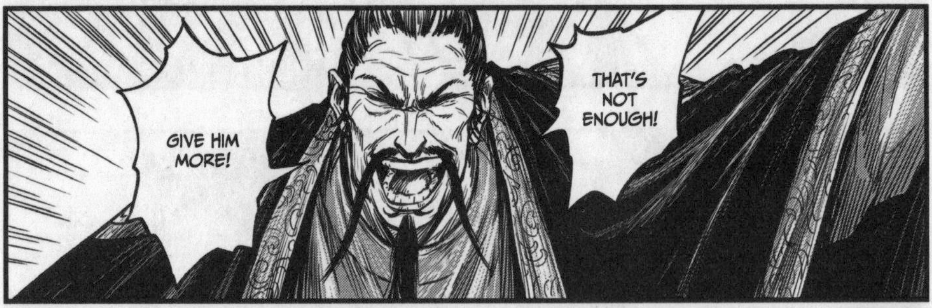
THAT'S NOT ENOUGH!
GIVE HIM MORE!

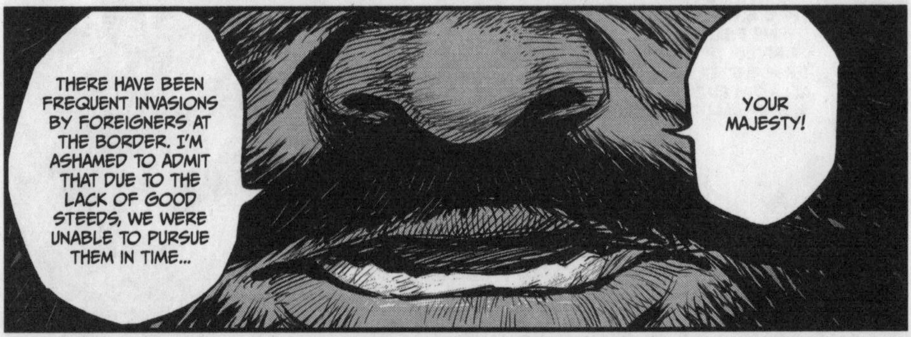
YOUR MAJESTY!
THERE HAVE BEEN FREQUENT INVASIONS BY FOREIGNERS AT THE BORDER. I'M ASHAMED TO ADMIT THAT DUE TO THE LACK OF GOOD STEEDS, WE WERE UNABLE TO PURSUE THEM IN TIME...

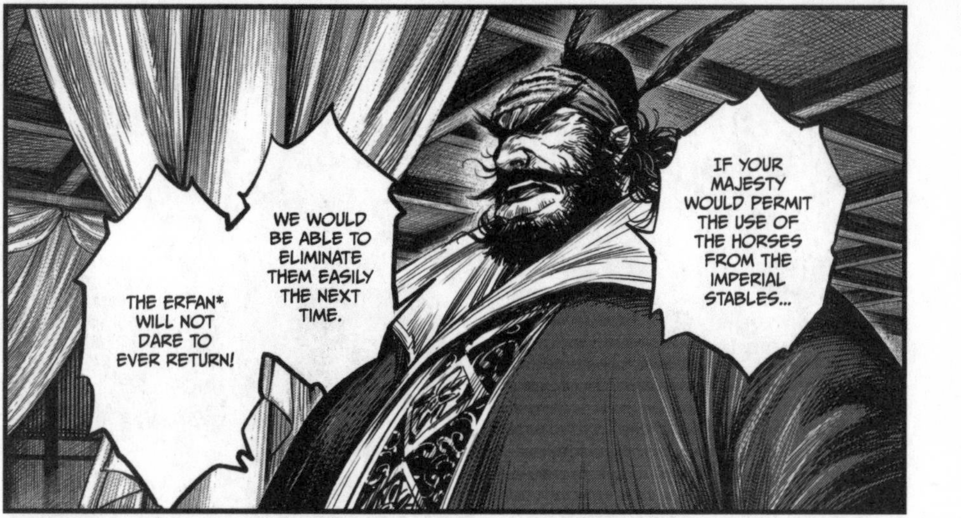
IF YOUR MAJESTY WOULD PERMIT THE USE OF THE HORSES FROM THE IMPERIAL STABLES...
WE WOULD BE ABLE TO ELIMINATE THEM EASILY THE NEXT TIME.
THE ERFAN* WILL NOT DARE TO EVER RETURN!

*ERFAN: KHITAN AND XI PEOPLE

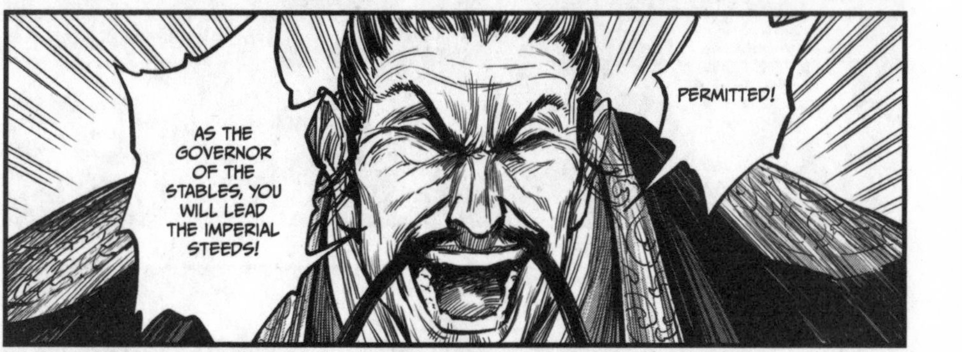
PERMITTED!
AS THE GOVERNOR OF THE STABLES, YOU WILL LEAD THE IMPERIAL STEEDS!

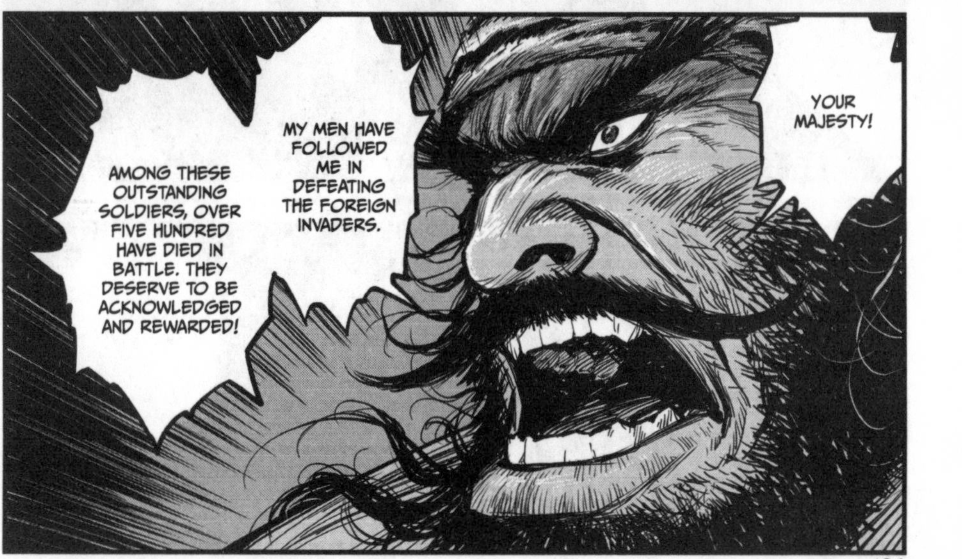
YOUR MAJESTY!
MY MEN HAVE FOLLOWED ME IN DEFEATING THE FOREIGN INVADERS.
AMONG THESE OUTSTANDING SOLDIERS, OVER FIVE HUNDRED HAVE DIED IN BATTLE. THEY DESERVE TO BE ACKNOWLEDGED AND REWARDED!

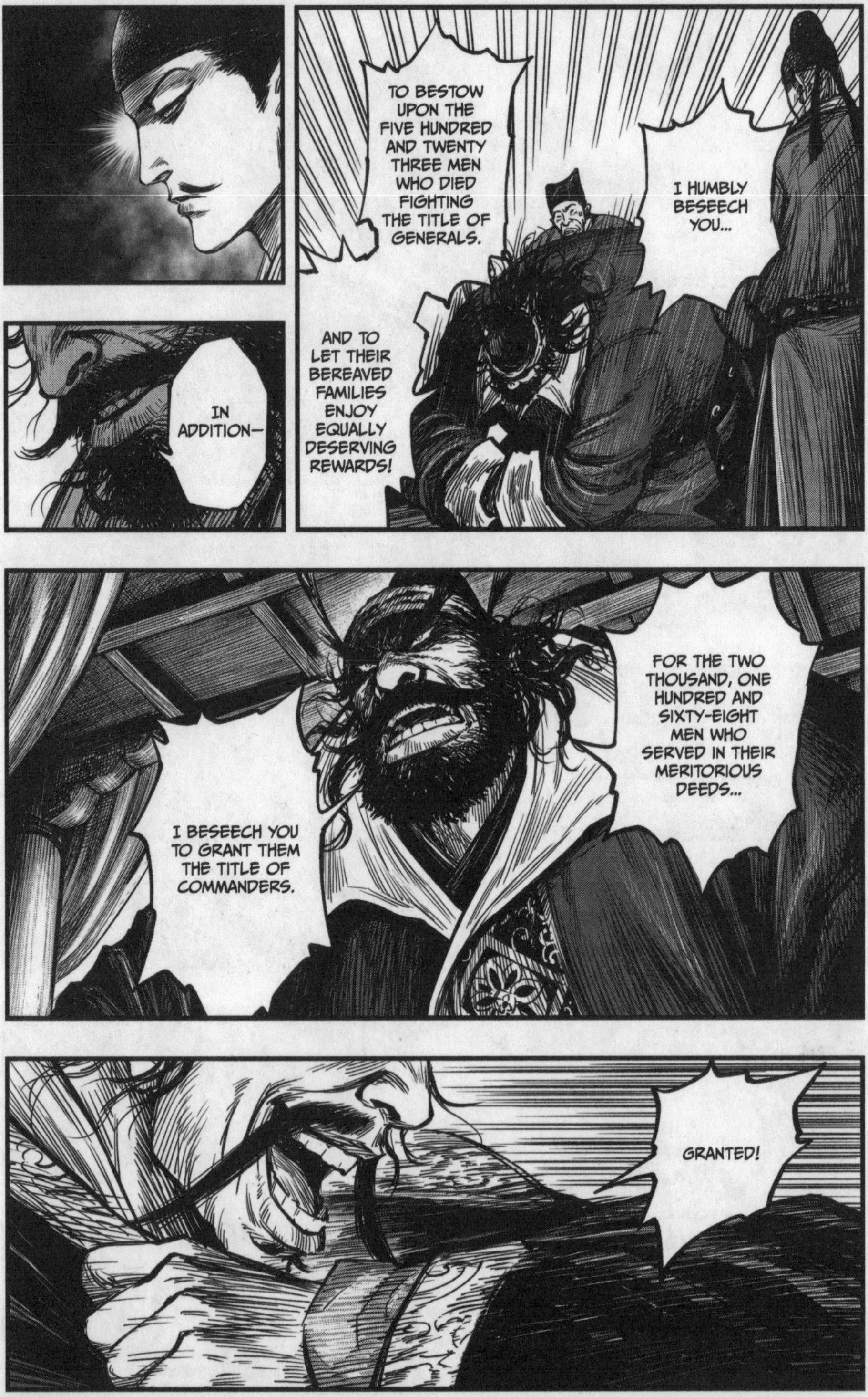
I HUMBLY BESEECH YOU...
TO BESTOW UPON THE FIVE HUNDRED AND TWENTY THREE MEN WHO DIED FIGHTING THE TITLE OF GENERALS.
AND TO LET THEIR BEREAVED FAMILIES ENJOY EQUALLY DESERVING REWARDS!
IN ADDITION—
FOR THE TWO THOUSAND, ONE HUNDRED AND SIXTY-EIGHT MEN WHO SERVED IN THEIR MERITORIOUS DEEDS...
I BESEECH YOU TO GRANT THEM THE TITLE OF COMMANDERS.
GRANTED!

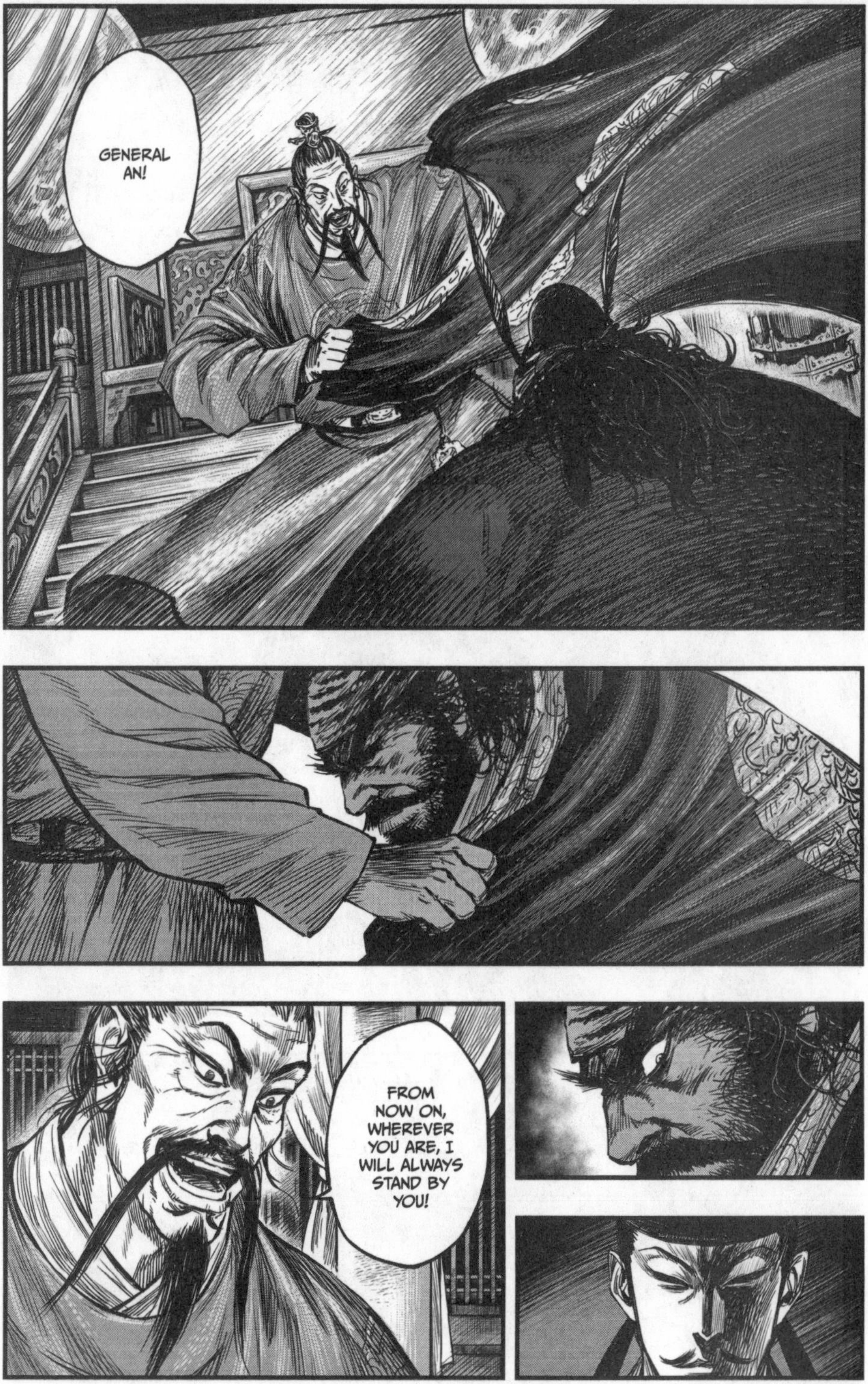
GENERAL AN!
FROM NOW ON, WHEREVER YOU ARE, I WILL ALWAYS STAND BY YOU!

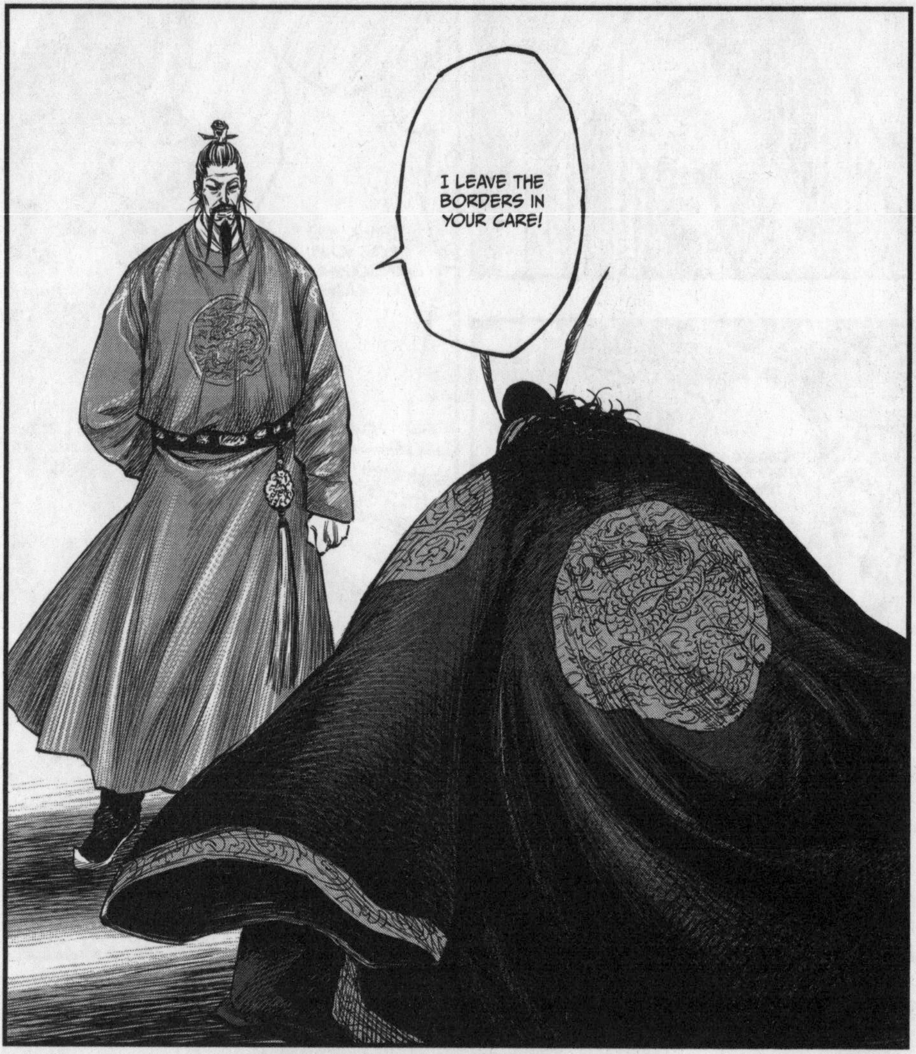
I LEAVE THE BORDERS IN YOUR CARE!

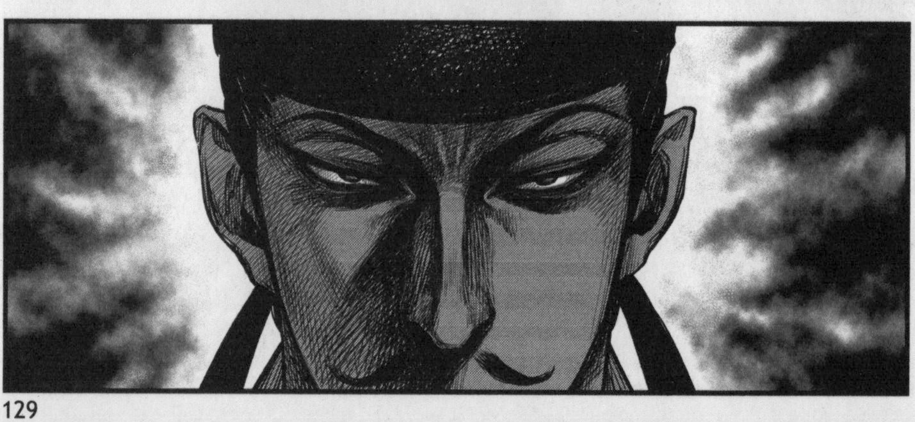

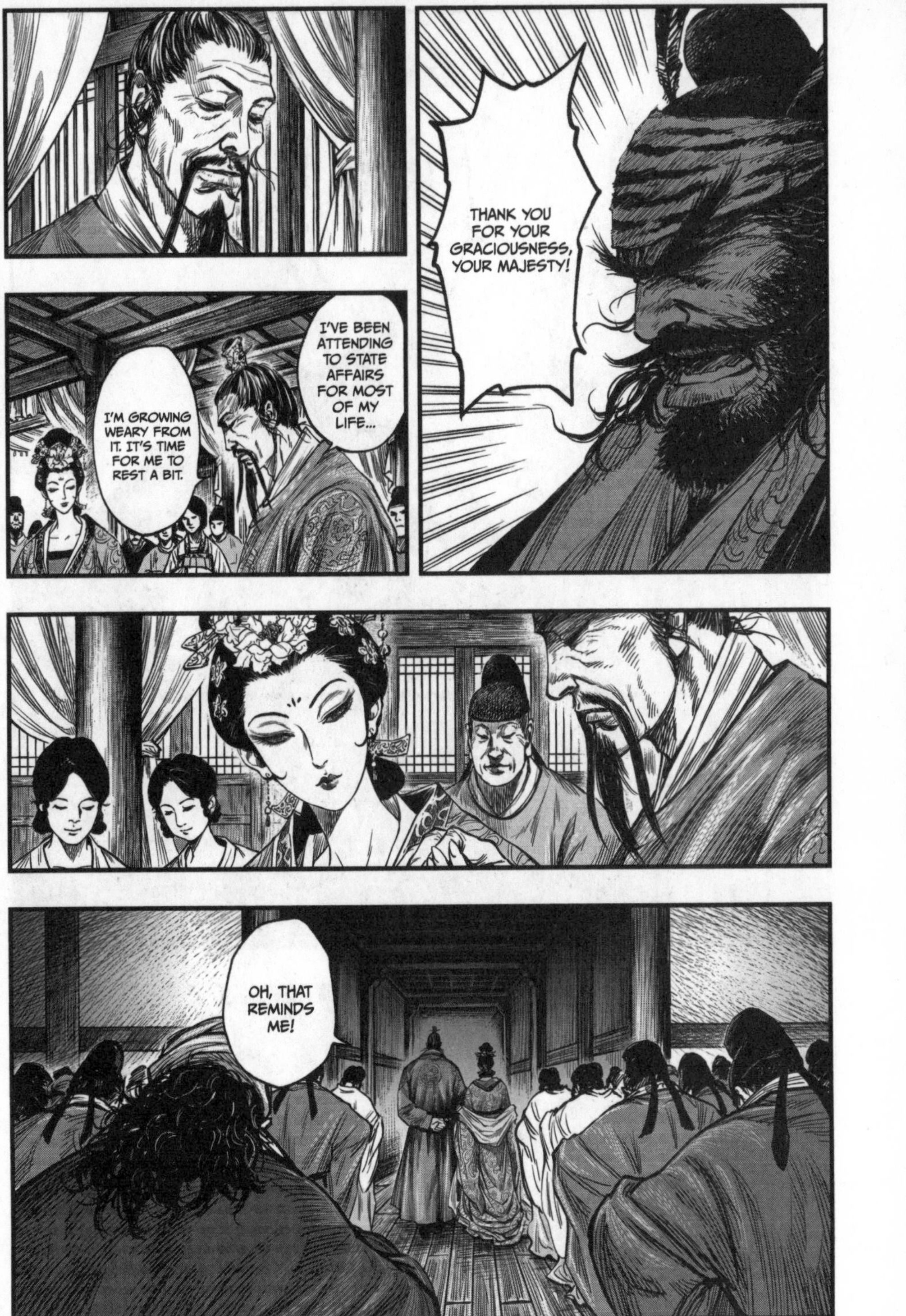
I'VE BEEN ATTENDING TO STATE AFFAIRS FOR MOST OF MY LIFE...
I'M GROWING WEARY FROM IT. IT'S TIME FOR ME TO REST A BIT.
THANK YOU FOR YOUR GRACIOUSNESS, YOUR MAJESTY!
OH, THAT REMINDS ME!

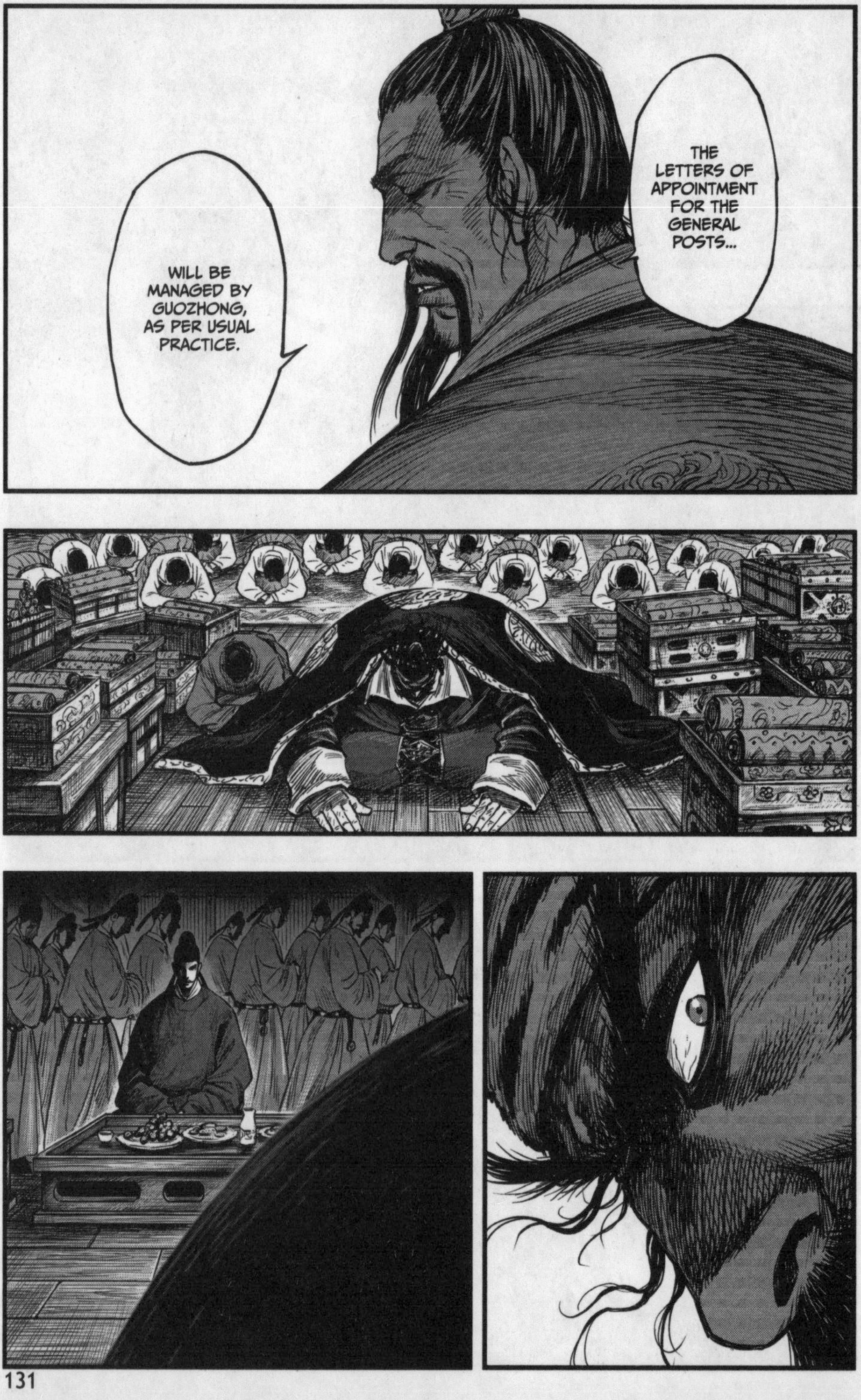
THE LETTERS OF APPOINTMENT FOR THE GENERAL POSTS...
WILL BE MANAGED BY GUOZHONG, AS PER USUAL PRACTICE.

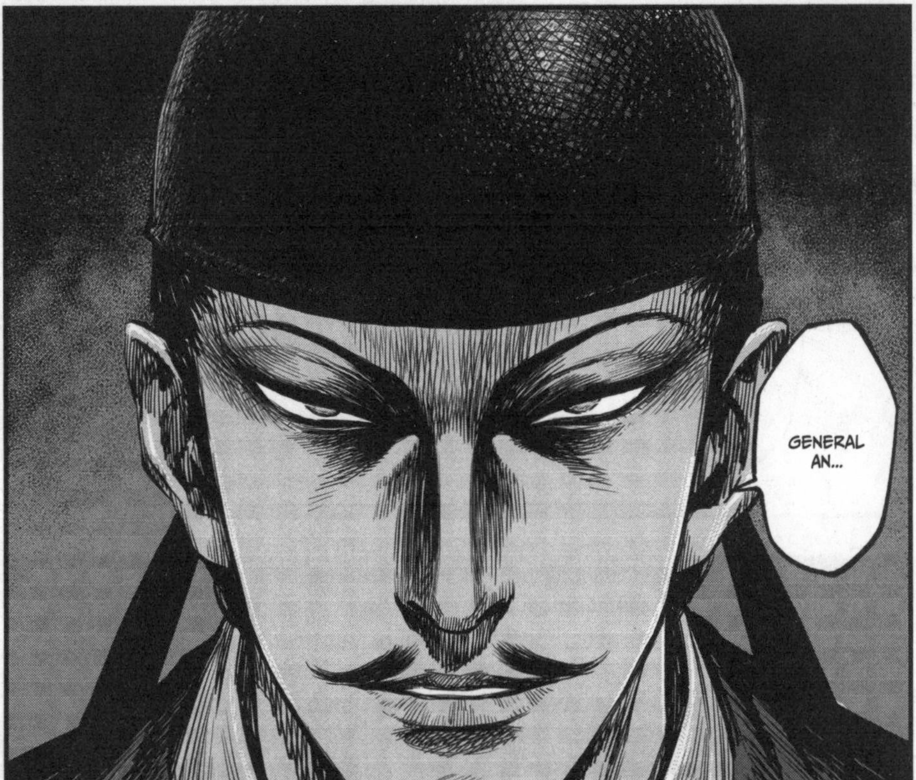
GENERAL AN...

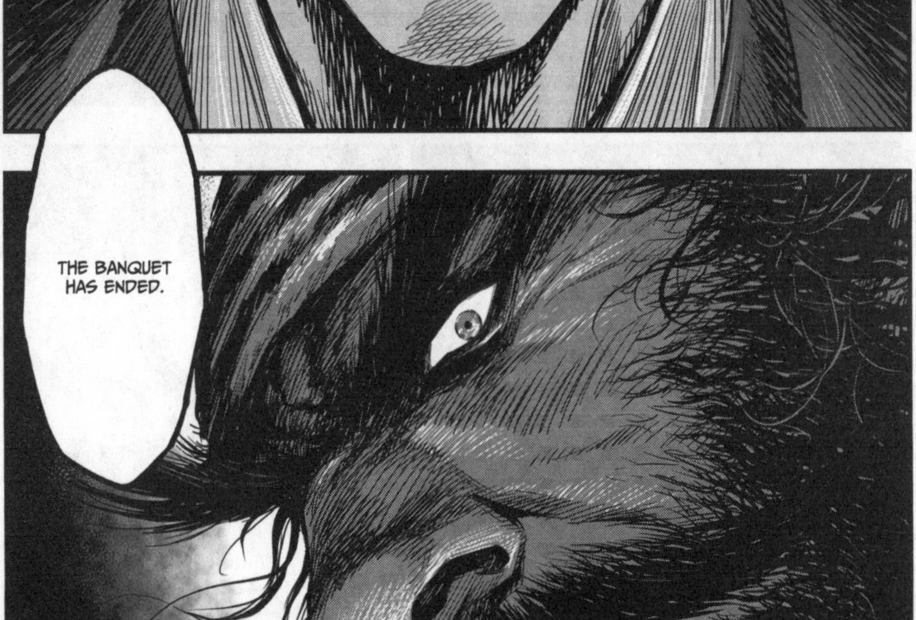
THE BANQUET HAS ENDED.

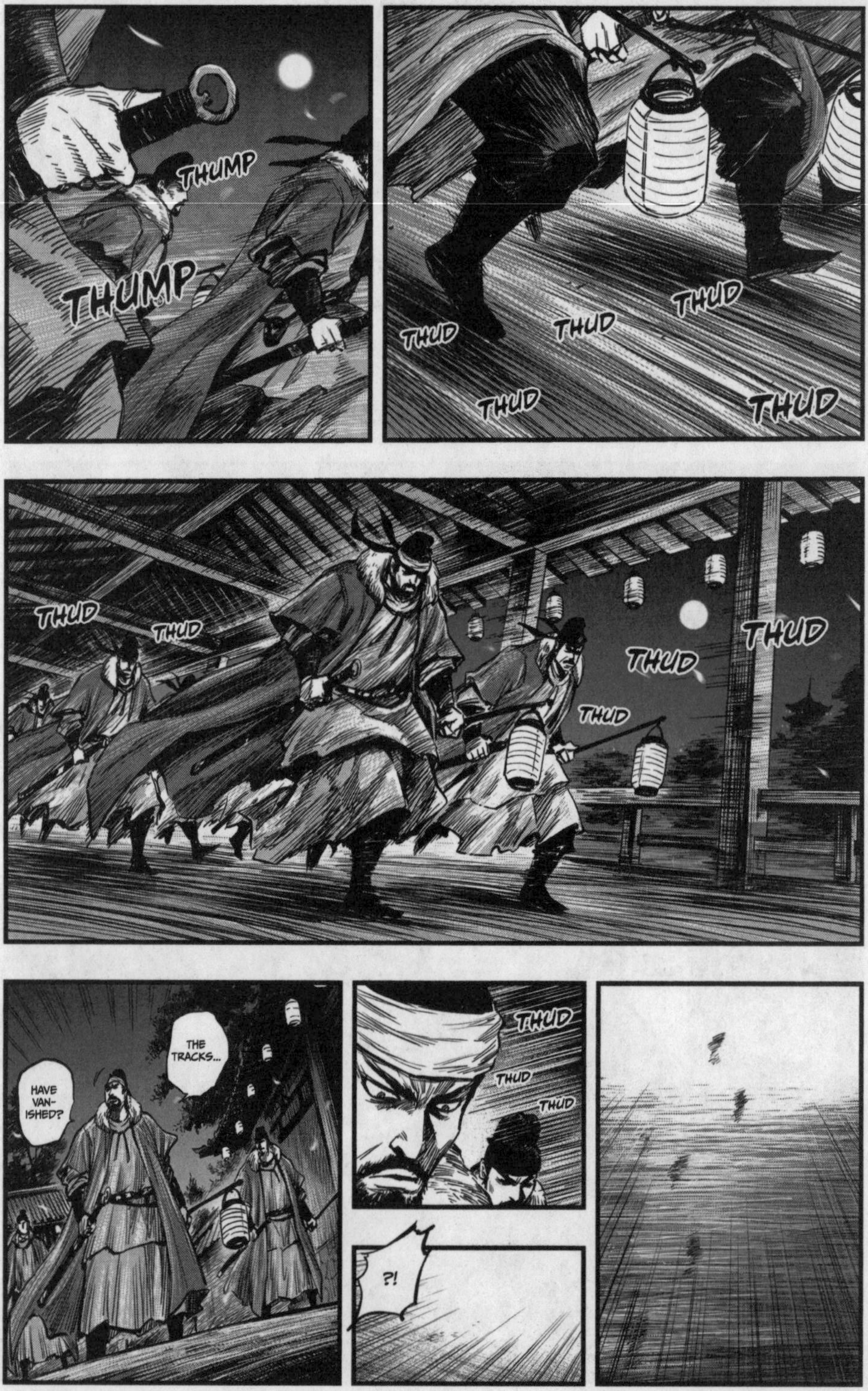
THUD
THUD
THUD
THUD
THUD
THUMP
THUMP
THUD
THUD
THUD
THUD
THUD
THUD
THUD
THUD
?!
THE TRACKS...
HAVE VAN-ISHED?

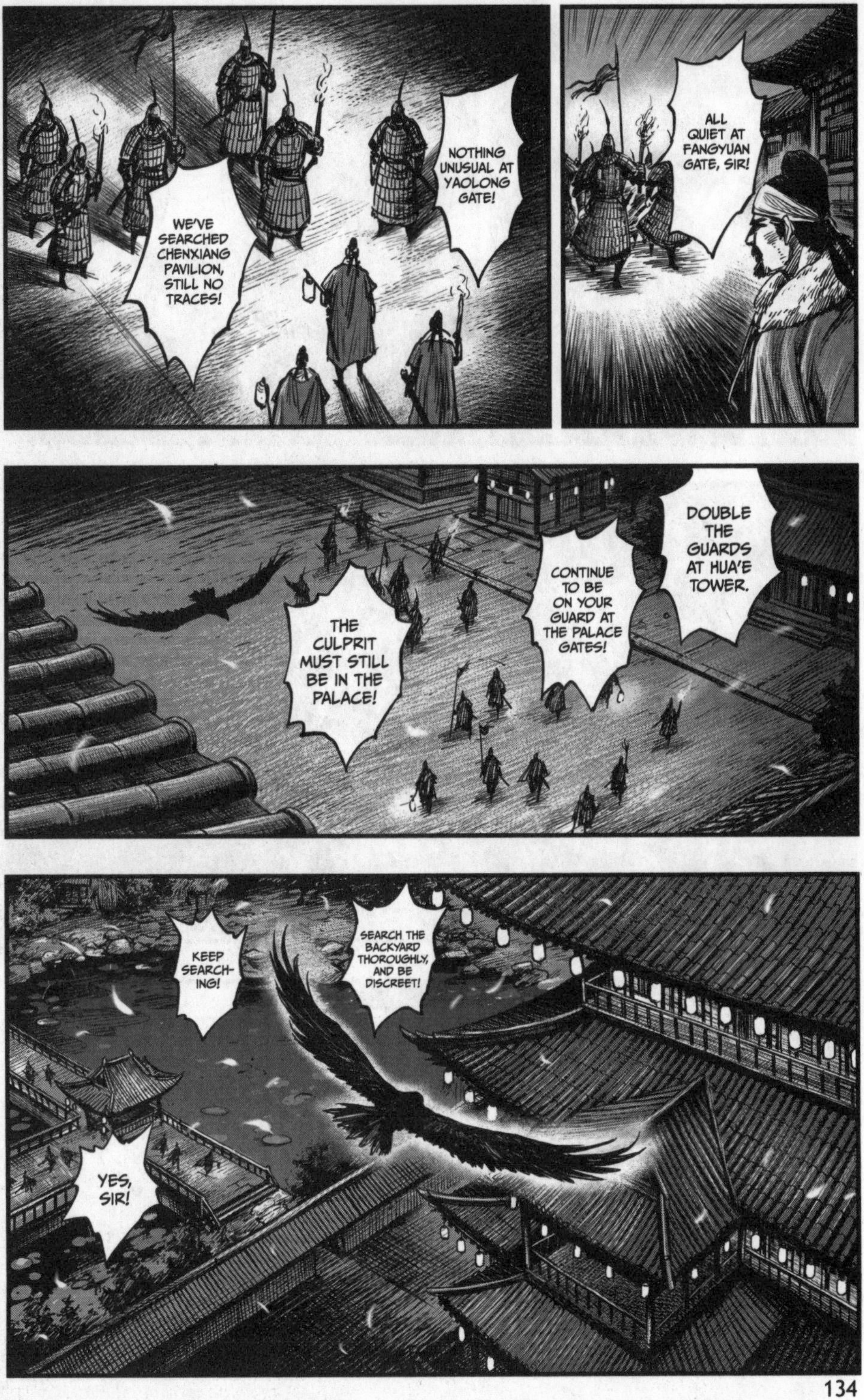
ALL QUIET AT FANGYUAN GATE, SIR!
NOTHING UNUSUAL AT YAOLONG GATE!
WE'VE SEARCHED CHENXIANG PAVILION, STILL NO TRACES!
DOUBLE THE GUARDS AT HUA'E TOWER.
CONTINUE TO BE ON YOUR GUARD AT THE PALACE GATES!
THE CULPRIT MUST STILL BE IN THE PALACE!
SEARCH THE BACKYARD THOROUGHLY, AND BE DISCREET!
KEEP SEARCHING!
YES, SIR!

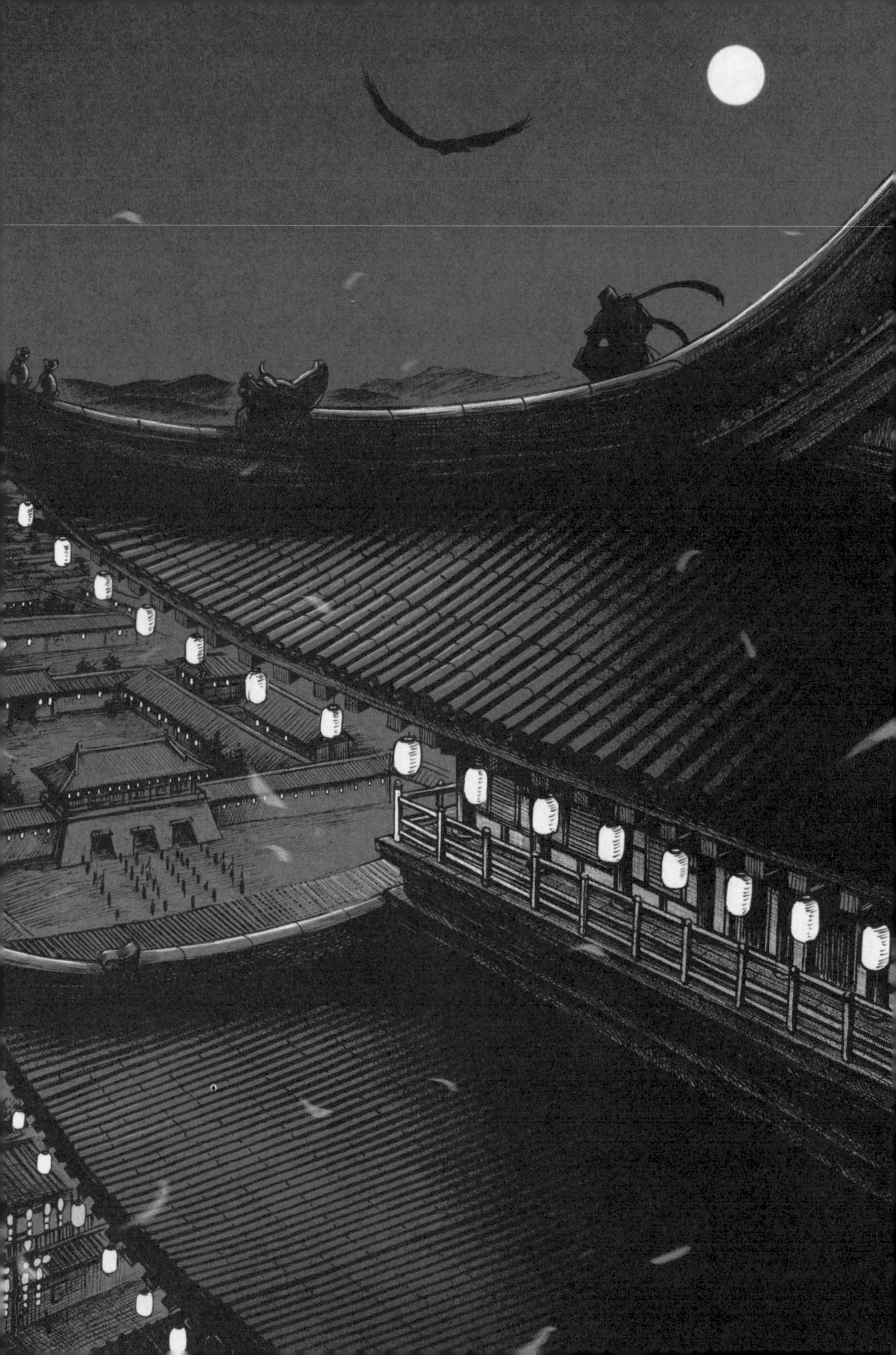

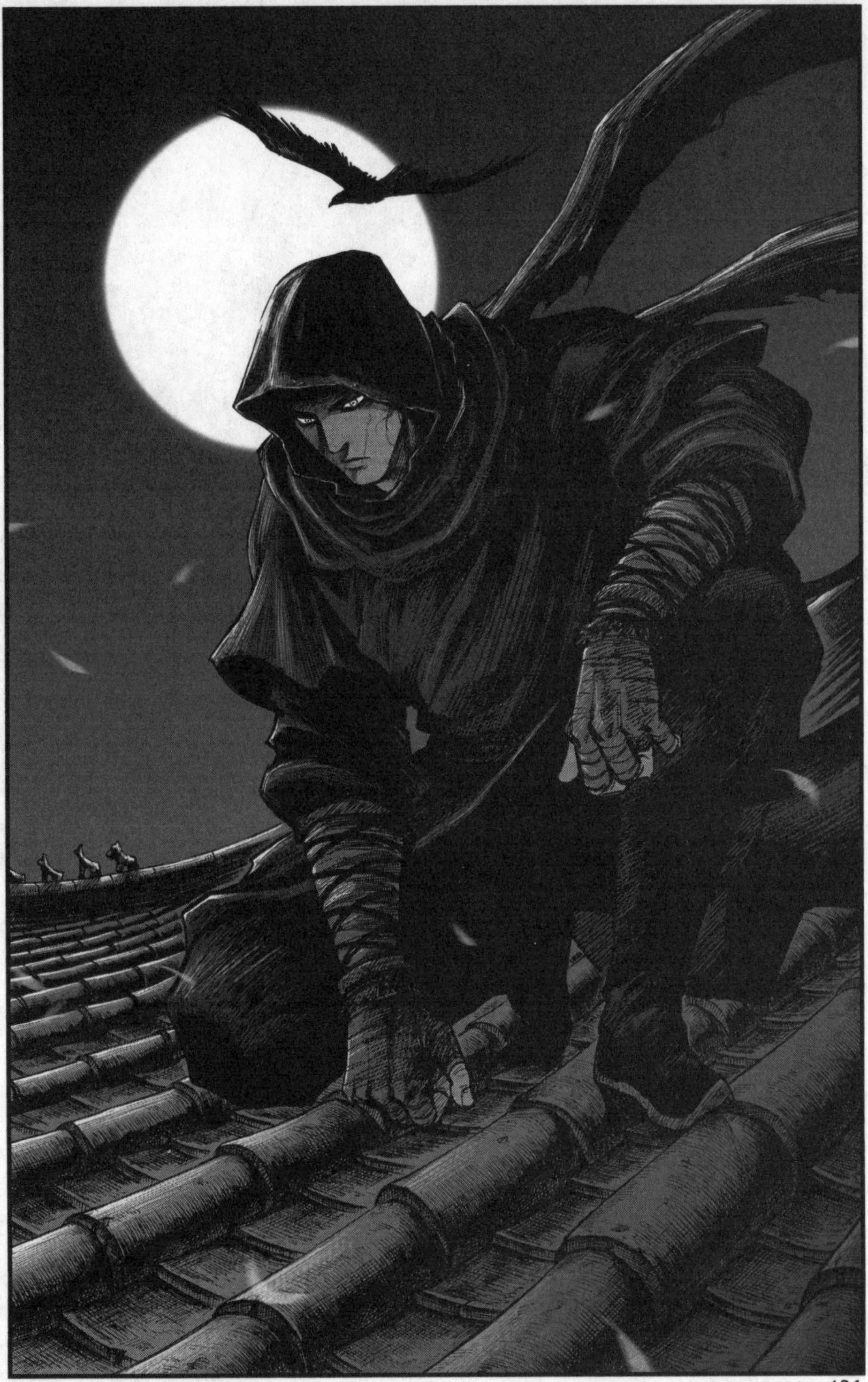

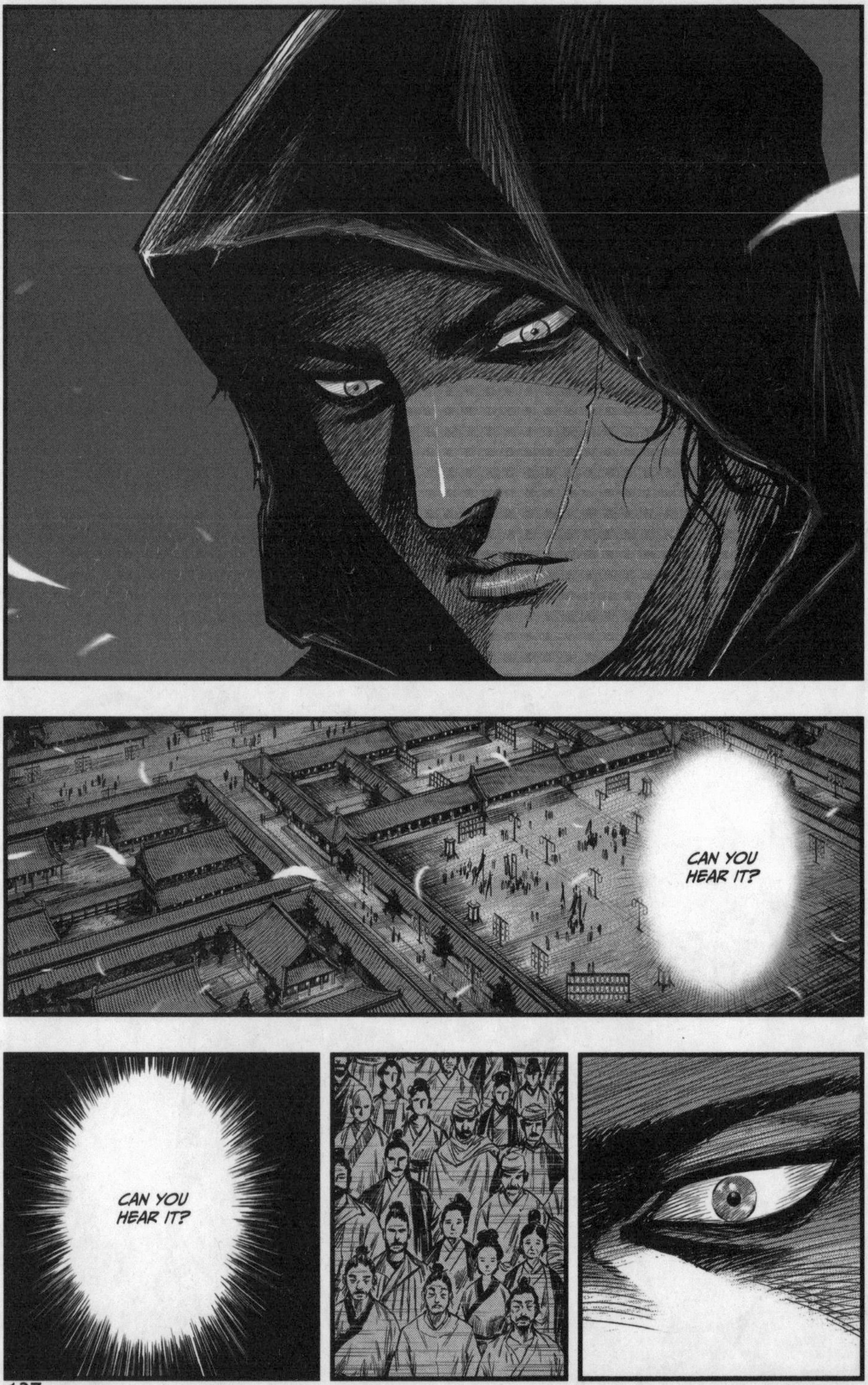
CAN YOU HEAR IT?
CAN YOU HEAR IT?

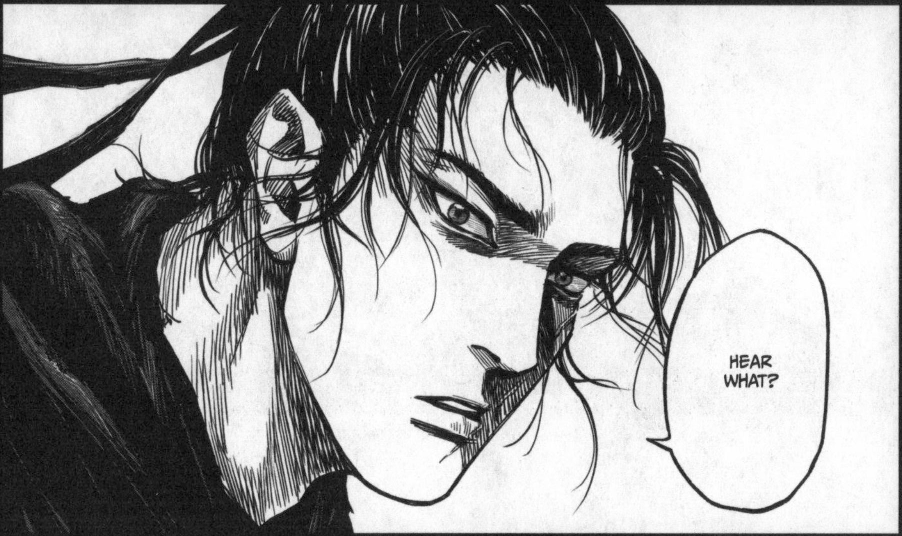
HEAR WHAT?

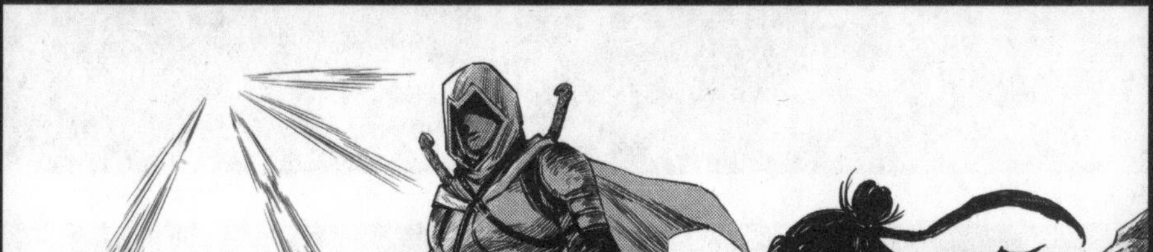

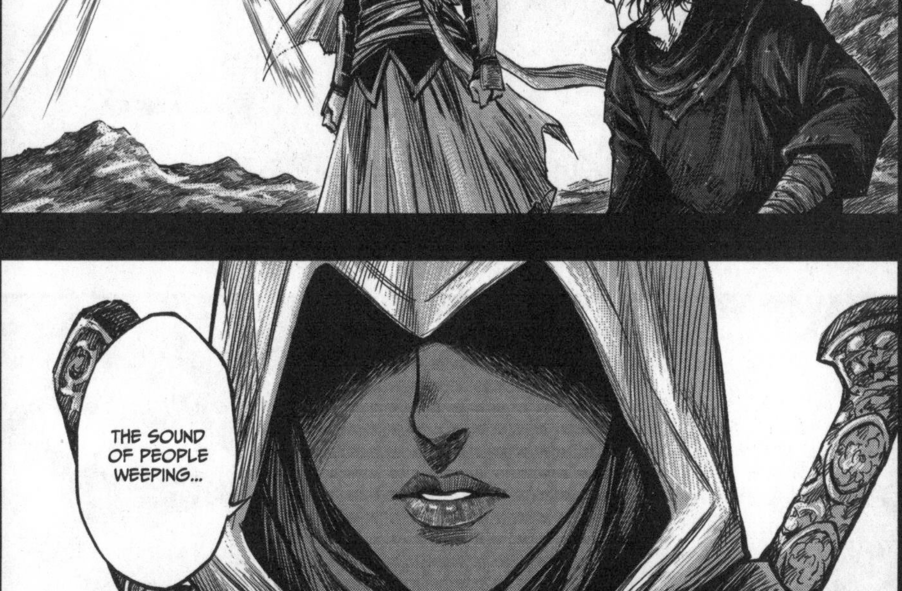
THE SOUND OF PEOPLE WEEPING...

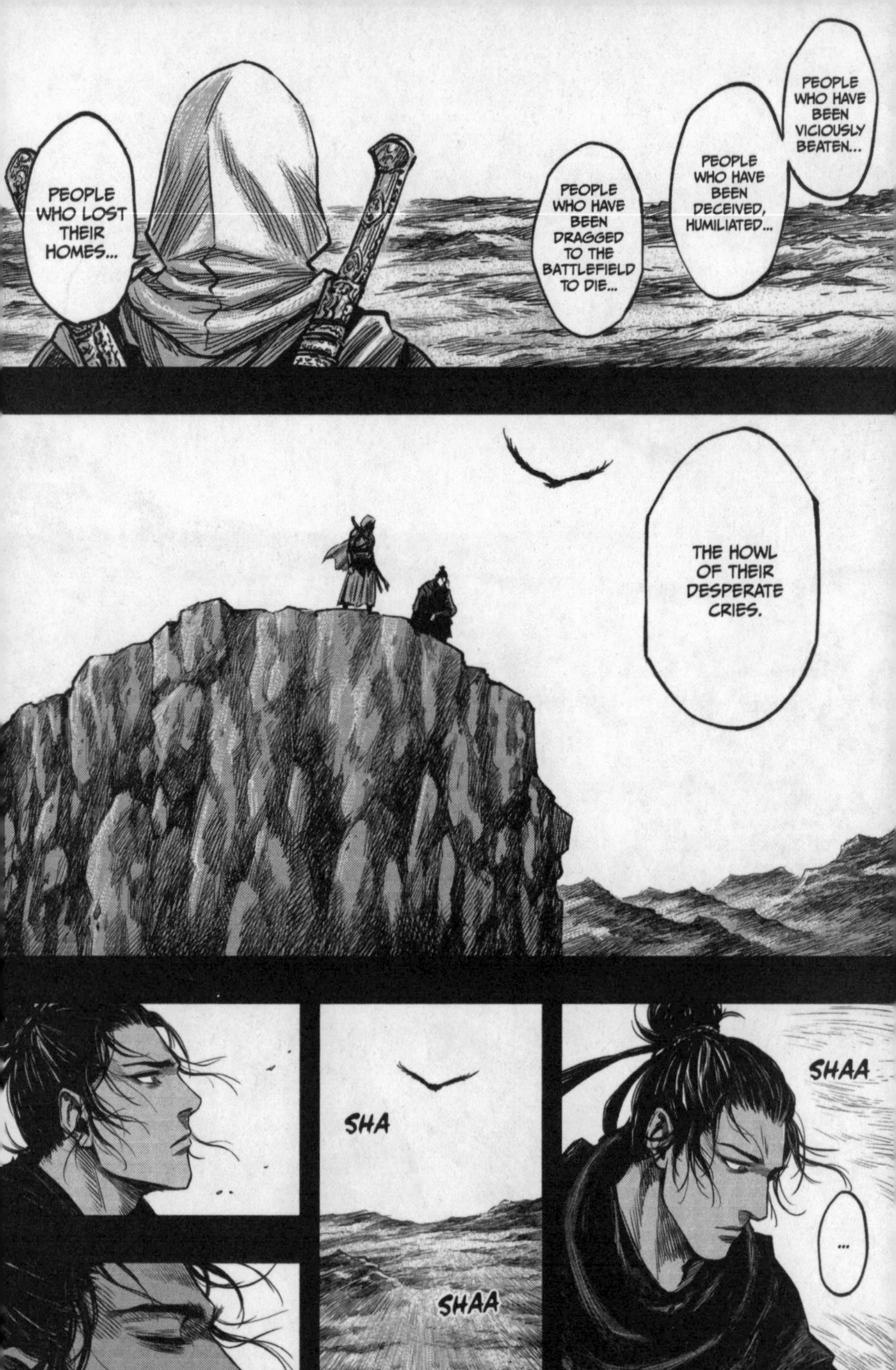
PEOPLE WHO HAVE BEEN VICIOUSLY BEATEN...
PEOPLE WHO HAVE BEEN DECEIVED, HUMILIATED...
PEOPLE WHO HAVE BEEN DRAGGED TO THE BATTLEFIELD TO DIE...
PEOPLE WHO LOST THEIR HOMES...
THE HOWL OF THEIR DESPERATE CRIES.
SHAA
...
SHA
SHAA

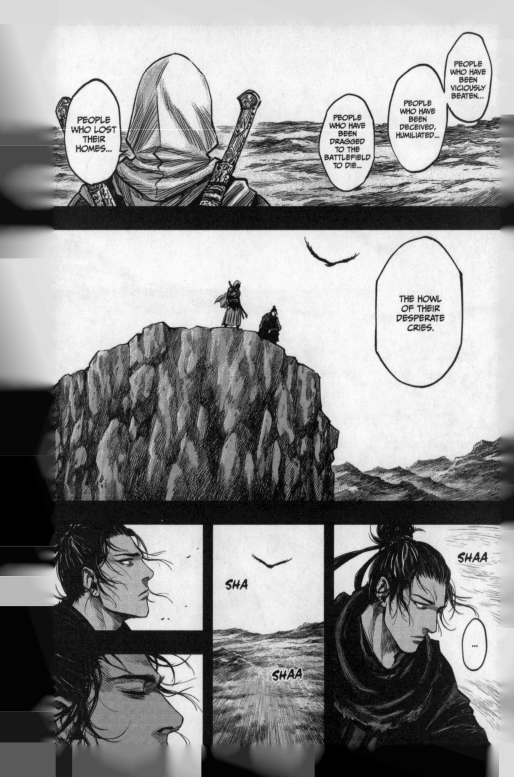

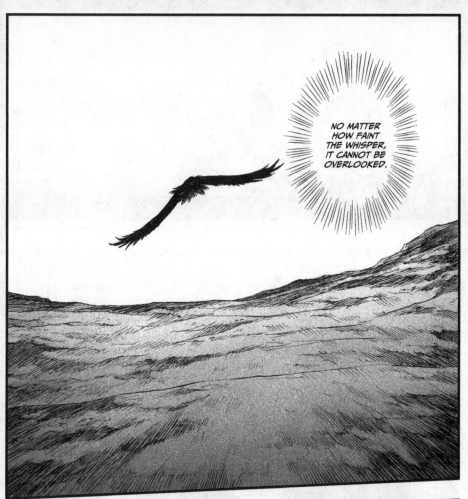

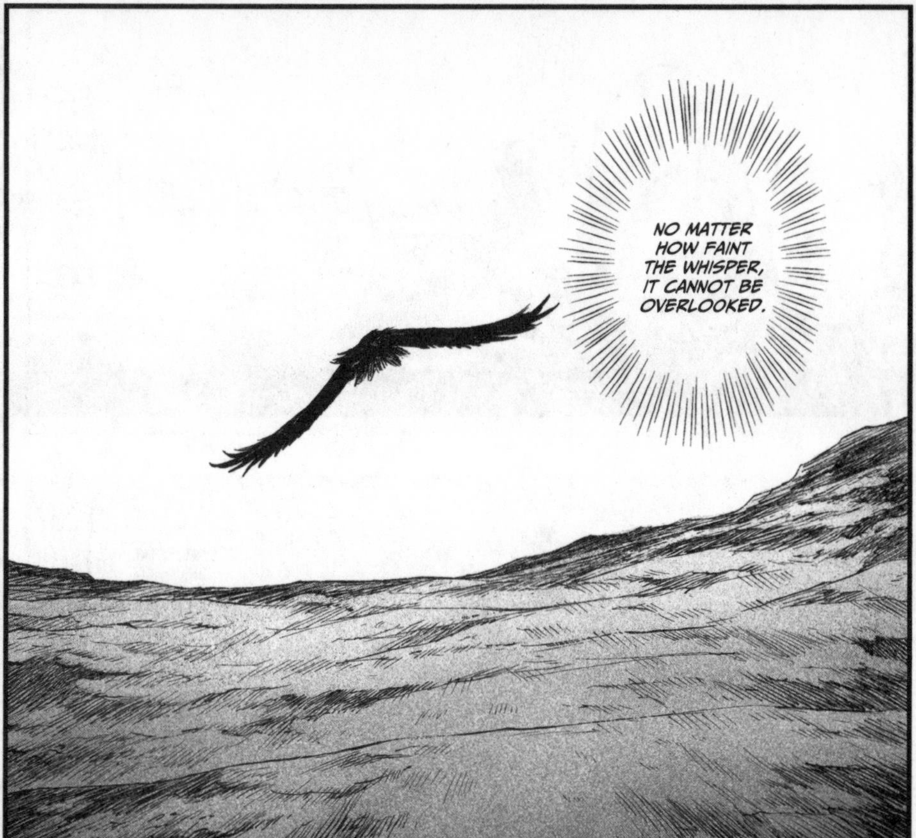
NO MATTER HOW FAINT THE WHISPER, IT CANNOT BE OVERLOOKED.
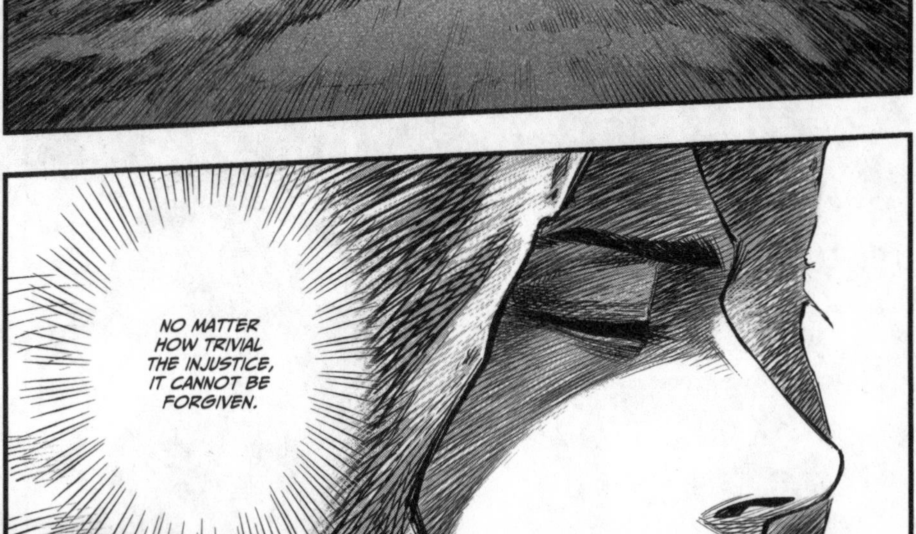
NO MATTER HOW TRIVIAL THE INJUSTICE, IT CANNOT BE FORGIVEN.

SCREECH—

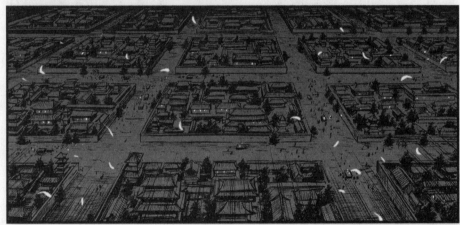

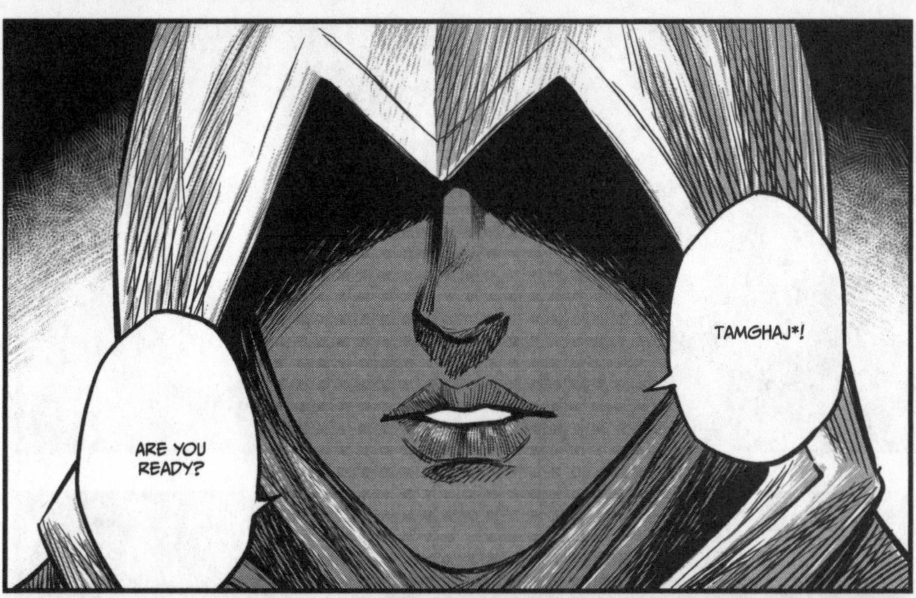
TAMGHAJ*!
ARE YOU READY?

*TAMGHAJ: THE TERM USED TO REFER TO CHINA BY THOSE IN CENTRAL ASIA AND WEST OF PERSIA DURING THE TANG DYNASTY. ALSO SPELLED AS TOMGHAJ, TOHGAJ.

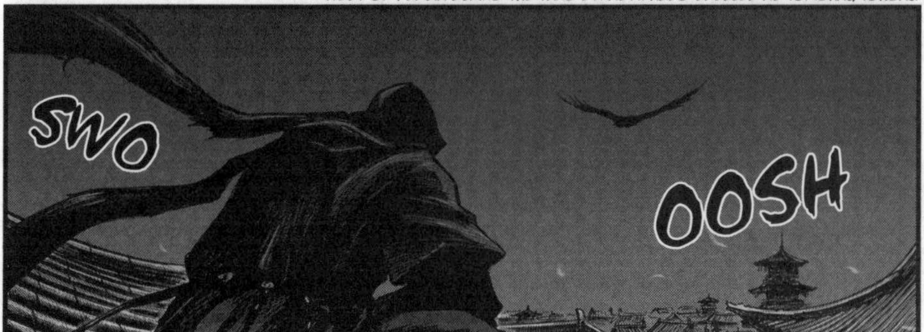
SWO
OOSH

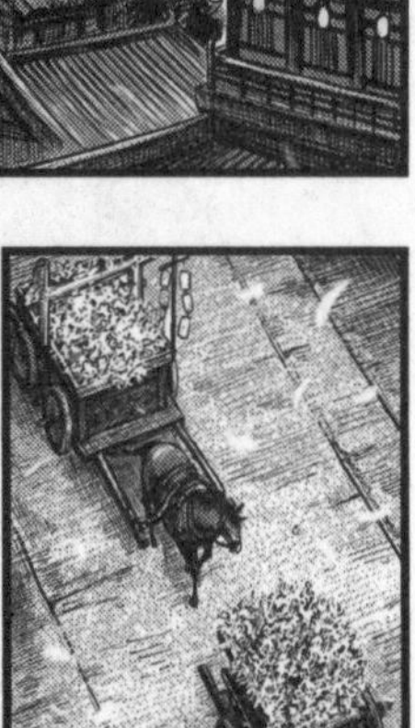

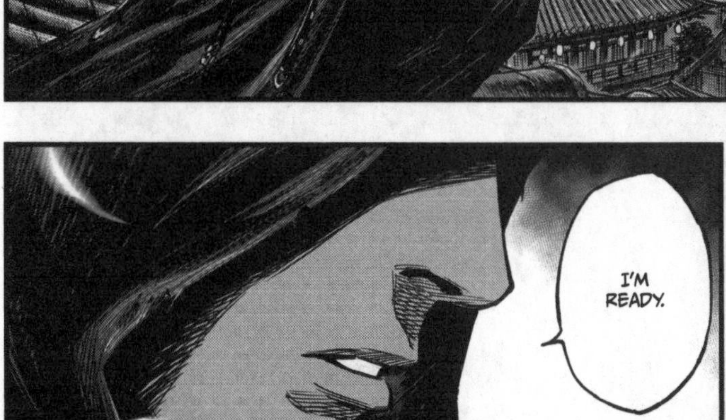
I'M READY.

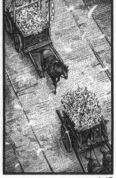

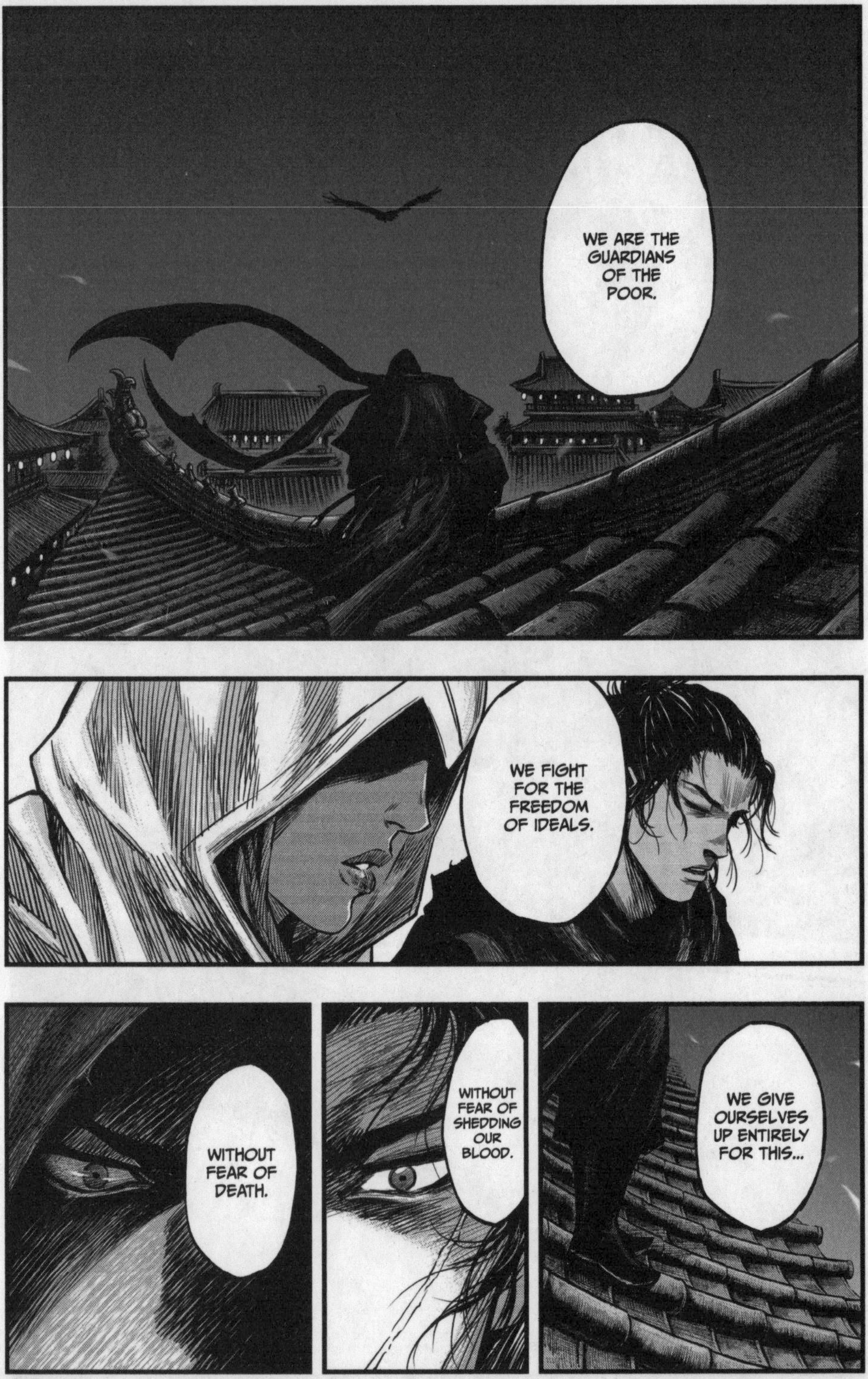
WE ARE THE GUARDIANS OF THE POOR.
WE FIGHT FOR THE FREEDOM OF IDEALS.
WE GIVE OURSELVES UP ENTIRELY FOR THIS...
WITHOUT FEAR OF SHEDDING OUR BLOOD.
WITHOUT FEAR OF DEATH.

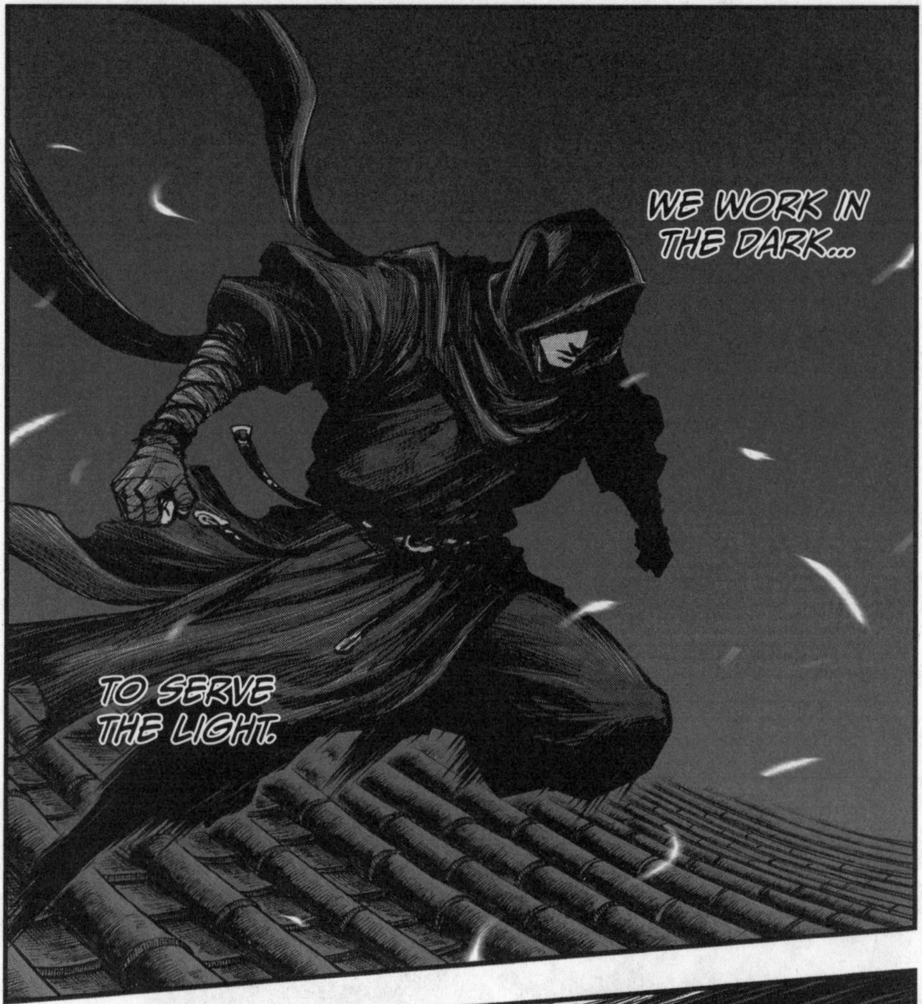
WE WORK IN THE DARK...
TO SERVE THE LIGHT.

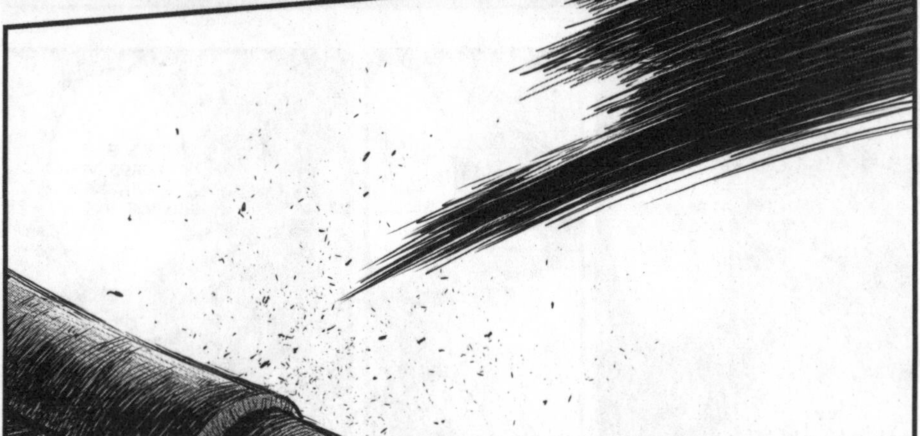

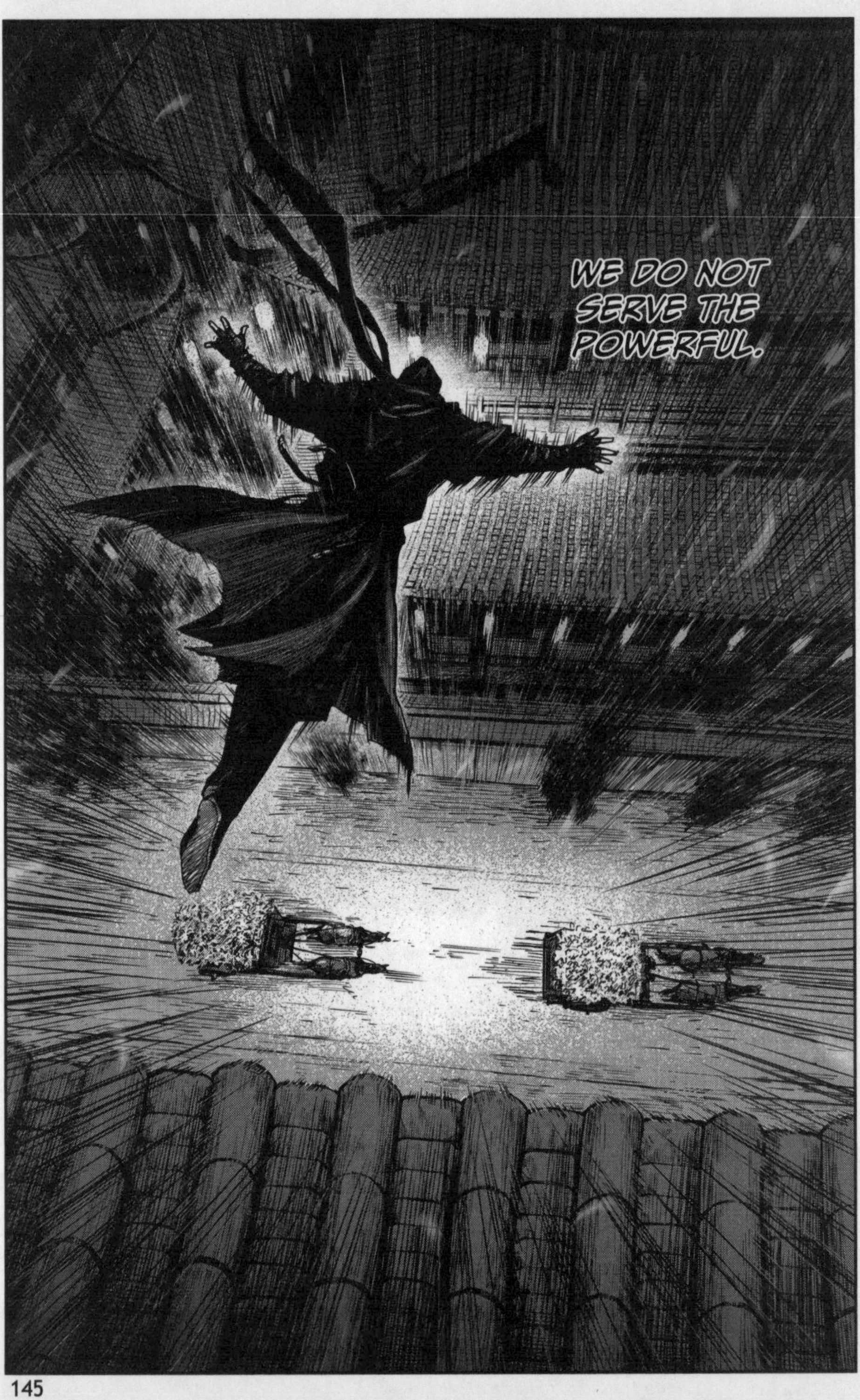
WE DO NOT SERVE THE POWERFUL.

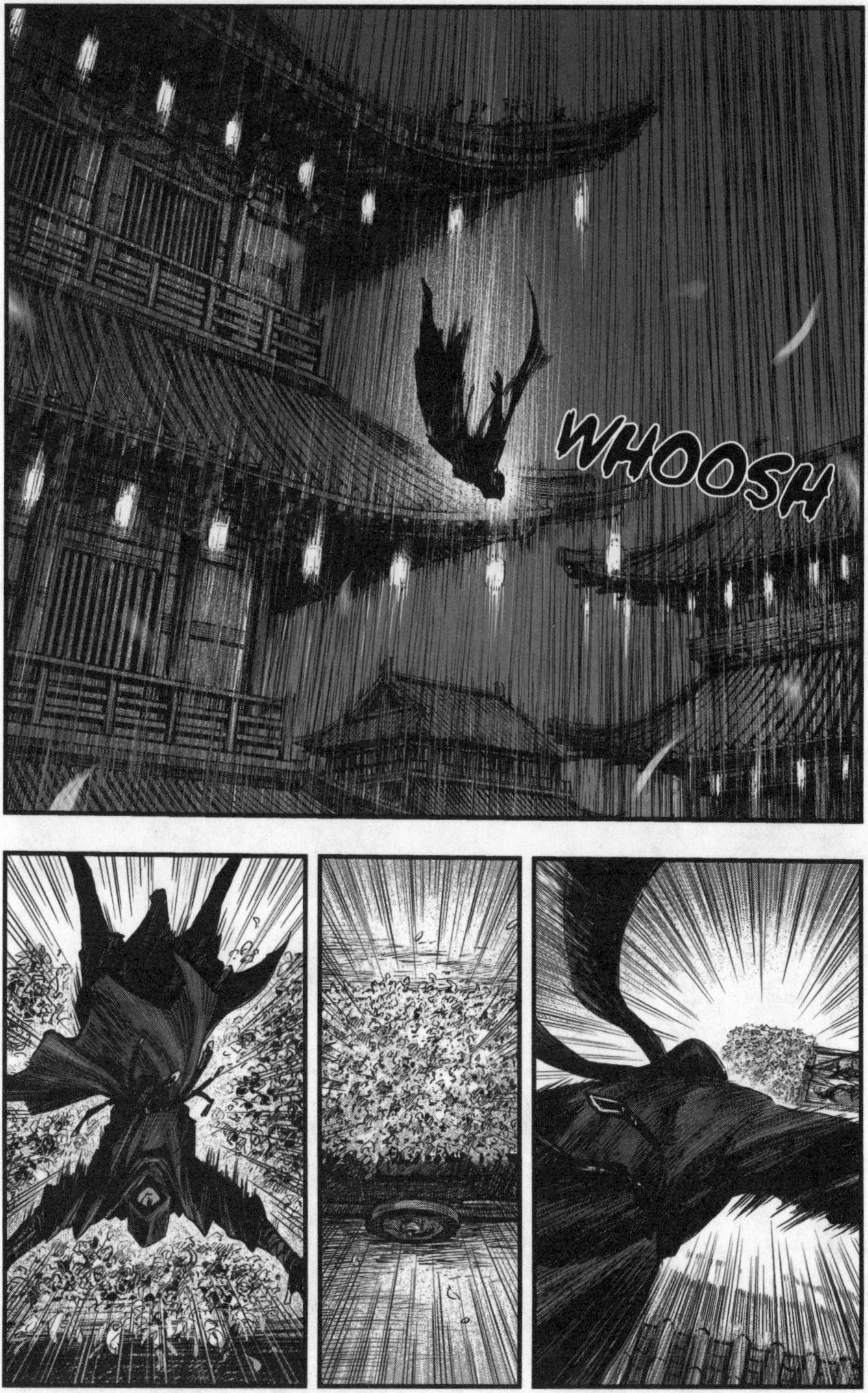
WHOOSH

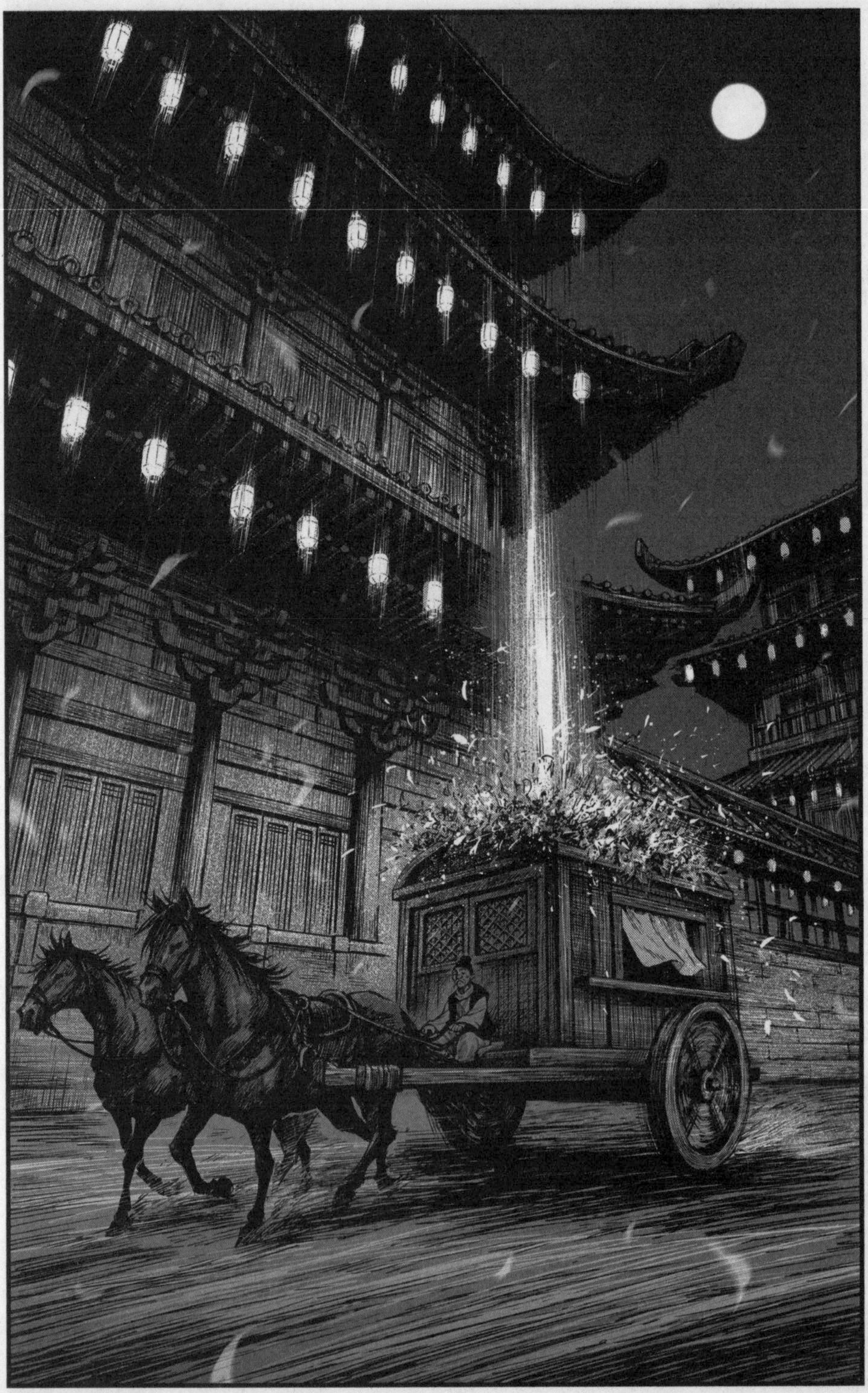

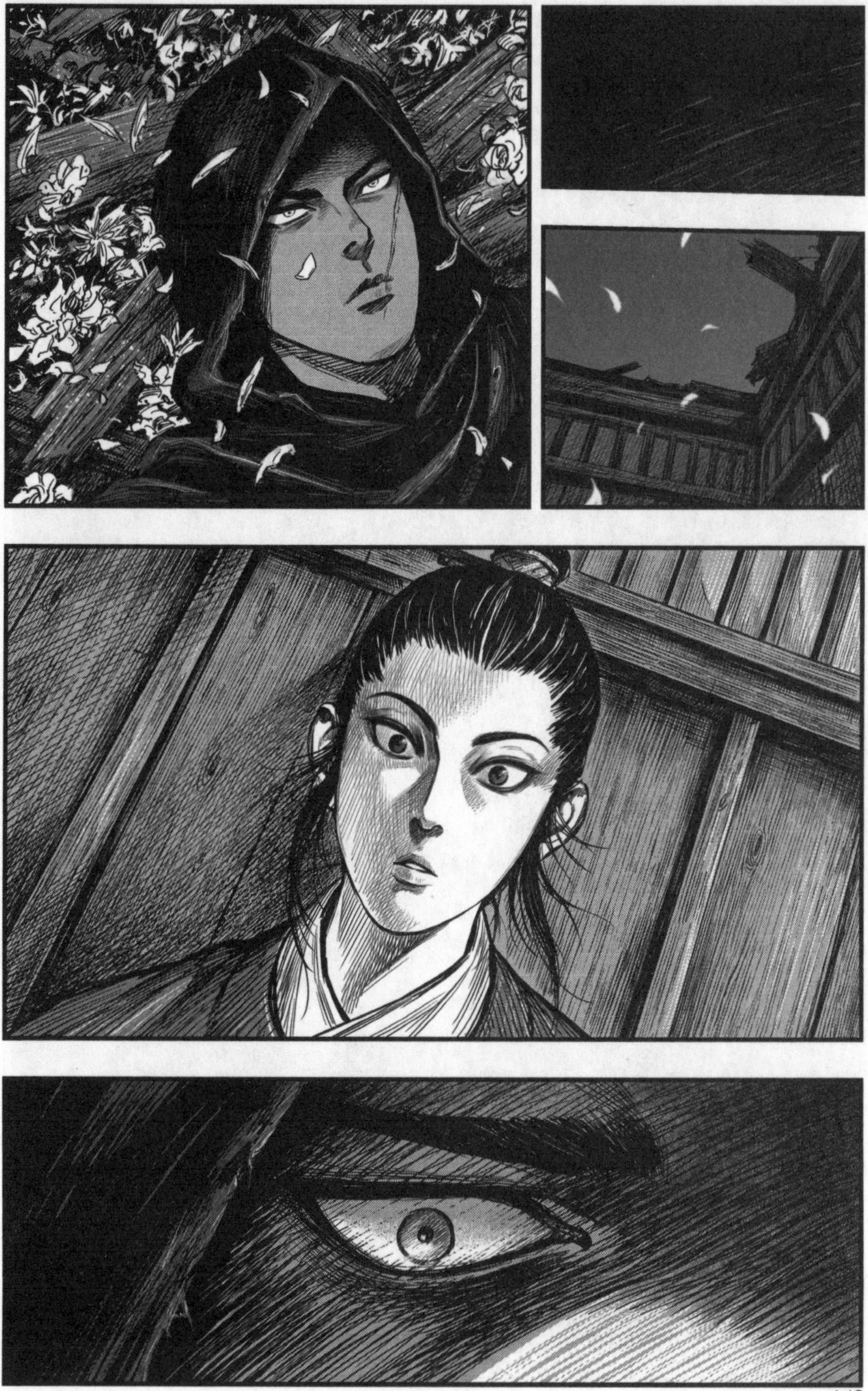

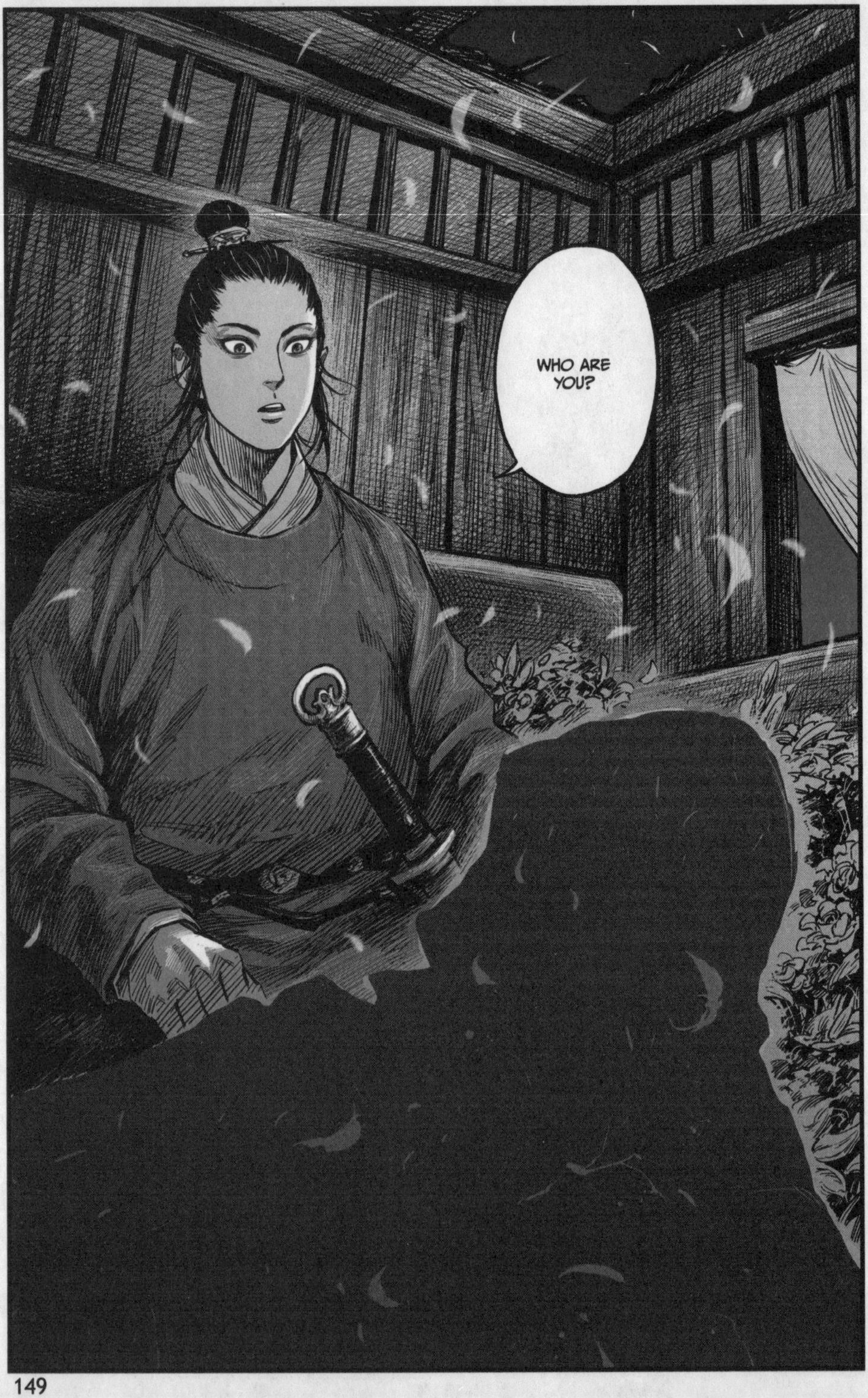
WHO ARE YOU?

ASSASSIN'S CREED

DYNASTY

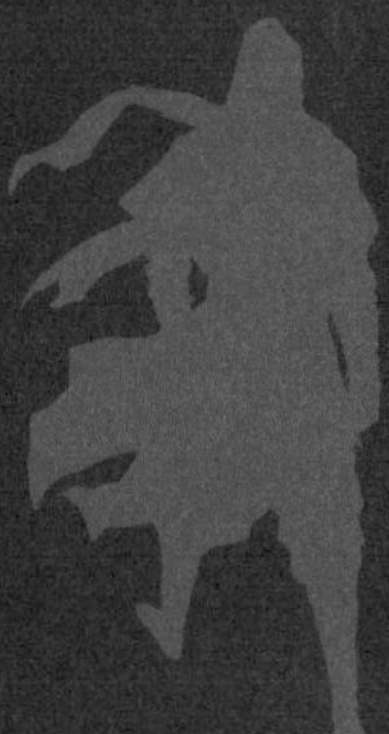

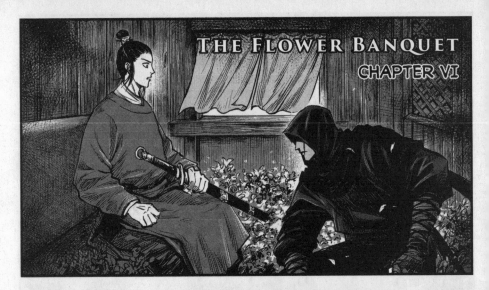

THE FLOWER BANQUET
CHAPTER VI

TREMBLE

TREMBLE

AHH...

AH...

HUFF

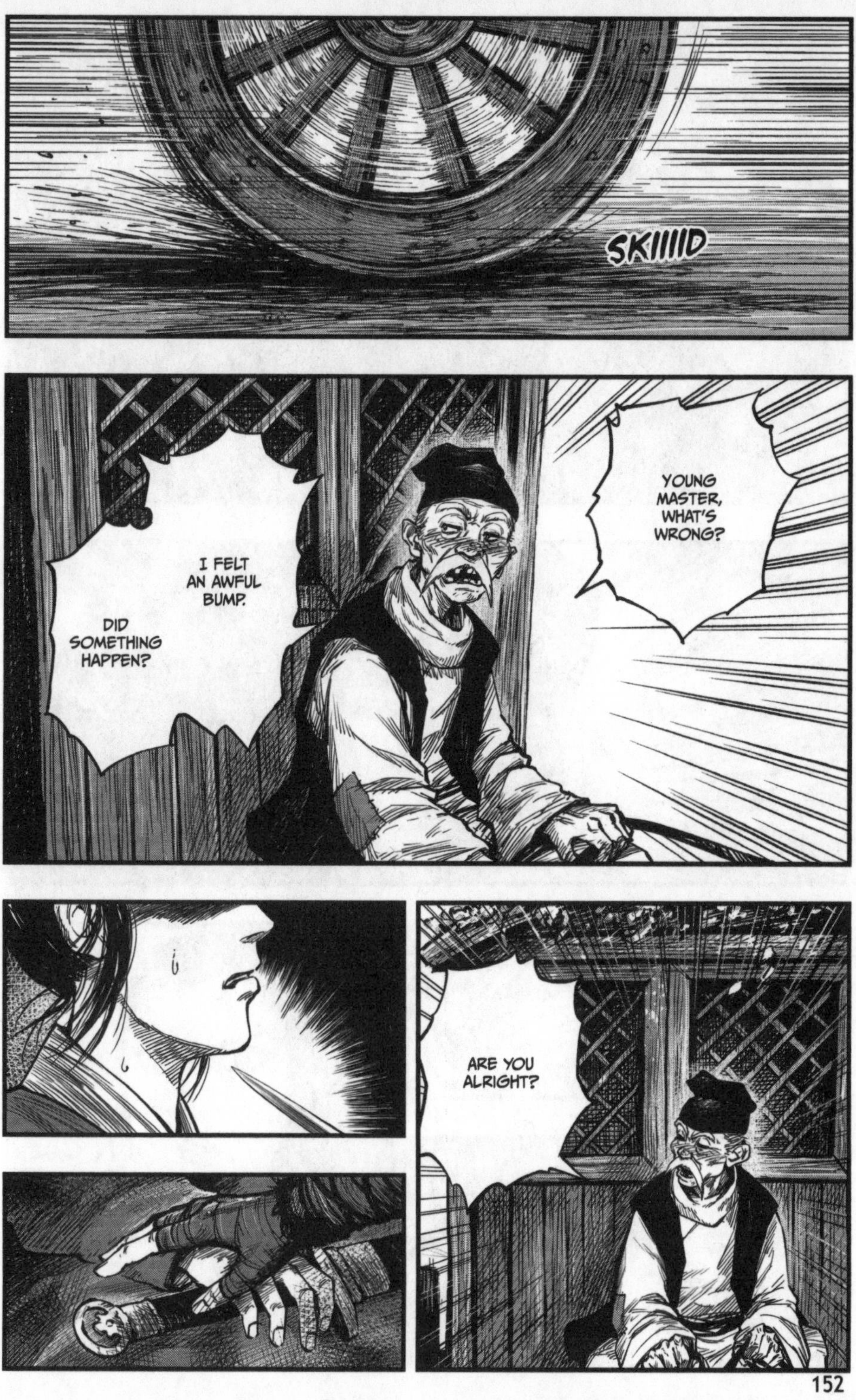
SKIIIID
YOUNG MASTER, WHAT'S WRONG?
I FELT AN AWFUL BUMP.
DID SOMETHING HAPPEN?
ARE YOU ALRIGHT?

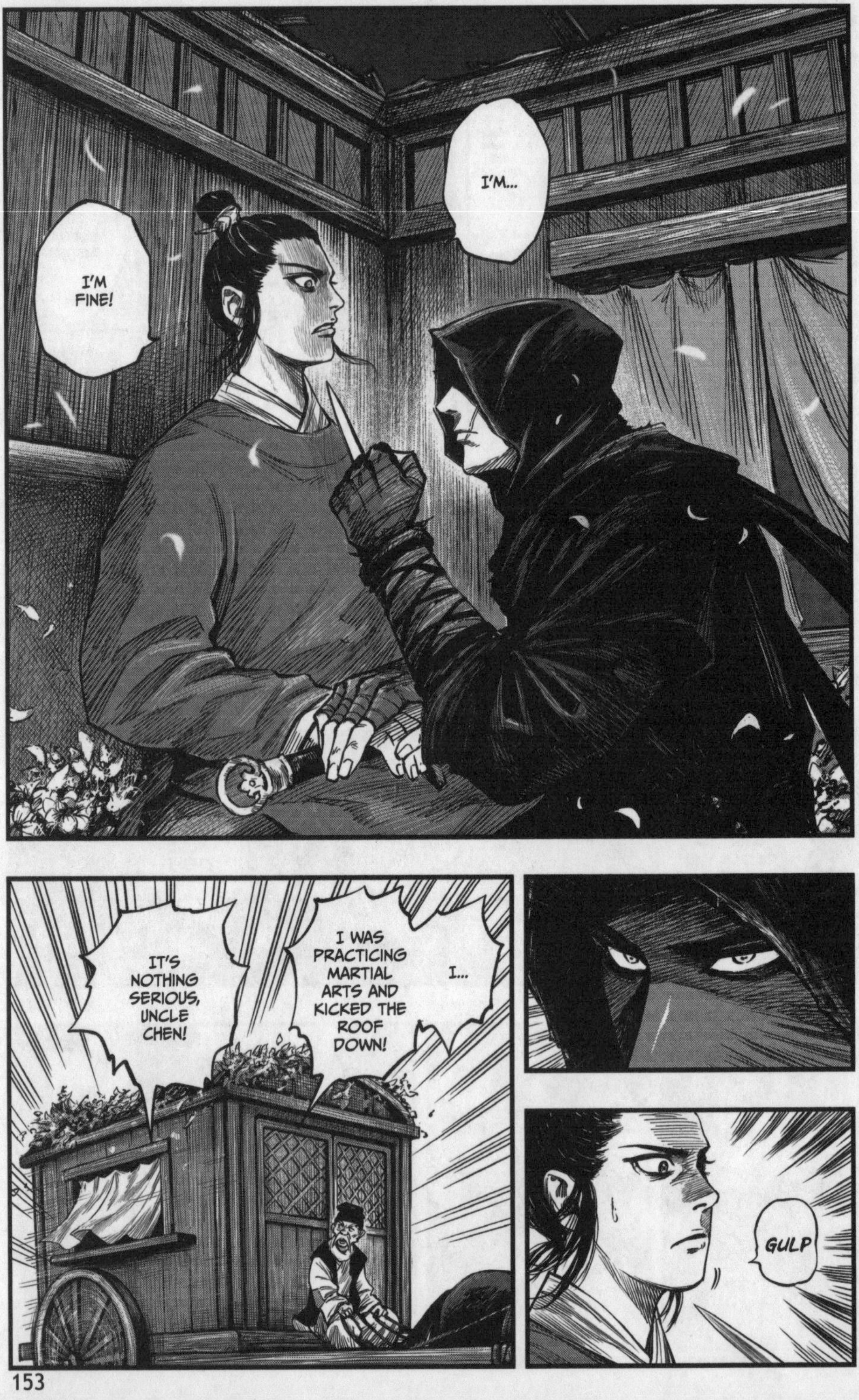
I'M...
I'M FINE!
GULP
I...
I WAS PRACTICING MARTIAL ARTS AND KICKED THE ROOF DOWN!
IT'S NOTHING SERIOUS, UNCLE CHEN!

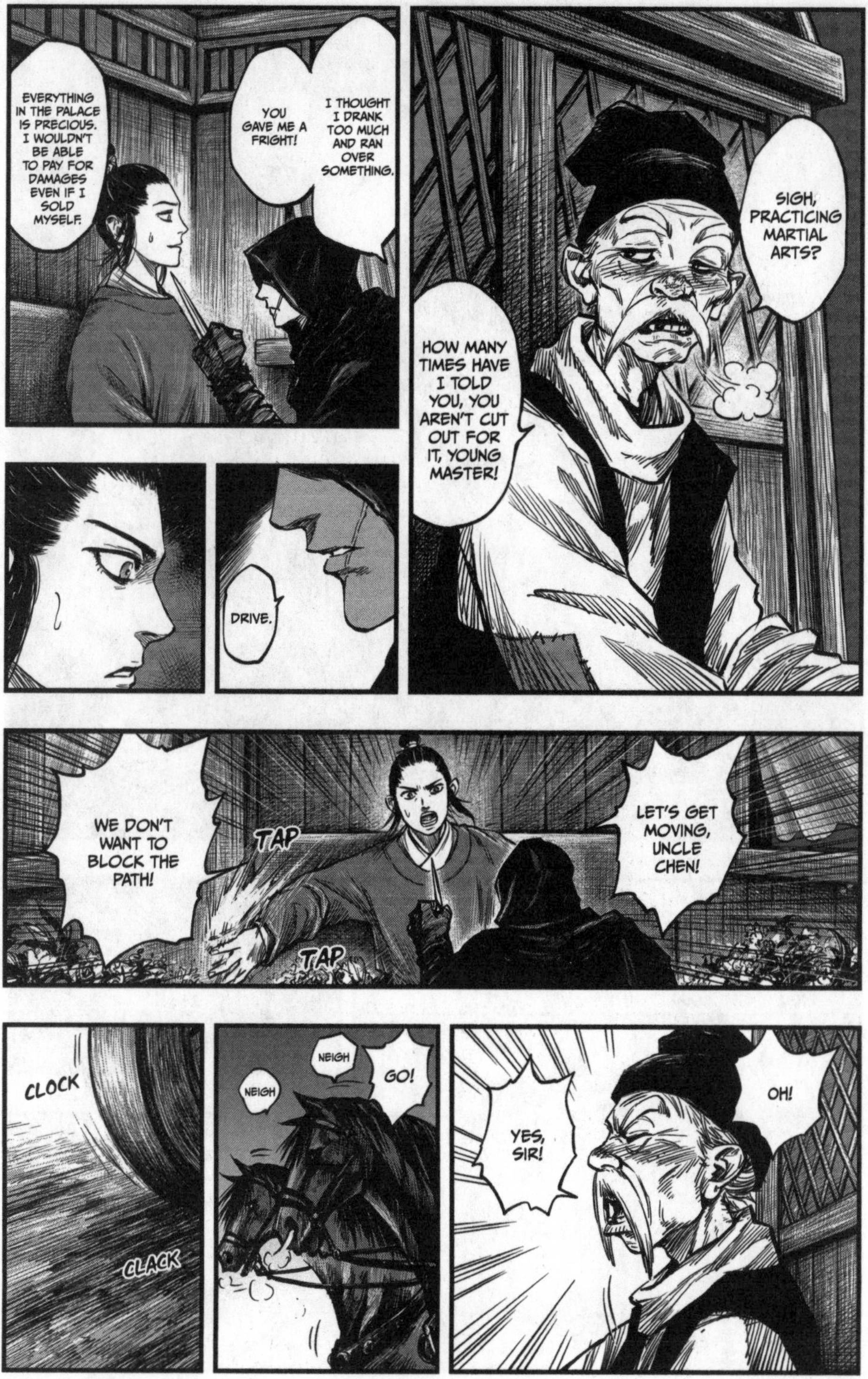
SIGH, PRACTICING MARTIAL ARTS?
HOW MANY TIMES HAVE I TOLD YOU, YOU AREN'T CUT OUT FOR IT, YOUNG MASTER!
YOU GAVE ME A FRIGHT!
I THOUGHT I DRANK TOO MUCH AND RAN OVER SOMETHING.
EVERYTHING IN THE PALACE IS PRECIOUS. I WOULDN'T BE ABLE TO PAY FOR DAMAGES EVEN IF I SOLD MYSELF.
DRIVE.
LET'S GET MOVING, UNCLE CHEN!
TAP
TAP
WE DON'T WANT TO BLOCK THE PATH!
OH!
YES, SIR!
GO!
NEIGH
NEIGH
CLOCK
CLACK

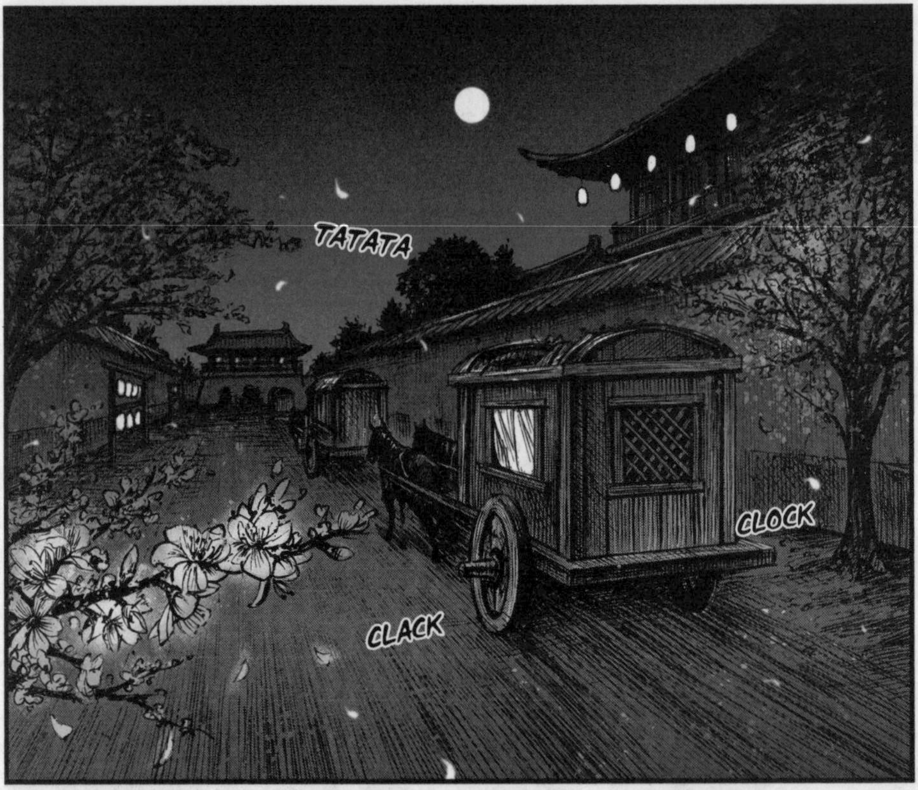
TATATA
CLOCK
CLACK
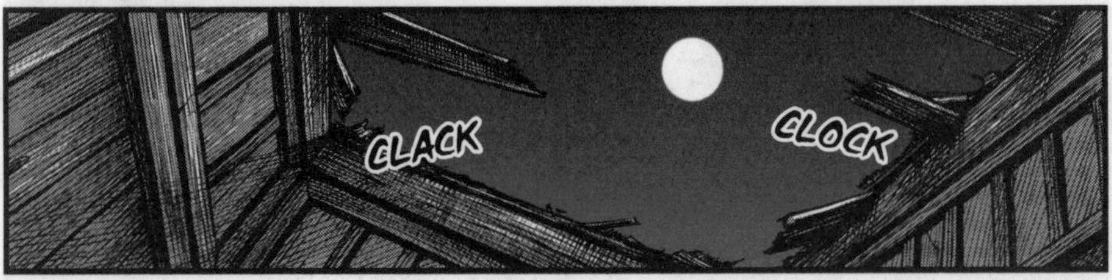
CLOCK
CLACK
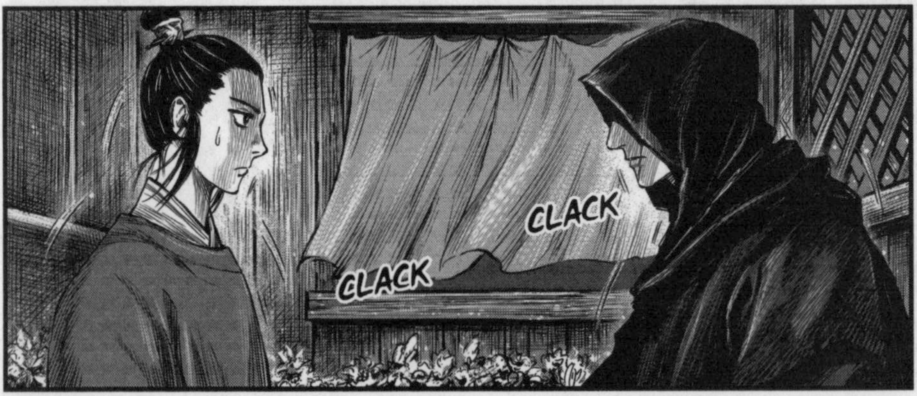
CLACK
CLACK

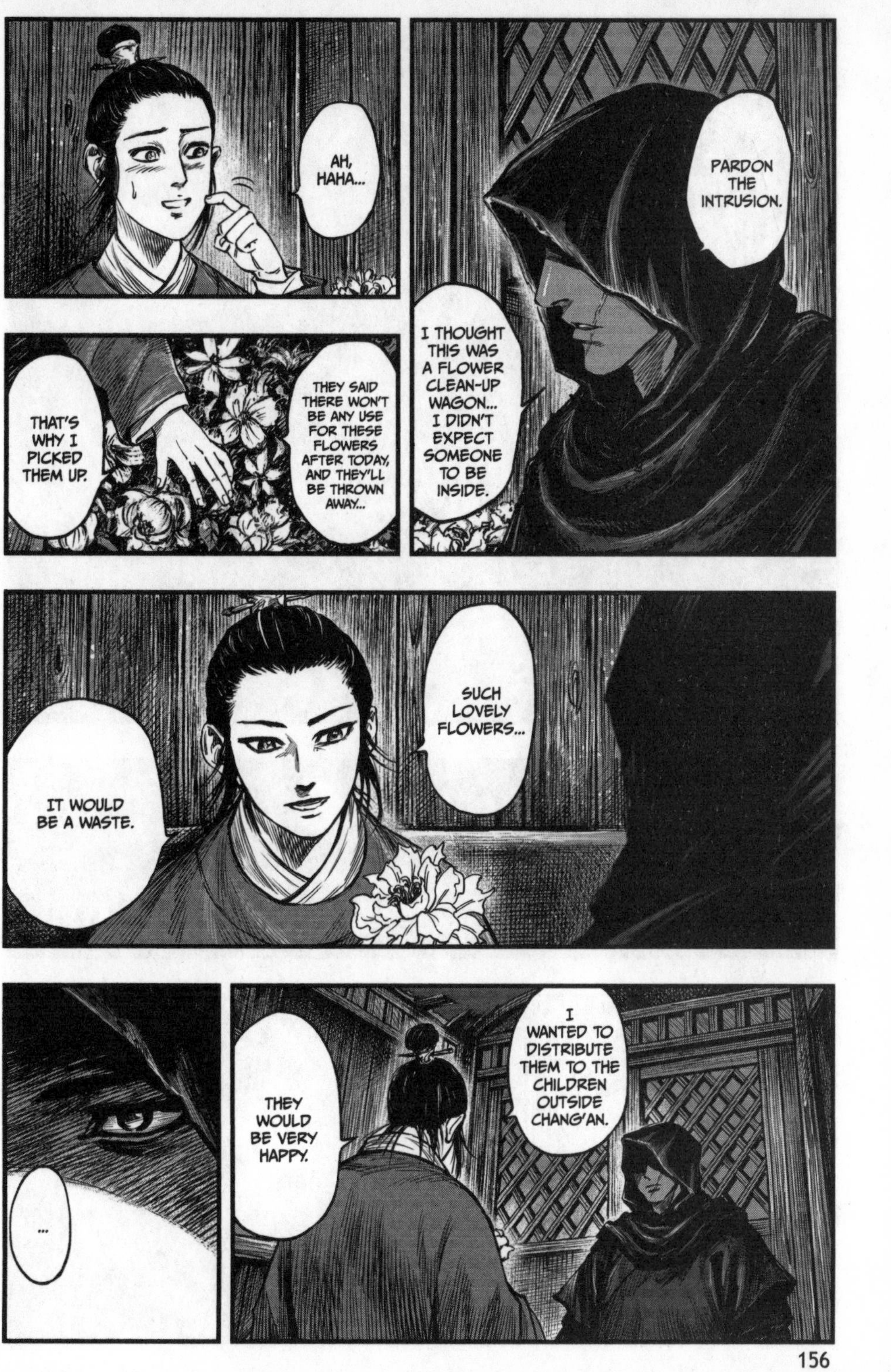

PARDON THE INTRUSION.
I THOUGHT THIS WAS A FLOWER CLEAN-UP WAGON... I DIDN'T EXPECT SOMEONE TO BE INSIDE.
AH, HAHA...
THEY SAID THERE WON'T BE ANY USE FOR THESE FLOWERS AFTER TODAY, AND THEY'LL BE THROWN AWAY...
THAT'S WHY I PICKED THEM UP.
SUCH LOVELY FLOWERS...
IT WOULD BE A WASTE.
I WANTED TO DISTRIBUTE THEM TO THE CHILDREN OUTSIDE CHANG'AN.
THEY WOULD BE VERY HAPPY.
...

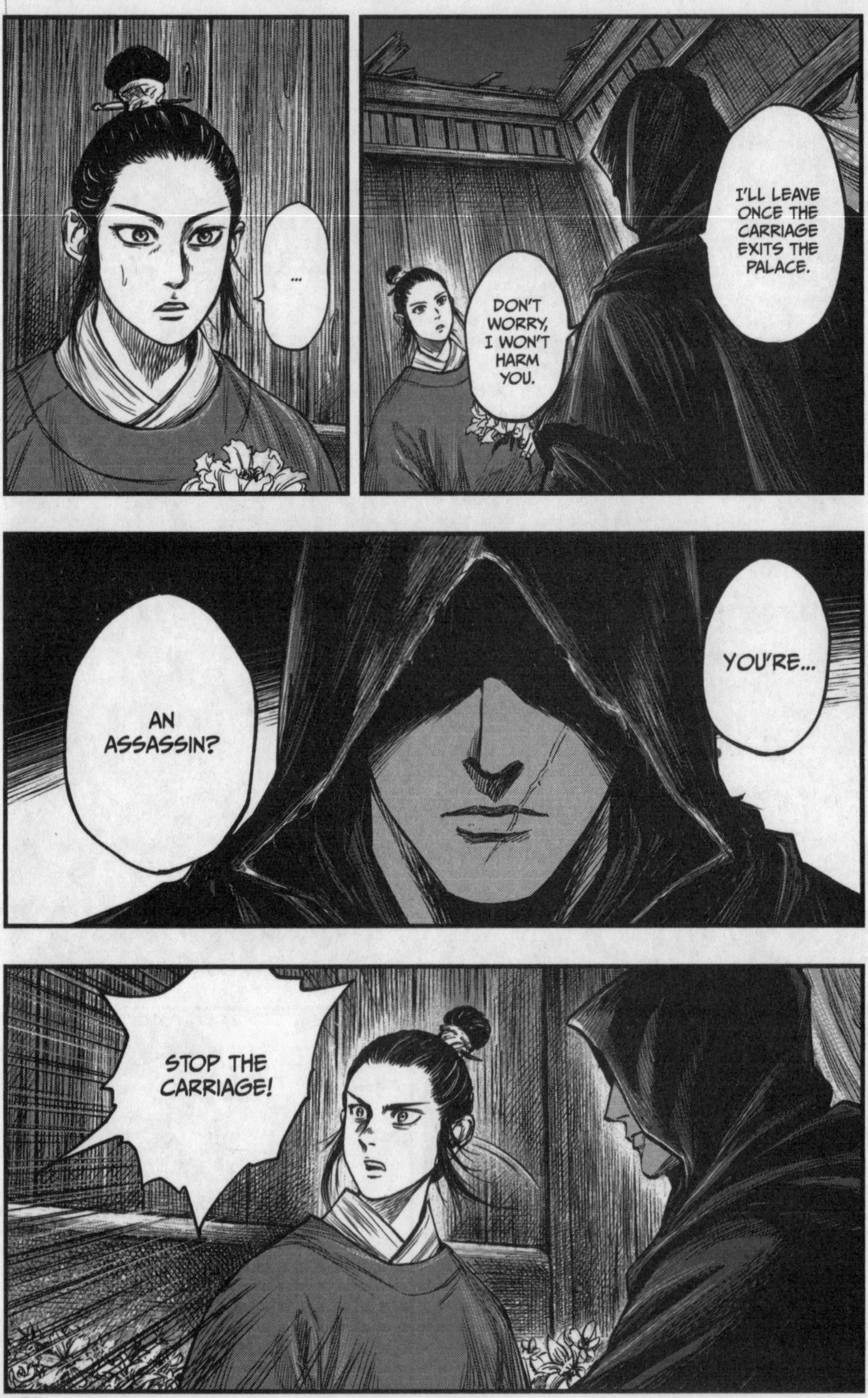
I'LL LEAVE ONCE THE CARRIAGE EXITS THE PALACE.
DON'T WORRY, I WON'T HARM YOU.
...
YOU'RE...
AN ASSASSIN?
STOP THE CARRIAGE!

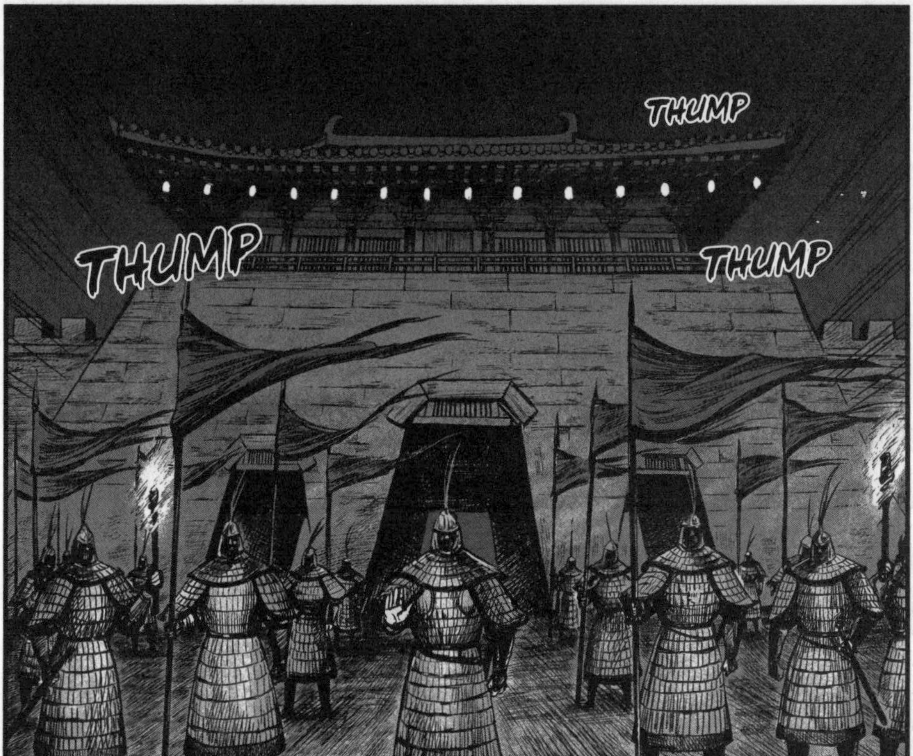
THUMP
THUMP
THUMP
THUMP
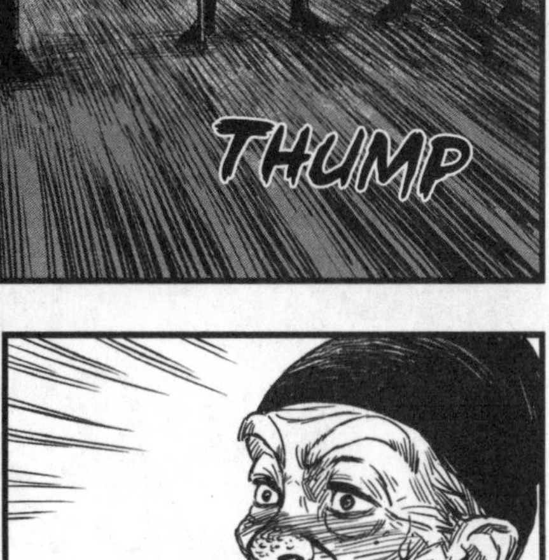
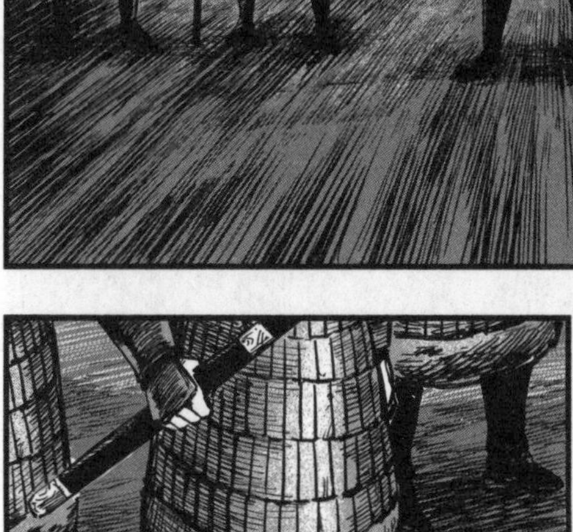
THUD
THUD
THUD

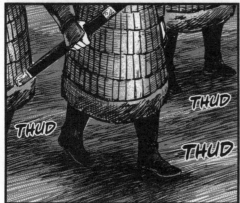

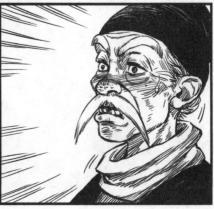

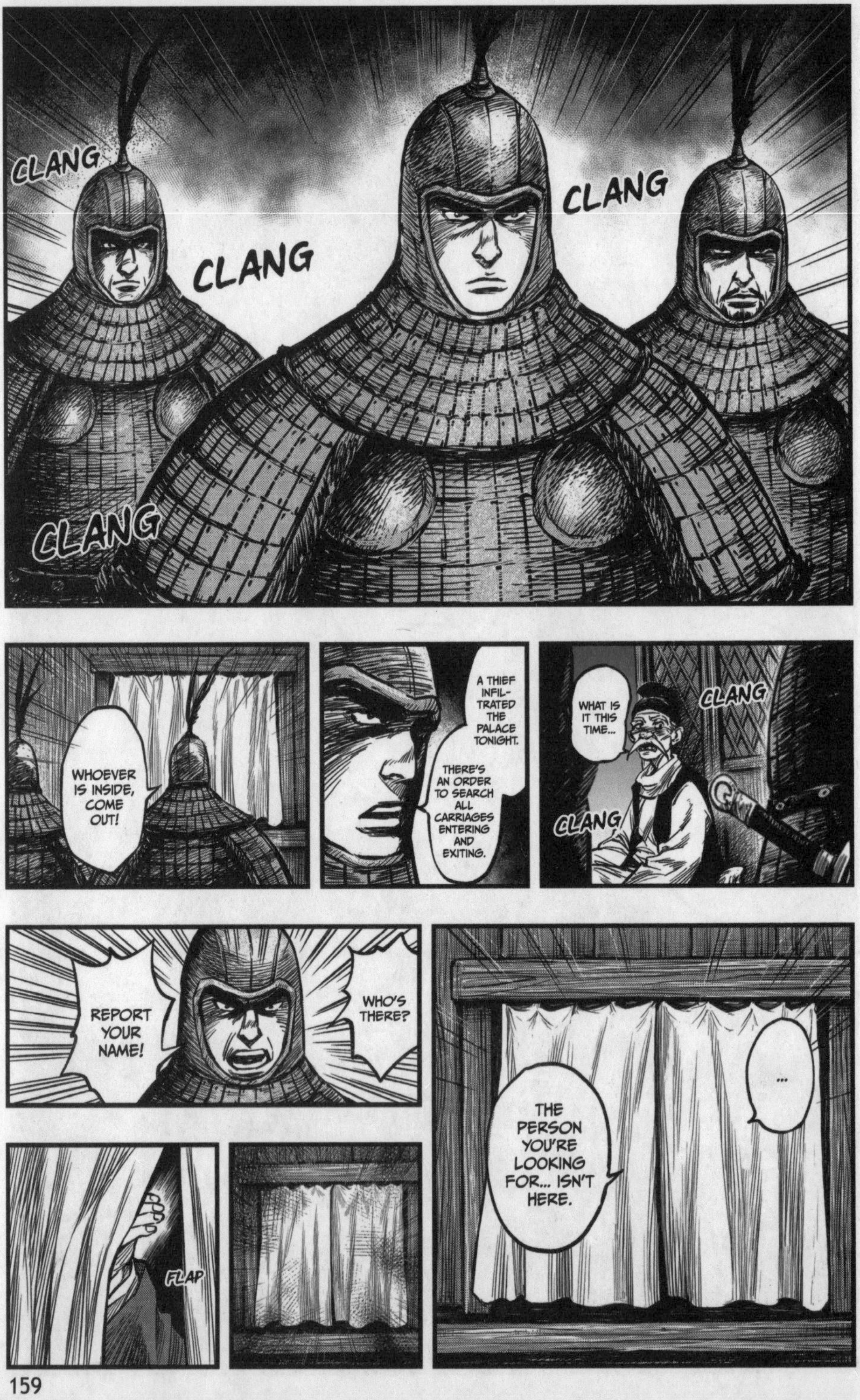
CLANG
CLANG
CLANG
CLANG
CLANG
CLANG
WHAT IS IT THIS TIME...
A THIEF INFILTRATED THE PALACE TONIGHT.
THERE'S AN ORDER TO SEARCH ALL CARRIAGES ENTERING AND EXITING.
WHOEVER IS INSIDE, COME OUT!
WHO'S THERE?
REPORT YOUR NAME!
...
THE PERSON YOU'RE LOOKING FOR... ISN'T HERE.
FLAP

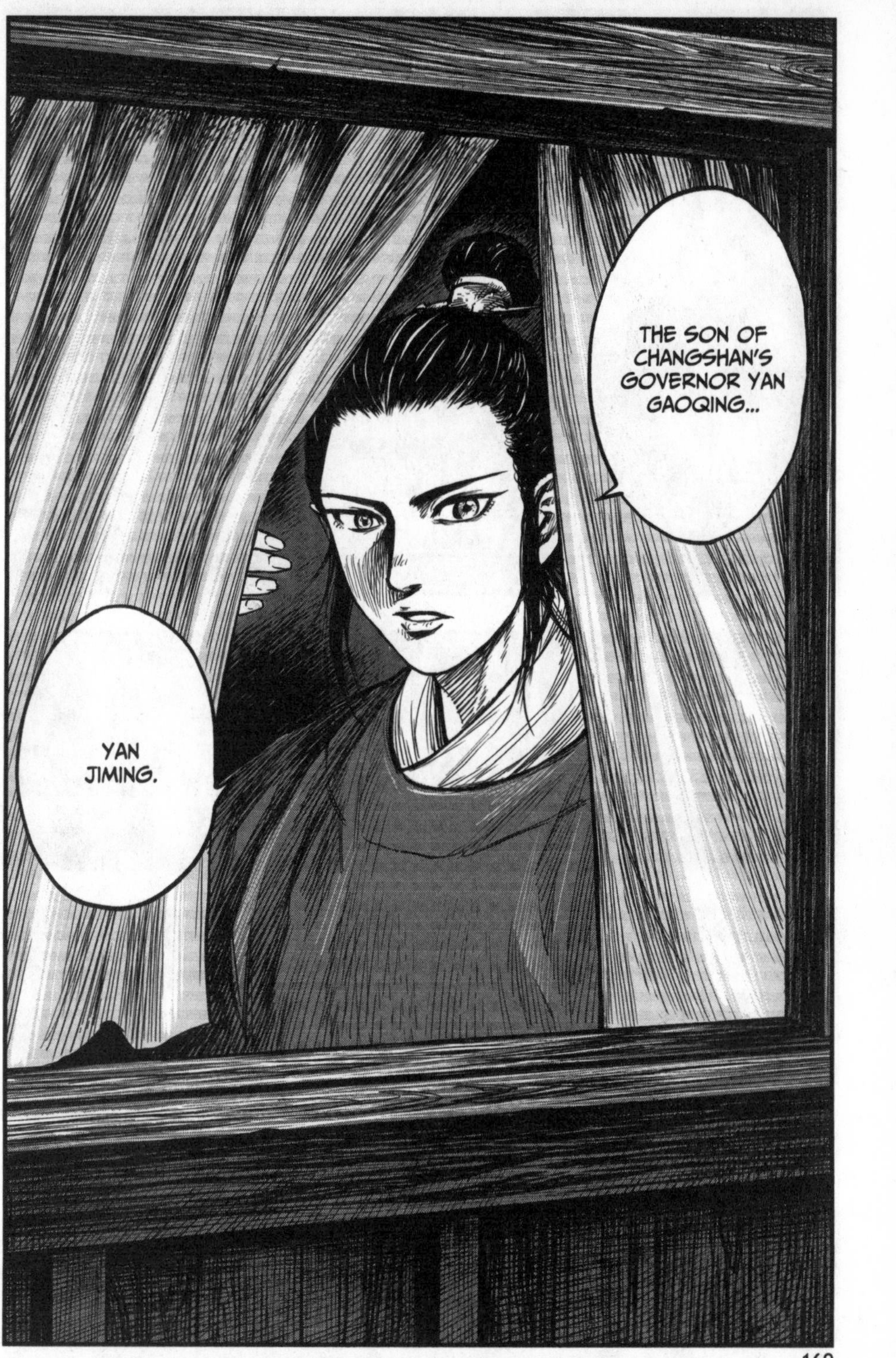
THE SON OF CHANGSHAN'S GOVERNOR YAN GAOQING...
YAN JIMING.

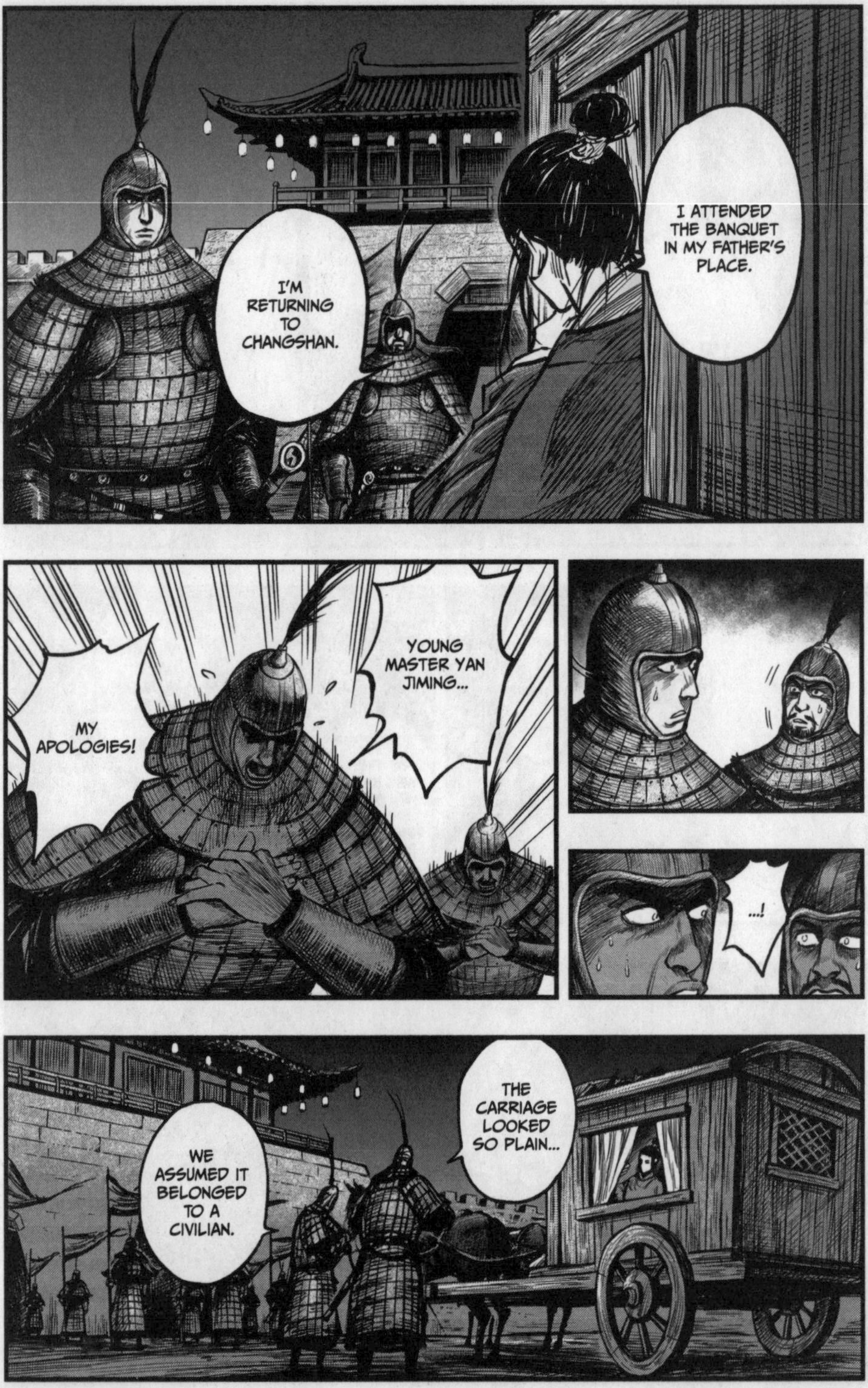
I ATTENDED THE BANQUET IN MY FATHER'S PLACE.
I'M RETURNING TO CHANGSHAN.
...!
YOUNG MASTER YAN JIMING...
MY APOLOGIES!
THE CARRIAGE LOOKED SO PLAIN...
WE ASSUMED IT BELONGED TO A CIVILIAN.

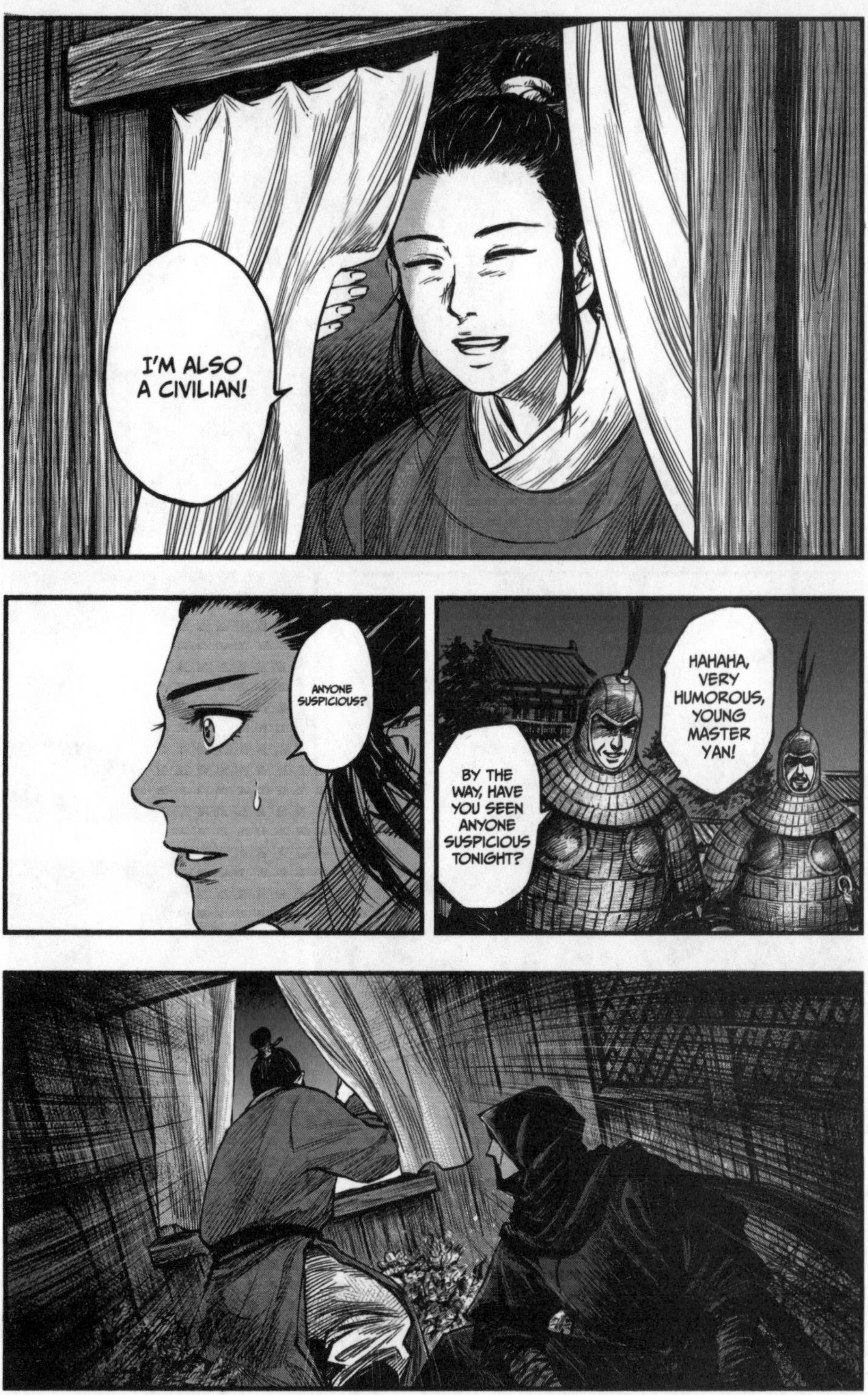
I'M ALSO A CIVILIAN!
HAHAHA, VERY HUMOROUS, YOUNG MASTER YAN!
BY THE WAY, HAVE YOU SEEN ANYONE SUSPICIOUS TONIGHT?
ANYONE SUSPICIOUS?

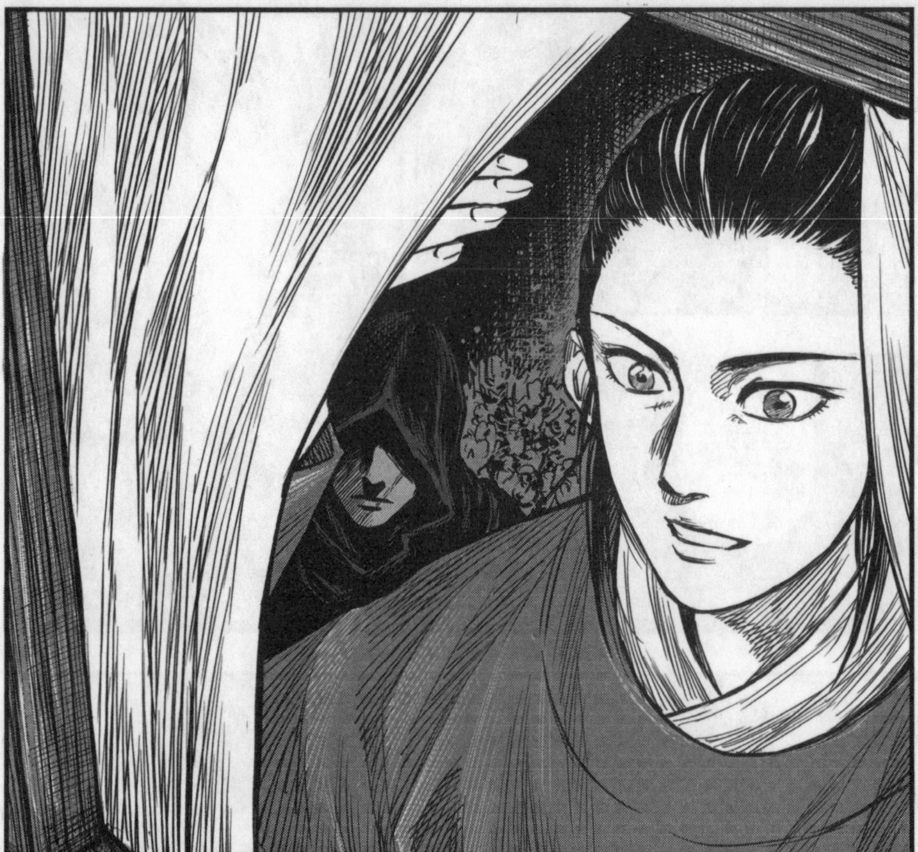

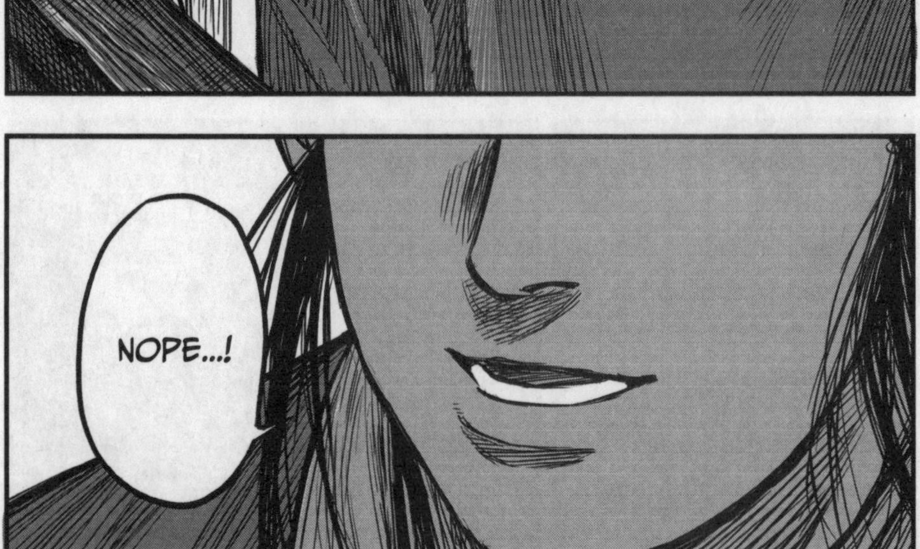
NOPE...!

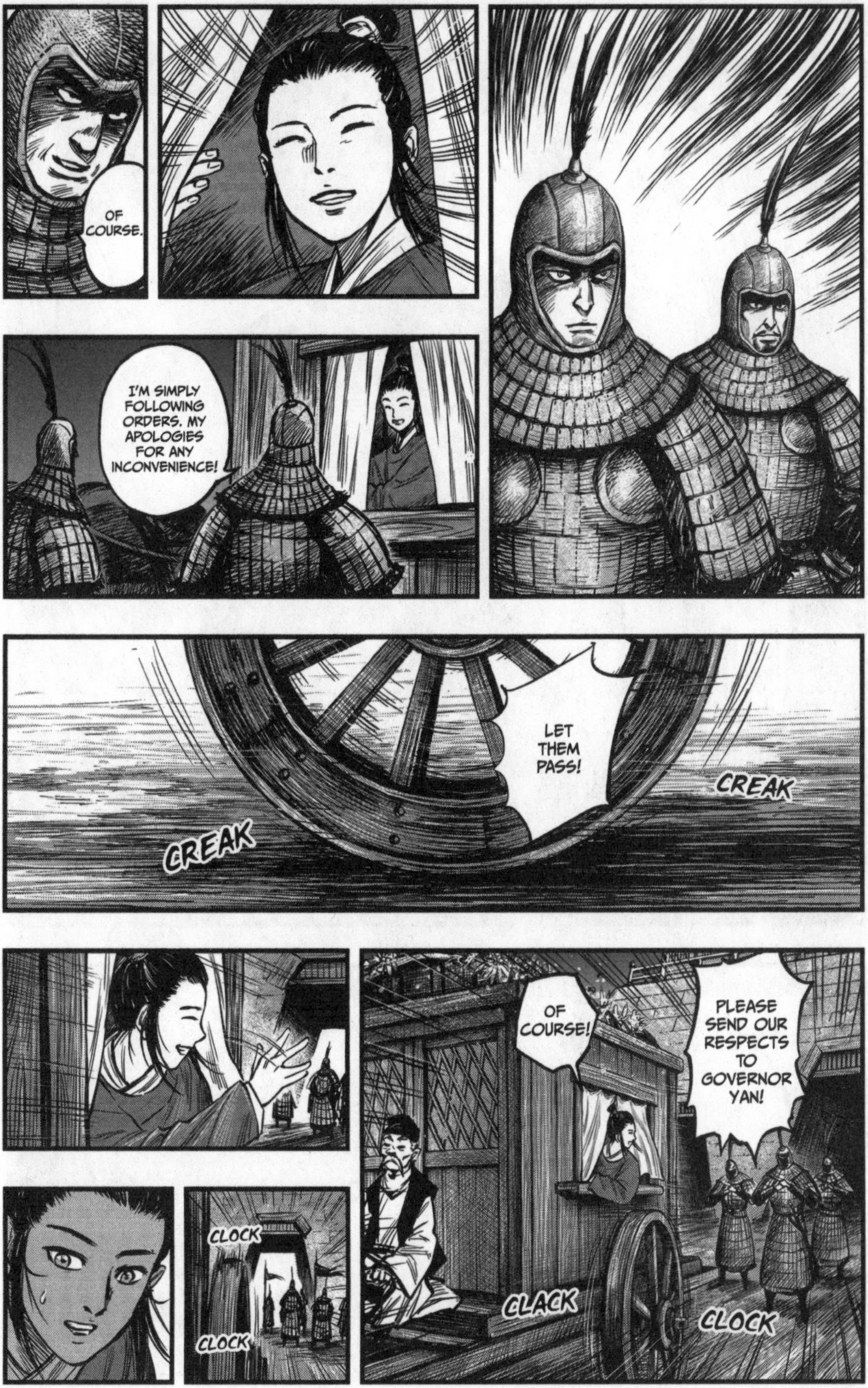
OF COURSE.
I'M SIMPLY FOLLOWING ORDERS. MY APOLOGIES FOR ANY INCONVENIENCE!
LET THEM PASS!
CREAK
CREAK
PLEASE SEND OUR RESPECTS TO GOVERNOR YAN!
OF COURSE!
CLOCK
CLACK
CLOCK
CLOCK

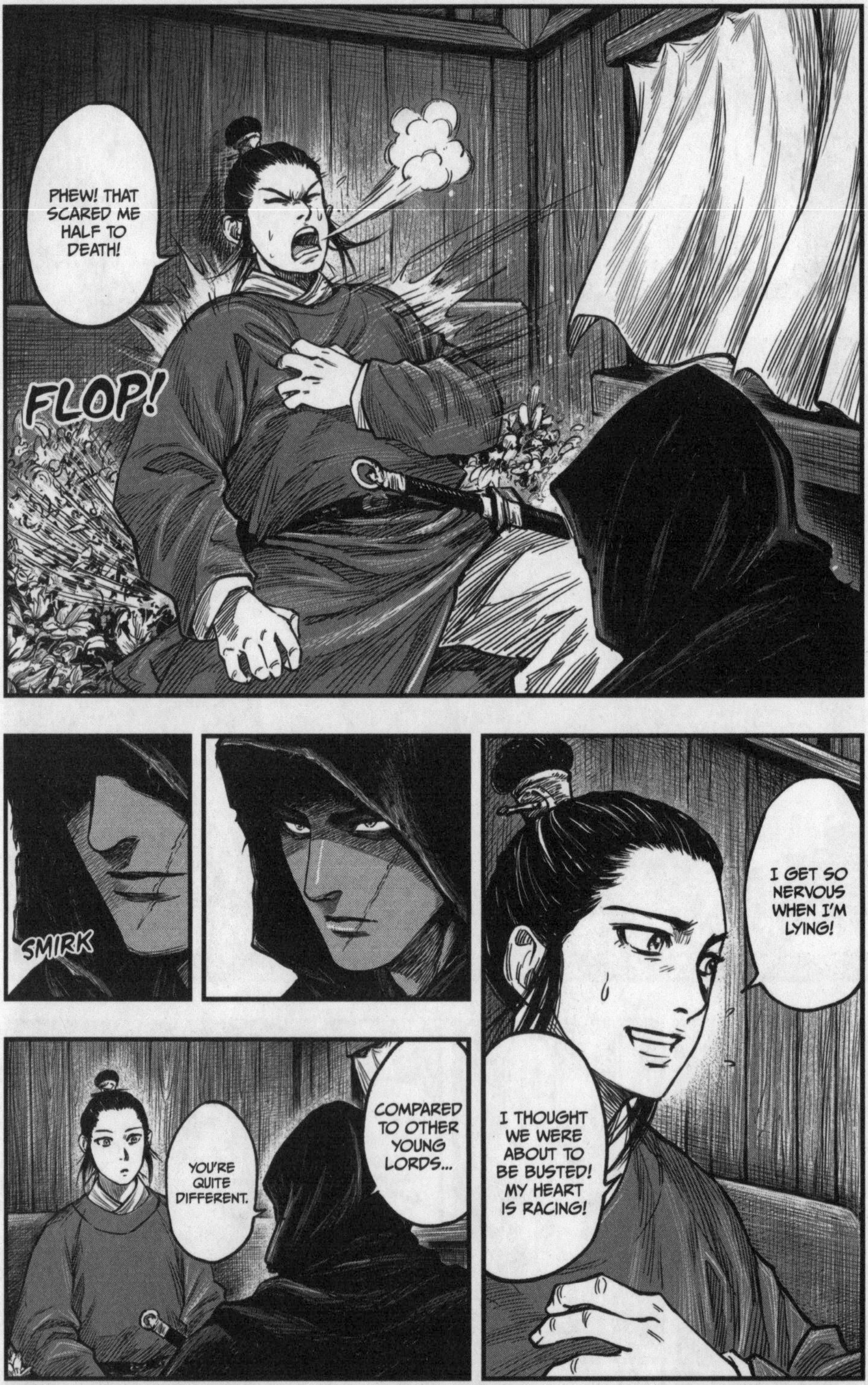
PHEW! THAT SCARED ME HALF TO DEATH!
FLOP!
I GET SO NERVOUS WHEN I'M LYING!
I THOUGHT WE WERE ABOUT TO BE BUSTED! MY HEART IS RACING!
SMIRK
COMPARED TO OTHER YOUNG LORDS...
YOU'RE QUITE DIFFERENT.

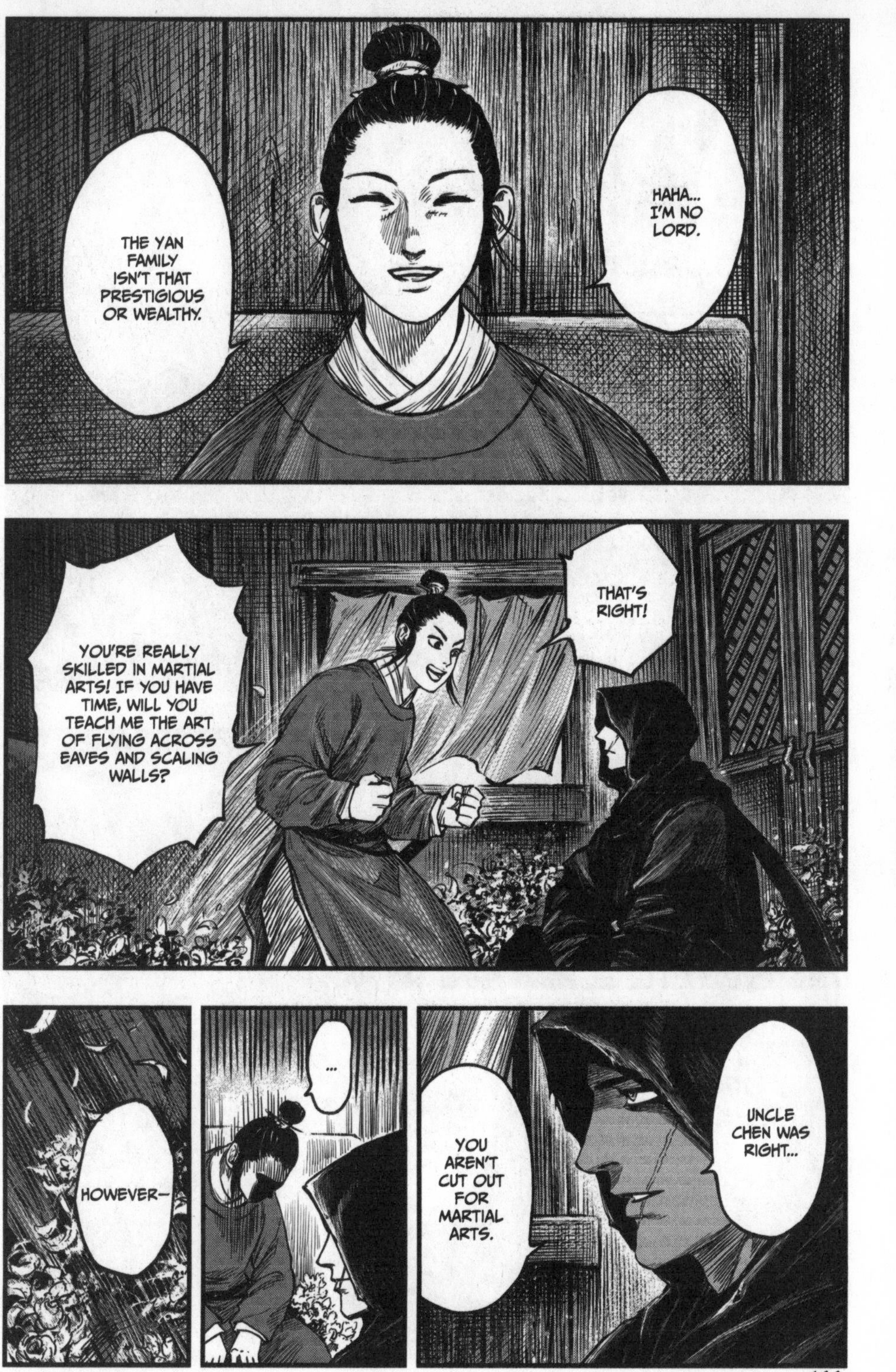
HAHA... I'M NO LORD.
THE YAN FAMILY ISN'T THAT PRESTIGIOUS OR WEALTHY.
THAT'S RIGHT!
YOU'RE REALLY SKILLED IN MARTIAL ARTS! IF YOU HAVE TIME, WILL YOU TEACH ME THE ART OF FLYING ACROSS EAVES AND SCALING WALLS?
UNCLE CHEN WAS RIGHT...
YOU AREN'T CUT OUT FOR MARTIAL ARTS.
...
HOWEVER–

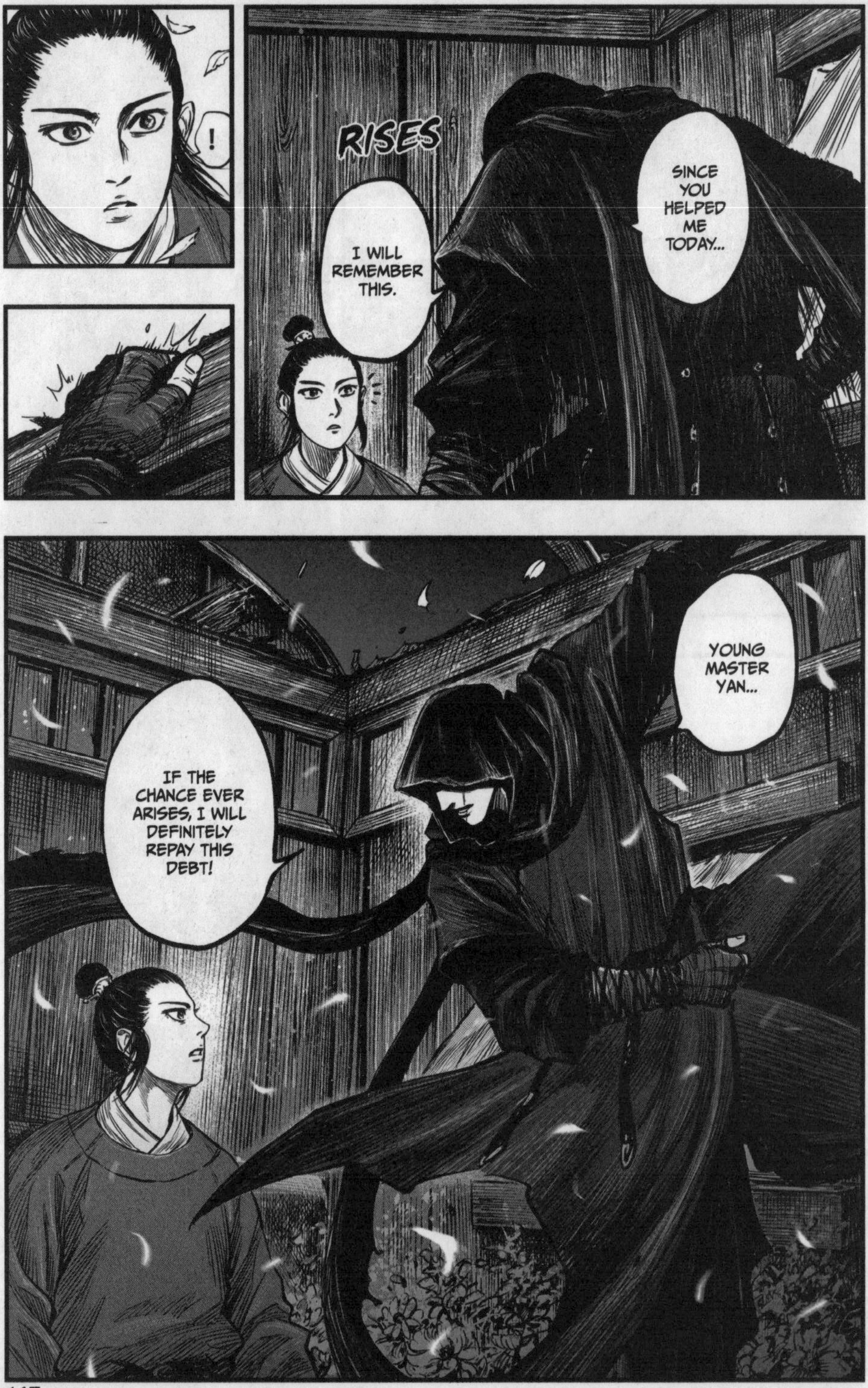
RISES
SINCE YOU HELPED ME TODAY...
I WILL REMEMBER THIS.
!
YOUNG MASTER YAN...
IF THE CHANCE EVER ARISES, I WILL DEFINITELY REPAY THIS DEBT!

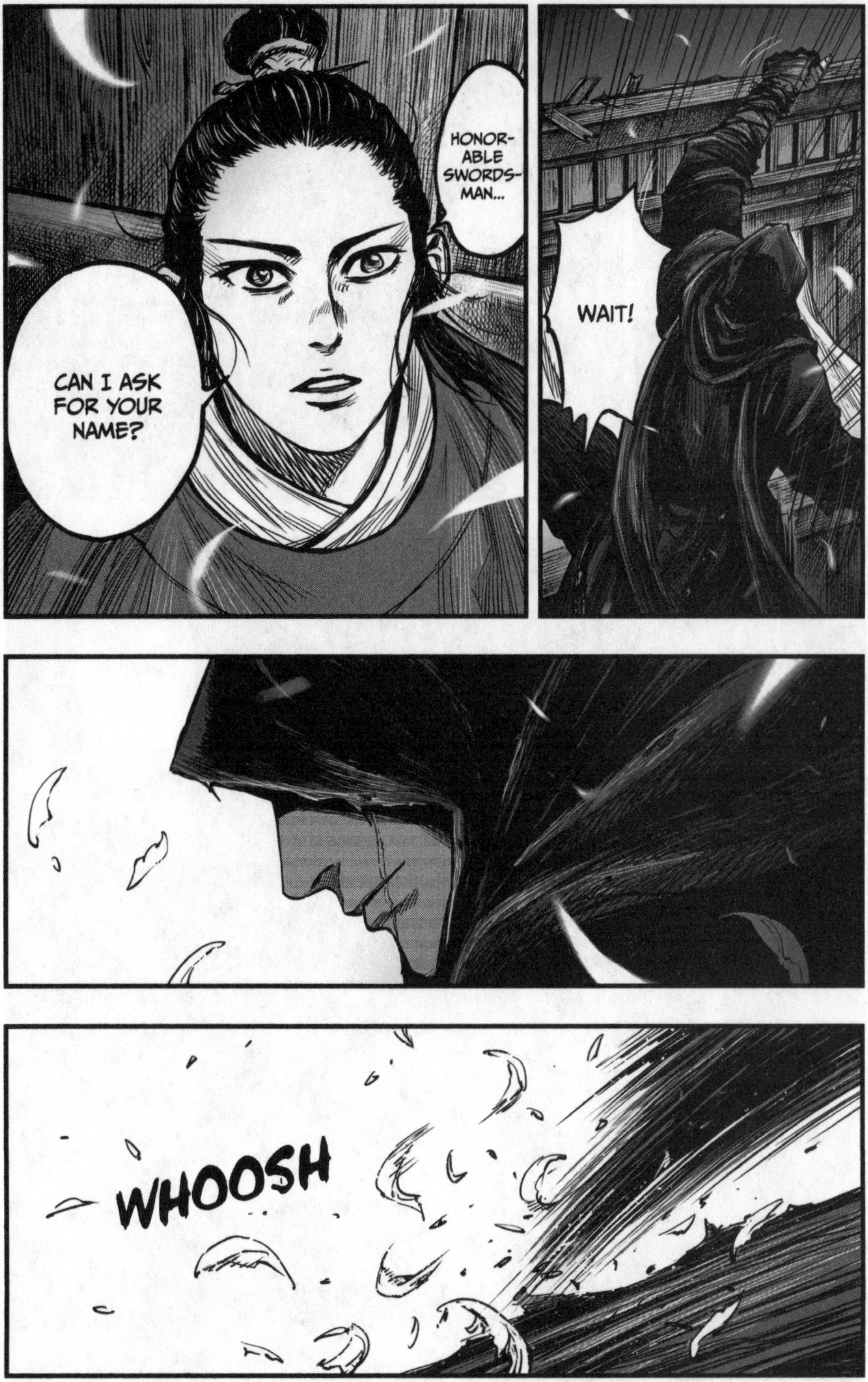
WAIT!
HONORABLE-ABLE SWORDS-MAN...
CAN I ASK FOR YOUR NAME?
WHOOSH

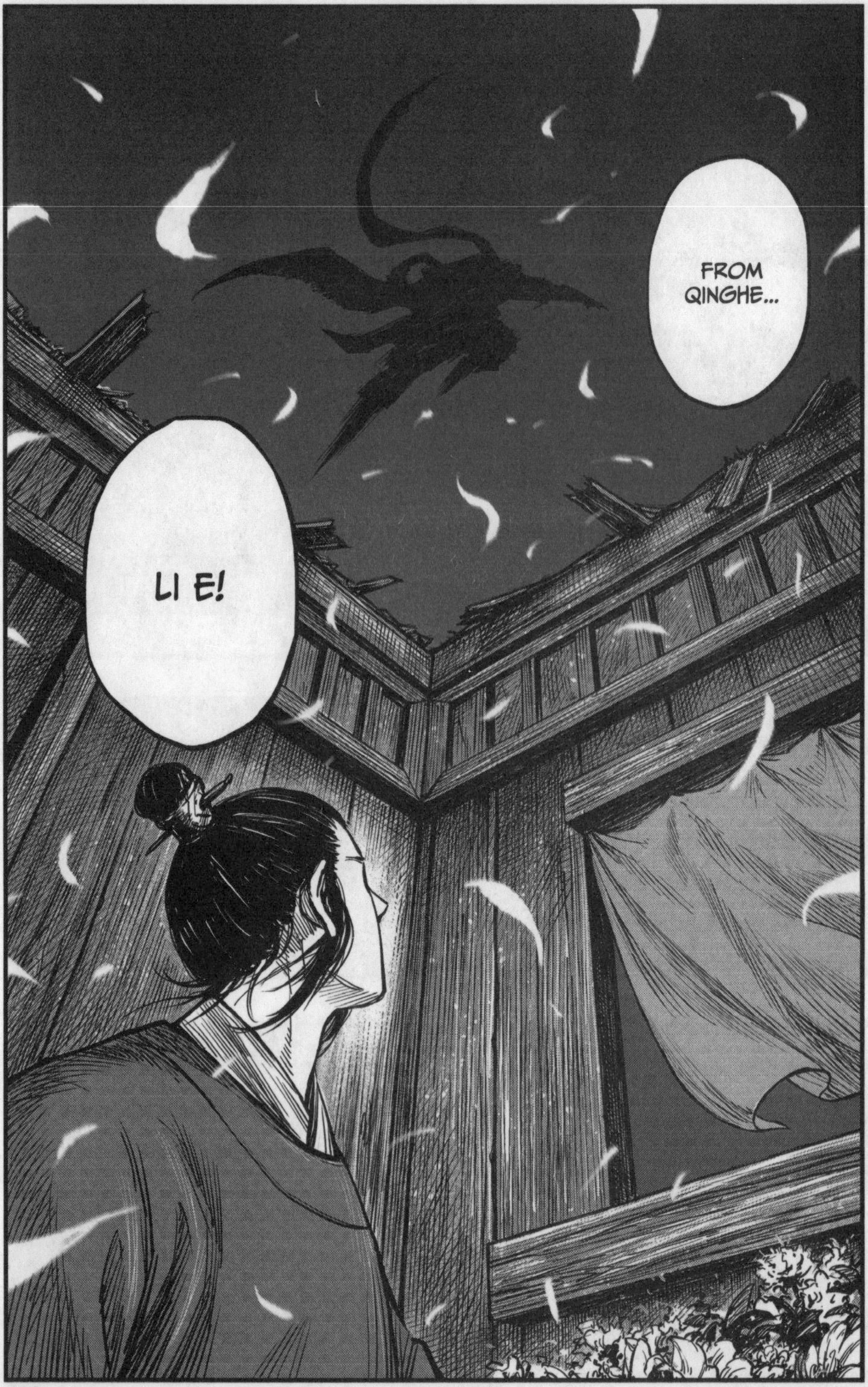
FROM QINGHE...
LI E!

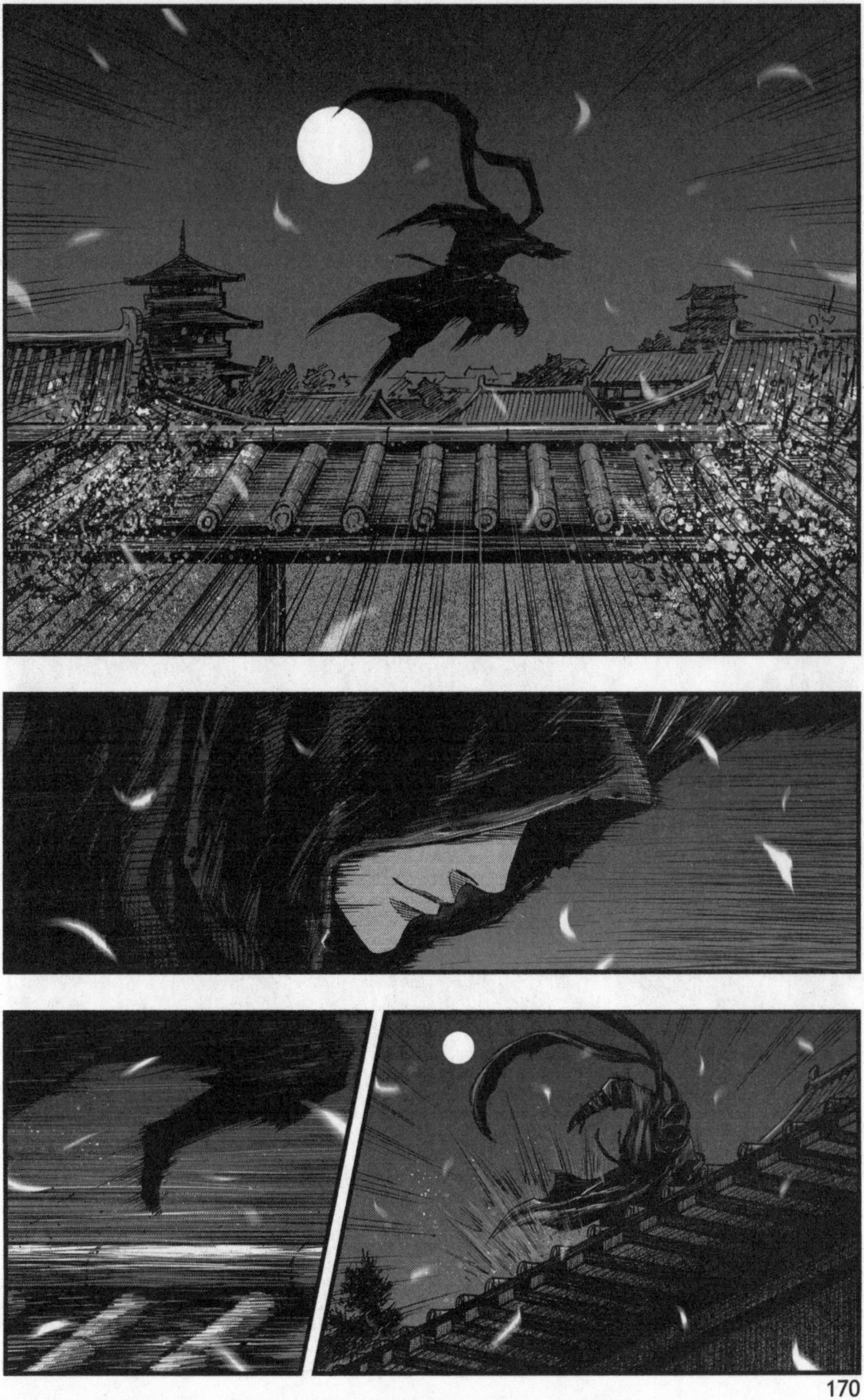

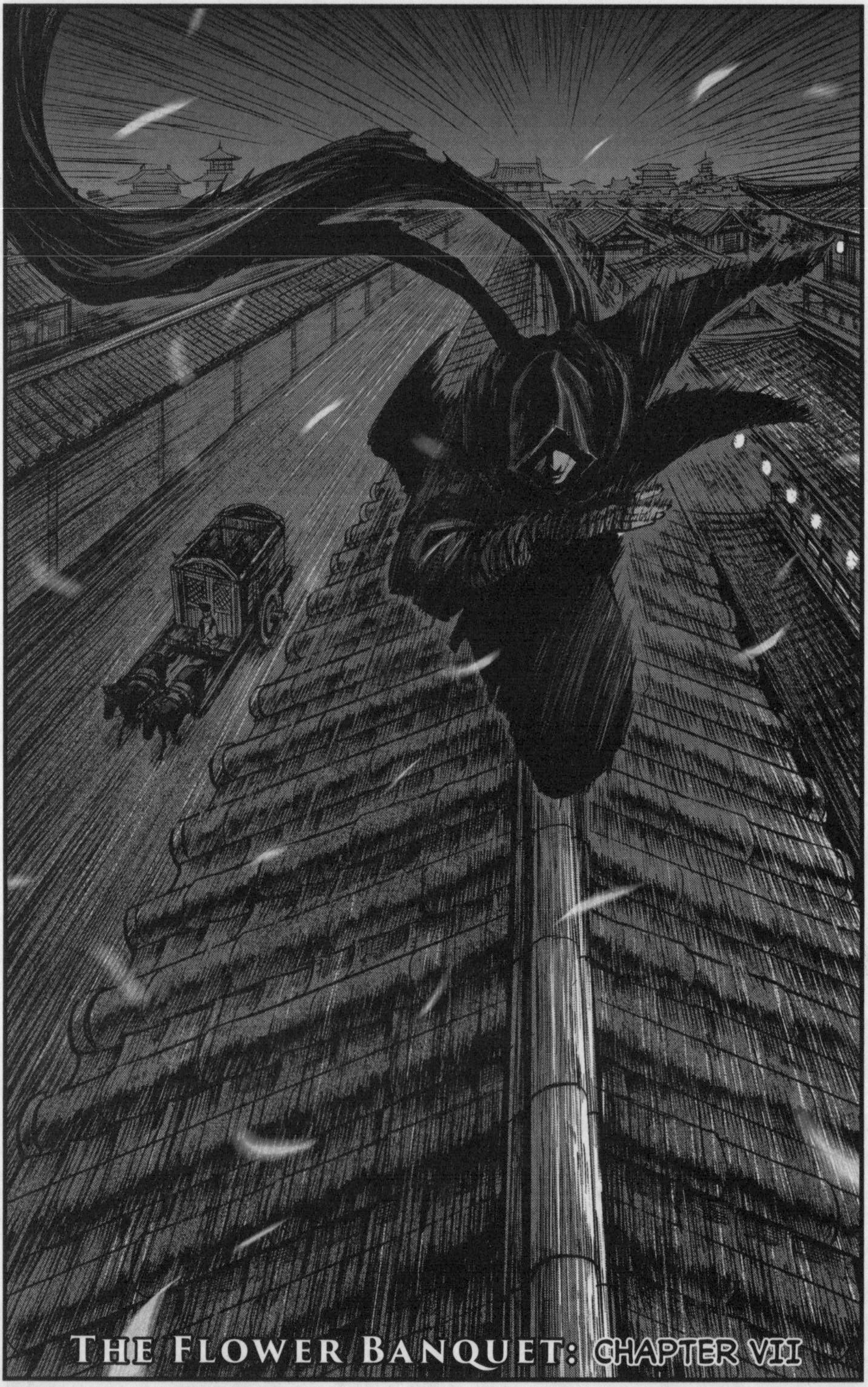
THE FLOWER BANQUET: CHAPTER VII

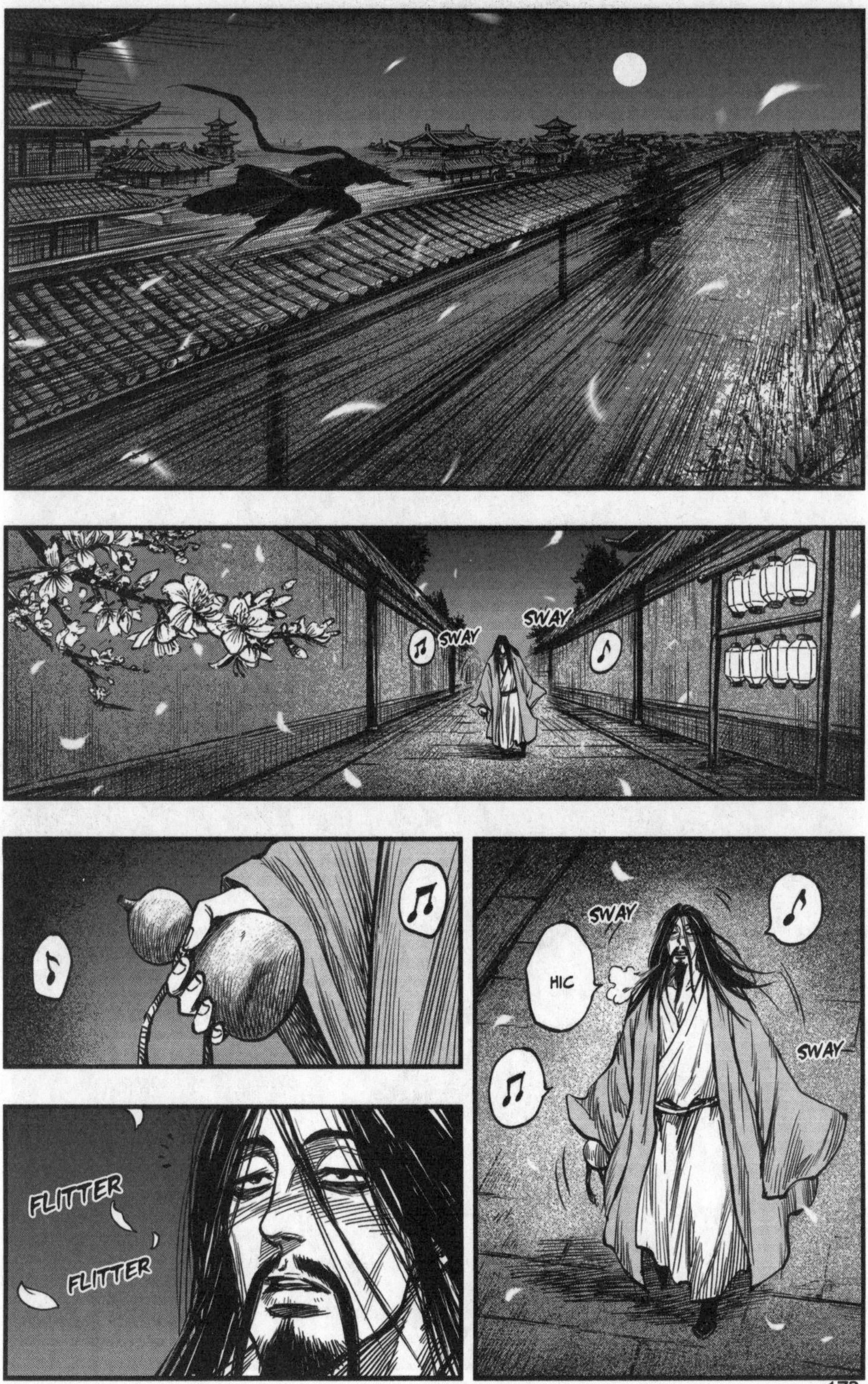
SWAY
SWAY
SWAY
HIC
SWAY
FLITTER
FLITTER

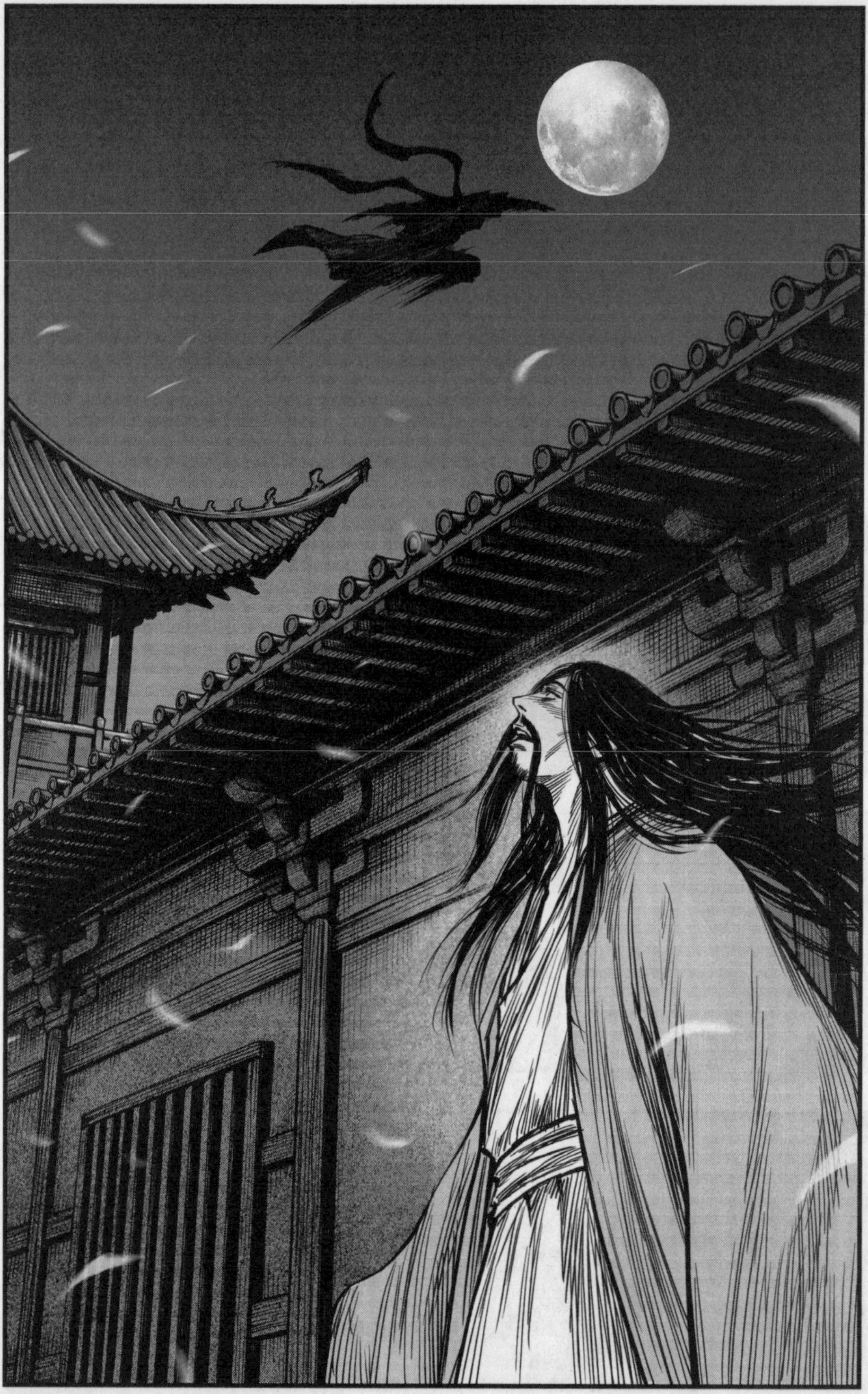

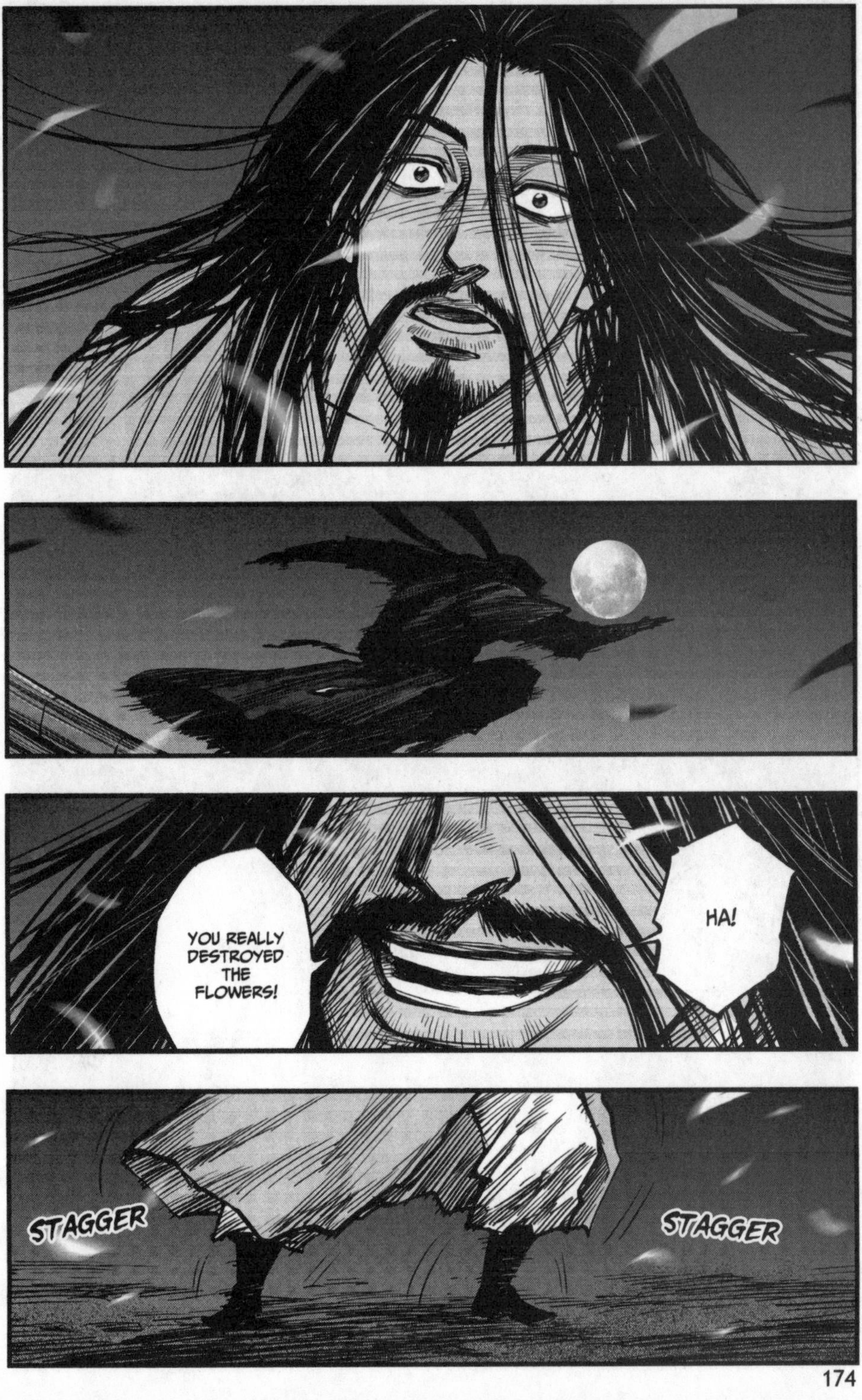
HA!
YOU REALLY DESTROYED THE FLOWERS!
STAGGER
STAGGER

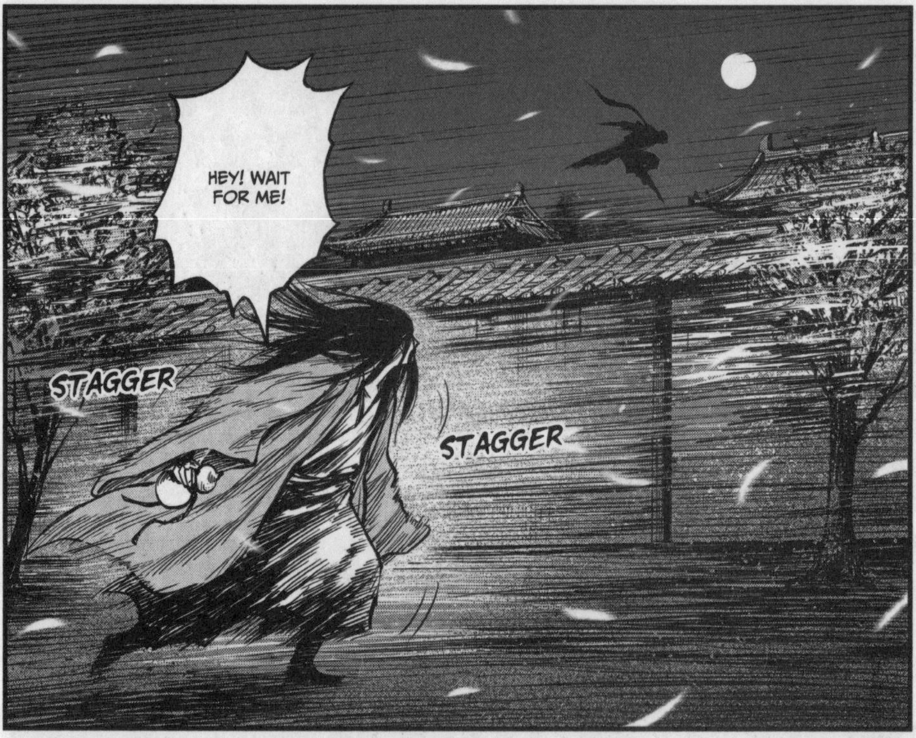
HEY! WAIT FOR ME!
STAGGER
STAGGER

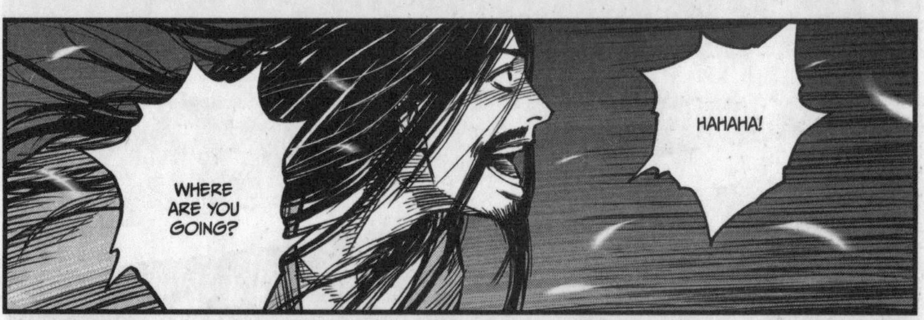
HAHAHA!
WHERE ARE YOU GOING?

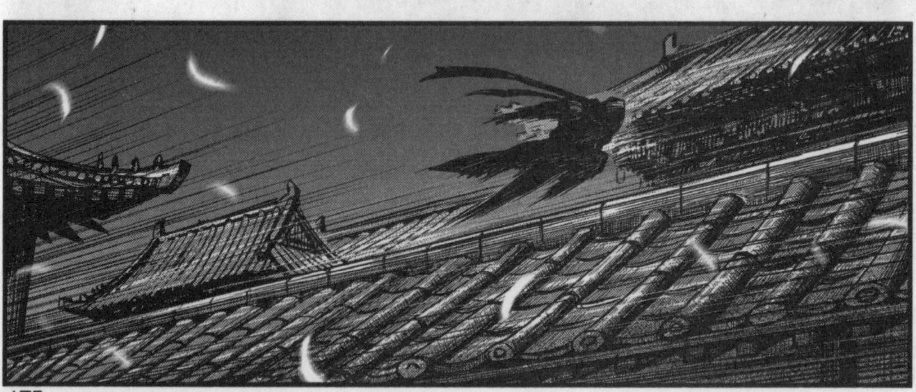

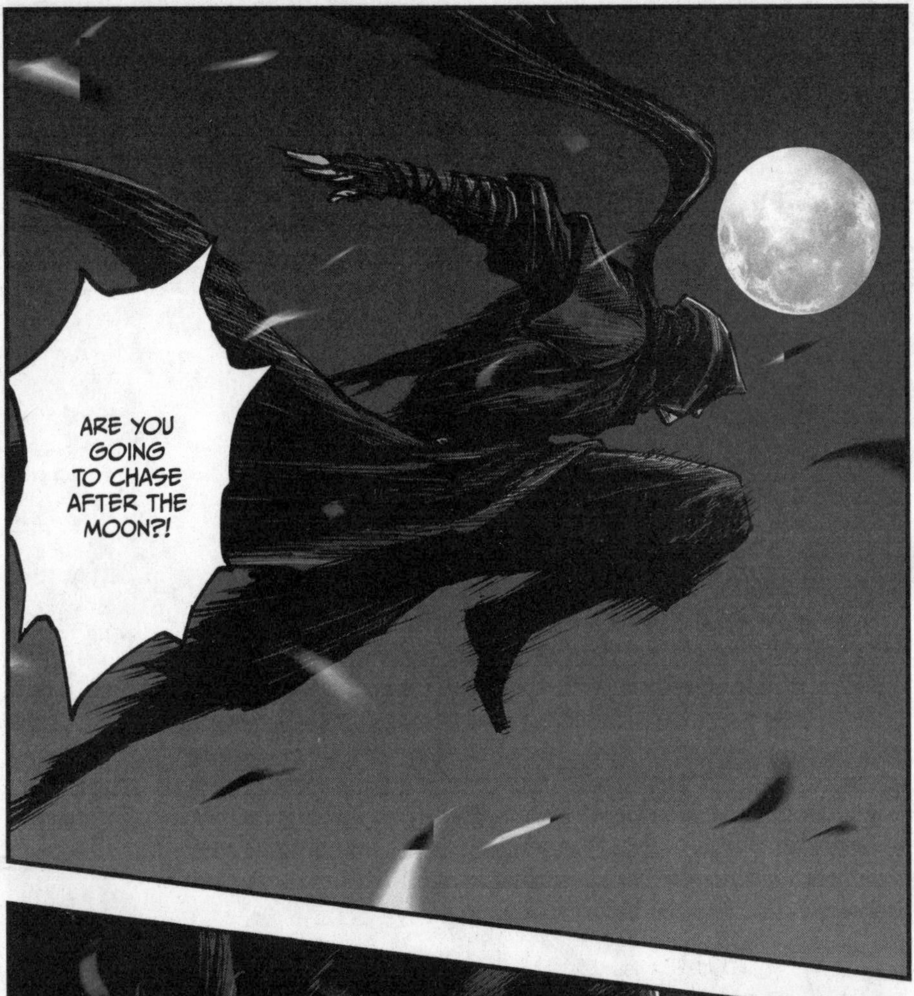
ARE YOU GOING TO CHASE AFTER THE MOON?!
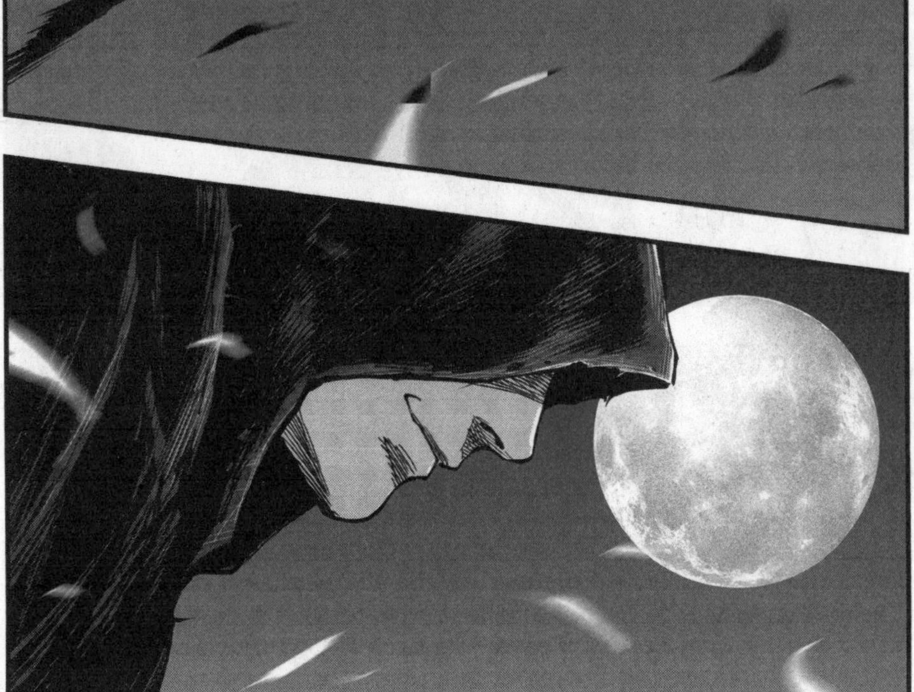

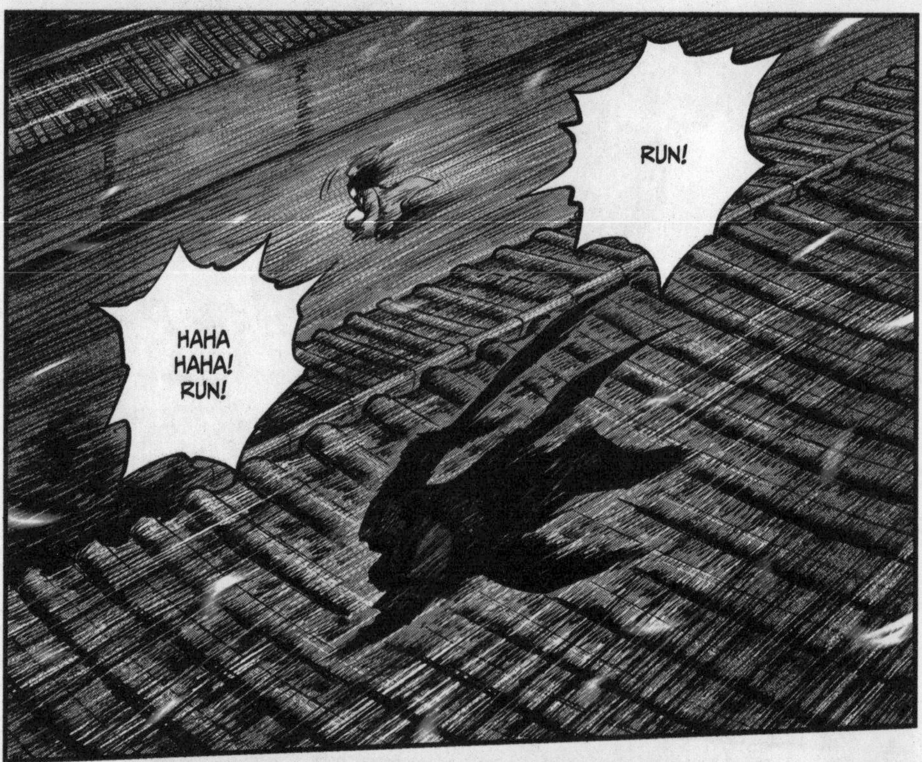
RUN!
HAHA HAHA! RUN!
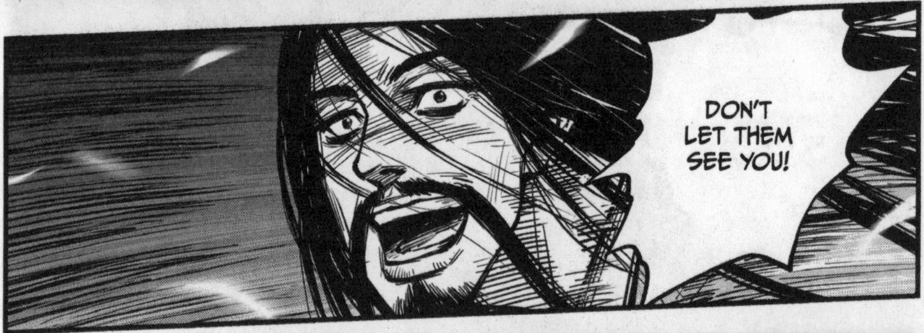
DON'T LET THEM SEE YOU!
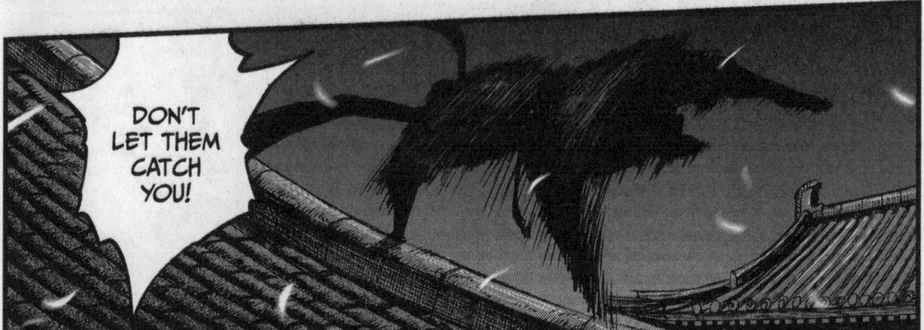
DON'T LET THEM CATCH YOU!

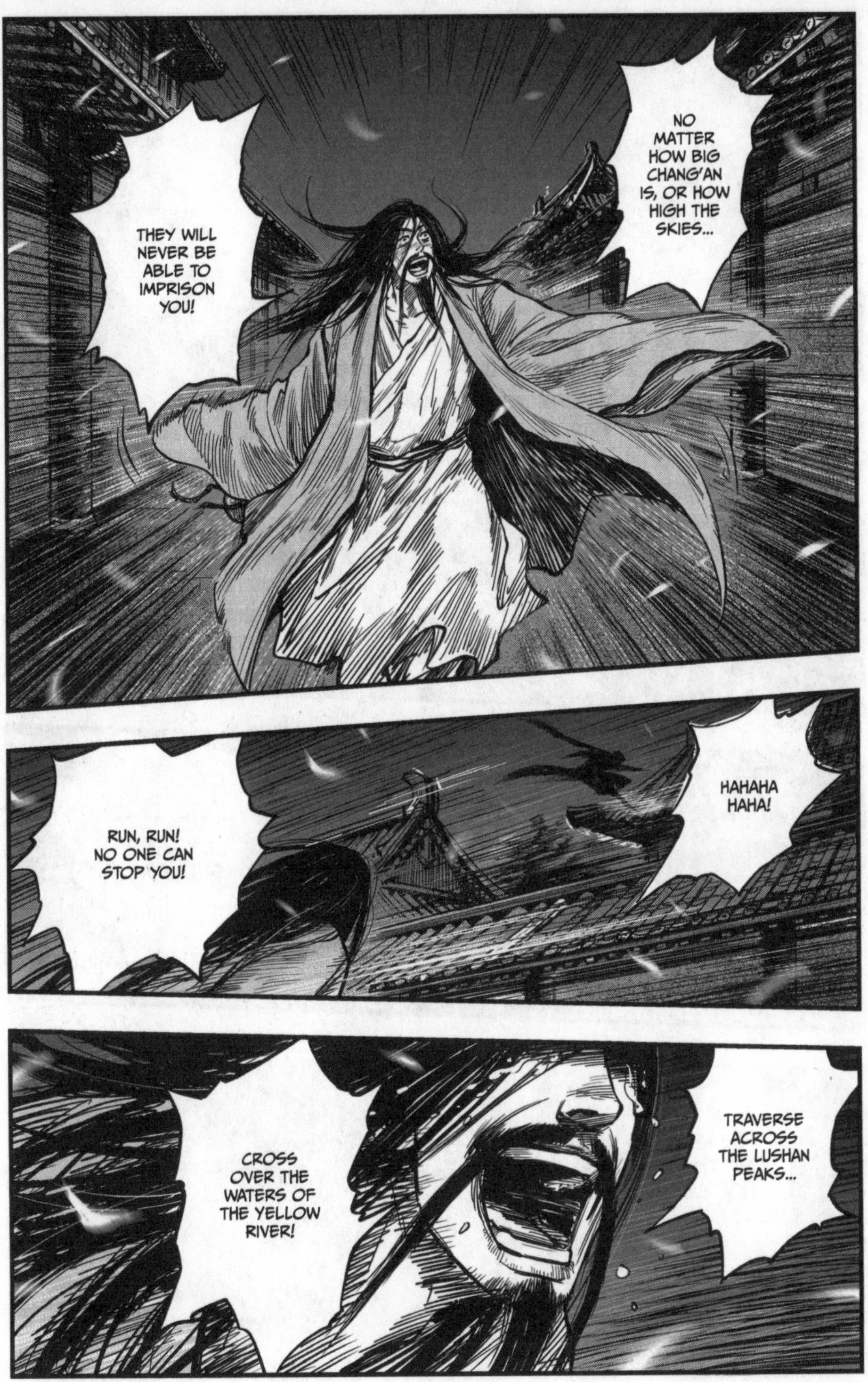
NO MATTER HOW BIG CHANG'AN IS, OR HOW HIGH THE SKIES...
THEY WILL NEVER BE ABLE TO IMPRISON YOU!
HAHAHA HAHA!
RUN, RUN! NO ONE CAN STOP YOU!
TRAVERSE ACROSS THE LUSHAN PEAKS...
CROSS OVER THE WATERS OF THE YELLOW RIVER!

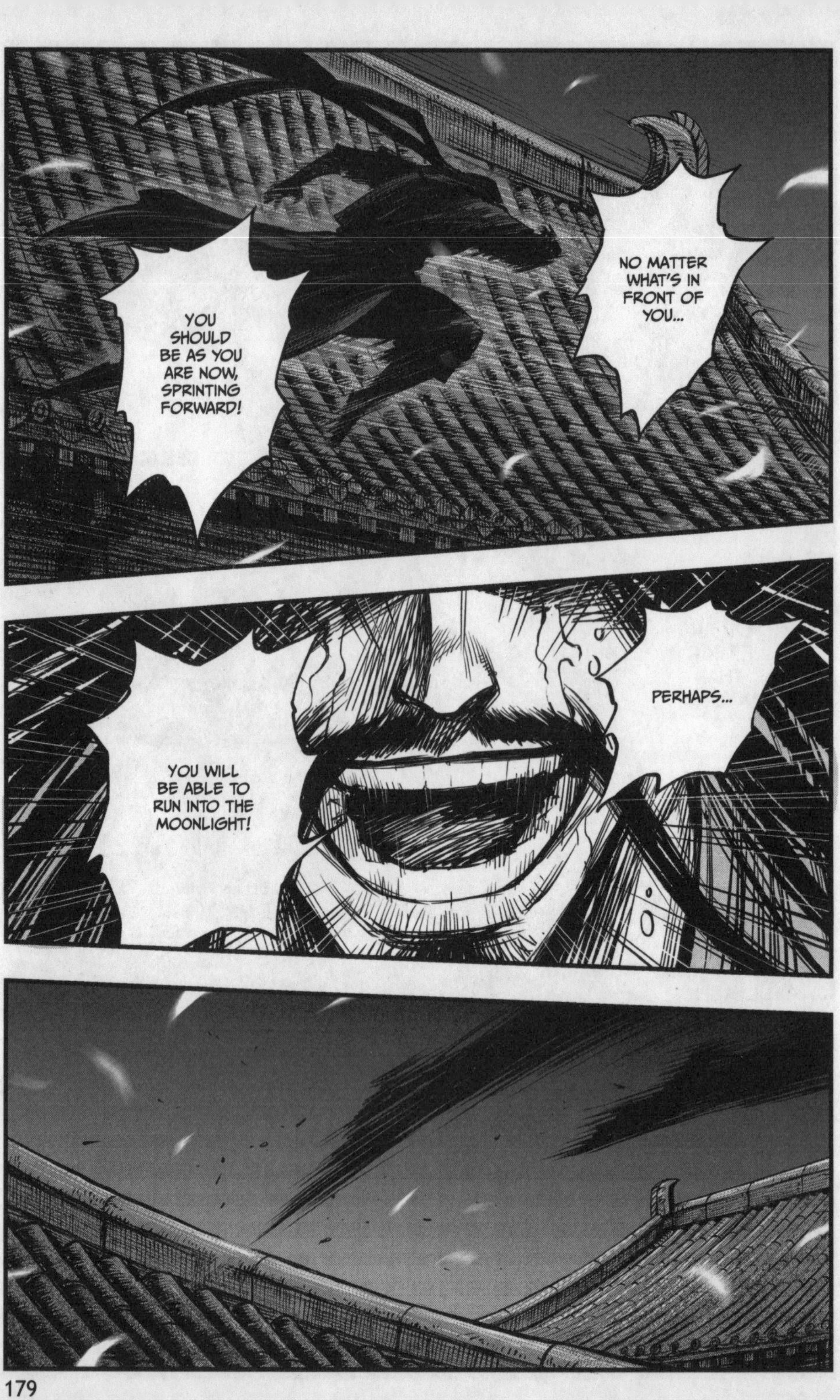
NO MATTER WHAT'S IN FRONT OF YOU...
YOU SHOULD BE AS YOU ARE NOW, SPRINTING FORWARD!
PERHAPS...
YOU WILL BE ABLE TO RUN INTO THE MOONLIGHT!

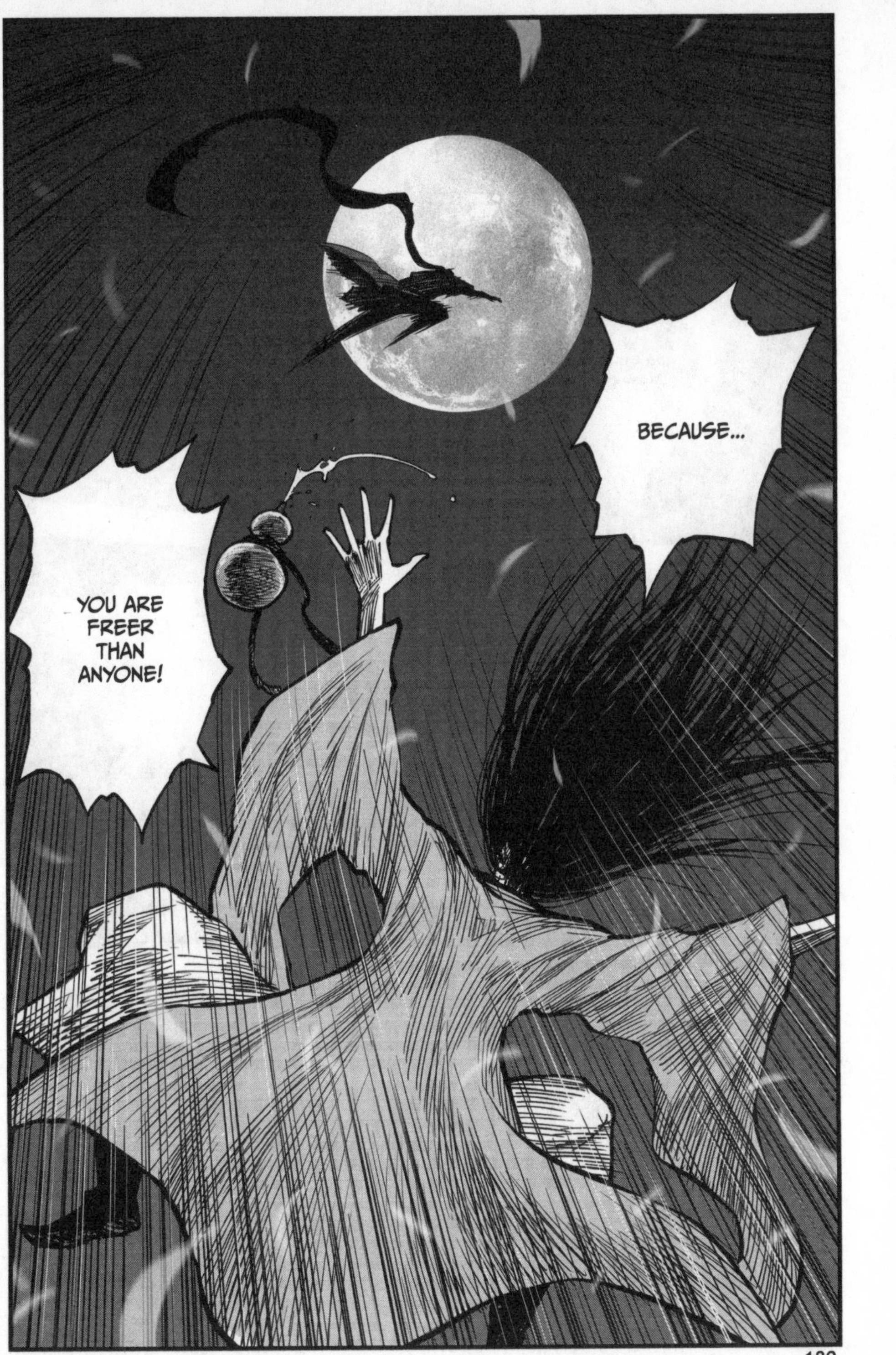
BECAUSE...
YOU ARE FREER THAN ANYONE!

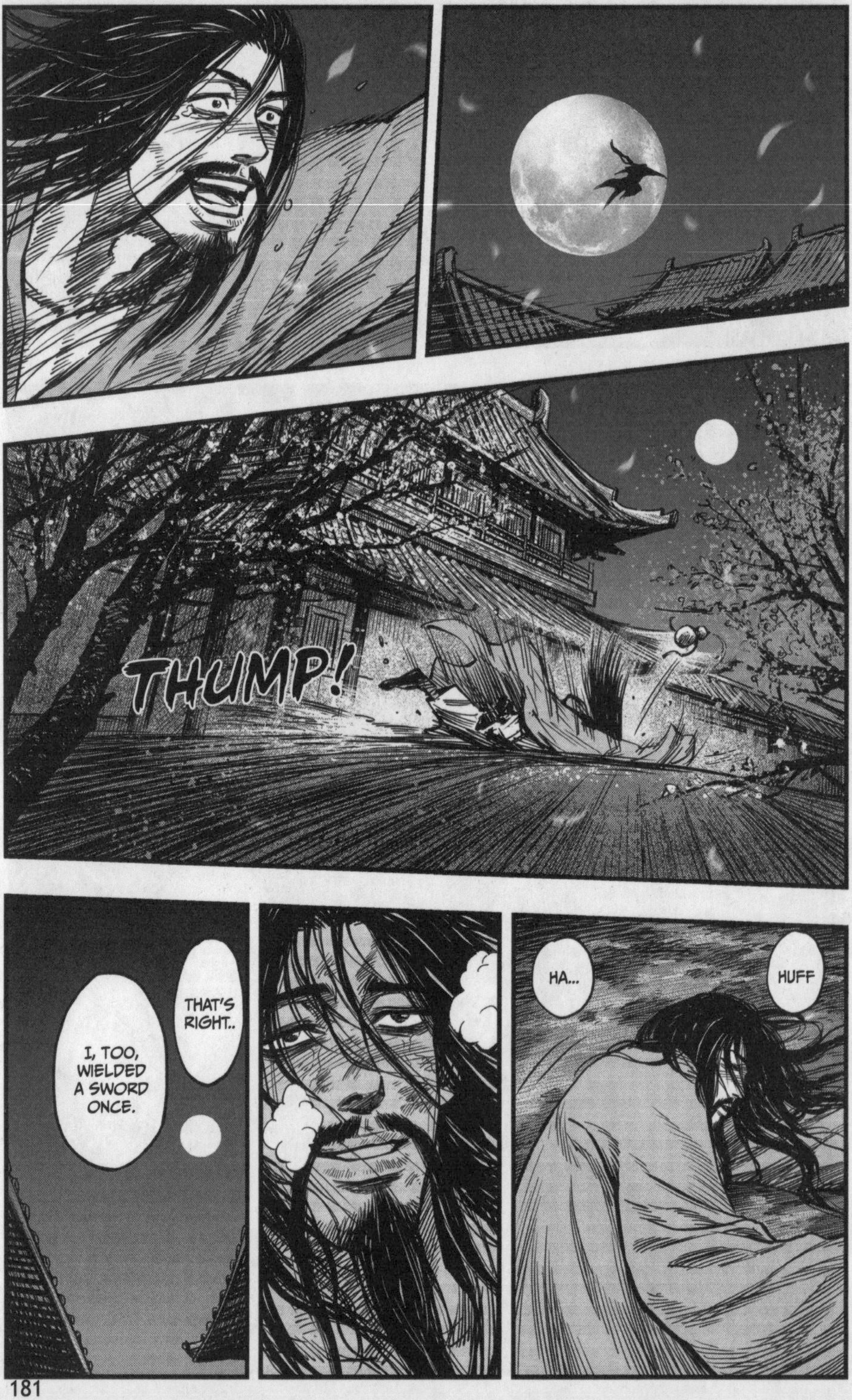
THUMP!
HUFF
HA...
THAT'S RIGHT..
I, TOO, WIELDED A SWORD ONCE.

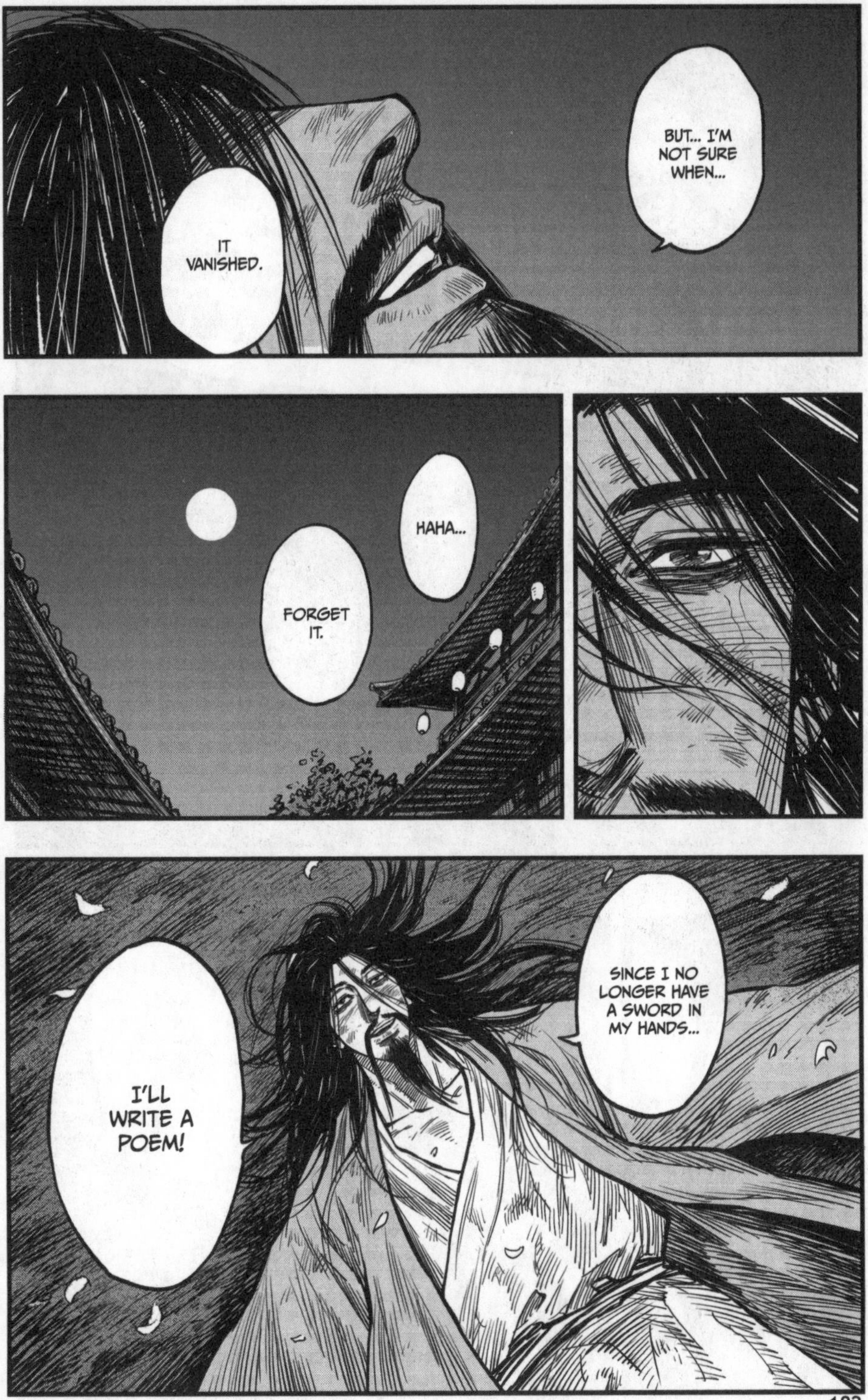
BUT... I'M NOT SURE WHEN...
IT VANISHED.
HAHA...
FORGET IT.
SINCE I NO LONGER HAVE A SWORD IN MY HANDS...
I'LL WRITE A POEM!

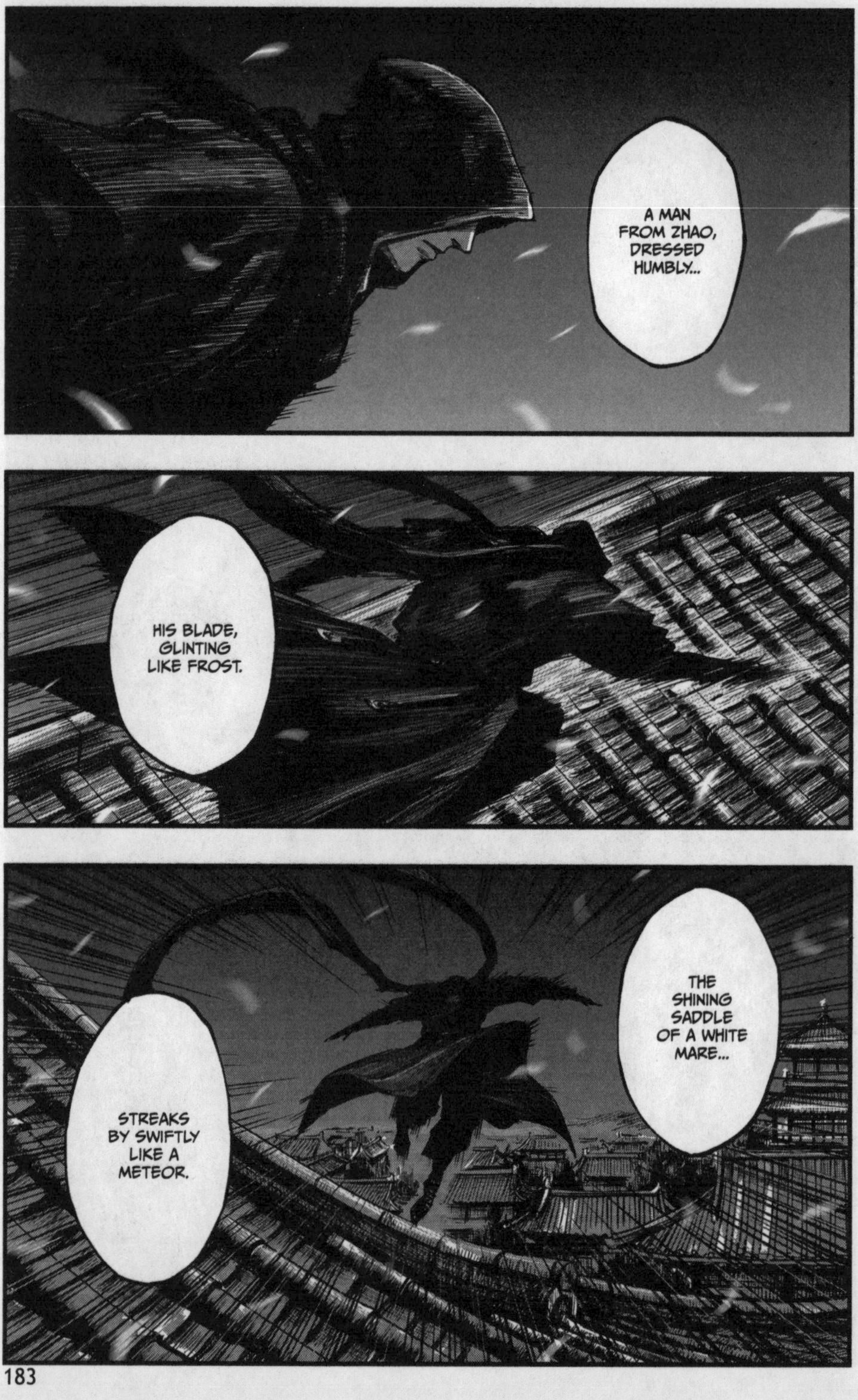
A MAN FROM ZHAO, DRESSED HUMBLY...
HIS BLADE, GLINTING LIKE FROST.
THE SHINING SADDLE OF A WHITE MARE...
STREAKS BY SWIFTLY LIKE A METEOR.

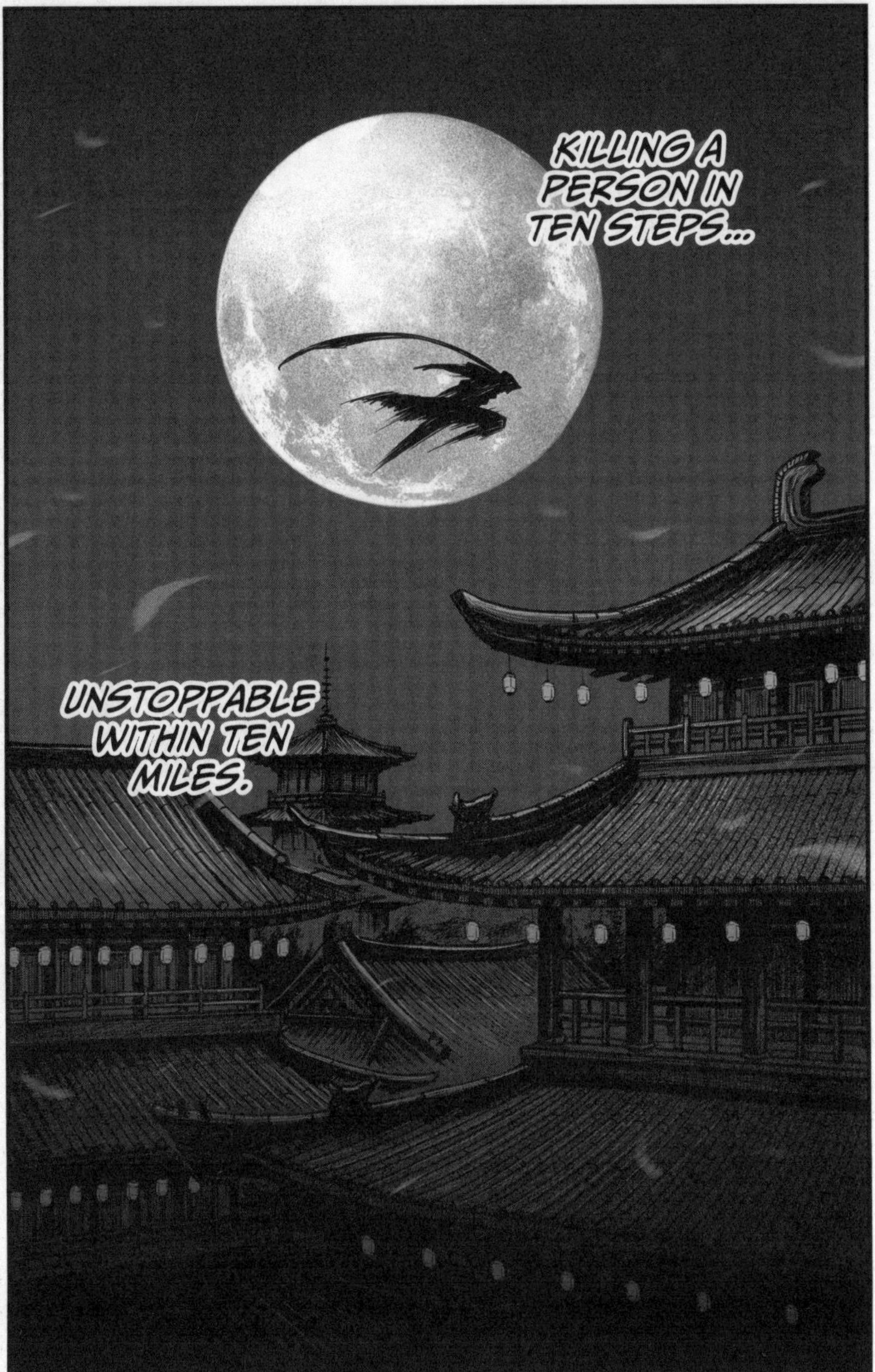
KILLING A PERSON IN TEN STEPS...
UNSTOPPABLE WITHIN TEN MILES.

HE DEPARTS ONCE THE DEED IS DONE, LEAVING BEHIND NO TRACES OR CARE FOR FAME.

— "ODE TO GALLANTRY" BY LI BAI

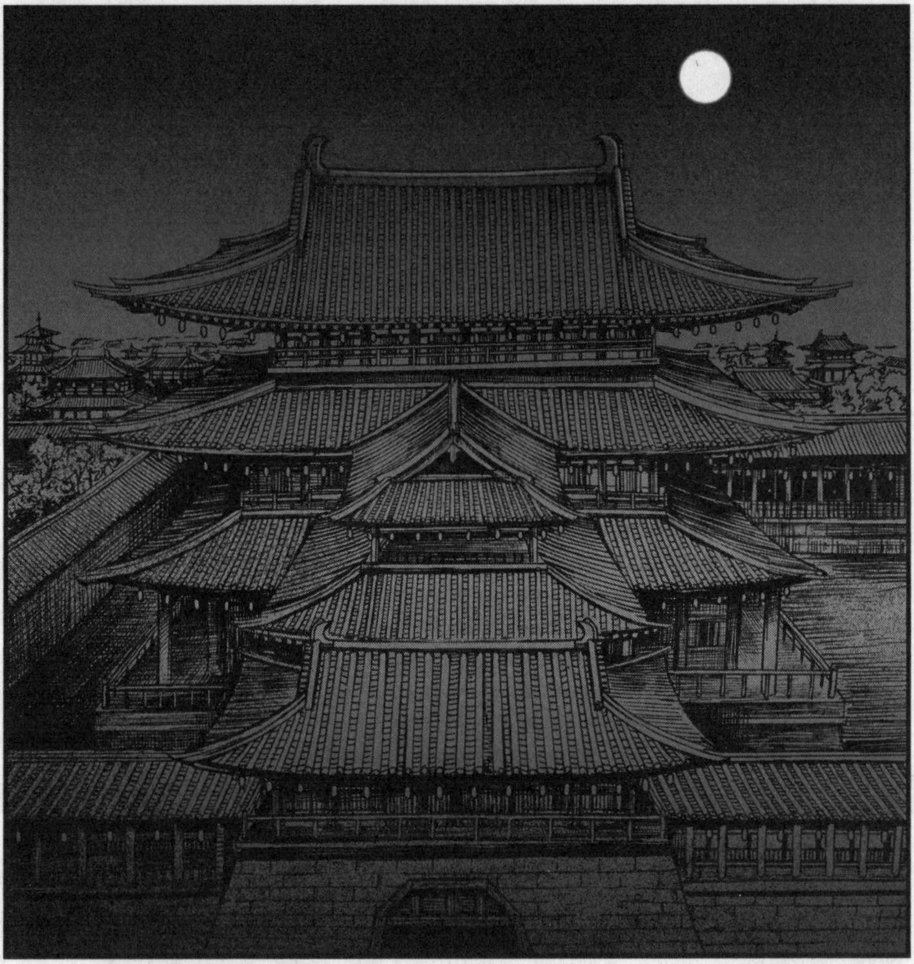
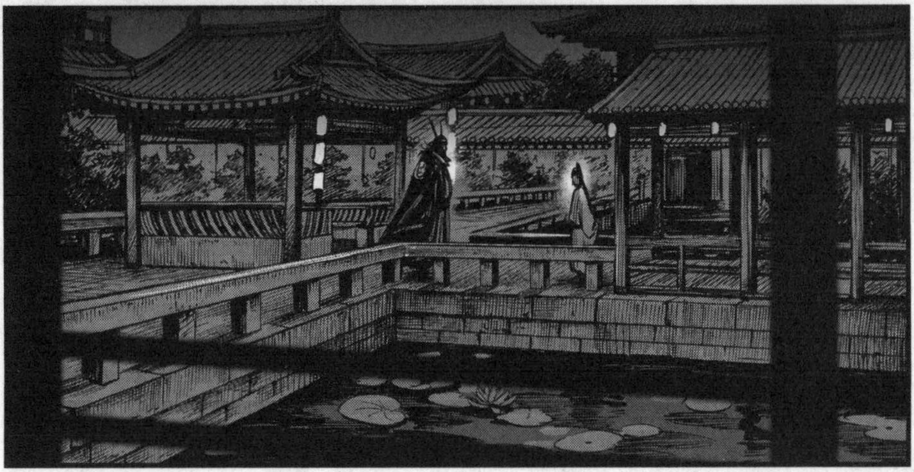

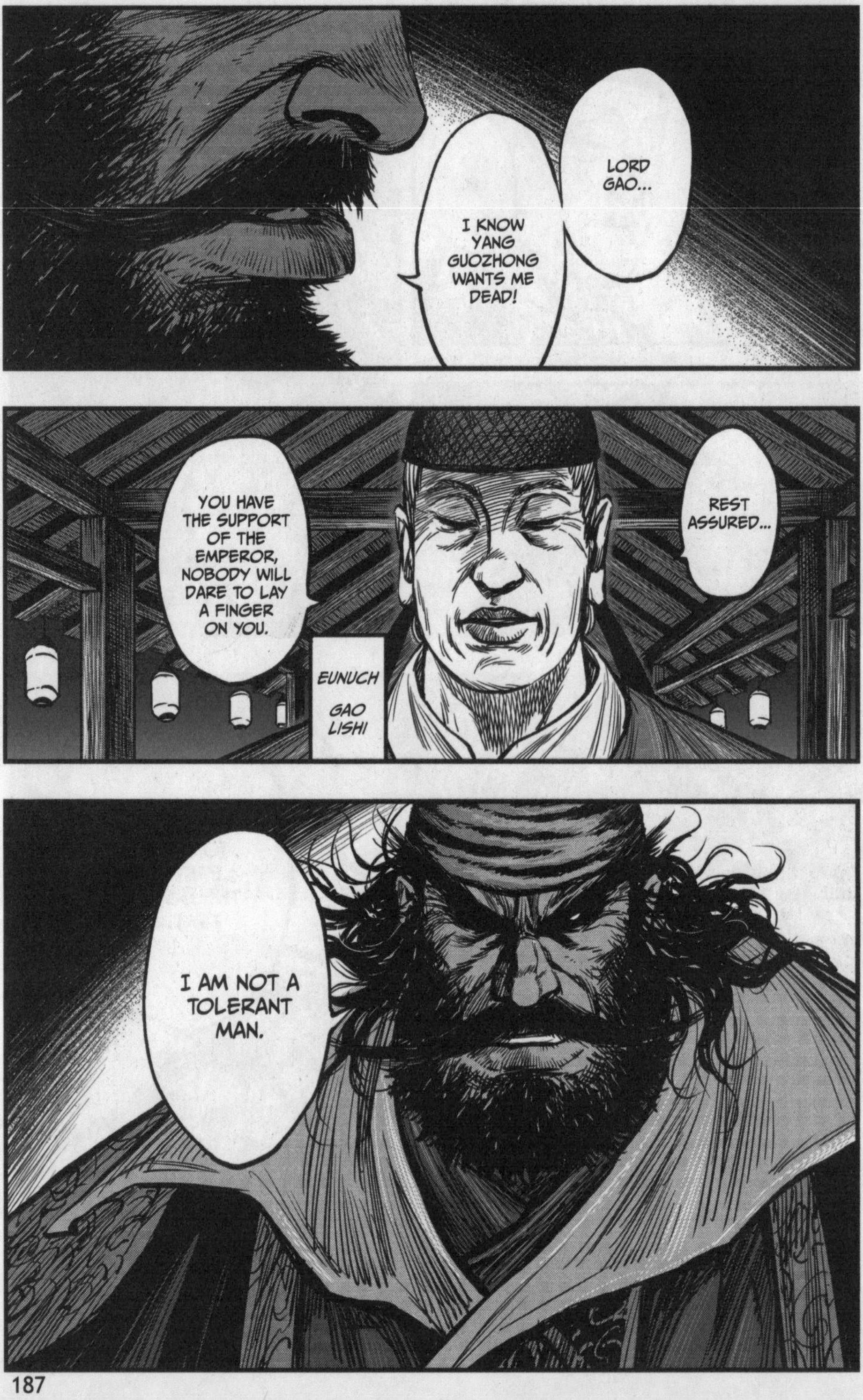
LORD GAO...
I KNOW YANG GUOZHONG WANTS ME DEAD!
REST ASSURED...
YOU HAVE THE SUPPORT OF THE EMPEROR, NOBODY WILL DARE TO LAY A FINGER ON YOU.
EUNUCH GAO LISHI
I AM NOT A TOLERANT MAN.

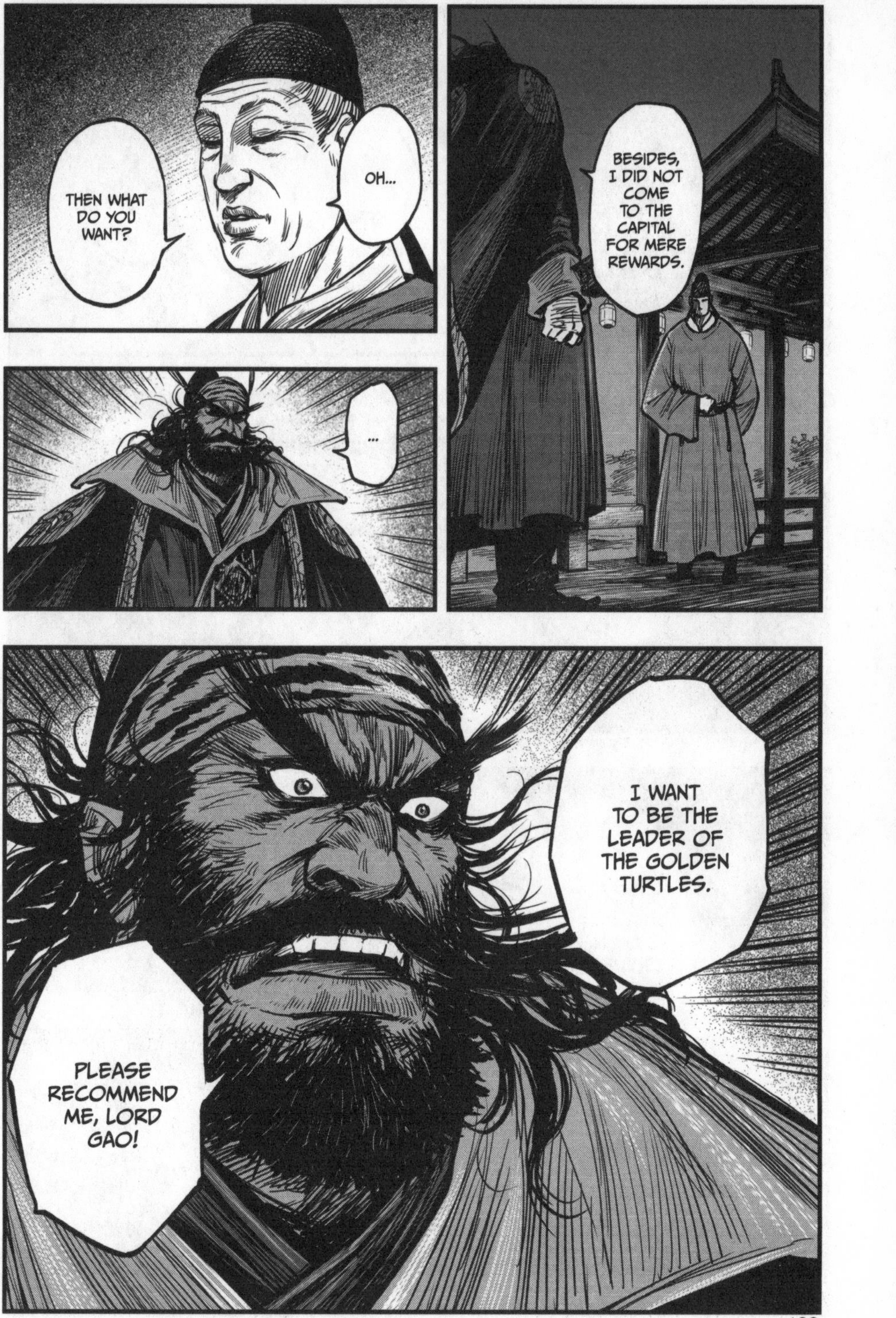
BESIDES, I DID NOT COME TO THE CAPITAL FOR MERE REWARDS.
OH...
THEN WHAT DO YOU WANT?
...
I WANT TO BE THE LEADER OF THE GOLDEN TURTLES.
PLEASE RECOMMEND ME, LORD GAO!

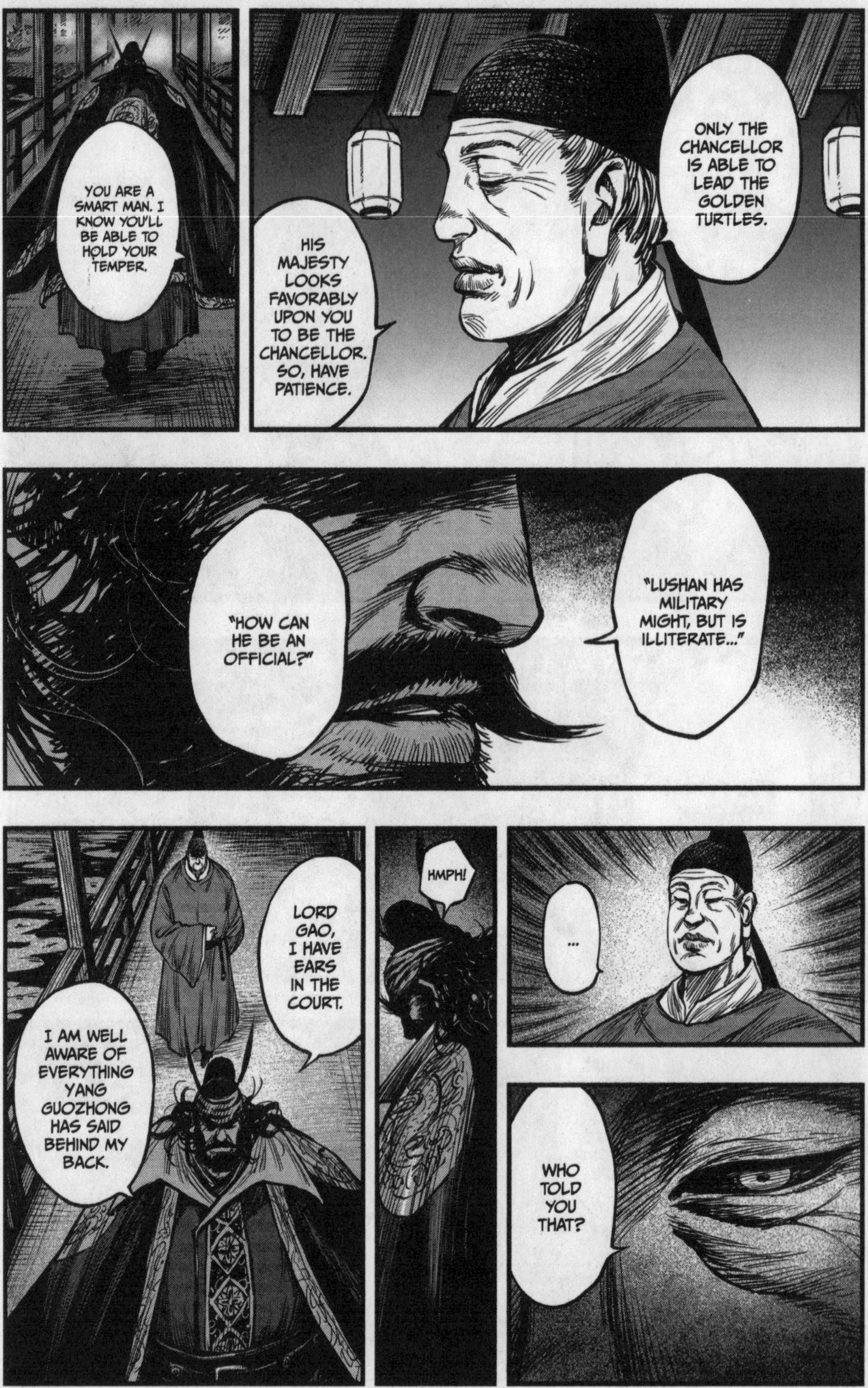
ONLY THE CHANCELLOR IS ABLE TO LEAD THE GOLDEN TURTLES.
HIS MAJESTY LOOKS FAVORABLY UPON YOU TO BE THE CHANCELLOR. SO, HAVE PATIENCE.
YOU ARE A SMART MAN. I KNOW YOU'LL BE ABLE TO HOLD YOUR TEMPER.
"LUSHAN HAS MILITARY MIGHT, BUT IS ILLITERATE..."
"HOW CAN HE BE AN OFFICIAL?"
...
WHO TOLD YOU THAT?
HMPH!
LORD GAO, I HAVE EARS IN THE COURT.
I AM WELL AWARE OF EVERYTHING YANG GUOZHONG HAS SAID BEHIND MY BACK.

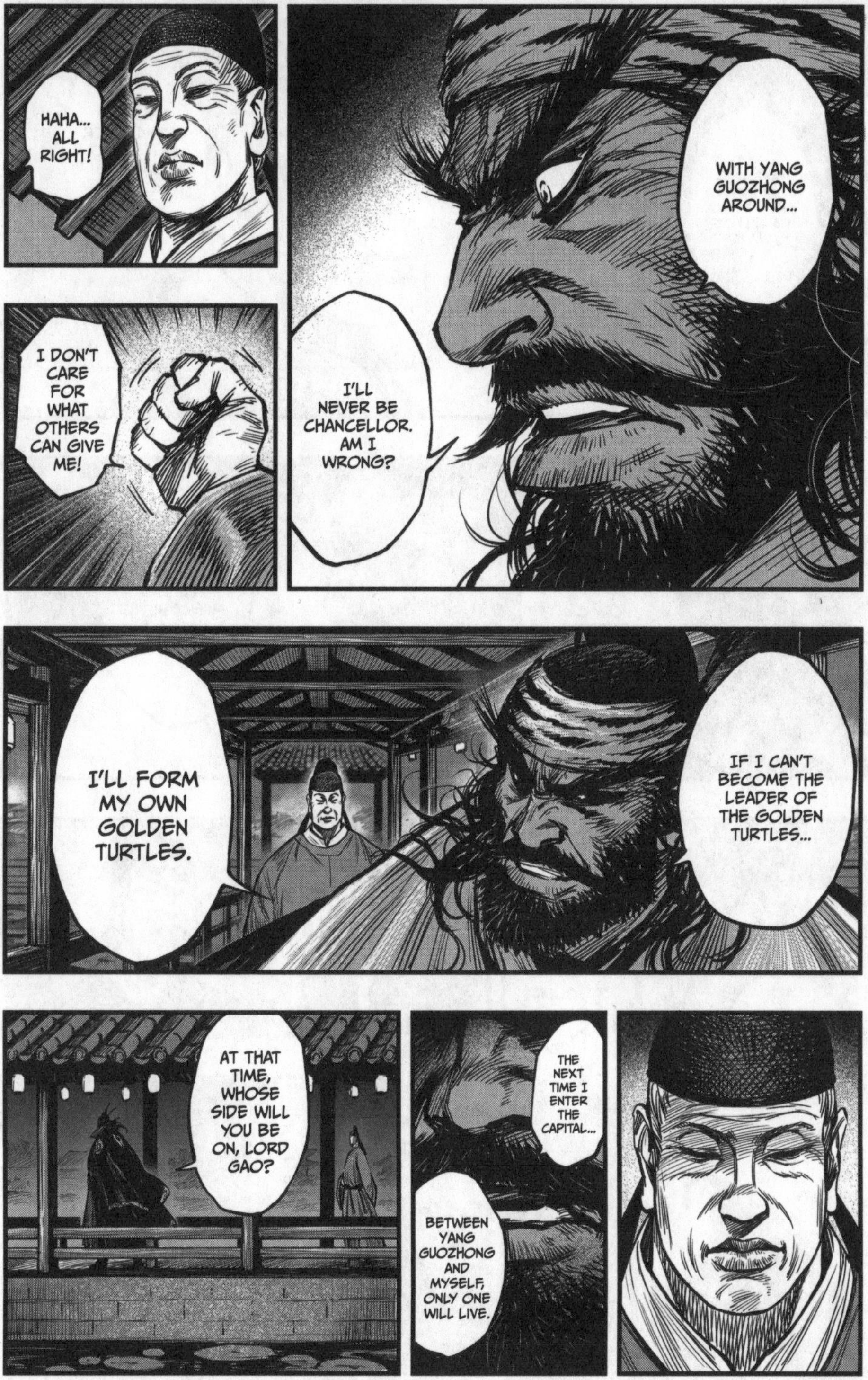
WITH YANG GUOZHONG AROUND...
I'LL NEVER BE CHANCELLOR. AM I WRONG?
HAHA... ALL RIGHT!
I DON'T CARE FOR WHAT OTHERS CAN GIVE ME!
IF I CAN'T BECOME THE LEADER OF THE GOLDEN TURTLES...
I'LL FORM MY OWN GOLDEN TURTLES.
THE NEXT TIME I ENTER THE CAPITAL...
BETWEEN YANG GUOZHONG AND MYSELF, ONLY ONE WILL LIVE.
AT THAT TIME, WHOSE SIDE WILL YOU BE ON, LORD GAO?

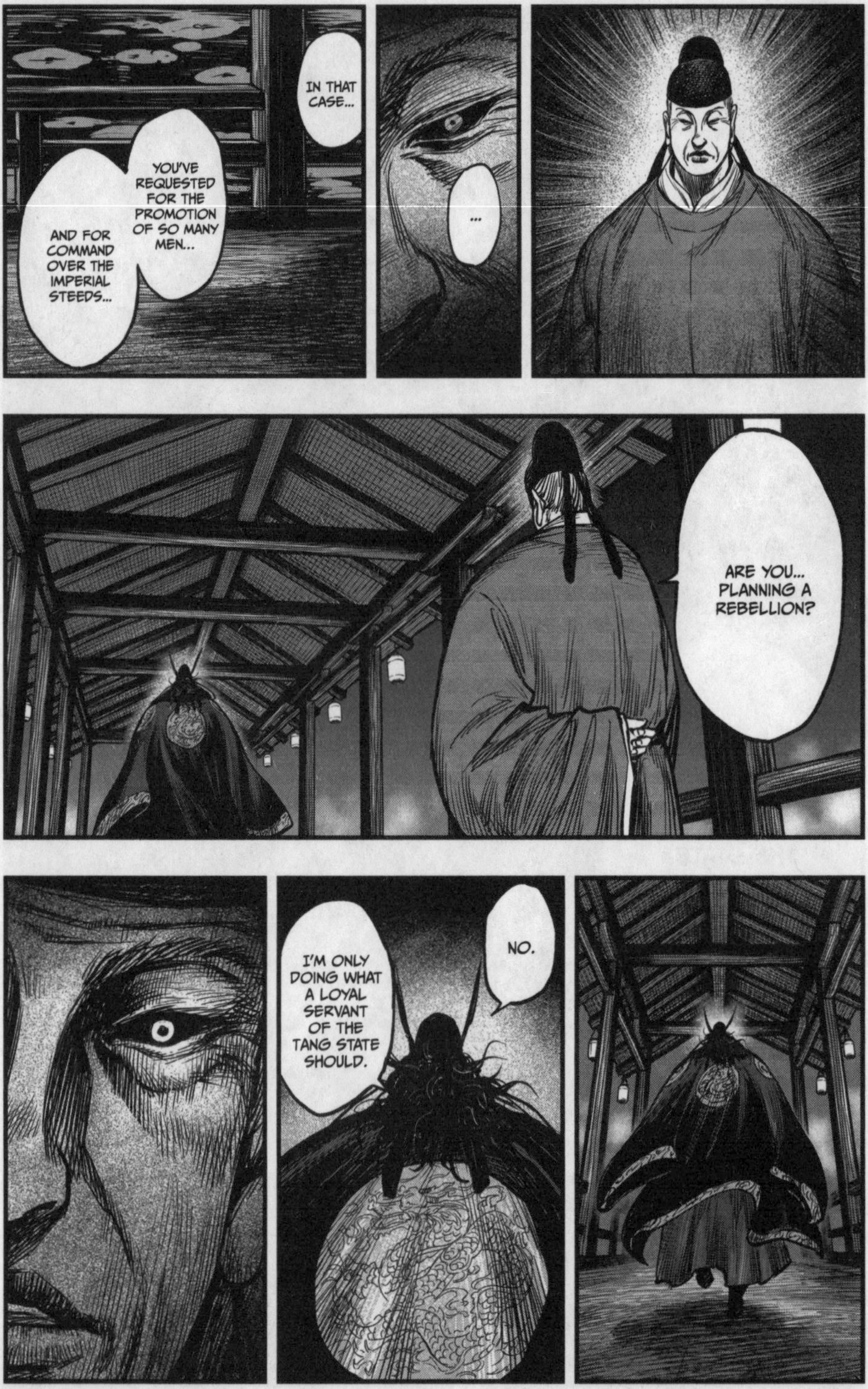
...
IN THAT CASE...
YOU'VE REQUESTED FOR THE PROMOTION OF SO MANY MEN...
AND FOR COMMAND OVER THE IMPERIAL STEEDS...
ARE YOU... PLANNING A REBELLION?
NO.
I'M ONLY DOING WHAT A LOYAL SERVANT OF THE TANG STATE SHOULD.

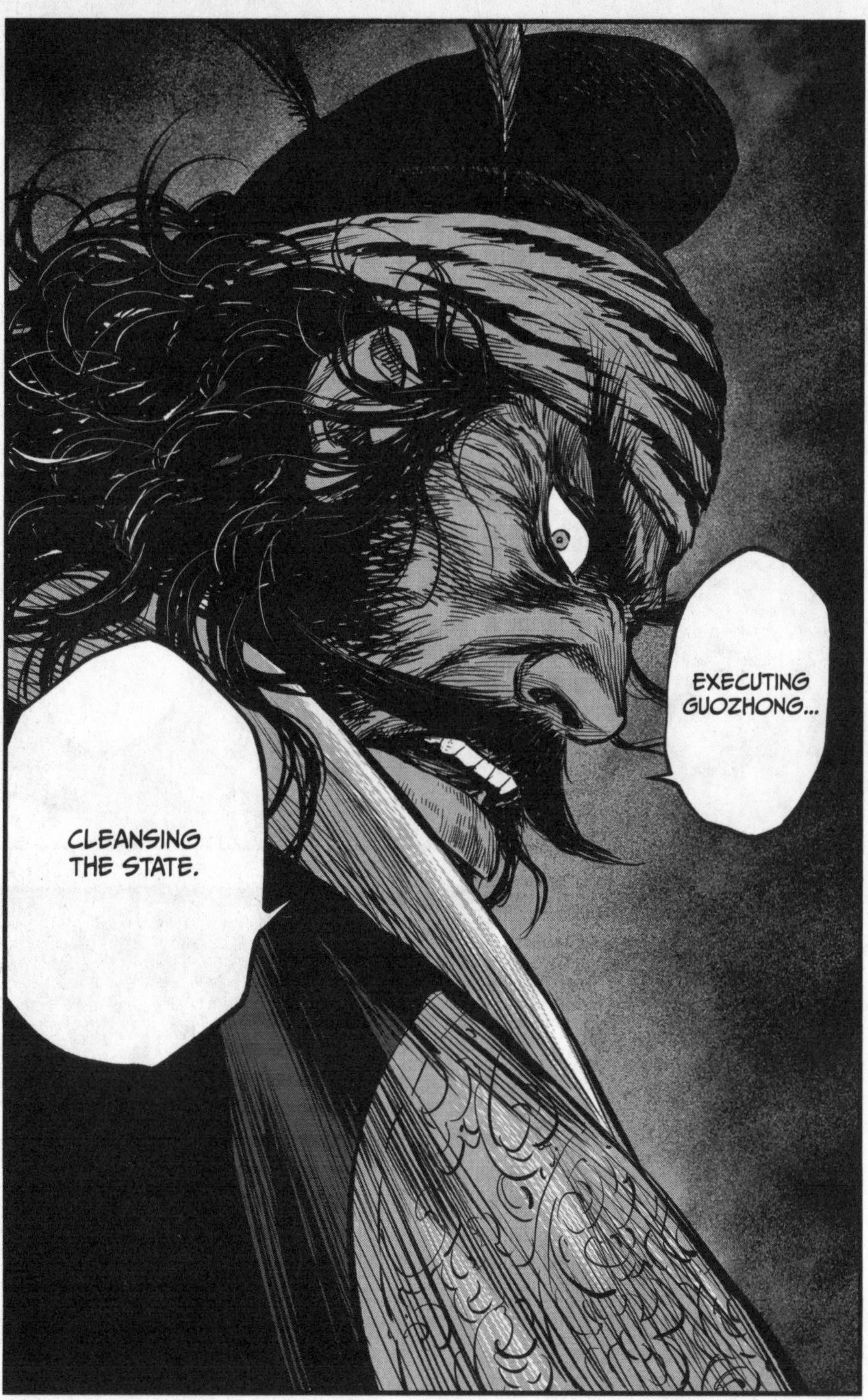
EXECUTING GUOZHONG...
CLEANSING THE STATE.

ASSASSIN'S CREED
DYNASTY

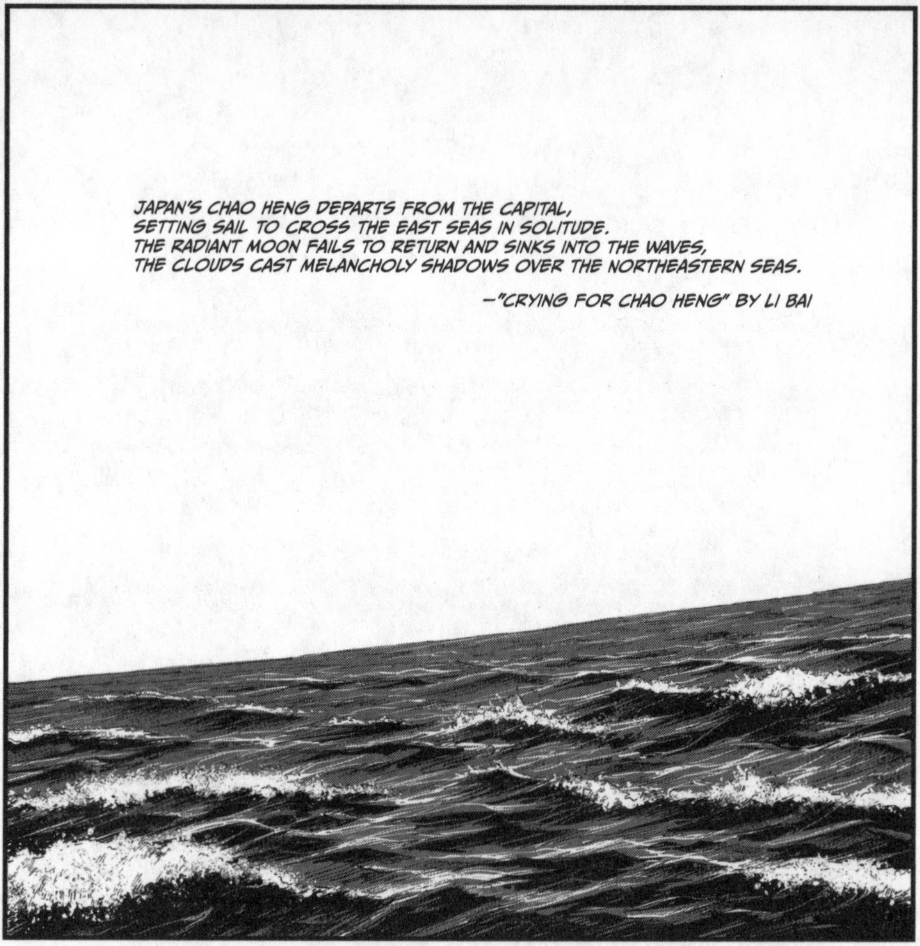
JAPAN'S CHAO HENG DEPARTS FROM THE CAPITAL,
SETTING SAIL TO CROSS THE EAST SEAS IN SOLITUDE.
THE RADIANT MOON FAILS TO RETURN AND SINKS INTO THE WAVES,
THE CLOUDS CAST MELANCHOLY SHADOWS OVER THE NORTHEASTERN SEAS.
—"CRYING FOR CHAO HENG" BY LI BAI
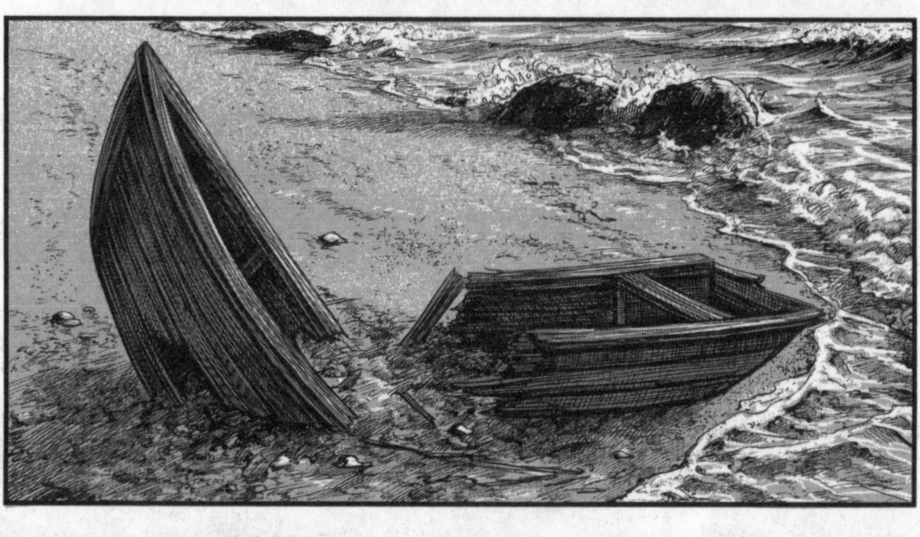

PAYING RESPECTS TO LI BAI

HOW HAVE YOU BEEN?
MANY MONTHS HAVE PASSED SINCE WE PARTED IN CHANG'AN IN OCTOBER LAST YEAR.

I REMEMBER WHAT YOU SAID TO ME WHEN YOU SAW ME OFF... "THIS FAREWELL WILL BE OUR LAST."

I ALSO REMEMBER, WHEN I FIRST ARRIVED AT THE TANG EMPIRE, I WAS ONLY A NINETEEN YEAR OLD BOY, OVERWHELMED BY ITS SPLENDOR. I AM ALREADY FIFTY. I HAVE WITNESSED THE LIVELINESS AND BEAUTY OF CHANG'AN, MADE MANY CLOSE FRIENDS, AND THE TANG HAVE ALSO BECOME A PART OF ME.

BUT AS I GROW OLD, I'M STARTING TO MISS THE TASTE OF MY HOMELAND.

HAVING SPENT THIRTY YEARS IN TANG, IT SEEMS LIKE A WONDERFUL DREAM. I ONLY WANT TO BE ABLE TO TASTE MY MOTHER'S COOKING ONE MORE TIME BEFORE I DIE.

THAT IS WHY I AM FOLLOWING LORD FUJIWARA'S ENVOY IN RETURNING TO JAPAN FOR THE PURPOSE OF FULFILLING THIS LAST WISH OF MINE.

BUT ASIDE FROM THAT, I HAVE ANOTHER TASK TO COMPLETE.

(NOTE: FOR THE EASE OF READING, THIS LETTER HAS BEEN TRANSLATED INTO MODERN TEXT.)

AS YOU MIGHT KNOW, I AM SOMEONE FILLED WITH CURIOSITY, AND MY CURIOSITY HAS LED ME TO LEARN OF SOME SECRETS.

IT SEEMS THAT THE BUDDHA THAT WE HAVE COME TO KNOW HAVE BEEN TERMED THE PRECURSOR.

IN ANCIENT HISTORY, THE PRECURSOR SHAKYAMUNI LED HIS DISCIPLES TO SPREAD THE DHARMA, AND HE WAS BELOVED AND RESPECTED BY MANY. THEREFORE, WHEN HE CHOSE TO ABANDON HIS FLESH TO ATTAIN NIRVANA, IT WAS A TRAGEDY TO THOSE AROUND HIM.

AFTER THE BUDDHA WAS CREMATED, HIS DISCIPLES FOUND A LARGE NUMBER OF MULTICOLORED BEADS IN HIS ASHES. THESE BECAME KNOWN AS "THE BUDDHA'S RELICS" AND EACH BEAD OF THE BUDDHA RELICS WERE INDESTRUCTIBLE, FILLED WITH SHAKYAMUNI'S MEMORIES FROM HIS PAST LIFE – THE TRUTH OF THE UNIVERSE.

THE BUDDHA'S RELICS TRAVELLED ALONG THE TRADE ROUTES FROM THE WESTERN REGIONS INTO HAN CHINA, WHERE THEY WERE PASSED ON FROM GENERATION TO GENERATION THROUGH THE TURMOIL OF THE AGES, KEPT AND PROTECTED BY RESPECTABLE MONKS.

PRESENTLY, THE BUDDHA RELICS AS WE KNOW THEM, ARE IN THE POSSESSION OF MONK JIANZHEN OF THE YANGUANG TEMPLE IN YANGZHOU.

MONK JIANZHEN IS A WISE MAN AND A HIGHLY RESPECTED MONK. EVEN IN TIMES OF PEACE, HE REMAINS TROUBLED.

LIKE YOU AND I, MONK JIANZHEN KNOWS OF THE GOLDEN TURTLES' EXISTENCE IN THE PALACE. THERE HAVE BEEN MANY HINTS OF A GREAT UPHEAVAL WITHIN OUR TIME, BUT WE KNOW NOT WHEN THIS MAY BE. SHOULD THE RELICS FALL INTO THE HANDS OF THE WICKED, TO BE USED FOR SOME AMBITIOUS SCHEME, THE CONSEQUENCES DO NOT BEAR IMAGINING.

MONK JIIANZHEN HOPES TO KEEP THE RELICS IN A DISCREET LOCATION, FAR AWAY FROM STRIFE AND TURBULENCE. HE SAYS THAT BUDDHISM KNOWS NO BORDERS, AND PERHAPS JAPAN MIGHT BE THE BEST PLACE TO HEAD TOWARDS.

MONK JIANZHEN HAS ATTEMPTED TO CROSS THE EAST SEA FIVE TIMES, BUT TO NO AVAIL, THOUGH THESE FAILURES HAVE LED HIM TO BE EVEN MORE DETERMINED.

I DESPERATELY HOPE TO BE ABLE TO ASSIST MONK JIANZHEN IN PROTECTING THE RELICS.

MOREOVER, HE CAN USE THIS OPPORTUNITY TO SPREAD BUDDHIST TEACHINGS IN JAPAN AND ENLIGHTEN THE MASSES. IT WOULD BE A GREAT MERIT IN THIS CASE.

AS SUCH, I REACHED OUT TO LORD FUJIWARA NO KIYOKAWA THAT HAD COME TO TANG ON AN EXPEDITION, TO BID FAREWELL TO CHANG'AN. WE ARE ESCORTING MONK JIANZHEN IN SECRET AND SAILING FOR JAPAN. IF WE ARE SO LUCKY AS TO HAVE OUR MOVEMENTS GO UNNOTICED BY THE GOLDEN TURTLES, IT WILL TRULY BE A FEAT.

WE HAVE SPLIT UP INTO FOUR SHIPS AND ARE SAILING SMOOTHLY ON THE QUIET SEAS. I CLOSE MY EYES AND I CAN ALMOST SMELL MY HOMELAND.

"LOOKING UP TOWARDS CHANG'AN,
I SPEED TOWARDS NARA'S SHORES.
UPON THE PEAK OF MOUNT MIKASA,
I PONDER THE RADIANCE OF THE MOON."

AS MY HOMELAND DRAWS CLOSER, I LOOK UP AT THE MOON, AND THINK OF THE PARTING WITH YOU, LI BAI. THAT HAS LED ME TO PEN THIS LETTER.

BUT AT THAT VERY MOMENT, A STORM BROKE OUT AT SEA.

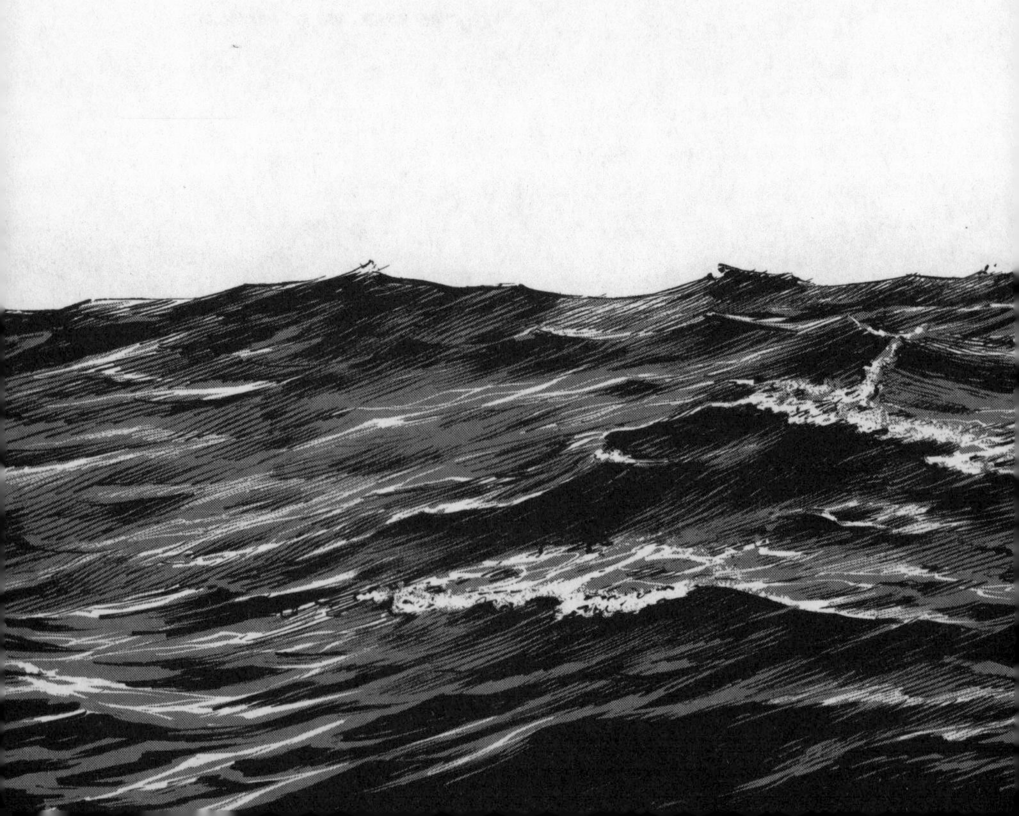

THE SHIP THAT LORD FUJIWARA AND I WERE ON HIT THE ROCKS AND
WE WERE UNABLE TO CONTINUE SAILING. WE LOST CONTACT WITH THE
OTHER THREE SHIPS, AND IN THE MIDST OF THE CRASHING WAVES,
I GRADUALLY LOST CONSCIOUSNESS.

WHEN I OPENED MY EYES, I FOUND MYSELF WASHED UP ON A SHORE. OUR
SHIP HAD BEEN TERRIBLY WRECKED AND WE DID NOT KNOW WHERE WE
WERE. TOGETHER WITH LORD FUJIWARA, WE LED THE MEN TO ABANDON OUR
SHIP AND SEARCH FOR HELP.

I WONDER IF THIS IS JAPAN OR THE TANG?

EVERYTHING IS UNKNOWN. I CAN ONLY TRUST THE GROUND BENEATH MY FEET.
IF I SHOULD NEVER BE ABLE TO RETURN HOME, I CAN ONLY ACCEPT MY FATE.

I CAN ONLY HOPE THAT MONK JIANZHEN'S SHIP IS SAFE.
I CAN ONLY HOPE THAT THE RELICS WILL ABLE ABLE TO REACH THEIR
DESTINATION UNHARMED.
I CAN ONLY HOPE THAT THE TANG AND JAPAN WILL REMAIN PEACEFUL.

......

I DO NOT KNOW WHEN I WILL BE ABLE TO SEND THIS LETTER, SO I WILL
KEEP IT WITH ME FOR THE TIME BEING. IF THERE IS A NEXT LIFE, I HOPE
I WILL BE ABLE TO SHARE A POT OF WINE WITH YOU ONCE MORE.

—CHAO HENG (ABE NO NAKAMARO)

ASSASSIN'S CREED

DYNASTY

“TIANBAO” (LASTING FROM THE FIRST LUNAR MONTH OF 742 A.D. TO THE SEVENT MONTH OF 756 A.D.) WAS THE ERA NAME COINED BY TANG DYNASTY EMPEROR L LONGJI. IN THE FIRST LUNAR MONTH OF THE THIRD YEAR OF TIANBAO, THE TERM FOR “YEAR” WAS CHANGED FROM “年 (NIAN)” TO “載 (ZAI)”.

DURING THE TIANBAO PERIOD, THE TANG EMPIRE GREW POWERFUL AND PROSPEROUS, PEACE REIGNING THROUGHOUT THE LAND. IT WAS A LIBERAL AND INCLUSIVE ERA, A GLORIOUS GOLDEN AGE OF OPTIMISM. NESTORIANS, ARABS, ZOROASTRIANS FROM SOGDIA (“FIRE-WORSHIPPERS”); FROM EVERY COUNTRY I CENTRAL ASIA AND WEST ASIA, MERCHANTS, MONKS, TAOIST PRIESTS, TRAVELING PERFORMERS AND ENTERTAINERS—ALL GATHERED IN THE CAPITAL OF CHANG’AN.

CHANG’AN SERVED AS THE CAPITAL OF THIRTEEN CHINESE DYNASTIES, AS WELL AS THE EASTERN TERMINUS OF THE SILK ROAD. THE CITY OF CHANG’AN WAS DEVELOPED THROUGH THE DESIGN OF THE SUI DYNASTY’S YUWEN KAI FOR THE SUI CITY OF DAXING. AFTER THE ESTABLISHMENT OF THE TANG DYNASTY, DAXING BECAME CHANG’AN. THE CITY OF CHANG’AN ADOPTED A GRID SYSTEM, WITH A TOTAL OF ONE HUNDRED AND NINE WARDS, AND TWO MARKETPLACES, ONE IN THE EAST AND ONE IN THE WEST. THE REGULAR GRID STRUCTURE AKIN TO A CHESSBOARD, THE CITY WAS DIVIDED BY ZHUQUE STREET, WITH CHANG’AN COUNT TO THE WEST AND WANNIAN COUNTY TO THE EAST.

GUANGHUA GATE
含光殿
DAMING PALACE
XIYUAN
修真 安定 修德 掖庭宫 玄武门 TAIJI PALACE 东宫 光宅 翊善 长乐 入苑
普宁 休祥 辅兴 广运门 承天门 长乐门 永昌 来庭 大宁 兴宁
义宁 金城 颁政 安福门 顺义门 IMPERIAL CITY 延喜门 景风门 永兴 安兴 永嘉
居德 醴泉 布政 含光门 朱雀门 安上门 崇仁 胜业 兴庆
群贤 WEST MARKET 延寿 太平 光禄 兴道 务本 平康 EAST MARKET 道政
怀德 光德 通义 通化 开化 崇义 宣阳 常乐
崇化 怀远 延康 兴化 丰乐 安仁 长兴 亲仁 安邑 靖恭
丰邑 长寿 崇贤 崇德 安业 光福 永乐 永宁 宣平 新昌
待贤 嘉会 延福 怀贞 崇业 靖善 靖安 永崇 升平 升道
永和 永平 永安 宣义 永达 兰陵 安善 昭国 修行 立政
常安 通轨 敦义 丰安 道德 开明 大业 晋昌 修政 敦化
和平 归义 大通 昌明 光行 保宁 昌乐 通善 青龙 曲江
永阳 昭行 大安 安乐 延祚 安义 安德 通济 曲池 芙蓉园
BORDER PATH
BORDER PATH
ANHUA GATE
MINGDE GATE
QIXIA GATE

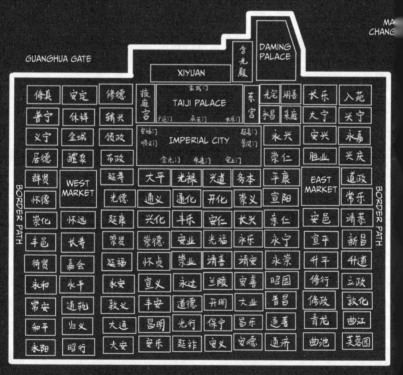

LI BAI

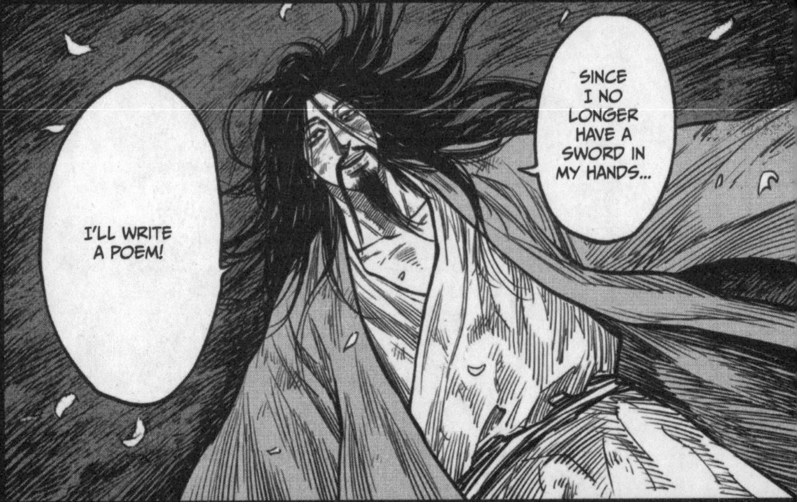
SINCE I NO LONGER HAVE A SWORD IN MY HANDS...
I'LL WRITE A POEM!

"A MAN MUST BEAR GREAT AMBITION. WITH ONLY HIS SWORD, HE MUST LEAVE HIS FAMILY TO JOURNEY FAR AND WIDE."

— RECORDS FOR GOVERNOR PEI OF ANZHOU, LI BAI

LI BAI WAS ONE OF THE GREAT ROMANTIC POETS OF THE TANG DYNASTY, NICKNAMED "THE BANISHED IMMORTAL". IN HIS YOUTH, LI BAI HELD CHIVALRIC HEROISM IN GREAT REVERENCE AND HAD GRAND PLANS, ASPIRING TO BECOME A PALACE OFFICIAL. IN THE FIRST YEAR OF TIANBAO (742 A.D.), EMPEROR XUANZONG SUMMONED LI BAI TO COURT, ORDERING HIM TO SERVE IN THE HANLIN ACADEMY, RETAINING HIM AS AN ENTERTAINER FOR BANQUETS AND TO COMPOSE POETRY AT THE IMPERIAL FAMILY'S PLEASURE.

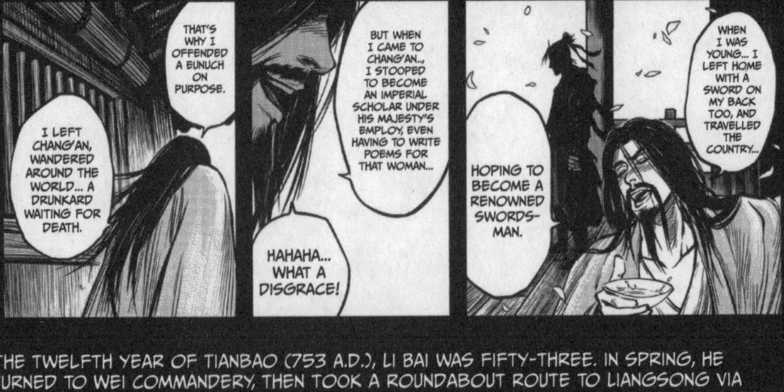
WHEN I WAS YOUNG... I LEFT HOME WITH A SWORD ON MY BACK TOO, AND TRAVELLED THE COUNTRY...
HOPING TO BECOME A RENOWNED SWORDS-MAN.
BUT WHEN I CAME TO CHANG'AN..., I STOOPED TO BECOME AN IMPERIAL SCHOLAR UNDER HIS MAJESTY'S EMPLOY, EVEN HAVING TO WRITE POEMS FOR THAT WOMAN...
HAHAHA... WHAT A DISGRACE!
THAT'S WHY I OFFENDED A EUNUCH ON PURPOSE.
I LEFT CHANG'AN, WANDERED AROUND THE WORLD... A DRUNKARD WAITING FOR DEATH.

IN THE TWELFTH YEAR OF TIANBAO (753 A.D.), LI BAI WAS FIFTY-THREE. IN SPRING, HE RETURNED TO WEI COMMANDERY, THEN TOOK A ROUNDABOUT ROUTE TO LIANGSONG VIA LUOYANG. FROM LIANGYUAN, HE CONTINUED SOUTH AND REACHED XUANCHENG IN THE AUTUMN, THEN HEADED NORTH AGAIN TO JINLING IN WINTER.

IN THE THIRTEENTH YEAR OF TIANBAO (754 A.D.), LI BAI WAS FIFTY-FOUR, TRAVELLING ACROSS GUANGLING. HE VISITED JINLING WITH WEI WAN, SAILING THE QINHUAI RIVER. IN JINLING, HE ENTRUSTED HIS LITERARY WORKS TO WEI WAN, WHICH WERE LATER COMPILED IN LI'S HANLIN COLLECTION. AFTER PARTING WAYS WITH WEI WAN, HE TRAVELLED BETWEEN XUANCHENG, QIUPU, NANLING, AND OTHER SUCH PLACES. HE ONCE TRAVELLED TO HUANGSHAN.

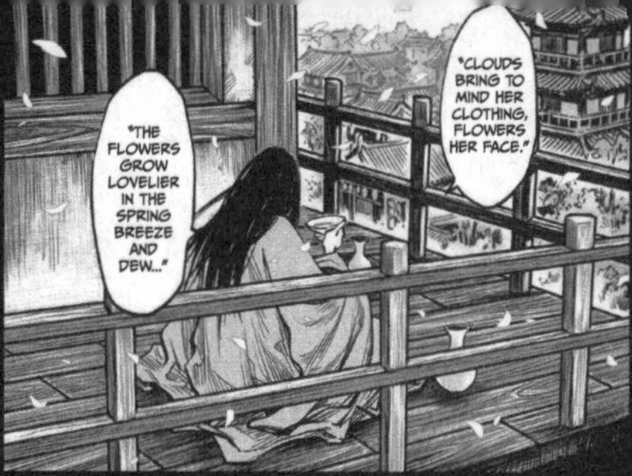
"CLOUDS BRING TO MIND HER CLOTHING, FLOWERS HER FACE."
"THE FLOWERS GROW LOVELIER IN THE SPRING BREEZE AND DEW..."

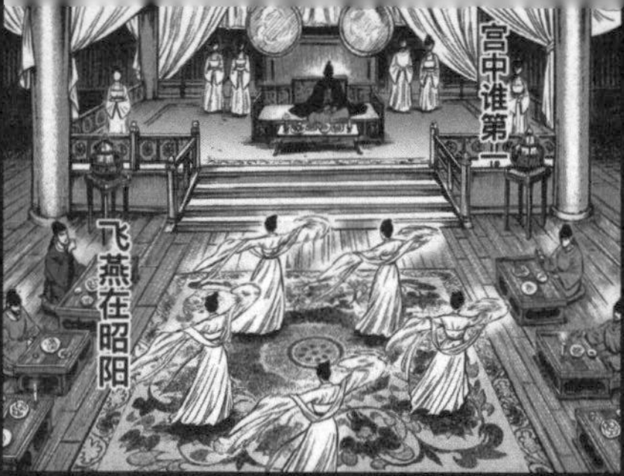
宫中谁第一
飞燕在昭阳

"CLOUDS BRING TO MIND HER CLOTHING, FLOWERS HER FACE. THE FLOWERS GROW LOVELIER IN THE SPRING BREEZE AND DEW.""

— SONG OF PEACE AND TRANQUILITY, ONE, LI BAI

"AND IN THE PALACE, THE FIRST IS LADY FEIYAN IN ZHAOYANG."

— LYRICS FOR WANDERING IN THE PALACE, LI BAI

AS AN IMPERIAL SCHOLAR IN THE COURT, LI BAI WROTE THE THREE VERSES THAT MAKE UP THE FAMOUS SONG, "SONG FOR PEACE AND TRANQUILITY," THE EIGHT VERSES OF "LYRICS FOR WANDERING IN THE PALACE," AND MANY OTHER POEMS THAT REMAIN WELL-KNOWN TO THIS DAY. HIS DREAMS OF BECOMING AN OFFICIAL SLOWLY DIED. THIS WAS REFLECTED IN MANY HISTORICAL RECORDS BOTH OFFICIAL AND INFORMAL, AS WELL AS IN HIS OWN WRITINGS.

"WHEN XUANZONG SUMMONED [WU] JUN TO COURT, JUN RECOMMENDED [LI BAI] TO THE COURT AS WELL, AND HE JOINED THE HANLIN ACADEMY WITH JUN. BAI WAS GREATLY ENJOYED DRINKING; EVERY DAY, HE WOULD DRINK HIMSELF INTO A STUPOR AT THE TAVERN WITH OTHER DRUNKARDS. XUANZONG HAD COMPOSED A MELODY AND WANTED LYRICS FOR IT. HE SUMMONED BAI URGENTLY, BUT BAI WAS ASLEEP IN THE TAVERN. BROUGHT IN, HIS FACE WAS SPLASHED WITH COLD WATER AND HE WAS ORDERED TO WRITE. HE IMMEDIATELY WROTE MORE THAN TEN VERSES, PLEASING THE EMPEROR GREATLY. ONCE, DRUNK IN COURT, HE STRETCHED HIS FOOT OUT AND DEMANDED THAT GAO LISHI REMOVE HIS BOOTS FOR HIM. HENCE, HE WAS FORCED TO LEAVE [CHANG'AN]. AFTER THIS, HE WANDERED THE WORLD, DROWNING HIMSELF IN DRINK ALL DAY."

— OLD BOOK OF TANG: RECORDS OF LI BAI

"I AM A FREE AND UNCONSTRAINED PERSON, BUT THE NARROW-MINDED MOCK ME."

— READING IN THE HANLIN ACADEMY AND SPEAKING MY HEART TO THE SCHOLARS OF JIXIAN ACADEMY, LI BAII

"LI BAI EXTENDED HIS FOOT AND ORDERED GAO LISHI: 'REMOVE MY SHOE!' LISHI WAS PUT IN A SPOT AND EVENTUALLY REMOVED THE SHOE. XUANZONG CRITICISED LI BAI, ACCORDING TO LISHI: 'HOW UNGRACIOUS.'"

— MISCELLANEOUS MORSELS FROM YOUYANG

LI BAI PRONOUNCED HIMSELF TO BE A "FREE AND UNCONSTRAINED PERSON". THOUGH HE HELD A POSITION OF LITTLE IMPORTANCE, HE CAME INTO CONFLICT WITH MANY IN THE PALACE, CAUSING HIM TO BE THE TARGET OF NUMEROUS CRITICISMS AND SLANDER. LI'S RECORDS OF HANLIN DETAILS HOW LI BAI WAS "BANISHED DUE TO ZHANG JI'S SLANDERS", AND LI BAI WROTE IN SELF-RECOMMENDATION TO ASSISTANT IMPERIAL COUNSELLOR SONG, "DUE TO SCHEMING OFFICIALS, I HAVE BEEN CAST OUT."

BEYOND ZHANG JI, GAO LISHI AND YANG YUHUAN ALSO PLOTTED TO SMEAR LI BAI'S REPUTATION. MISCELLANEOUS RECORDS FROM THE PINE WINDOW RECORDS HOW GAO LISHI, DISGRACED BY THE BOOT-REMOVING INCIDENT, SOWED DISCORD BETWEEN LI BAI AND YANG YUHUAN, LISHI EXPLAINED THAT IN "SONG OF PEACE AND TRANQUILITY", "IN COMPARING YOUR HIGHNESS TO ZHAO FEIYAN, HE IS INSINUATING THAT YOU ARE LOWLY BORN." AS A RESULT, LI BAI LOST YANG YUHUAN'S FAVOR. XUANZONG HAD INTENDED TO BESTOW THE TITLE OF AN OFFICIAL TO LI BAI THRICE, BUT YANG YUHUAN HAD INTERVENED THRICE TO PREVENT THIS FROM COMING TO FULFILMENT. FURTHERMORE, IN XUANZONG'S EYES, LI BAI WAS SIMPLY "UNGRACIOUS", LEADING LI BAI TO BE "DISMISSED WITH REWARDS OF GOLD". HENCE, LI BAI WAS LEFT TO WANDER

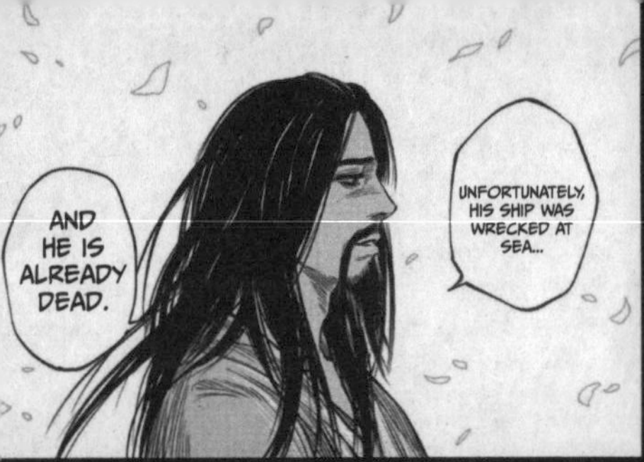
UNFORTUNATELY, HIS SHIP WAS WRECKED AT SEA...
AND HE IS ALREADY DEAD.

"LIFE IN THIS WORLD DOES NOT HEED ONE'S DESIRES, I WOULD MUCH RATHER LOOSEN MY HAIR AND RIFE UPON A RIVER BOAT THE NEXT MORNING."

— FAREWELL FOR SHU YUN AT XUAN ZHOU'S XIE TIAO HOUSE, LI BAI

"JAPAN'S CHAO QING DEPARTS FROM THE CAPITAL, SAILING AROUND THE [FABLED EASTERN ISLE OF] PENGHU."

— CRYING FOR CHAO HENG, LI BAI

LI BAI HAD A WIDE CIRCLE OF FRIENDS. THE EMISSARY TO THE TANG DYNASTY ABE NO NAKAMARO (CHINESE NAME CHAO HENG) WAS ONE OF HIS CLOSE FRIENDS. IN THE WINTER OF THE TWELFTH YEAR OF TIANBAO (753 A.D.), A FEW MONTHS BEFORE THIS STORY TAKES PLACE, CHAO HENG, ALONG WITH THE DELEGATION OF TANG EMISSARY FUJIWARA NO KIYOKAWA, WERE RETURNING TO JAPAN WHEN THEY MET WITH DISASTER AT SEA. WORD HAD SPREAD THAT ABE NO NAKAMARO HAD PASSED AWAY. LI BAI WROTE "CRYING FOR CHAO HENG" IN HIS DESPAIR.

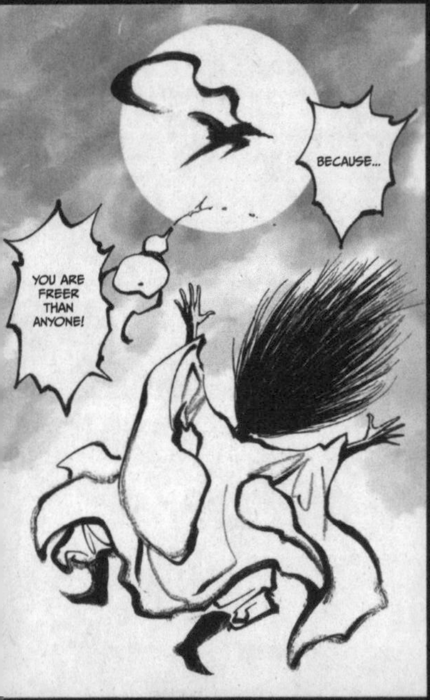
BECAUSE...
YOU ARE FREER THAN ANYONE!

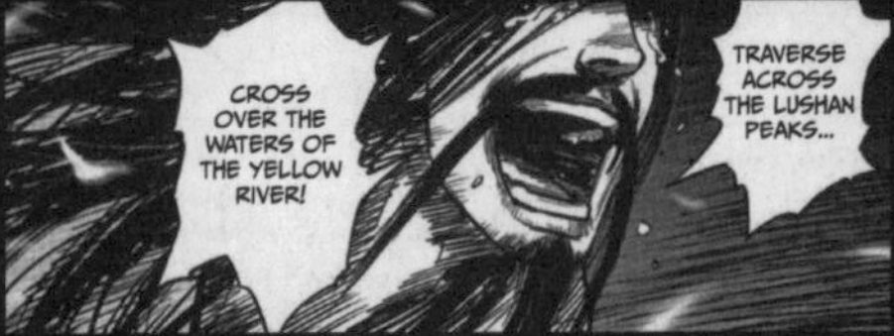
CROSS OVER THE WATERS OF THE YELLOW RIVER!
TRAVERSE ACROSS THE LUSHAN PEAKS...

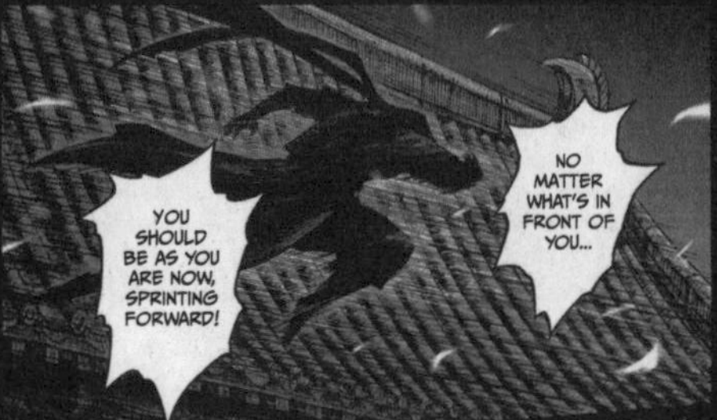
NO MATTER WHAT'S IN FRONT OF YOU...
YOU SHOULD BE AS YOU ARE NOW, SPRINTING FORWARD!

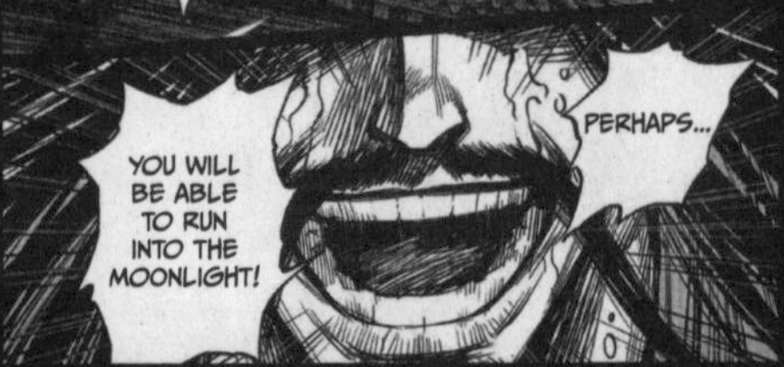
PERHAPS...
YOU WILL BE ABLE TO RUN INTO THE MOONLIGHT!

IT IS NOT CLEAR WHEN "ODE TO GALLANTRY" WAS WRITTEN, BUT IT IS THE MOST WELL-KNOWN POEM OF LI BAI'S WANDERING SWORDSMAN COLLECTION. FORMAL HISTORICAL RECORDS DETAIL THAT LI BAI HAD COLLAPSED AND EVENTUALLY PASSED AWAY IN XUANCHENG FROM DRINKING TOO MUCH ALCOHOL. FOLK LEGEND HAS IT THAT WHILE DRUNK, LI BAI LEAPT

ABE NO NAKAMARO AND MONK JIANZHEN

ABE NO NAKAMARO (698–770)

IN THE OLD BOOK OF TANG, THE CHAPTER "BIOGRAPHIES ONE HUNDRED AND FORTY-NINE" STATES: "THE COUNTRY OF NIPPON IS DISTINCT FROM THE COUNTRY OF WA. BECAUSE THE COUNTRY IS NEAR THE SUN, IT WENT BY THE NAME OF 'NIPPON' (日本, JAPAN OR LAND OF THE RISING SUN). SOME SAY THAT THE PEOPLE OF WA DISLIKED THE OFFENSIVE NAME 'WA' (倭, WHICH HAS CONNOTATIONS OF SUBMISSIVENESS OR SMALL STATURE), AND CHANGED IT TO NIPPON'. OTHERS SAY THAT NIPPON WAS FORMERLY A SMALL COUNTRY THAT LATER COMBINED WITH THE LAND OF WA."

AN EMISSARY TO THE TANG, ABE NO NAKAMARO CAME TO THE TANG DYNASTY IN THE FIFTH YEAR OF KAIYUAN (717). ADMIRING CHINESE CULTURE, HE WAS UNWILLING TO LEAVE, STAYING IN CHANG'AN AND ADOPTING THE CHINESE NAME "CHAO HENG". HE WAS A GOOD FRIEND OF LI BAI. IN OCTOBER 753, AT THE AGE OF 55, ABE NO NAKAMARO JOINED THE MISSION OF FUJIWARA NO KIYOKAWA ON THEIR RETURN TRIP TO JAPAN. THE PEOPLE OF CHANG'AN, FROM THOSE IN THE IMPERIAL COURT TO CIVILIANS, GATHERED TO SEND THEM OFF. THE MONK JIANZHEN OF YANGZHOU WENT EAST TO JAPAN WITH THEM TO SPREAD BUDDHIST TEACHINGS. ABE NO NAKAMARO'S SHIP WAS CLOSE TO RYUKYU WHEN THEY MET WITH DISASTER, LOSING CONTACT WITH THE MONK JIANZHEN'S SHIP. THEY DRIFTED TO THE REGION OF ANNAN (PRESENT DAY VIETNAM). A FALSE RUMOR SPREAD THROUGHOUT CHANG'AN, CLAIMING THAT ABE NO NAKAMARO HAD PASSED AWAY, LEADING LI BAI TO COMPOSE "CRYING FOR CHAO HENG."

JIANZHEN (688–763)

ALSO KNOWN AS THE SEA-VOYAGING MONK, A GREAT MONK OF THE TANG DYNASTY. BORN IN JIANGYANG, YANGZHOU, IN THE TANG DYNASTY (PRESENT DAY JIANGSU, YANGZHOU), HIS FORMER NAME WAS CHUNYU. HE LEFT HOME TO JOIN DAYUN TEMPLE AT FOURTEEN. AT THE AGE OF EIGHTEEN, HE TOOK HIS BODHISATTVA VOWS WITH THE TANG MONK DAO'AN AND DEVOTED HIMSELF TO THE STUDY OF RISSHŪ BUDDHISM. AT TWENTY-ONE, HE TOOK HIS UPASAMPADÁ VOWS IN CHANG'AN. HE TRAVELLED CHANG'AN AND LUOYANG, STUDYING THE TRIPITAKA SCRIPTURES, WITH A FOCUS ON RISSHŪ. HE LATER TAUGHT THE MONASTIC COMMANDMENTS IN DAMING TEMPLE IN YANGZHOU, BECOMING A FAMOUS TEACHER OF THE COMMANDMENTS IN AND AROUND THE JIANGHUAI REGION. IN THE FIRST YEAR OF TIANBAO (742), AT THE INVITATION OF THE JAPANESE MONKS YOEI AND FUSHŌ, WHO HAD COME TO THE TANG TO LEARN BUDDHISM, HE TRAVELED EAST TO JAPAN WITH HIS DISCIPLES, INCLUDING XIANGYAN AND SITUO. FIVE ATTEMPTS TO CROSS THE SEA FAILED ONE AFTER ANOTHER. OVER THE AGE OF SIXTY, BLIND IN BOTH EYES, HE REMAINED DETERMINED. IN THE TWELFTH YEAR OF TIANBAO, HE WAS INVITED TO JAPAN ONCE AGAIN. WITH THE BHIKKHUS FAJIN AND XIANJING, THE NUN ZHISHOU, THE UPÁSAKA PAN XIANTONG AND OTHERS, HE FINALLY SUCCEEDED ON THE SIXTH TRIP WITH TANG EMISSARY FUJIWARA NO KIYOKAWA'S FLEET, MAKING LANDFALL IN AKIZUMA YAURA IN SATSUMA, KYUSHU (PRESENT-DAY AKIME IN KAGOSHIMA, SOUTHERN KYUSHU).

THE FESTIVAL OF FLOWERS

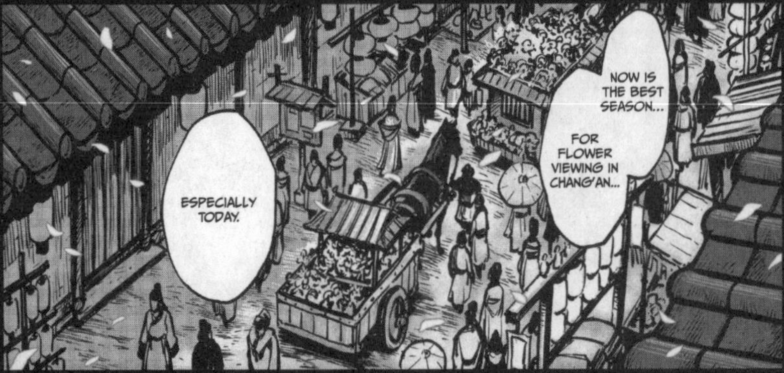
NOW IS THE BEST SEASON...
FOR FLOWER VIEWING IN CHANG'AN...
ESPECIALLY TODAY.

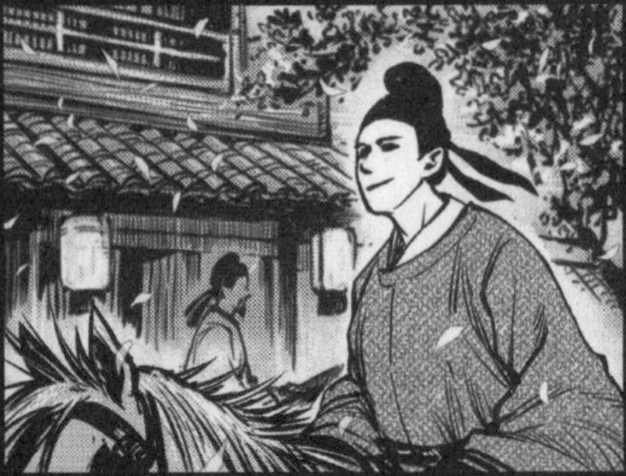

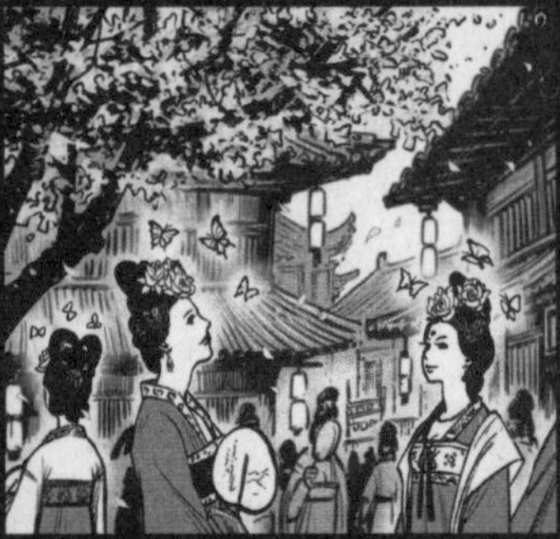

IN THE FIRST CHAPTER, THE SCENE OF CHANG'AN'S STREETS DEPICT THE PRACTICE OF "FLOWER VIEWING" AND "NOBLE LADIES VYING FOR FLOWERS". THE YOUTH OF CHANG'AN WANDER THE STREETS IN ADMIRATION OF THE FLOWERS AND THE LADIES COMPETE TO SEE WHO CAN GATHER THE LARGEST OFFERINGS OF FLOWERS.

"AT SPRING EACH YEAR, THE YOUTH IN CHANG'AN WOULD GATHER WITH THEIR FRIENDS, SADDLING PONIES DECORATED IN BROCADES AND STROLL BY THE FLOWERS AND TREES."

— KAIYUAN TIANBAO RECORDS: FLOWER VIEWING

"THE ROYAL GARDENS FILL WITH THOUSANDS OF NEW BLOSSOMS. THE EMPEROR PICKS ONE AND PLACES IT IN THE CONCUBINE'S PRECIOUS COIFFURE, SAYING, 'THIS FLOWER HIGHLIGHTS YOUR BEAUTY.'"

— KAIYUAN TIANBAO RECORDS: FLOWERS TO AID BEAUTY

"THE LADIES OF CHANG'AN VIE WITH FLOWERS IN SPRING, THOSE EARNING THE MOST EMERGE VICTORIOUS. THOUSANDS OF GOLD PIECES ARE EXCHANGED FOR FAMOUS FLOWERS TO BE PLANTED IN THE IMPERIAL GARDENS, TAKING ADVANTAGE OF SPRING."

— KAIYUAN TIANBAO RECORDS: VYING WITH FLOWERS

PEONIES

THE PEOPLE OF TANG LOVED PEONIES THE MOST. PEONIES STARTED TO GROW IN POPULARITY WITHIN THE TWENTY YEARS FROM APPROXIMATELY THE SIXTH YEAR OF THE YONGHUI ERA (655 A.D.) TO THE FIRST YEAR OF THE HONGDAO ERA (682 A.D.) UNDER THE RULE OF EMPEROR GAOZONG.

— LI SHUTONG, THE TANG PEOPLE'S LOVE OF PEONIES

TANG POEMS AND HISTORICAL RECORDS STAND AS EVIDENCE FOR HOW PEONIES WERE HIGHLY VALUED AT THAT TIME. OUT OF THESE WRITINGS, THE MOST FAMOUS WOULD BE, "A SINGLE PEONY IS WORTH A THOUSAND GOLD PIECES."

"A SINGLE PEONY IS WORTH A THOUSAND GOLD PIECES, A DEEPER SHADE EMBODYING GREATER BEAUTY."

— COMPLETE TANG POETRY: PEONIES, ZHANG YOUXIN

BESIDES PEONIES, OTHER TYPES OF FLOWERS THAT WERE POPULAR DURING THE TANG DYNASTY INCLUDE CHINESE PEONIES, CHRYSANTHEMUMS, ORCHIDS, BABY ROSES, RHODODENDRONS, CAMELLIAS, AND LOTUS FLOWERS.

THE DOMINEERING FLOWER CARRIAGE

"GUOZHONG HAS ONCE AGAIN BUILT HIS PAVILION WITH AGARWOOD, WITH THAT OF THE BRANCHES AS ITS FRAME, THE SMELL OF MUSK AND FRANKINCENSE MIXED INTO THE SOIL TO FORM ITS WALLS. EVERY SPRING WHEN THE PEONIES ARE IN BLOOM, HE GATHERS GUESTS IN THIS PAVILION TO ADMIRE THE FLOWERS AND STREETS. NO OTHER CAN COMPARE WITH THE MAGNIFICENCE OF THIS PAVILION."

— KAIYUAN TIANBAO RECORDS: FOUR FRAGRANCE PAVILION

SNATCHING THE VICTORY WITH THE FLOWER CARRIAGE, "SHIFTING SPRINGS"

"EVERY SPRING, THE MEN WHO SERVE YANG GUOZHONG GATHER FAMOUS PLANTS AND FLOWERS FOR HIS CARRIAGE. WITH A BOARD BASE AND WOODEN WHEELS, IT ROLLS ALONG AS IT IS CARRIED BY HIS MEN. THE CARRIAGE DRAWS THE ADMIRATION OF OTHERS DUE TO ITS DESIGN AND HAS THUS BEEN TERMED THE SHIFTING SPRINGS CARRIAGE."

— KAIYUAN TIANBAO RECORDS: SHIFTING SPRINGS

THERE'S NO HARM!
EVEN IF WE'RE MISSING ONE, OUR "SHIFTING SPRINGS" FLOWER CARRIAGE IS STILL THE MOST BEAUTIFUL.

FLOWER FARMERS OF DULING

THE VILLAGE OF DULING IS A REAL VILLAGE THAT EXISTED DURING THE TANG DYNASTY, MADE UP OF A COMMUNITY OF FLOWER FARMERS. THEY MADE THEIR LIVING SELLING FLOWERS. FLOWER MARKETS WERE ALREADY WELL ESTABLISHED DURING THE TANG DYNASTY, WHERE VALUABLE FLOWERS WOULD FETCH EXORBITANT PRICES, BUT THESE MARKETS WERE STILL LOVED BY THE NOBLES OF CHANG'AN.

THE FLOWER FARMERS IN DULING...
WE TOOK THEIR FLOWERS...

"THE PEOPLE OF DULING VILLAGE DON'T HARVEST CROPS, THE VALLEY AND A STREAM LEADS YOU TO THE DESTINED PLACE. THE GRASS AND TREES OF NANSHAN EVERY SPRING BRINGS THE REWARDS OF GOLD AND JADES."

— SONG FOR BUYING FLOWERS, LIU YANSHI

"A SINGLE CLUSTER OF DEEPLY COLORED BLOOMS, TEN FACTIONS OF THIEVING MEN."

— BUYING FLOWERS, BAI JUYI

"WHAT PERSON DOES NOT LOVE PEONIES? IT POSSESSES THE GLORY OF THE ALL CITY'S BEAUTY."

— COMPLETE TANG POETRY: PEONIES, XU NING

HUA'E TOWER AT XINGQING PALACE

XINGQING PALACE IS LOCATED TO THE EAST OF THE IMPERIAL CITY. WITHIN THE PALACE STANDS XINGQING HALL, THE GOVERNMENT BUILDING, HUA'E XIANGHUI TOWER, CHENXIANG PAVILION AND MORE. HUA'E TOWER WAS PROCLAIMED TO BE THE WORLD'S FOREMOST TOWER, WHERE XUANZONG OFTEN HOSTED BANQUETS AND ENJOYED ENTERTAINMENT WITH HIS PEOPLE.

"ON THE DAY OF GUIHAI IN THE EIGHTH MONTH, THE DAY OF THE EMPEROR'S BIRTH, HUNDREDS OF OFFICIALS GATHERED UNDER HUA'E TOWER."

"THE DAY OF DINGMAO, OFFICIALS ARE IN ATTENDANCE AT THE BANQUET OUTSIDE CHUNMING GATE, BY THE POND OF NING WANGXIAN. THE EMPEROR INVITES THEM TO RIDE UP TO HUA'E TOWER BEFORE GIVING THE ORDER TO BEGIN THE CELEBRATIONS. THE GENEROSITY OF REWARDS WAS MEASURED BY ONE'S DANCE."

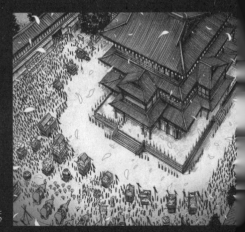

"ON THE DAY OF DINGHAI IN THE EIGHTH MONTH, AT HUA'E TOWER, THE EMPEROR REWARDS HIS MANY OFFICIALS IN THE NAME OF QIANQIU FESTIVAL. FOURTH RANKING OFFICIALS AND ABOVE WERE BESTOWED WITH GOLD MIRRORS, BAGS OF PEARLS AND COLORED SILK, WHILE THOSE OF THE FIFTH RANK AND BELOW WERE REWARDED WITH BOLTS OF PLAIN SILK."

— OLD BOOK OF TANG, BOOK EIGHT: XUANZONG, ONE OF TWO

"THE CUSTOM IN AUGUST IS TO GATHER AT HUA'E TOWER, WHERE MANY FEAST TO THEIR HEART'S CONTENT CELEBRATING QIANQIU."

— COLLECTION OF SONGS AND SHORT POEMS: FESTIVITIES OF QIANQIU, ZHANG HU

AN LUSHAN ENTERS THE IMPERIAL COURT

THE THIRTEENTH YEAR OF TIANBAO, FIRST MONTH OF THE LUNAR CALENDAR, AN LUSHAN ENTERS THE IMPERIAL COURT.

"THE FIFTH MONTH OF THE THIRTEENTH YEAR, SPRING, THE DAY OF JIHAI, AN LUSHAN ENTERS THE IMPERIAL COURT. YANG GUOZHONG EXPRESSED HIS CONVICTION THAT LUSHAN WOULD DEFINITELY STIR A REBELLION, STATING, 'EVEN IF YOUR MAJESTY WERE TO ISSUE AN IMPERIAL EDICT SUMMONING HIM, HE WOULD NOT COME.' HENCE, THE EMPEROR ORDERED MEN TO SUMMON AN LUSHAN. UPON HEARING THE SUMMON, AN LUSHAN HURRIED TO THE IMPERIAL CITY. ON THE DAY OF GENGZI, AN LUSHAN MADE HIS APPEARANCE AT HUAQING PALACE, EXCLAIMING, 'I AM A PERSON OF HU WHO HAS RECEIVED CONSIDERABLE FAVOR FROM HIS MAJESTY. TO BE ABLE TO SERVE FOR THE COUNTRY, I CAN DIE WITH NO REGRETS!' WITH SUCH AN APPEAL, LUSHAN WAS REWARDED HANDSOMELY AND DUE TO THE EMPEROR'S TRUST IN HIM, GUOZHONG'S WORDS WERE IN VAIN. THE CROWN PRINCE KNEW OF LUSHAN'S REBELLION AND WARNED THE EMPEROR, BUT HIS WORDS FELL ON DEAF EARS."

— COMPREHENSIVE MIRROR IN AID OF GOVERNANCE

"GUOZHONG FORWARDED THE INVESTIGATION INTO LUSHAN'S REBELLION... BUT HIS SUBORDINATE ACCEPTED A BRIBE FROM AN LUSHAN, LEADING HIM TO SING PRAISES OF AN LUSHAN WHEN HE RETURNED. GUOZHONG ALSO ACCUSED AN LUSHAN OF 'NOT HEEDING IMPERIAL ORDERS, EVEN WHEN SUMMONED,' ACTING PURELY ON HIS OWN WILL. IN THE FIRST MONTH OF THE THIRTEENTH YEAR, LUSHAN ENTERED HUAQING PALACE. WEEPING HE SAID, 'I AM AN ILLITERATE BARBARIAN, YET YOUR MAJESTY HAS PROMOTED ME AGAIN AND AGAIN, CAUSING GUOZHONG TO WANT TO KILL ME.' XUANZONG TRUSTED HIM DEEPLY, BESTOWING UPON HIM THE TITLE OF RIGHT CHIEF ADMINISTRATOR BEFORE ALLOWING HIM TO LEAVE. IN THE SAME MONTH, HE ALSO APPLIED TO BE HEAD OF THE IMPERIAL STABLES AND COMMANDER OF LONGSHI CIRCUIT. HE ALSO REQUESTED FOR JI WEN TO BE THE DEPUTY MINISTER FOR THE MILITARY, AS WELL AS GIVING HIM THE TITLE OF IMPERIAL COUNSELLOR AND LATER VICE GOVERNOR IN SERVICE OF HIS OWN OFFICE. LUSHAN ALSO REQUESTED TO BE ALLOWED TO ASSIST IN THE OFFICE OF GENERAL AFFAIRS. WITH CONTROL OVER THE STABLES, HIS MILITARY PROWESS WAS STRENGTHENED. HE TOOK ADVANTAGE OF THIS, ACQUIRING THE FINEST STEADS FOR HIMSELF FROM THE LOUFAN AND ZHANG WENYAN'S STABLES. ON THE FIRST DAY OF THE THIRD MONTH, HE RETURNED TO FANYANG, WITH WORD BEING SPREAD THAT HE WAS TO CROSS THE BORDERS. HE TRAVELLED FOR DAYS OVER A DISTANCE OF BETWEEN THREE AND FOUR HUNDRED MILES TOWARDS FANYANG. XUANZONG WOULD FLY INTO A RAGE WHENEVER ANYONE MENTIONED LUSHAN'S REBELLION, AND THEY WOULD BE BOUND AND SENT TO AN LUSHAN. IN THE FOURTEENTH YEAR, XUANZONG SUMMONED HIM TO THE IMPERIAL CITY BUT HE REPORTED THAT HE HAD FALLEN ILL AND WAS UNABLE TO ATTEND. WHEN THE EMPEROR OFFERED A MARRIAGE PROPOSAL FOR AN LUSHAN'S SON, ORDERING HIM TO ATTEND, HE ALSO REFUSED."

— OLD BOOK OF TANG, SCROLL TWO HUNDRED, BIOGRAPHIES ONE HUNDRED AND FIFTY: AN LUSHAN

YANG GUIFEI'S ENTRANCE

WHEN THE IMPERIAL PALACE DOORS WERE OPEN TO THE PUBLIC, THE CIVILIANS WERE WELCOMED WITH VIBRANT ENTERTAINMENT TROUPES AND THEIR ILLUSIONS, AS WELL AS RHINOCEROS AND ELEPHANTS.

"ENTERTAINERS WERE COMMON ACROSS EVERY DYNASTY, CAPABLE OF A VARIETY OF MUSICAL AND DANCE PERFORMANCES. WHEN THE EMPEROR DESCENDED FROM THE HEAVENS TO THE ORCHESTRATION OF MUSIC, THE BEAST SHE LI WOULD COME FROM THE WEST. PLAYING IN THE PALACE COURTYARD, IT WOULD TRANSFORM INTO A FLOUNDER WITHIN THE POND, LEAPING THROUGH THE WATERS, CONJURING CLOUDS OF MIST, FINALLY TURNING INTO A DRAGON EIGHT FEET LONG. IT WOULD DANCE IN THE WATERS, GLISTENING IN THE SUN'S RAYS. TWO FEMALE PERFORMERS WOULD DANCE UPON A ROPE STRUNG ACROSS TWO POLES, A LENGTH OF MANY ZHANG, BRUSHING SHOULDERS BUT NEVER LOSING THEIR FOOTING. SUCH WERE THE DIVERSITY OF PERFORMANCES, COUNTLESS IN THEIR TRICKS."

— OLD BOOK OF TANG, CHRONICLE NINE: MUSIC, TWO

"THE ANIMAL HANDLERS LEAD THE ELEPHANTS, AS OFFERINGS OR PART OF THE DANCE, ENERGIZING THE CROWD TOGETHER WITH THE MUSIC."

— OLD BOOK OF TANG, CHRONICLE EIGHT: MUSIC, ONE

"THE MINISTER OF CEREMONIES WOULD LEAD THE CEREMONIAL MUSIC, WHILE THE ANIMAL HANDLERS WOULD LEAD THE ELEPHANTS AND RHINOCEROSES IN TO DANCE IN HONOR OF THE EMPEROR. IT WAS COMMON FOR THOSE IN THE PALACE TO DON THEIR FINEST WEAR OF EMBROIDERED SILKS, AND THE CELEBRATIONS TO BE ENLIVENED BY THE WAVING OF FLAGS AND THE THUNDERING OF DRUMS."

— NEW BOOK OF TANG: RITES AND MUSIC, TWELVE

HALCYONS NEST UPON THE PALACE ROOFS...

MANDARIN DUCKS SETTLE WITHIN THE PALACE PONDS.

IN PART TWO, WHEN THE BANQUET OFFICIALLY BEGINS, THE MALE MUSICIAN PLAYING THE PIPA (CHINESE LUTE) AND SINGING LI BAI'S "LYRICS FOR WANDERING IN THE PALACE" IS THE FAMOUS TIANBAO ERA MUSICIAN LEI HAIQING (716 A.D. - 755 A.D.)

HISTORICAL RECORDS STATE THAT AN LUSHAN HAD A STOUT BUILD AND OFTEN NEEDED OTHERS TO SUPPORT HIM AS HE WALKED. HOWEVER, WHEN HE PERFORMED THE SOGDIAN WHIRL, HE WOULD BE MAGNIFICENT LIKE THE WIND. THE DANCE HE PERFORMED DURING THE BANQUET IS NOT TYPICALLY AN INDIVIDUAL PERFORMANCE, BUT IS USUALLY ACCOMPANIED BY A GROUP OF FEMALE DANCERS.

牛馬散北海
割鮮若虎餐

"IN HIS LATER YEARS, HE WOULD BE OF A STAUNCH BUILT, WITH A BELLY HANGING PAST HIS KNEES. AT A WEIGHT OF THREE HUNDRED AND THIRTY JIN, HE WOULD NEED TO BE LIFTED FROM HIS ARMS ON BOTH THE LEFT AND RIGHT TO BE ABLE TO WALK, AND EVERY STEP REQUIRED EFFORT. BEFORE XUANZONG, HIS PERFORMANCE OF THE SOGDIAN WHIRL WOULD BE A ROBUST AND BREATH-TAKING SIGHT."

– OLD BOOK OF TANG, BIOGRAPHIES ONE HUNDRED AND FIFTY: AN LUSHAN

XUANZONG'S JIEGU

HISTORICAL RECORDS STATE THAT XUANZONG HAD AN EXCELLENT UNDERSTANDING OF MUSICAL RHYTHM, AND WAS ESPECIALLY GOOD WITH THE JIEGU (WETHER DRUM).

"THE JIEGU LOOKED SIMILAR TO A BUCKET, AND COULD BE PLAYED BY DRUMMING WITH BOTH HANDS. IT ORIGINATED FROM THE JIE TRIBE AND WAS HENCE TERMED THE JIEGU. IT CAN ALSO BE PLAYED WITH TWO STICKS."

– OLD BOOK OF TANG: MUSIC, TWO

XUANZONG, WHO WAS VERSED IN MUSICAL RHYTHM AND HAD A DEEP LOVE FOR DHARMIC SONGS, ESTABLISHED THE PEAR GARDEN TO TRAIN THREE HUNDRED PERFORMERS. THE EMPEROR WOULD CORRECT ANY MISTAKES HE NOTICED, AND HENCE THEY WERE CALLED THE 'EMPEROR'S DISCIPLES AT THE PEAR GARDEN.' THERE WERE A HUNDRED PALACE MAIDS WHO WERE ALSO PART OF THE PEAR GARDEN DISCIPLES, AND THEY RESIDED IN THE YICHUN NORTH YARD. THERE WERE ONLY THIRTY SINGERS WHO FORMED A SMALL MUSICAL GROUP DEVOTED TO THE PRACTICE OF FA MUSIC AT THE PEAR GARDEN. IMPRESSED BY MOUNT LI, THE EMPEROR ORDERED THIS MUSICAL GROUP TO PERFORM AT THE IMPERIAL COURT ON YANG GUIFEI'S BIRTHDAY. THE NEW SONG THAT THEY PERFORMED HAD YET TO BE WELL KNOWN TO OTHERS, BUT BECAUSE OF THE LYCHEES BROUGHT IN FROM THE NORTH, WOULD BE TITLED, 'FRAGRANCE OF LYCHEES.' THE EMPEROR WAS ALSO FOND OF THE JIEGU, AND THE PRINCE OF NING ENJOYED PLAYING THE SIDE-BLOWN FLUTE. UNDER THE ADMIRATION OF THE COURT OFFICIALS, THEY WOULD PERFORM JOYOUSLY. THE EMPEROR OFTEN CLAIMED, 'THE JIEGU PRODUCES THE BEST OF THE EIGHT TONES AND THERE IS NO OTHER WHICH CAN COMPARE TO IT.' BELONGING ORIGINALLY TO THE MINORITY TRIBES, THEY INVOLVED A PORTION OF THE TONES FROM THE TAICU SCALE, INCORPORATING NOTES FROM KUCHA, GAOCHANG, SHULE, TIANZHU, PRODUCING A ROBUST AND UNIQUE FOLK SOUND."

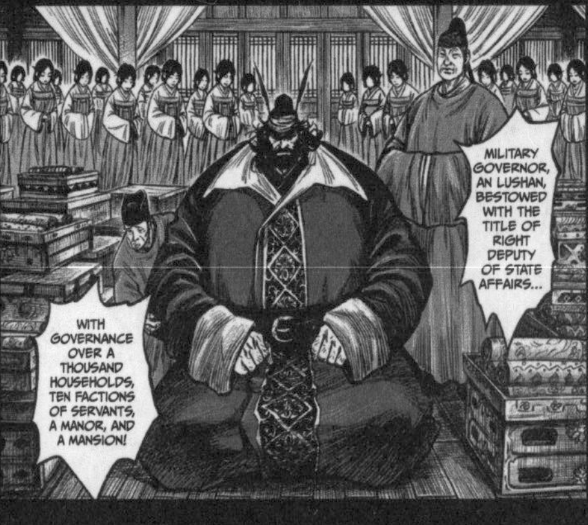
MILITARY GOVERNOR, AN LUSHAN, BESTOWED WITH THE TITLE OF RIGHT DEPUTY OF STATE AFFAIRS...
WITH GOVERNANCE OVER A THOUSAND HOUSEHOLDS, TEN FACTIONS OF SERVANTS, A MANOR, AND A MANSION!

AN LUSHAN'S REWARDS

"ON THE DAY OF YISI, AN LUSHAN WILL BE BESTOWED THE TITLE OF RIGHT CHIEF ADMINISTRATOR, WITH GOVERNANCE OVER A THOUSAND FACTIONS OF SERVANTS, A MANOR, AND A MANSION; WITH AN ADDITION OF GOVERNANCE OVER THE XIANJIU, WU FANG EUNUCHS, IMPERIAL GARDEN, THE REGION OF LONGYOU, AS WELL AS HAVING DEPUTY MINISTER OF THE MILITARY TO BE HIS VICE GOVERNOR. HE IS TO RETURN TO THE CAPITAL ON THE DAY OF BINGWU. ON THE DAY OF GUIYOU OF THE SECOND MONTH, HE IS TO ATTEND THE IMPERIAL COURT AT DAQING PALACE, BY THE ORDERS OF THE EMPEROR, HIS MAJESTY THE GREAT AND HEAVENLY ANCESTOR OF THE LANDS."

— OLD BOOK OF TANG, BOOK NINE: XUANZONG, TWO OF TWO

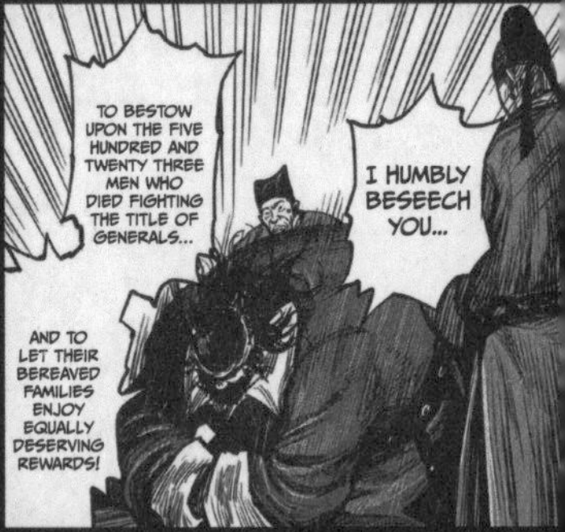
I HUMBLY BESEECH YOU...
TO BESTOW UPON THE FIVE HUNDRED AND TWENTY THREE MEN WHO DIED FIGHTING THE TITLE OF GENERALS...
AND TO LET THEIR BEREAVED FAMILIES ENJOY EQUALLY DESERVING REWARDS!

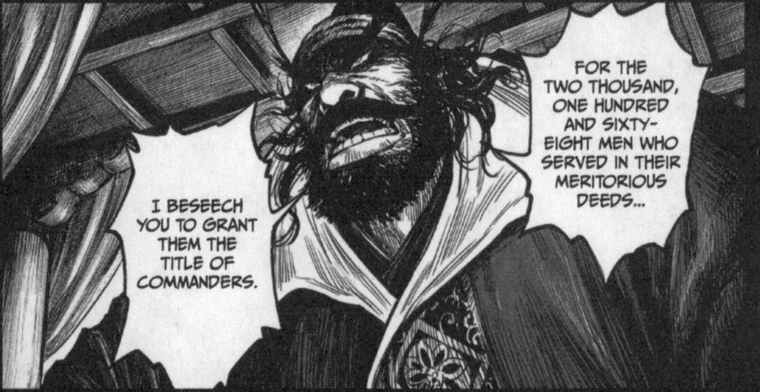
FOR THE TWO THOUSAND, ONE HUNDRED AND SIXTY-EIGHT MEN WHO SERVED IN THEIR MERITORIOUS DEEDS...
I BESEECH YOU TO GRANT THEM THE TITLE OF COMMANDERS.

"THE DAY OF YIHAI, THE EMPEROR VISITED XINGQING COURT TO BE NAMED. THE PUNISHMENT FOR ONE OF HIS OFFICIALS HAD BEEN PARDONED, AND HE WAS SENT BACK TO HIS HOME UPON NEWS OF HIS PARENTS' PASSING. THE EXISTING TITLES OF WUSHU HAD BEEN CHANGED TO WUTAI. THE GOVERNORS AND OFFICIALS WERE RAISED A TITLE. ALL THIRD RANKING MILITARY AND SCHOLARLY OFFICIALS WERE ALSO ABLE TO MOVE A RANK UP. FOURTH RANKING OFFICIALS TO MOVE UP A TIER. A FEAST WAS HELD FOR THREE DAYS. THE DAY OF WUYAN, THE TITLE OF CHANCELLOR, MINISTER OF CIVIL AFFAIRS, AND MINISTER OF LAND AND SEA WAS BESTOWED ON YANG GUOZHONG, WITH NO FURTHER CHANGES IN THE OTHER OFFICIAL POSTS. ON THE DAY OF JIASHEN, YANG GUOZHONG WAS GIVEN HIS TITLES AND THE SKY POURED DOWN HEAVILY, DRENCHING THE ROBES OF ALL. BEFORE COMING TO THE IMPERIAL COURT, AN LUSHAN HAD LED THE MILITARY EXPEDITION AND SPRUNG AN ATTACK ON THE KITHAN, EARNING RECOGNITION AS A WORTHY GENERAL. HE REQUESTED FOR MORE MEN THAN HE WAS ASSIGNED, AND CONTINUED TO DESIRE FOR A PROPER WRITTEN APPOINTMENT TO OFFICE. AS A RESULT, HE WAS REWARDED WITH MORE THAN HE ASKED FOR, WITH FIVE HUNDRED GENERALS AND TWO THOUSAND COMMANDERS."

— OLD BOOK OF TANG, BOOK NINE: XUANG ZONG, PART TWO OF TWO

"ON THE DAY OF JICHOU, AN LUSHAN EXCLAIMED, 'A NUMBER OF MY SOLDERS WILL BE TRAVELING TO XI, KITHAN, JIUXING, TONGLUO AND MORE, WHICH LEAVES THEM IN THE PATH OF DANGER, BEYOND WHAT THEY ARE USED TO. IT WOULD BE BEST IF THEY WERE GIVEN AN IMPERIAL AMULET FOR THEIR EASY TRAVELS.' HIS WORDS EARNED THIS HONOR FOR HIS FIVE HUNDRED GENERALS AND TWO THOUSAND COMMANDERS. LUSHAN WAS PLANNING A REBELLION AND THIS HELPED HIM WIN THE HEARTS OF MANY."

— COMPREHENSIVE MIRROR IN AID OF GOVERNANCE: TANG RECORDS, THIRTY-THREE

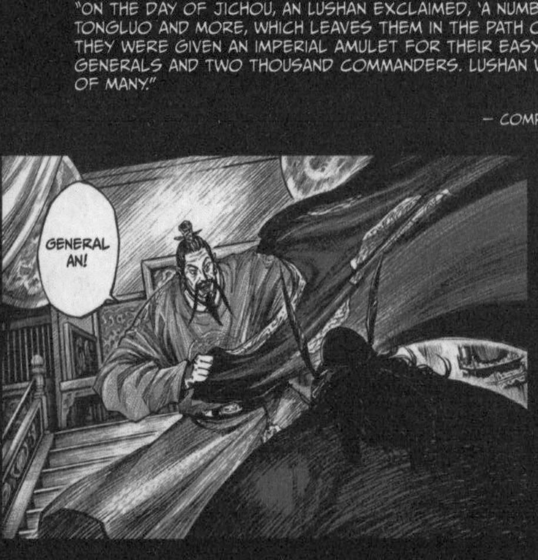
GENERAL AN!

"THE THIRD MONTH, THE BEGINNING OF THE DAY OF DINGYOU, LUSHAN RETURNED TO FANYANG. THE EMPEROR OFFERED HIM HIS ROBES AS A REWARD, DELIGHTING THE SURPRISED LUSHAN."

— COMPREHENSIVE MIRROR IN AID OF GOVERNANCE: TANG RECORDS, THIRTY-THREE

YANG GUOZHONG'S POWER

THE POLITICALLY AMBITIOUS YANG GUOZHONG HAD A DEEP HATRED TOWARDS AN LUSHAN. DURING AN LUSHAN'S FINAL VISIT TO THE IMPERIAL COURT, THEIR CONFLICT FINALLY EXPLODED.

GUOZHONG WAS COLD AND NEUROTIC. HIS STRENGTH WAS HIS WAY WITH WORDS; THIS SKILL WON HIM THE POSITION OF CHANCELLOR. HE HANDLED CONFIDENTIAL MATTERS DECISIVELY, WITHOUT A SHADOW OF DOUBT. IN COURT, WITH A SHAKE OF HIS SLEEVES AND A TURN OF HIS WRISTS, HE WOULD ORDER THE OFFICIALS BELOW HIM ABOUT. ALL WERE AFRAID OF HIM.

AT THE TIME, AN LUSHAN RECEIVED GREAT FAVOR FROM THE EMPEROR, HOLDING MILITARY POWER. GUOZHONG KNEW HE WAS PRIDEFUL, AND DID NOT OVERSTEP BEFORE HIM, DECIDING INSTEAD TO TELL THE EMPEROR AGAIN AND AGAIN OF HIS REBELLIOUS NATURE. THE EMPEROR DID NOT BELIEVE HIM. THIS TIME, LUSHAN HAD ALREADY ESTABLISHED HIS AUTHORITY IN HEBEI, RIDING OUT TO GATHER TROOPS IN YOUZHOU IN PREPARATION TO REVOLT, THOUGH THE REASON WAS STILL UNCLEAR. AFTER WISHING THE EMPEROR LONGEVITY AT THE QIANQIU FESTIVAL, HE WAS FURIOUS AND DOMINEERING. SEEING THAT GUOZHONG HAD CONTROL AND THINKING THAT THINGS WERE NOT IN HIS FAVOR, LUSHAN TOOK ON THE ROLE OF HEAD OF THE IMPERIAL STABLES FROM AFAR, PLACING MILITARY MINISTER JI WEN IN THE POSITION OF THE PROVISIONAL GOVERNOR AND IMPERIAL CENSOR WHILE GATHERING INFORMATION IN AND AROUND THE CAPITAL TO UNDERSTAND THE SITUATION IN THE IMPERIAL COURT. GUOZHONG SENT JIAN ANG AND HE YING TO UNCOVER LUSHAN'S SECRET AFFAIRS, SURROUNDING HIS HOME. THEY FOUND THAT LI CHAO, AN DAI AND OTHERS, AND HAD THE IMPERIAL OFFICIAL ZHENG ANG SENTENCE THEM TO DEATH BY STRANGULATION. HE APPEALED TO HAVE JI WEN DEMOTED TO HEPU, ENRAGING LUSHAN. HAVING SUCCESSFULLY PROVOKED LUSHAN, HE ATTEMPTED TO OBTAIN THE EMPEROR'S TRUST ON THIS, BUT THE EMPEROR REMAINED UNMOVED. HENCE, LUSHAN WAS INTIMIDATED AND USED THE EXCUSE OF KILLING GUOZHONG TO RALLY THE TROOPS.

– OLD BOOK OF TANG, BIOGRAPHIES FIFTY-SIX: LI LINFU, YANG GUOZHONG

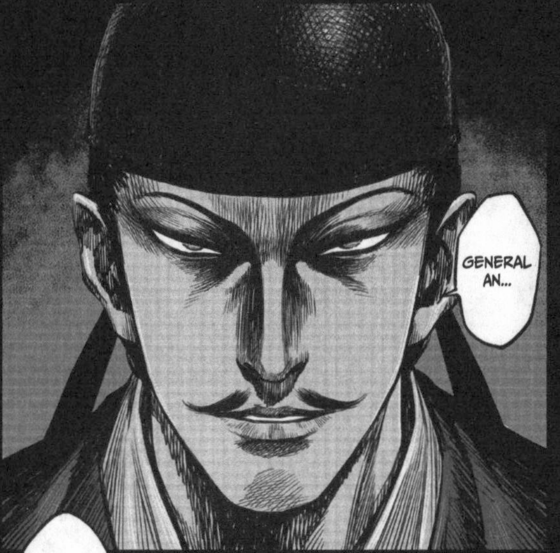
GENERAL AN...

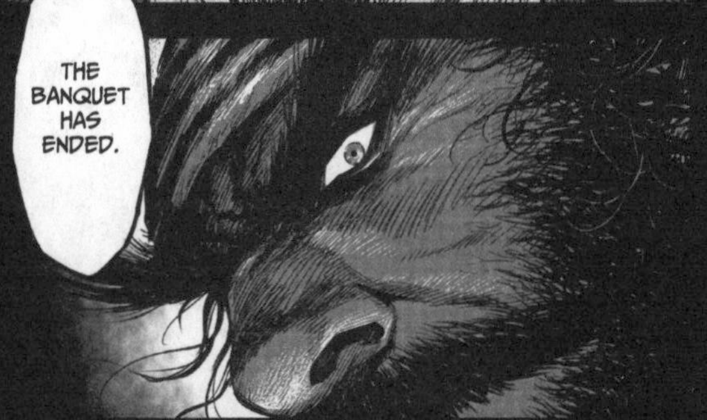
THE BANQUET HAS ENDED.

YANG GUOZHONG MOBILIZES THE YÜLIN IMPERIAL GUARDS

[WANG] HAN'S GOOD FRIEND XING ZAI PLANNED TO KILL THE LONGWU GENERAL WITH THE LONGWU TROOPS, CAUSING THE TROOPS TO REVOLT AND CALL FOR THE DEATH OF LI LINFU, CHEN XILIE AND YANG GUOZHONG. THIS WAS LEAKED TWO DAYS BEFORE THE INCIDENT. IN SUMMER, ON THE DAY OF YIYOU IN THE FOURTH MONTH, AT COURT, THIS REPORT WAS READ TO [WANG] HONG, WITH A WARRANT FOR HIS ARREST. THINKING HAN WAS WITH ZAI, HONG SENT SOMEONE TO SUMMON HIM. LATE IN THE DAY, HE ORDERED JIA JILIN TO ARREST ZAI. ZAI LIVED IN JINCHENGFANG. WHEN JILIN AND HIS MEN REACHED, ZAI AND HIS MEN, TEN PEOPLE, SUDDENLY ATTACKED WITH BLADES AND BOWS. HONG AND YANG GUOZHONG LED THE TROOPS THERE. XING'S GUARD WARNED, "YOU ARE NOT TO HARM LORD WANG AND HIS MEN." YANG GUOZHONG'S GUARD TOLD HIM IN SECRET, "THESE TRAITORS ARE SPEAKING IN CODE. DO NOT CROSS SWORDS WITH THEM." XING FOUGHT HIS WAY OUT TO THE SOUTH WEST OF THE IMPERIAL CITY.

– COMPREHENSIVE MIRROR IN AID OF GOVERNANCE: XUANZONG, ELEVENTH YEAR OF TIANBAO

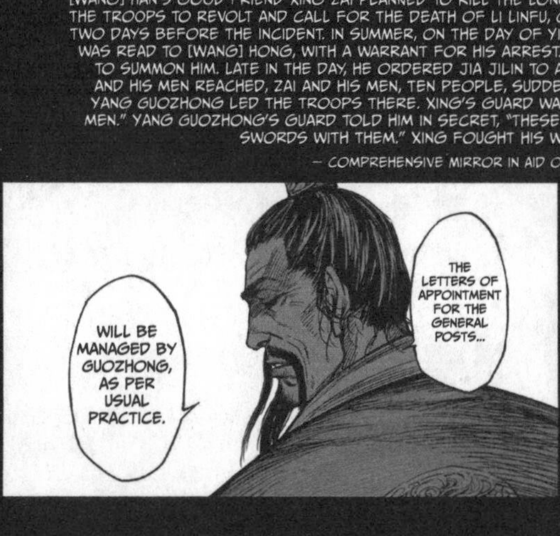
THE LETTERS OF APPOINTMENT FOR THE GENERAL POSTS...
WILL BE MANAGED BY GUOZHONG, AS PER USUAL PRACTICE.

YANG GUOZHONG'S NEPOTISM

SPRING, THE FIRST MONTH, THE DAY OF RENXU, GUOZHONG SUMMONED THE RIGHT CHANCELLOR CHEN XILIE, THE JISHIZHONG, AND ALL OTHER MINISTERS TO BE GATHERED AT THE DOCUMENTS OFFICE TO DECIDE ON POTENTIAL CANDIDATES. ONLY A DAY WAS NEEDED TO REACH A CONCLUSION. HE SAID, "SINCE THE RIGHT CHANCELLOR AND GEI SHI ZHONG ARE BOTH PRESENT, WE CAN ASSUME WE HAVE ALREADY PASSED THE INSPECTION OF INTERNAL AFFAIRS." THE CANDIDATES SELECTED HAD A LARGE DISPARITY IN THEIR CAPABILITIES, BUT NONE DARED TO OFFER THEIR OPINION.

– COMPREHENSIVE MIRROR IN AID OF GOVERNANCE, SCROLL TWO HUNDRED AND SIXTEEN: RECORDS OF TANG, THIRTY-TWO, XUAN ZONG, TWELFTH YEAR OF TIANBAO

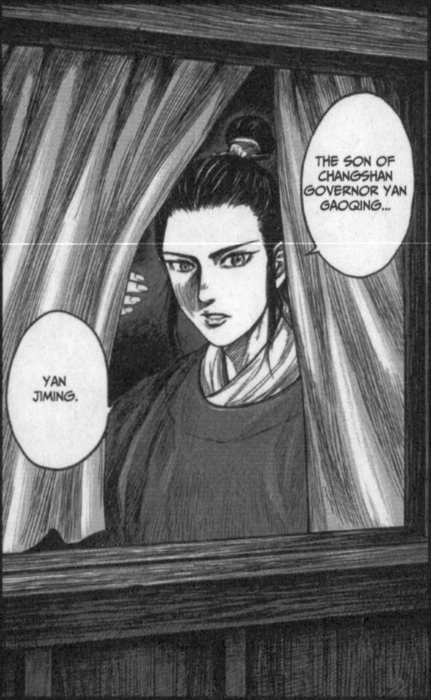
THE SON OF CHANGSHAN GOVERNOR YAN GAOQING...
YAN JIMING.

YAN JIMING

YAN JIMING WAS THE THIRD SON OF CHANGSHAN COMMANDER YAN GAOQING. HE WAS ALSO THE NEPHEW OF RENOWNED CALLIGRAPHER YAN ZHENQING.

"YAN GAOQING, OF LINYI IN LANGYA. HE WAS A HEREDITARY OFFICIAL, UPRIGHT AND CAPABLE. IN THE FOURTEENTH YEAR OF TIANBAO, HE WAS GIVEN THE POSITION OF CHANGSHAN COMMANDER."

— OLD BOOK OF TANG, SCROLL ONE HUNDRED AND EIGHTY-SEVEN, ONE OF TWO, BIOGRAPHIES ONE HUNDRED AND THIRTY-SEVEN: YAN GAOQING

"YAN GAOQING, COURTESY NAME XIN, WAS RELATED TO ZHENQING UNTO THE FIFTH DEGREE, AND DESCENDED FROM A SCHOLARLY FAMILY. HE WAS UPRIGHT AND CARRIED OUT HIS DUTIES IRREPROACHABLY. ONCE QUESTIONED BY A REGIONAL INSPECTOR, HE WAS ESPECIALLY FRANK AND UNBENDING. IN THE ERA OF KAIYUAN, HE AND HIS BROTHERS CHUNQING AND YAOQING HAD EXTRAORDINARY PENMANSHIP AND LITERARY TALENT, CAUSING XI YU, THE ASSISTANT MINISTER OF APPOINTMENTS, TO SIGH IN ADMIRATION. HENCE, HE WAS PROMOTED TO THE POSITION OF REGISTRAR IN THE COUNTY OF FANYANG. HEARING OF HIM, AN LUSHAN PROPOSED FOR HIM TO TAKE THE ROLE OF MILITARY MAGISTRATE AND DESIGNATED GOVERNOR OF CHANGSHAN.

— NEW BOOK OF TANG, SCROLL ONE HUNDRED AND NINETY-TWO, BIOGRAPHIES ONE HUNDRED AND SEVENTEEN: YAN GAOQING

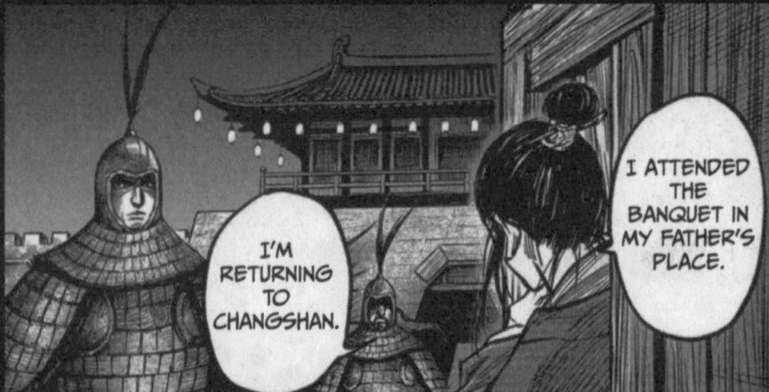
I ATTENDED THE BANQUET IN MY FATHER'S PLACE.
I'M RETURNING TO CHANGSHAN.

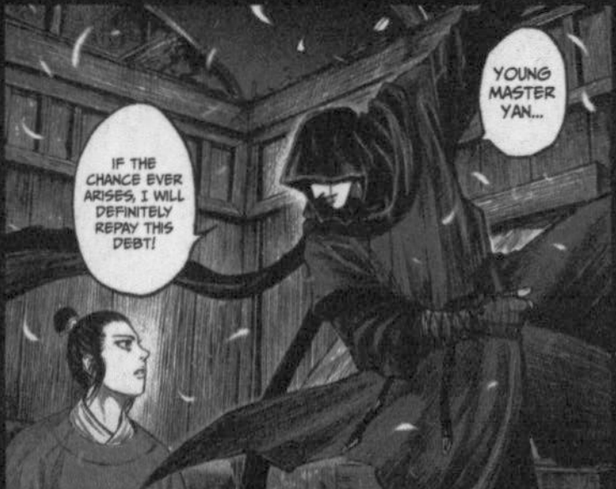
YOUNG MASTER YAN...
IF THE CHANCE EVER ARISES, I WILL DEFINITELY REPAY THIS DEBT!

THERE ARE NO RECORDS OF LI E IN HISTORY. HOWEVER, IN THE RECORDS OF YAN ZHENQING, HE WAS BRIEFLY NOTED AS A VISITOR FROM QINGHE.

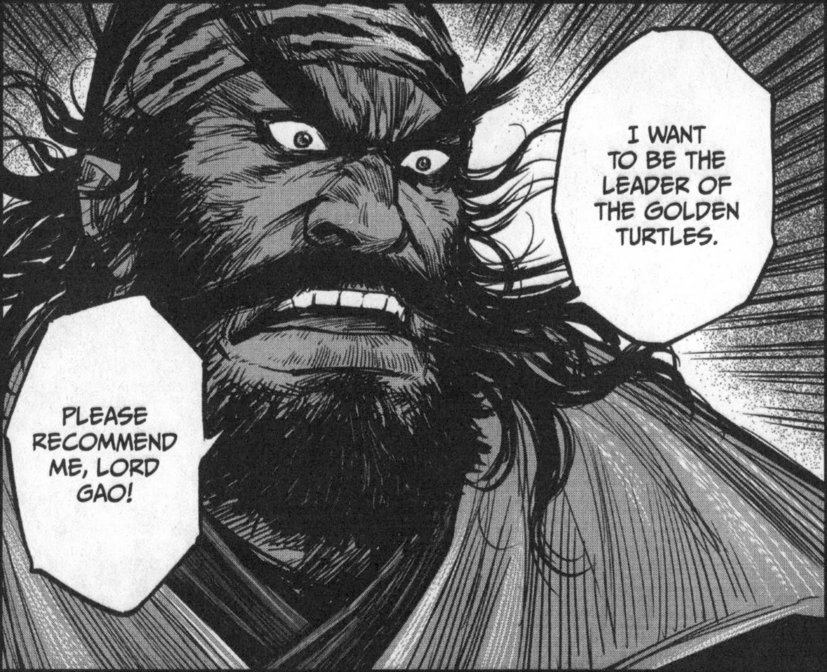
I WANT TO BE THE LEADER OF THE GOLDEN TURTLES.
PLEASE RECOMMEND ME, LORD GAO!

GOLDEN TURTLES

IN THE NINTH MONTH OF THE FIRST YEAR OF WUDE UNDER GAOZU'S RULE, THE OFFICIAL TOKEN OF AUTHORITY, THE SILVER RABBIT, WAS CHANGED TO THE SILVER FISH. IN THE FIFTH MONTH OF THE SECOND YEAR OF YONGHUI, UNDER GAOZONG'S RULE, TOP-RANK OFFICIALS, OFFICIALS OF THE CENTRAL GOVERNMENT BOTH MILITARY AND CIVIL, FOURTH- AND FIFTH-RANK OFFICIALS, WERE ALL TO CARRY THE FISH ON THEIR PERSON. IN THE FIFTH MONTH OF THE THIRD YEAR OF XIANHENG, OFFICIALS OF THE FIFTH RANK AND ABOVE WERE NEWLY BESTOWED FISH BROCADES, DECORATED WITH SILVER. THIRD-RANK OFFICIALS AND ABOVE WERE EACH BESTOWED GILDED BLADES AND WHETSTONES. IN THE FIRST MONTH OF THE SECOND YEAR OF CHUIGONG, COMMANDERS AND REGIONAL INSPECTORS OF ALL PREFECTURES WERE TO CARRY FISH BROCADES ALONG WITH CENTRAL GOVERNMENT OFFICIALS.

IN THE NINTH MONTH OF THE FIRST YEAR OF TIANSHOU, THE FISH TOKENS WERE CHANGED TO TURTLES. IN THE TENTH MONTH OF THE FIRST YEAR OF JIUSHI, THIRD-RANK OFFICIALS AND ABOVE CARRIED TURTLE SACHETS WITH GOLD ORNAMENTATION, FOURTH-RANK OFFICIALS USED SILVER, AND FIFTH-RANK OFFICIALS COPPER.

IN THE SECOND MONTH OF THE FIRST YEAR OF SHENLONG, OFFICIALS OF THE FIFTH RANK AND ABOVE, WITHIN AND WITHOUT THE CENTRAL GOVERNMENT, BORE THE FISH BROCADE AS BEFORE. IN THE SIXTH MONTH, REGIONAL AND HEREDITARY LORDS WERE ALLOWED TO BEAR GOLDEN FISH BROCADES. IN THE EIGHTH MONTH OF THE THIRD YEAR OF JINGLONG, SPECIAL PERMISSION WAS NEEDED TO BEAR THE FISH. THE SPECIAL BENEFITS OF BEARING THE FISH BEGAN. STARTING IN THE WUDE ERA, ALL OFFICIALS, FROM THE WATCHTOWER GUARDS UPWARDS, WOULD CARRY THE FISH BROCADE. FROM ZETIAN AND ZHONGZONG'S TIME ONWARD, SUPERVISORS AND INSPECTORS, THOSE WHO WERE NOT OFFICIALS, WOULD NOT CARRY THE FISH. THOUGH OFFICIALS CARRIED THEM, THEY WOULD GIVE THEM UP UPON RETIREMENT OR REMOVAL FROM OFFICE. THIS LASTED UNTIL THE NINTH YEAR OF KAIYUAN, WHEN ZHANG JIAZHEN IN HIS POSITION AS ZHONGSHU ORDERED THAT ALL RETIREES MAY CARRY THE FISH WITH THEM TILL THE END OF THEIR LIVES, AS A SYMBOL OF PRIDE AND FAVOR. THOSE WHO WERE REMOVED FROM OFFICE FOR ADEQUATE REASONS WERE ALSO ALLOWED TO WEAR THE FISH BROCADE. SINCE THOSE OF MERIT WERE GIVEN ROBES OF RED AND PURPLE, ALONG WITH THE FISH BROCADE, AS FORMAL DRESS, MANY CARRIED THE FISH BROCADE AND WORE ROBES OF CINNABAR AND PURPLE.

– OLD BOOK OF TANG, SCROLL FORTY-FIVE, CHRONICLE TWENTY-FIVE: RITES OF DRESSING

OFFICIALS IN THE TANG DYNASTY USED FISH-EMBROIDERED SACHETS AS A TOKEN TO IDENTIFY THEIR AUTHORITY. THE FISH TOKEN WAS CHANGED TO A TURTLE TOKEN UNDER WU ZETIAN'S RULE, THEN CHANGED BACK TO A FISH TOKEN WHEN ZHONGZONG RETURNED TO THE THRONE. WITH THE END OF WU ZETIAN'S RULE, THE TURTLE TOKEN'S AUTHORITY WAS ALSO ABOLISHED AFTER FIVE BRIEF YEARS. NEVERTHELESS, GOLDEN TURTLES ENDURED AS A SYMBOL OF NOBILITY, GIVING BIRTH TO THE SAYING "GOLDEN-TURTLE SON-IN-LAW" IN REFERENCE TO WEALTHY SON-IN-LAWS.
FIFTY YEARS LATER, "THE GOLDEN TURTLES" WAS THE NAME OF A SECRET IMPERIAL ORGANIZATION.

AN LUSHAN AND GAO LISHI

IT IS A HISTORICAL FACT THAT XUANZONG HAD HOPED TO PROMOTE AN LUSHAN TO BE AN OFFICIAL, AND EVEN A CHANCELLOR, BUT ULTIMATELY DID NOT DO SO DUE TO YANG GUOZHONG'S OPPOSITION. A COURTIER SECRETLY CONVEYED THIS TO AN LUSHAN, AND AN LUSHAN WAS GREATLY DISPLEASED. THE EUNUCH GAO LISHI WAS ORDERED TO SEND OFF AN LUSHAN DURING HIS DEPARTURE FROM CHANG'AN AND BECAME AWARE OF THIS.

"LUSHAN HAS MILITARY MIGHT, BUT IS ILLITER-ATE..."
"HOW CAN HE BE AN OFFICIAL?"

"THE EMPEROR HOPED TO PROMOTE AN LUSHAN TO THE RANK OF AN OFFICIAL AND HAD ALREADY WRITTEN THE EDICT FOR IT. HOWEVER, YANG GUOZHONG SAID TO HIM, 'AN LUSHAN HAS SERVED WELL AS A MILITARY MAN, BUT HE IS ILLITERATE. HOW CAN HE BE CHANCELLOR? IF YOU LET THIS COME TO PASS, THE TANG DYNASTY WILL BE BELITTLED BY THE OTHER NATIONS.' AS A RESULT, THE EMPEROR RELUCTANTLY OVERWROTE HIS INITIAL INTENTIONS. ON THE DAY OF YISI, THE EMPEROR BESTOWED LUSHAN THE TITLE OF RIGHT CHIEF ADMINISTRATOR, AS WELL AS REWARDING ONE OF HIS SONS WITH THE POST OF A THIRD RANKING OFFICIAL, AND ANOTHER WITH THE POST OF A FOURTH RANKING OFFICIAL."

— COMPREHENSIVE MIRROR IN AID OF GOVERNANCE

"WHEN LUSHAN LEFT CHANG'AN, THE EMPEROR ORDERED GAO LISHI TO SEND HIM OFF UP TO CHANGLE HILL. UPON GAO LISHI'S RETURN, THE EMPEROR ASKED, 'WAS AN LUSHAN SATISFIED?' GAO LISHI REPLIED, 'I SAW THAT HE DID NOT SEEM PLEASED. HE MUST KNOW THE REASON THAT THE PLAN TO MAKE HIM CHANCELLOR WAS QUASHED.' THE EMPEROR INFORMED GUOZHONG, WHO SAID, 'THIS PLAN WAS NOT KNOWN TO OTHERS, SO IT MUST HAVE BEEN ZHANG JI AND HIS BROTHERS WHO INFORMED HIM OF IT.' ENRAGED, THE EMPEROR DEMOTED ZHANG JUN TO GOVERNOR OF JIAN'AN, ZHANG JI TO MARSHAL OF LUXI, AND JI'S YOUNGER BROTHER, IMPERIAL ATTENDANT CHU, TO MARSHAL OF YICHUN."

— COMPREHENSIVE MIRROR IN AID OF GOVERNANCE

"HENCE, LUSHAN WAS INTIMIDATED AND USED THE EXCUSE OF KILLING GUOZHONG TO RALLY THE TROOPS."

— OLD BOOK OF TANG, BIOGRAPHIES FIFTY-SIX: YANG GUOZHONG

EXECUTING GUOZHONG...
CLEANSING THE STATE!

Feng Zi Su

ASSASSIN'S
CREED

VALHALLA

BLOOD BROTHERS

ACTION

Not long before the exploits of Eivor Wolf-Kissed, Jarl Stensson and his sons, Ulf and Björn, make their way to England at the behest of Halfdan Ragnarsson and Ivarr the Boneless. Filled with excitement, confidence and bloodlust, the two brothers are eager to go to war against Aelfred the Great and his Anglo Saxon army. But they would do well not to underestimate what awaits them on those green shores...

UBISOFT

TOKYOPOP

LAUGHING UNDER THE CLOUDS, VOLUME 1

KarakaraKemuri

LAUGHING UNDER THE CLOUDS

1

KarakaraKemuri

FANTASY

In the early Meiji era, against civil unrest and the end of the samurai way of life, Japan's crime rate skyrocketed. As prisons overflow, the government has no choice but to build a new, inescapable prison. This prison is Gokumonjo, located in the center of Lake Biwa, which means it relies on the three sons of the Kumo family to transport criminals to it. But is Gokumonjo truly just a prison for petty criminals...?

ADVENTURE

When Lizel finds himself in a city that bears odd similarities to his own but clearly isn't, he quickly comes to terms with the unlikely truth: this is an entirely different world. Even so, laid-back Lizel isn't the type to panic. He sets out to learn more about this strange place, and to help him do so, hires a seasoned adventurer named Gil as his guide and protector. Until he's able to find a way home, Lizel figures this is a perfect opportunity to explore a new way of life adventuring as part of a guild. Might as well enjoy the otherworldly vacation for now!

SUPERNATURAL

Yamagishi and Sendo are schoolmates, but that's about all they have in common: one is a down-to-earth guy in the boxing club, while the other is a brainy, bookish conspiracy nut. But when they stumble across something weird and inexplicable after class one evening, it seems they'll have to set their differences aside in order to uncover the truth behind the mysterious creatures and strange figure prowling the school grounds.

KAMO
PACT WITH THE SPIRIT WORLD
TOKYOPOP
1
Ban Zarbo

KAMO: PACT WITH THE SPIRIT WORLD, VOLUME 1

Ban Zarbo

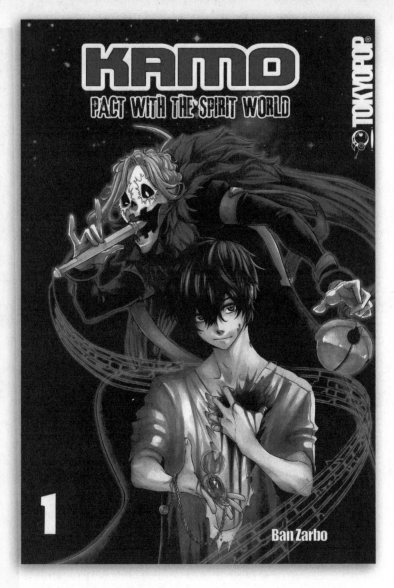

FANTASY

Born with a failing heart, Kamo has fought death his whole life, but to no avail. As his body weakens and he readies to draw his final breath, he's visited by a powerful spirit named Crimson who offers him a deal: defeat and capture the souls of twelve spirits in exchange for a new heart. It seems too good to be true... and maybe it is.

A pact with the spirit world... what could possibly go wrong?

TOKYOPOP

UNDEAD MESSIAH, VOLUME 1

Gin Zarbo

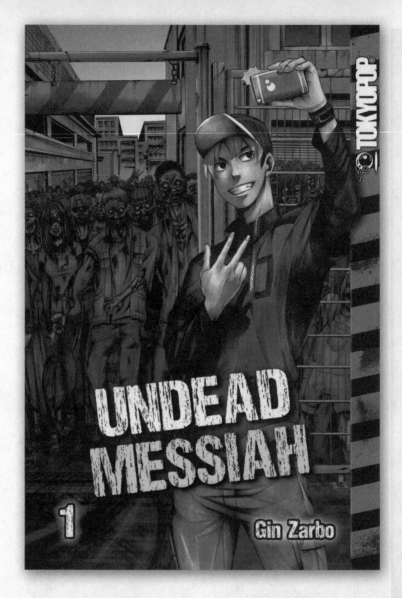

ACTION

A pregnant woman is pursued by a supernatural creature. On the internet, videos of a bandaged hero surface. 15-year-old Tim Muley makes a terrible discovery in his neighbor's garden. Three seemingly unrelated events, all of which seem to point to an imminent zombie apocalypse! But this time the story's not about the end of mankind; it's about a new beginning...

YA MANGA
ASSASSINS CREED
491-1536

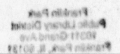

Assassin's Creed® Dynasty, Volume 1

Story by Xu Xianzhe
Art by Zhang Xiao

Assistant Artists	-	Zhou Peican, Lin Lin, Yuan Yuan
Consulting Historian	-	Meng Xianshi
Produced by	-	New Comics
Special thanks	-	Mia Zhang and the Ubisoft Film and Television team, Aymar Azaïzia, Fatiha Chellali and Etienne Bouvier
Translator	-	Karen Lam
Proofreaders	-	Tay Weiling, Alex Lam
Editor	-	Lena Atanassova
Copy Editor	-	Kae Winters
Marketing Associate	-	Kae Winters
Cover Design & Graphic Artist	-	Sol DeLeo
Editorial Associate	-	Janae Young
Retouching and Lettering	-	Vibrraant Publishing Studio
Licensing Specialist	-	Arika Yanaka
Editor-in-Chief & Publisher	-	Stu Levy

A  Manga

TOKYOPOP and ⊙ are trademarks or registered trademarks of TOKYOPOP Inc.

TOKYOPOP Inc.
5200 W. Century Blvd. Suite 705
Los Angeles, 90045

E-mail: info@TOKYOPOP.com
Come visit us online at www.TOKYOPOP.com

f www.facebook.com/TOKYOPOP
🐦 www.twitter.com/TOKYOPOP
📷 www.instagram.com/TOKYOPOP

ISBN: 978-1-4278-6882-4
First TOKYOPOP Printing: January 2022
Printed in CANADA

STOP

THIS IS THE BACK OF THE BOOK!

How do you read manga-style? It's simple! Let's practice -- just start in the top right panel and follow the numbers below!

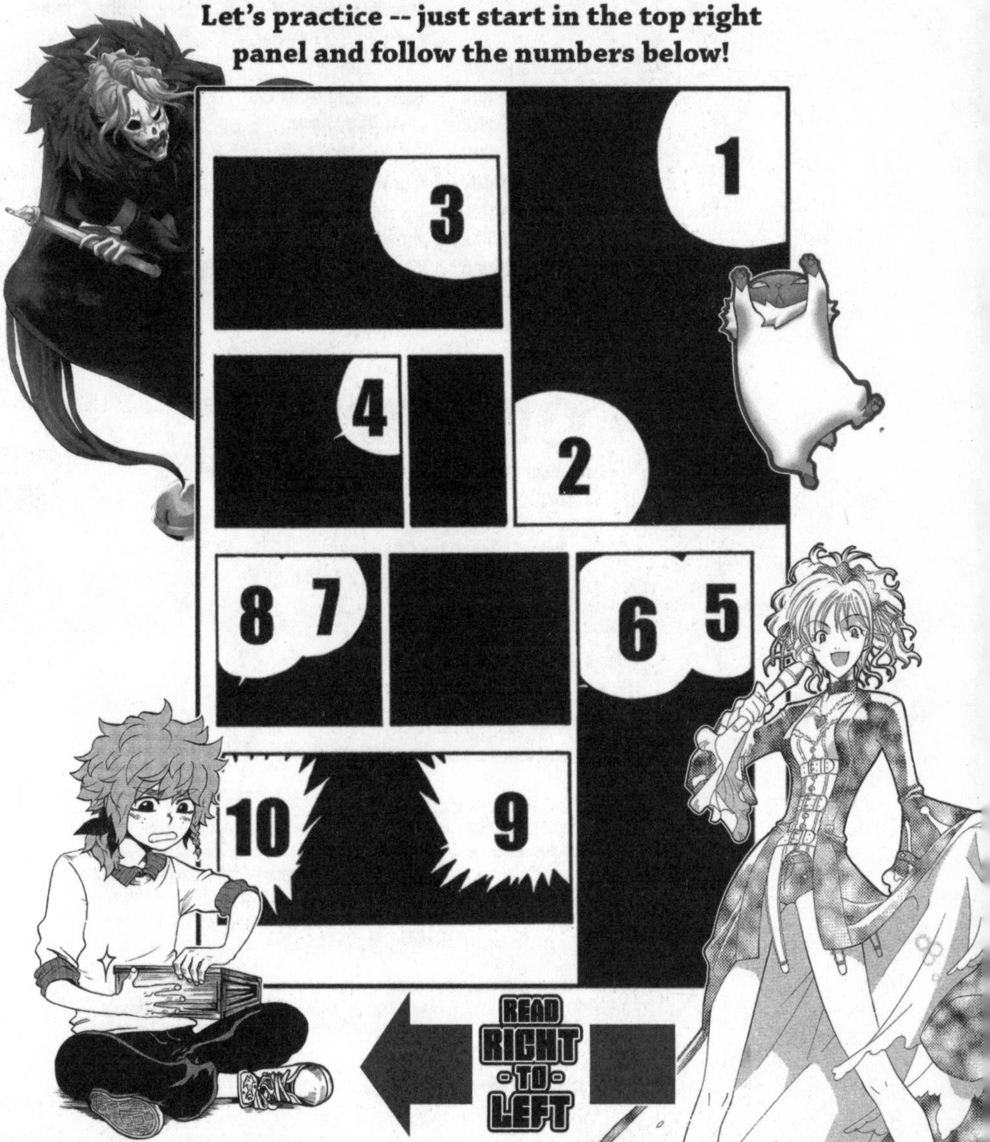
1
2
3
4
5
6
7
8
9
10
READ
RIGHT
-TO-
LEFT

Crimson from ***Kamo*** / Fairy Cat from ***Grimms Manga Tales***
Morrey from ***Goldfisch*** / Princess Ai from ***Princess Ai***